*PHILOSOPHIES OF EDUCATION:*
*AN INTRODUCTION*

# Philosophies of Education: An Introduction

G. Max Wingo
*The University of Michigan*

D. C. HEATH AND COMPANY
Lexington, Massachusetts • Toronto • London

*To Mary, who spends her days
in the schools doing the things
her husband mostly talks about*

# PREFACE

In this edition I have retained the basic orientation of the original volume. Those who are familiar with the previous edition will note, however, that certain changes have been made. The first chapter has been rewritten almost in its entirety. The second chapter has been eliminated, but some of the material in it has been incorporated in various contexts in other chapters. The material on philosophy and educational conservatism has been consolidated into a single chapter and some of the original material eliminated. The concluding chapter is completely new.

I wish to reiterate here what I wrote in the preface to the original edition. When a student approaches a field as diverse and extended as philosophy of education, he needs something to help him fit together the things he reads, the ideas he hears in lectures, and the practices he observes in schools. A textbook can help him identify the important problems in the field of educational theory, together with the solutions that have been proposed to solve these problems. Thus, a textbook can be a means for orientation in a complex field of study.

Since virtually all instruction at the college and university level is necessarily group instruction, both teacher and students need something that provides a common base of experience from which other inquiries and studies can develop. The textbook, properly used, provides an organization that prevents aimless wanderings through the vast literature of a field, yet encourages individual and group initiative in discussing and analyzing ideas and branching out to consider in detail issues that the text does not develop fully.

It is important for students (and their instructors as well) to realize the inherent limitations of a textbook. There is no substitute for firsthand contact with the classic works of a field of knowledge. A textbook can help by identifying important original sources for the student and by assisting him in interpreting and analyzing these works. If a book does these things well, and if the student in reading the text is encouraged to push his own way into the fundamental literature of the field, then the most important purpose of the textbook has been achieved.

The function of a textbook is not to tell people what they should think and believe; in my opinion, this is most certainly true in the philosophy of education. A textbook serves its real purpose when it helps a student to understand the significant questions and the variant answers that have been given. There is ample room in the literature of a field for books that advocate acceptance of particular ideas. When a book is designed in this way, however, it is no longer a textbook and it cannot serve the peculiar function of a textbook.

I express my gratitude to students and colleagues for the many helpful comments and suggestions accorded this book. I wish also to express appreciation to the Macmillan Company, Yale University Press, the National Society for the Study of Education, and the American Educational Research Association for their generous permission to quote extensively from their publications.

Finally, I give heartfelt thanks to Miss Mary Catherine O'Malley, who assisted me with various tasks in preparing the manuscript.

G. Max Wingo

# CONTENTS

PHILOSOPHIES OF EDUCATION:
AN INTRODUCTION

# chapter ONE

# PHILOSOPHY AND EDUCATION

*The investigation of the truth is in one way hard, in another easy. An indication of this is found in the fact that no one is able to attain the truth adequately, while, on the other hand, we do not collectively fail, but everyone says something true about the nature of things, and while individually we contribute little or nothing of the truth, by the union of all a considerable amount is amassed. Therefore, since the truth seems to be like the proverbial door, which no one can fail to hit, in this respect it must be easy, but the fact that we can have a whole truth and not the particular part we aim at shows the difficulty of it.*

—ARISTOTLE

Our common concern is American education. Our primary interest, therefore, is in the institutions and traditions that make up our schooling system from the lowest to the topmost levels. We are interested in the programs the schools conduct, the purposes the programs are designed to serve, and the methods and materials of instruction teachers use in their work. However, we do not intend to study these matters in isolation as if they were independent phenomena. Our understanding and assessment of them will have meaning only as we see them in the context from which they have emerged and in which they operate. An educational system is more than the concrete embodiment of philosophic or scientific or economic ideas, though in some measure it includes these and many more as well. The school has often been said to represent ultimately a crystallization of ideas (and ideals) about man and his place in the universe.

The school is an institution responsible for certain specialized services involved in inducting the young into social life. The school can never transmit the entire intellectual and social heritage. Choices must always be made about the knowledge to be transmitted, the intellectual and practical skills to be developed, and the values to be stressed. These choices tend to be made according to values that prevail in society; those values that are dominant will be expressed in choices about the purposes and programs of the school.

In relatively stable societies, agreement about the parts of the cultural heritage to transmit by formal educational means can usually be widespread. Educational theory in such societies operates as a rationale and a synthesis of prevailing and accepted modes of education. Friction and debate on educational questions are minimal. But in societies that are undergoing transition and disruption, the case is very different. A widely accepted thesis of cultural anthropology is that societies in transition suffer a loss of traditional values and that this loss abets cultural confusion and social crisis. Ralph Linton, for example, has pointed out that stability of a society largely depends on wide acceptance of a common core of values and beliefs. Outside this common core are various peripheral ideas and ideals among which men are free to choose. When social change is accelerated, the common core becomes indistinct and men no longer clearly perceive the central universals. The allegiances of citizens are pulled in many directions. The alternatives become confused with the constants, and the result leads to increasing social disorganization.[1]

Under such social conditions, the stresses and dissensions in society find ready expression in debate over educational policy. Those who resent

---

[1] See Ralph Linton, *The Study of Man* (New York: Appleton-Century-Crofts, 1936), pp. 282 ff.

fundamental changes in the social structure and who feel threatened by them make heavy demands on the school to preserve the status quo. People who oppose the old order and who welcome change demand in turn that the school throw its influence towards new curricula, new services, and changed values. Friction grows, name calling becomes common, and the educational theory loses its detachment and becomes evangelical. The view represented here is that stability of society is not a function of the prevailing modes of education. Their relation lies in the manifestation that the modes of education give to the stabilities and instabilities of the social order.

Our thesis is that American society is involved in a great transition, in which our whole way of life is being transformed. The common core of ideas and beliefs that once represented cultural solidarity is dissolving. We can no longer perceive clearly what is constant and what is open to choice. The turmoil, therefore, that is so evident in American education is reflecting the confusion in American society. This educational confusion and conflict cannot be understood, nor can a way out of it be found, until we learn about the underlying conditions that generate it. Education is always a function of the total social pattern, and there is no point in examining philosophies of education as if they existed in isolation, independent of any social context. Many traditions have helped to develop American society, and much instability of present-day life is owing to the fundamental incompatibility of the most important of these traditions. The conflicts and uncertainties the incompatibilities generate are the source of our educational controversies.

Various approaches to studying the theory and practice of education are possible. The approach of this study represents an effort to construct a comprehensive view of educational activity *in its social context*. To some, philosophic thinking at its best is concerned primarily, if not exclusively, with the specialization, intellectual rigor, and concern for detail that characterize scientific analysis. Others would add that at the same time philosophy is concerned with wholeness and with the effort to synthesize experience. Decided differences of opinion exist regarding the proper role of philosophy in the modern world, as we shall see.

We are now ready to embark on a long and complicated inquiry into this character of the educational enterprise in America. We can expect that our task will not be simply one of identifying a common body of beliefs and practices that can be labeled "the philosophy of American education." Rather we are committed to a study of various conceptions about education that in these days are contesting for acceptance by our citizens. Some of the differences among these conceptions are the source of controversies that are deep and bitter. Whether they are capable of being resolved remains for the time being, at least, an open question. How can philosophy help us in understanding education in America?

## THEORY AND PRACTICE

A common characteristic of everyday discourse is the distinction between theory and practice. Individuals vary in their attitudes toward the importance of the two components. Some people profess a strong preference for practice, emphasizing that the work of the world is done by practical people, the "doers" who get things accomplished. On the other hand, there are people who reserve their greatest admiration and approval for the theorist—the man of ideas, whose work must go on often without much immediate reference to the practical consequences of theory. The doer is interested in bringing about change, influencing events in the world, and bringing new events into being. The theorist is more interested in ideas per se, and his search is for discovery, understanding, and synthesis in the realms of fact and of value.

Present-day science is commonly the setting for clashing ideas about the respective values of theory and practice. Although the achievements of science rest ultimately on basic, or "pure," research—that is, research not connected immediately with any practical or applied situation—this is not always understood by the layman nor even by all scientists. Traditionally, it has been easier for scientific workers to get support for practical and technological research than for pure research, although occasionally there are signs that this condition is changing somewhat towards greater appreciation of basic theoretical work.

If a situation of this kind occurs in the field of natural science, dependent as it is on pure research, consider what it must be in a field of endeavor such as teaching, which manifestly is a practical occupation. Those who are responsible for the work of the educational world are doers. They are teachers and administrators and members of boards of education. It is their business to make decisions and to act, and they usually have little time for speculation and disinterested analysis. After all, schools must be maintained, school programs must be planned and established, and there must be teachers in classrooms with some plans and methods for carrying out the work. Typically, the really important matters so far as teachers are concerned are teaching method (including social discipline), curriculum, and instructional materials. To administrative personnel, the important matters are curriculum, personnel, finance, and public relations. All of these areas are practical. They are the primary concerns of the doer. It is not unusual for the practical educator to harbor deep-seated feelings of suspicion toward those who are the theorists of educational activity. The attitude of the practicing teacher or administrator may sometimes be similar to that of the practical businessman when he asks about some economic or social theorist, Has he ever met a payroll?

This same attitude more often than not is encountered by instructors in professional courses for the training of teachers. Typically, the courses students like best are those in which they can see most clearly the relation between what is done in college classes and the specific work they will have to do as teachers. It is not surprising, therefore, that student teaching and similar work that brings the student into contact with the reality of the school are generally the most popular courses in teacher-preparation programs.

Teachers in preparation, as well as those already practicing, find little difficulty in enumerating the things they really want to know about. They want a good mastery of the subject matter they will be called on to teach. They want to know about good methods for teaching the material they are charged with teaching. They are interested in materials to use in the classroom. There is universal concern among teachers about the problems of social control of students—usually called discipline. All teachers want to know in general what is expected of them, what objectives they are supposed to achieve, and how their work will be evaluated by the administration and ultimately by the community.

It would be possible to make a similar list of the practical concerns of educational administrators. The administrator's mind-set of practicality is not fundamentally different from that of the teacher, nor is there any reason to believe that his attitude towards educational theory is really any different.

These attitudes are important and should be respected within the teaching profession, as well as in institutions that prepare people for educational work. After all, if an individual cannot master the elements of the craft to a reasonable degree, he cannot be a teacher. If he cannot in some way fashion a tenable approach to teaching method, if he cannot devise a workable program for his classes, if he cannot manage the relations in his classrooms so that a reasonable degree of social discipline is maintained, he cannot be a teacher. He cannot even hold a position and collect a salary. It is no wonder, then, that these considerations usually occupy the attention of teachers often to the exclusion of more abstract matters.

Does this mean that theory really has nothing to do with the practical work of the practicing educator? Does it mean that teacher-education institutions should concern themselves exclusively with teaching the practical aspects of the teacher's art? Is it reasonable to expect that those who serve society as teachers should be thoughtful about their role and that their concern should go beyond the immediate problems of the day-by-day routine of the school? In a time of cultural transition, with the resulting upheavals in society, can teachers and school officials content themselves with established ideas and established routines, as important as these may be? It is peculiar to a time of social disorganization that all men are called to make decisions they would not be faced with making in more settled times. Educators, since they occupy positions of strategic importance in society, are called on to make decisions that will inevitably affect many people, and these decisions are becoming increasingly difficult to make.

Behind every approach to teaching method, behind every plan for administrative organization of the schools, behind the structure of every school curriculum stands a body of accepted doctrine—assumptions, concepts, generalizations, and values. In short, every practical approach to the art of teaching is shored up by some constellation of accepted *ideas*. Very often, however, the very presence of this body of ideas goes unnoticed. Its acceptance is largely unconscious and based on tradition. Only rarely is it subjected to careful critical analysis, and on the occasions of such analysis there are certain to be outcries from various segments of society; men always find it difficult to see their cherished ideas submitted to objective scrutiny.

Although it is doubtful that complete agreement has ever existed about the ends and means of education, it is possible that in a time of relative cultural stability accepted modes of education and their attending ideology can operate with reasonable satisfaction. If this is true, it is largely because in such settled periods the cultural focus seems clear and distinct. Men find but little difficulty in perceiving what is focal and essential and what is peripheral and secondary. In such times, theory and practice can be united, though the unity may be unconscious in the minds of most practitioners. Thus, under these conditions, teachers teach as they do because their ways are the "right ways," the established ways. The subject matter they teach is what "everybody knows" we ought to teach in school. The values teachers seek to transmit to their students, whether by precept or example, are those "eternal verities" to which all "good citizens" give allegiance.

Under such conditions as these, very little strain is put on the teacher's reflective and analytic powers. There is no reason for him to feel impelled to reflect on the body of accepted ideas that determine what he does as a teacher; in truth, he might very well find such speculative activity frowned on in his community. Generally in his training as a teacher he is told what the correct subject matters are, how they should be presented, and to what end. The emphasis is placed on his development of facility in the practical affairs of teaching, not on the analysis of ideas. Similarly, the administrator and the members of the school board see their task as implementing the "wishes of society." These "wishes," it is maintained, are not only worthy but also reasonably clear.

In these circumstances, the life of the teacher can be comfortable and secure—though perhaps sometimes on the dull side. But this security of life and of professional conviction depends on a corresponding stability in the pattern of culture, and no culture is ever completely stable. Truly stable conditions have been rare or nonexistent certainly for more than a century and perhaps really in the whole postmedieval world. The division of theory and practice in education exists because certain momentous developments in modern culture have opened to question the accepted modes of education. For example, the influence of natural science and scientific method has been at work undermining, at least in the minds of increasing numbers of people, the old certainties about the ends, the contents, and the means of education. Altered conceptions of human nature, new theories of social and political life, and profound developments in pure science and consequently in technology have robbed the old traditions of some of their vitality and influence.

And so theory necessarily becomes a matter of real concern not only to the educational reformer, who seeks to transform, but also to the conservative, whose deepest desire is to retain and consolidate the existing pattern. Whether we think of ourselves as liberal or conservative, radical or regressive, we cannot escape in these times the necessity of attending to our basic ideas. The luxury of operating our schools on the basis of ideas "everybody knows are right" is gone, provided that it ever really existed at all. The educational conservative now finds that he must advocate his cause not merely through the reiteration of the accepted "truths" of educational practice, but also through a demonstration that the implications of these "truths" are coherent and consistent.

And in the same way, the would-be reformer finds it necessary not merely to advocate certain new ideas about practical concerns, but also to explain the body of doctrine related to these ideas. A certain lag between theory and practice is probably always present in any period. Today's question, however, is not so much the relation of certain practices to an accepted body of theory; it is rather what practices and consequently what theories are to be accepted. Thus, in unsettled times, at least, the theory of education becomes controversial and dialectical. In this sense, it becomes philosophical.

## THE GROWTH OF PHILOSOPHY

Historically, philosophy is one of the oldest and most respected provinces of knowledge. In the Western tradition, it has been regarded as the great synthesizing and speculative discipline; and the history of philosophy is a record of achievement of some of the greatest intellects of the West. It has been common for philosophers to insist that philosophy is first of all an autonomous discipline, that it concerns itself with certain subject matter and certain kinds of questions and that it has provided its own methods of inquiry and analysis—contentions, by the way, that are denied by various modern philosophers. It is possible to study philosophy with virtually no attention to any practical implications nor any concern for them, just as one can study mathematics or physics as "pure" sciences independent of their practical ramifications. Plato said that a philosopher is a spectator of all time and all existence. To Aristotle, the philosopher was one who is concerned with the "first causes" of things. The history of philosophy is replete with definitions like this, which portray philosophy as love of wisdom in the grand manner.

Traditionally, Western philosophy has concerned itself with certain categories of questions. These conventional categories of philosophy usually number three:

1. *Metaphysics*, which deals with questions relating to the nature of reality. Metaphysical questions are concerned with the nature of Being in itself, as contrasted with being in the form of the entities with which, for example, physics or some other science deals. Metaphysics is often thought of as the search for what is ultimately real. To many traditional philosophers metaphysics raises the ultimate philosophical question. Very often in philosophical writing the term is made synonymous with *ontology* and readers will find the two terms used interchangeably. There are distinctions between the terms, but these are not of great importance in the matters with which we are dealing.

*Cosmology*, which is often thought of as a subcategory in metaphysics, deals with questions about the ultimate nature of the universe as a whole.

2. *Epistemology*, usually referred to as "the theory of knowledge." It is concerned with the nature and limits of human knowledge. Some important questions in epistemology are about (a) the nature of cognitive processes; (b) the sources of human knowledge; and (c) methods of validating ideas.

3. *Axiology*, which concerns questions of value. General axiological questions are those about the source and the nature of standards (norms) for value and the processes by which these standards are applied in making judgments (the process of valuation). Axiology is considered to have two subcategories, *ethics* and *aesthetics*. Ethics deals with the problem of value as applied to human conduct. Aesthetics deals with value as applied to works of art, criteria for beauty as opposed to ugliness, and experience when it is concerned with beauty.

To these categories we should add *logic*, a field of study in philosophy that deals with the rules of inference. Conventionally, logic is thought of as *formal* and *deductive* and as *scientific* and *inductive*.

It should be understood that questions originating in any of the philosophical categories are interrelated. Thus, problems that are considered primarily to be axiological generally have important implications in epistemology and metaphysics. Metaphysical questions most always involve important questions in epistemology and axiology, and so on.

Customarily, the common man—the doer—thinks he has little in common with the philosopher, whose concerns so obviously are with matters that go beyond ordinary vision and understanding. Though the ordinary man may often harbor deep-seated doubts about the "practicality" of the philosopher's speculations, nonetheless he has usually stood in awe of them. And this awe is only slightly diminished when he hears of such recondite subjects as philosophy of law, philosophy of science, and philosophy of education. To the unphilosophic person, *law, science,* and *education* are understandable terms; above all, they imply practical matters, pursuits that make a difference in human lives. To be sure, science is known to have its basic theories, law its general principles of jurisprudence, and education its theories of objectives, curriculum, and method. But what has philosophy to do with these? Of what use is philosophy in conducting our schools? What kind of bread can philosophy bake for education?

Those who ask this question are entitled to a reasoned answer and indeed, there is more than one answer. To understand the varying ways in which philosophy is viewed at the present time, we briefly consider three conceptions, each of which has its adherents. If we can grasp how philosophy itself is conceived, then perhaps we shall be better able to think about the role philosophy can play in education.

## PHILOSOPHY AS SYSTEM BUILDING

Western philosophy began in Greece at a time when men had become sophisticated enough to cast off at least part of the superstition and animism that had served to make men feel at home in the universe. It was the beginning of an effort to understand and to organize knowledge about the natural world, about man, and about his place in the scheme of things.

In those days there was no distinction between philosophy and science. Philosophy was "the love of wisdom" and the Greeks understood, as some of us today do not, the difference between wisdom and erudition. Even for the earliest philosophers, the pre-Socratics, the business of the philosopher was synthesis, not simply observation, classification, and categorization. What is the nature of the universe? they asked. Is there a "basic stuff" that is the ultimate explanation of the cosmos? Are there basic processes that, acting lawfully, are responsible for the operations of nature?

The answers these early cosmologists gave may seem quaint and intellectually innocent to us of a later day, as we read them superficially and only as a prologue to the work of the great Athenians. But these early thinkers, from Thales to Empedocles, had set the pattern, not only for Greek philosophy but also for all of Western philosophy, at least well into the nineteenth century. They tried to *understand.* And in the effort to understand, they developed systems (perhaps today we should call them models), that would make possible an encompassing conception of the world. Their achievement should not go unnoticed and misunderstood.

They had developed *philosophy*, and as Edward Zeller has pointed out, not every people—not even every highly civilized people—has done that.[2] At the root of their achievement was the casting off of religion; at the least, they came to understand its essentially artistic, mythological character, and to substitute for myth and mysticism the play of human reason.

With Socrates, the focus of inquiry shifted from cosmology to man and the central question became ethics, not physics. But the original spirit prevailed: to inquire, to synthesize, and to understand. Out of this intellectual environment, the great system builders Plato and Aristotle emerged. More than any others, they set the course philosophy was to follow for more than two thousand years. They posed the questions and they provided the answers, many of which are still objects of admiration. All human knowledge was grist for their mills, from metaphysics to psychology, ethics, politics, and education. With the characteristic Greek urge for order, they sought to bring these divergent elements into a pattern—a system that would constitute a unified view of the universe and man's place and prospects within it.

This is philosophy in "the grand manner," an expression not always devoid of opprobrium in these days. But with the close of the nineteenth century, the character of the philosophic enterprise changed and "the mother of sciences" found herself playing a more restricted and mundane role.

## PHILOSOPHY AS INQUIRY AND THE
## EFFORT TO SYNTHESIZE KNOWLEDGE

The role of philosophy changed gradually with the progression of Western history. One momentous development was the success of medieval scholars, who had recovered the important works of the Greek philosophers, in infusing philosophy into Christian theology in the effort to provide a rational basis for the doctrines of the Church. In this process, philosophy for the most part kept its synthesizing, system-building role, but that role became subordinate: philosophy came to serve as the "handmaiden" of the most important science—theology.

The fundamental alteration began toward the end of the fifteenth century as a result of the increase in knowledge at the close of the medieval era and the consequent scholarly specialization that inevitably followed. The first disciplines to leave the philosophic fold were the physical sciences, beginning particularly with astronomy. By the seventeenth century, new

---

[2] Edward Zeller, *Outlines of History of Greek Philosophy* (Cleveland and New York: World Publishing Co., 1955), p. 18.

ways of looking at the world and new methods of studying natural phenomena were well advanced. Observation and experimentation increasingly superseded speculation. As these methods were developed and refined, one by one the remaining natural sciences split off and became disciplines in their own right. This process took more than two centuries but by the middle of the nineteenth century it was all but complete. And the conviction was increasingly widespread that only two legitimate methods of inquiry exist: for natural phenomena, hypothesis and experimentation, and for mathematical and logical problems, careful deduction based on the rules of inference.

Hegel is generally regarded as the last of the great system builders, although some would include Whitehead and perhaps even John Dewey and William James. In any event, before the middle of the present century the mission of philosophy had changed until it was hardly recognizable to anyone except professional philosophers.

One way to look at it, at least in the manner of some, is that philosophy simply had run out of business. The Greeks did not distinguish science from philosophy. There were various reasons for this; one of them lay in their conception of the term *science*, which they regarded as encompassing *any* organized body of knowledge in which cause-and-effect relations are incorporated. Thus, metaphysics was a science in the Greek mind. Theology was a science as far as the medievals were concerned. Another reason the Greeks failed to acknowledge separate disciplines stemmed from the failure of their philosophy to distinguish clearly between questions dealing with fact, which required settlement on factual and experimental grounds, and matters concerning logical systems, which required deduction from some set of assumed premises for a solution. By the end of the last century it was perceived that the ultimate in confusion can result when these two methods are intermingled uncritically in the effort to solve factual problems.

The upshot of the matter is that in the twentieth century, philosophy, having seen its fledglings mature and leave the nest, is faced with the question of what there is left to do. The response to the question has been varied but, under the risk of some oversimplification, it seems generally agreed that there are perhaps two tasks left for the philosophic enterprise. One is concerned with axiology (ethics and aesthetics) and the other with the analysis of the nature and function of language (analytic philosophy). The empirical problems belong to the several sciences and the formal problems to the logicians and the mathematicians.

However satisfactory this state of affairs may seem to philosophers, it has not seemed satisfactory to the entire intellectual community, nor even to all philosophers. A chief source of the dissatisfaction lies in the fragmentation of knowledge that has occurred, recently reaching astonishing proportions. The term *knowledge explosion* is by now a cliché, but there is no one who seems inclined to deal with the phenomenon or who would know what to do even if he were so inclined.

One can have the highest admiration for the achievements of the experimental sciences, just as one can appreciate the contributions of analytic philosophy in expurgating many of the pseudoproblems with which traditional philosophy struggled. Men for centuries have looked to philosophy for certain kinds of guidance, for inspiration, for synthesis of knowledge, and for wisdom. They also have done the same with theology, and in certain historical periods most of them probably could not tell one from the other. However, as the argument goes, in view of the course on which present-day philosophy is embarked and apparently is destined to continue, there is little chance that nonphilosophers, even if they have generous intellectual gifts, can look to philosophy for the kind of contribution that philosophers used to make.

One of these contributions is the synthesizing, organizing role that has already been described as a principal characteristic of traditional philosophy. The thought has occurred to many people that if philosophy has abandoned this role, then where is a man to look for help in making sense of it all? Those who argue in this view do not necessarily advocate a return to armchair speculation and the construction of vast metaphysical systems with no regard for the achievements of natural science. They maintain, however, that although the common man is not concerned with specialization and the scientist typically is not concerned with wholeness, the philosopher ought to be concerned with both. And they add that while there may be dangers in attempting to construct an encompassing world view, the risks may be no greater than those of the increasingly narrow technical specialization that characterizes present knowledge.

To this argument may be added that reflective thinking and inquiry have long been fostered by philosophy, and although the method they extol is not the sole possession of philosophy, it is, as John Dewey insisted, the most reliable philosophic tool. This method, it is held, can make possible the achievement of a reasoned view of man and his place in nature, while minimizing the danger of speculative excesses. In brief, this view of philosophy stresses the synthesizing, holistic function of the discipline. It maintains that philosophy can still help man to fashion a view of himself and his place in the universe, and that this can be accomplished by methods of inquiry and reflection that can lead men to wisdom.

## PHILOSOPHY AS ANALYSIS OF LANGUAGE

Various stages have led British and American philosophy to its present state. It is generally agreed that the first stage took place shortly after

World War I with the formation of the "Vienna Circle." The Circle was made up of philosophers, usually referred to as logical positivists, who were concerned with the relation of philosophy and science. The orientation of this group was weighted heavily toward the sciences, and while the group repudiated the traditional metaphysical system-building role of philosophy, they were interested in discovering whether philosophy still had any role to play in the intellectual enterprise, and if so, what that role might be.

Perhaps the most famous idea to emerge from the Vienna Circle was what is usually known as the verifiability principle.[3] This is one form of semantic empiricism and it is built on the idea we have already considered, namely, that propositions about nature and society can be tested only through experience. This idea provides a basis for dealing with meaning, which is the main concern of present-day philosophers. Logical positivists regarded the theory of meaning as crucial: they contended that "big questions" of traditional philosophy (in metaphysics and epistemology, for example) had not been solved and that any promise of solution was remote because those questions were meaningless to begin with. Manifestly, the positivists argued, it is not possible to answer questions or test propositions that in themselves mean nothing.

They proposed, therefore, that a big contribution would be to formulate a principle that would enable us to distinguish between meaningful statements and statements without meaning. We could then eliminate the meaningless questions and concentrate on those questions that have meaning. The principle enunciated by the logical positivists was that (1) a proposition is meaningful if it is testable through experience, *and* (2) the meaning of a proposition is knowable only in terms of the method required to test it. Obviously, if the verifiability principle is valid, many traditional questions of philosophy can be eliminated forthwith.

Logical positivism is not the only form of semantic empiricism, and the theory of meaning had been important long before the Vienna Circle was formed.[4] There had been much debate and controversy over the verifiability principle and fundamental differences of opinion had developed. However, the work done by the Circle had a profound influence on philosophers, particularly in emphasizing the importance of language.

---

[3] Semantic empiricism is the position that meaning depends on experience. For a proposition to be meaningful, it must be possible to relate it to experience as a test of its truth. Abraham Kaplan in his book *The Conduct of Inquiry: Methodology for Behavioral Science* (San Francisco: Chandler Publishing Co., 1964) describes three forms of semantic empiricism.

[4] The pragmatism of Charles Sanders Peirce is also a form of semantic empiricism. It will be discussed in Chapter Seven.

Language is the greatest achievement of the race, for without it we should be little different from the beasts. But as the linguistic philosophers have been at pains to demonstrate, it can also be a great deceiver. The matter is indeed complex. Suffice it here to say that there are various ways in which we can be deceived—or deceive ourselves—by uncritical use of language. For example, we can (and do) make statements that appear to be statements of fact but are really disguised value judgments. Similarly, we can make statements in the interrogative form that look and sound like real questions because they are constructed according to ordinary rules of grammar; but application of the verifiability rule indicates that they are meaningless statements disguised as questions. As these attributes of language came to light, it began to be accepted that the function of language must be a principle concern of philosophy, replacing the overriding concern with metaphysical and epistemological problems. This brings us to the second stage in the development of linguistic analysis.

The second stage occurred partly as a result of analyzing and criticizing issues raised from logical positivism and the verifiability principle. From philosophy's inception, its thoughts had always been expressed in ordinary language, which many philosophers thought lacked necessary precision and clarity because of its general nature. So it seemed only reasonable to conclude that a way out of the difficulties posed by natural language would be to construct some kind of artificial language that would be free of the ambiguities of natural language. It was believed that if this could be accomplished, then philosophical statements could be translated into the new language and issues could be settled once and for all. The extremely sophisticated and determined efforts to solve the language problem through artificial language were not successful. And today, philosophers have turned again to a reconsideration of ordinary language. Modern linguistic philosophers disagree over many issues, but in spite of the differences, there is basic agreement.

From the general perspective of analytic philosophy, the function of philosophy is not speculation, whether in metaphysics or epistemology or any of the conventional categories of philosophy. Philosophy's mission according to this view is not to tell us what is good or how we ought to live or how we ought to conduct scientific inquiry—or educate our children or do any of the things that are necessary for maintaining social life. The purpose of philosophy is held to be clarifying the uses to which we put language, with the view of ensuring the greatest possible precision of meaning. To the degree that this can be accomplished, we shall supposedly be able to analyze the conceptual and methodological bases on which various forms of human inquiry are conducted. This is what the analysts tell us that philosophy is all about.

We have now considered briefly three ways of conceiving philosophy, from traditional system building to analysis of language. Our main interest is the philosophy of education and its relation to these conceptions of pure philosophy. Before we turn to this question it may be useful to look at the matter in a slightly different way.[5]

## THE FUNCTIONS OF PHILOSOPHY

Philosophy may be said to have three main functions: (a) the descriptive; (b) the normative; and (c) the analytic. When a person studies philosophy, he may approach it in any of these ways. He may approach it simultaneously in all three ways, but when he does he is doing three different kinds of things. Knowing each of these ways will be helpful when we examine the varying conceptions of the philosophy of education.

A person who engages in the study of philosophy from the descriptive standpoint is concerned with learning what has been said and done by various philosophers or in various schools of philosophic thought. Working piecemeal, he may seek to understand Plato's revelations on the nature of the real or the basic principles of Aristotle's metaphysics or even what Wittgenstein was up to in the *Tractatus*. In short, the student is concerned with what is (and has been) in the field of philosophy. Working comprehensively, he is trying to picture the general development of philosophical thought. A good many present-day philosophers would be inclined to think that what the student probably is doing is studying intellectual history. One reason for their view is that they discriminate between *studying about* what philosophers have said and *doing* philosophy, by which they mean analyzing and clarifying concepts and the language in which ideas are expressed. It is possible that the student might be doing both kinds of things.

A person who approaches philosophy in the normative sense is concerned in some way with value (axiology). His interest may be focused on ethics or aesthetics. He will be involved with advocating some ends or objectives (values) that he believes to be desirable and with explaining the reasons for their desirability. He may also be involved in suggesting means for achieving these values. His main concern is not what is, but what ought to be.

The third kind of approach is the analytic, with which we are now familiar. The analytic philosopher professes to be *doing* philosophy; that is, he purports to be engaged in the analysis of language, concepts, theories, and so on.

---

[5]  Christopher J. Lucas has collected in compact and useful form statements of various points of view about the philosophy of education. One section of the anthology concerns general philosophy. See his *What Is Philosophy of Education?* (Toronto: Collier-Macmillan Canada, 1969).

Now it may be argued that while these three functions of philosophy may be isolated and separately conceived, there is no good reason to believe them mutually exclusive. Surely there are few, if any, competent normative philosophers who are ignorant of the history of ethics. And in the same sense, what would ethical theory be without the process of analysis? The greatest danger for philosophy appears to lie in the deliberate effort to make any one of the functions independent of the others, particularly when this effort involves the elevation of one and the denigration of one or both of the others.

## THE RELATION OF PHILOSOPHY TO EDUCATION

Exactly what do we mean by *education?* When we use the term, we usually refer to one of two things. On the one hand, there is the practical meaning, which denotes the activity of teaching (curricula, method, and so forth), the experience of the student who is going through the process, and the ends achieved; in short, we mean by *education* what goes on in schools. We may use *education* in other contexts, however, meaning our thinking about education in general, wherein we critically examine the field and formulate principles, theories, and organized knowledge about it.[6]

Since education is primarily a practical activity, its practitioners' interests understandably are practical and only secondarily theoretical if at all. Teachers, like anybody else engaged in some practical process, have to make decisions. They have to decide, when various options present themselves, that it is better (or probably better) to do one thing instead of another. Obviously, the same thing is true of administrative officials. When people have a choice, they must have some reason for deciding to do one thing instead of another, and behind every set of school policies, which are more or less formalized, and organized statements of chosen directives for action stands some set of accepted ideas and ideals.

It would appear that one of the proper functions of philosophy of education would be to inquire into these sets of ideas and ideals, discover what they are, subject them to critical scrutiny, test them for logical consistency, and judge their adequacy. One writer in considering this matter has suggested that the choices individual teachers make, and by implication the formation of school policies, while not entirely fortuitous, "may more often be made on grounds of customs of the teaching service, on

---

[6] This distinction has been spun out at great length by various writers. It appears to the present author that the distinction as presented by William K. Frankena is brief, eminently sensible, and quite adequate for the purpose here as well as elsewhere. See his *Philosophy of Education* (New York: Macmillan Co., 1965), p. 2.

grounds of expediency, requirements (rules, regulations, directives) or in terms of psychological or sociological research than in terms of socio-political traditions or philosophies." [7]

This statement has a ring of cynicism about it, and probably was so intended. What it seems to say is that philosophic, or even social-political, ideas have a negligible influence on educational decision making, if they have any at all. While this may or may not be cynical, it certainly may very well be true. Obviously it is an empirical statement and the only way to test its truth is by empirical means.

Suppose we were to investigate and find that the statement is true, that is, that decisions about teaching and administration are actually made on some such grounds. Certain questions could then properly be raised. For example, it might be asked whether or not this is a desirable state of affairs—whether such grounds are adequate for making decisions in a field of endeavor as complex and important as education. Even if we concede that some day-to-day decisions of relatively minor importance may be made on simple pragmatic grounds, that is, that such-and-such a method appears to "work," there are still other questions of considerably greater import that go unanswered. There is, for example, the question of what a teacher or a school is trying to do by using certain methods. What objectives govern the process? After all, methods of teaching can be little else than means to achieve something. How are we to decide what these objectives ought to be? What is teaching for?

It is submitted that this is a normative question, that it is an extremely important one, and that it cannot be answered on simple factual or pragmatic grounds. It is possible that teachers and other school people do let their decisions about objectives rest on customs of the service or on "grounds of expediency," but once again the question is whether such a practice is desirable—or even tolerable.

The issue that is raised here is one of the most important and disputed questions in philosophy of education; it is the problem of the relation of means to ends. Philosophers of education, as well as thoughtful people who make no pretensions to be philosophers but who do reflect on basic educational issues, rarely question the idea that values are involved in some way in education. The question is not about the presence of values but rather the way in which they function. This is not the only question with which philosophy of education is concerned but it is one of the most important, and it serves as an example of the kind of problems with which the discipline is concerned.

Today, the philosophy of education is conceived and practiced in three

[7]   George L. Newsome, Jr., in *Studies in Philosophy and Education*, vol. 5, no. 1 (Winter 1966–67), p. 166.

ways. These three ways are roughly parallel to the three forms of general philosophy that have already been sketched. As in the case of general philosophy, each of these approaches has its proponents and its critics. On some issues there are differences that probably are irreconcilable.

## EDUCATIONAL PHILOSOPHY AS DEDUCTION FROM PHILOSOPHICAL PREMISES

One of the occasional uses of philosophy is to construe it as the original source of certain ideas from which the practical matters of education are held *to be derived by a series of logical inferences.* For example, suppose we learn from philosophy (that is, from some philosophical "system") that ultimate reality is of such-and-such a nature. Say that we learn from Plato that ultimate reality is of the nature of universal ideas, or *Forms,* and that these Forms are knowable only through the rational operations of the mind, not through the senses. We learn further that although the things and events we encounter in our sensory experience depend on the Forms for their very existence and character, those things that we know through the senses are not real in the sense that the Forms are real.

From these ideas (which we are taking as demonstrated philosophic "truths"), it is held, we can deduce certain principles for education. We can say for one thing that the existence known by the mind is of a higher order than that known through the senses. And we can infer, further, that the activity of the intellect, which opens the way to an understanding of that which is ultimately real, is higher than physical activity that deals merely with the world of sense. It must follow then that education should be concerned with the training of the mind, that is, with man's rational powers, and that this should take precedence over any training in manual and manipulative pursuits.

Now if these things are true, it is said to follow that the curriculum of the school should be one designed for intellectual training, that it should be based on abstractions and symbolic materials—that is, on ideas—rather than on things. And it follows from this that teaching method should emphasize the training of the powers of reason and it should communicate to the students those Truths that hold on all occasions, regardless of time, place, or circumstance.[8]

---

[8] The derivation of a scheme for practical educational ideas from a set of metaphysical assumptions is far more complicated than this account would indicate. However, my purpose at this point is not to give a complete exposition but to indicate the general direction of thought such philosophizing takes. For examples of this conception of the

If Platonism can be described accurately as philosophy in the "grand manner," perhaps we can describe the logical derivation of practical ideas for education from metaphysical premises as philosophy of education in the "grand manner." To some practitioners in the field of educational philosophy this is what the term really means, but their numbers are dwindling. In their judgment, this logical mating of theory and practice is the only sound conception of the uses of philosophy in the educational enterprise. It must be admitted that intellectually this is a tidy approach to educational philosophy. By this approach it is possible to build a whole system of ideas about what educational practices ought to be without once troubling to observe the character of any existing school or the social context in which the schools exist.

An instructor, therefore, looking at the matter in this way will often begin with the study of certain epistemological and metaphysical theories; and after an analysis of these philosophical matters he will demonstrate that certain propositions in metaphysics or epistemology or ethics imply logically certain conclusions about the objectives of education, the character and content of the curriculum, and the principles of educational methodology.

Such an inferential process furnishes a ready-made device for judging the validity of practical educational ideas. Plainly, under this view, false ideas about education are either those that are derived from false premises, or those that are false because formal errors have been made in their logical derivation. Therefore, it is possible to say, as indeed one writer once said, that certain educational practices (in this case those of progressivism) are *necessarily* bad because they are related in the logical sense to an untenable and false philosophy, namely pragmatism. Since there can scarcely be anything more convincing than logical necessity, it does not appear worth while, according to this view, to spend time considering educational practices that are already known to be false. The wise thing to do would be summarily to dismiss these ideas and search for others whose validity can be inferred from a firm philosophical base.[9]

As neat and attractive as this approach to philosophy of education may seem, certain questions need to be raised about it. For one thing, the whole enterprise depends on the correctness of the assumption that the

---

uses of philosophy, see Harry S. Broudy, "How Philosophical Can Philosophy of Education Be?" *Journal of Philosophy* 52 (October 27, 1955): 612–22; Kingsley Price "Is a Philosophy of Education Necessary?" *Journal of Philosophy* 52 (October 27, 1955): 622–33; Richard K. Morris, "The Philosophy of Education: A Quality of Its Own," *Harvard Educational Review* 26 (Spring 1956): 142–44.

[9] See Albert Lynd, "Who Wants Progressive Education?" *Atlantic Monthly* 191 (April 1953): 35 ff.

relation between, say, propositions in metaphysics and ideas about school practice is a logical one, logical that is, in the sense of a necessary relation between premise and conclusion.[10]

According to its critics, there is a further source of evidence of the untenability of this perception of the role of philosophy of education. The whole idea presumes some set of metaphysical (or epistemological or ethical) premises that are known to be true and that imply logically certain educational practices and not others. If this is true, where are we to look for these universal, foolproof philosophical premises? Certainly there seems to be little point in looking for them in the history of Western philosophy, for if there is a field of knowledge that involves more disagreement on basic issues than philosophy it is hard to know what it is. Whose premises are we to take? Those of Plato, Aristotle, Locke, Kant, Hegel, Descartes, James, Dewey—whose? How are we to know which to select? While all of them may be mistaken, there is no possibility they can all be right, for they are obviously contradictory of each other on many important issues. If we accept the idea that philosophical premises can be made to yield conclusions about the practices of education, it seems clear that unless we all begin with the same premises we cannot hope to emerge with the same conclusions. Since there is no promising sign that we are very near to agreeing on philosophical premises, how can we hope ever to agree on practical educational issues?

A book of essays on educational theory written by eminent philosophers of the day provides an instructive example of what happens when educational ideas are conceived as logical implications of certain philosophical premises.[11] At least three of the authors of essays in this volume come to near-perfect agreement on what the curriculum of the schools should be. But these conclusions are arrived at supposedly by way of three different philosophical systems: idealism, realism, and existentialism.[12]

How are we to account for this curious situation? Historically, adherents of idealism and realism have believed the two traditions to be poles apart as philosophical systems. Certainly it is a common notion that existentialism developed, partly at least, as a serious protest against the in-

10 For a study of this question, see Hobart W. Burns, "The Logic of the 'Educational Implication,'" *Educational Theory* 12 (January 1962): 53–63. See also Sidney Hook, "The Scope of Philosophy of Education," *Harvard Educational Review* 26 (Spring 1956): 145–48.

11 John S. Brubacher, ed., *Modern Philosophies and Education*, 54th Yearbook of the National Society for the Study of Education (Chicago: University of Chicago Press, 1955).

12 Readers may find it an interesting intellectual exercise to trace, if they can, the paths of reasoning that led the idealist Theodore Greene, the realist John Wild, and the existentialist Ralph Harper to their substantial agreement on the character of the school curriculum. See ibid., chaps. 2, 4, and 7.

fluence of older philosophical systems. If educational theories are related to philosophical premises in the logical sense, we should ordinarily expect that different philosophical premises would yield different educational conclusions. In this case, they do not. Why?

One possibility is that the philosophical premises with which the three authors begin are really identical, although expressed in different words. This would account for the identity of their conclusions; but it is doubtful that this idea will hold up under analysis because it is possible to demonstrate that there are genuine philosophical differences among idealism, realism, and existentialism as systems of thought. The reasonable conclusion seems to be that the three essayists really arrived at their conclusions about the curriculum on some basis other than inferences from propositions in metaphysics and epistemology. In other words, this case furnishes no clear evidence that the relation between philosophical premise and practical conclusion is one of logical entailment.[13] Perhaps the trouble lies ultimately in an original and unwarranted assumption that the only respectable approach to philosophy of education is the effort to imitate philosophy in the grand manner, that is, through trying to derive ideas about education from great systems of speculative thought.

## PHILOSOPHY OF EDUCATION AS DETERMINATION OF THE ENDS AND MEANS OF EDUCATION

A second way in which philosophy of education may be approached is by identifying it with the ends and means of education. This is a normative approach, reflecting many ideas and attitudes that are implicit in the normative approach to general philosophy. By and large, those who take this approach repudiate conceiving philosophy of education as logically deduced from philosophic premises. They do believe, however, that philosophy of education, like general philosophy, should retain its function of synthesis and that it can and should be one source of guidance to action. "To the extent that fundamental ideas determine our actions," says Sidney Hook, "they flow from our basic commitments. Philosophy is a mode of thought which analyzes our presuppositions and assumptions in every field of action and thought. It enables us to make explicit our allegiances

---

[13] In an interesting paper, Joe R. Burnett argues that propositions in philosophy and theology can have a logical relation to propositions about practical school operations without this relation's being a strict one of premise to conclusion. See Burnett, "An Analysis of some Philosophical and Theological Approaches to Formation of Educational Policy and Practice," *Proceedings of the Seventeenth Annual Meeting of the Philosophy of Education Society*, published by the Society, 1961.

to the ideals in behalf of which we are prepared to live, to fight, sometimes even to die." [14]

Those who look at philosophy of education in this light, thus do not conceive it in "the grand manner" but rather as a process of inquiry into ideas and basic beliefs that will enable us to form reasoned attitudes about the important issues of our time. By and large, they agree that there are many ways in which educational issues may be approached fruitfully. Education, they say, being the complex kind of social enterprise that it is, has psychological, sociological, and political dimensions that are of great importance. Adherents of the normative approach point out, however, that there is one kind of question that is not in the province of these empirical disciplines—the question of determining the ends of education. For example, Sidney Hook has observed: "The only distinctive theme with which the philosophy of education has concerned itself from Plato to Dewey is: What should the aims or goals of education be?" [15] Hook has also argued, as most of those have who agree with this position, that the means of education must be considered not in isolation from but in conjunction with the question of ends. John Dewey, for example, inveighed throughout his career against the dualism of ends and means, viewing it as one of the deepest pitfalls of philosophy and hence of philosophy of education.

Those who are committed to this general position point out that determination of the ends and means of education is no simple task. Certainly they do not see it as a matter of personal taste or the result of revealed truth from some transcendental source. They see it as a process of inquiry, of analysis, and of evaluation. They recognize that science, particularly the social and behavioral sciences, must play an important role, but they also hold that the basic problem is philosophical. Max Black once said:

> All serious discussion of educational problems, no matter how specific, soon leads to consideration of educational aims, and becomes a conversation about the good life, the nature of man, the varieties of experience. But these are the perennial themes of philosophical investigation. It might seem a hard thing to expect educators to be philosophers, but can they be anything else? [16]

---

[14] Sidney Hook in *Saturday Review* 50 (November 11, 1967): 21–23, reprinted in Lucas, *What Is Philosophy of Education?* Here Hook is speaking of philosophy in the broad sense. The general thrust of his statement is applicable to educational philosophy.

[15] Sidney Hook, *Education for Modern Man* (New York: Alfred A. Knopf, 1963), p. 51.

[16] Max Black, "A Note on Philosophy of Education," *Harvard Educational Review* 26 (Spring 1956): 154–55.

This conception of philosophy of education is not without its critics. Traditionalists assail it because of what they consider its cavalier attitude towards metaphysics and epistemology and its suspicions about speculative system building. From what we know about the views of traditional schools of educational philosophy, it is not hard to foresee the general trend of their criticism. As might also be expected, there is criticism from the other group—the analytic philosophers.

## EDUCATIONAL PHILOSOPHY AS ANALYSIS OF THE LANGUAGE OF EDUCATION

Among analytic philosophers of education, certain differences of opinion and approach prevail. The analytic philosophers' attitude towards traditional philosophy leads us to expect that they would reject a philosophy of education based on the traditional approach. This rejection does not mean necessarily that they think nobody should ever read Rousseau or Plato or any other illustrious person in the history of philosophy who has concerned himself with education. It implies that when we read these traditional works, we should view them as a record. In other words, we are reading history. Whether or not as a group they think we can learn anything useful by studying history, useful in the sense that it applies to our own times and problems, is difficult to determine. Evidently there are differences of opinion on this point. At any rate, they seem to agree that this is by no means the chief activity with which educational philosophy is concerned.

Some analytic educational philosophers regard the normative dimension as a proper province of the philosophy of education; others express doubt about the contribution philosophers of education can make in the ethical domain.[17] Suspicion is often expressed that when educational philosophers are engaged in normative discourse about education they tend to speak *ex cathedra*, in the manner of their traditional forebears.

There is no good reason, critics of this procedure say, for thinking that philosophers are any more moral in their own lives or any wiser about good and evil than the rest of us. Ethics, they hold, is too important a matter to be left to the philosophers alone, since they do not have any exclusive option on moral wisdom or sensitivity and they should not pretend that they do.

A general tendency among analytic educational philosophers seems to be the adopting of a morally neutral stance, at least as neutral as possible.

---

[17] For example, see George L. Newsome, Jr., "Educational Knowledge and Philosophy of Education," *Educational Theory* 17 (January 1957): 48–55.

Such a stance, it is held, will then free the philosophic mind for its real task, which is an objective, rational, analytic study of the conceptual and linguistic aspects of education. It is their view that when educational philosophers work in this way, they will perform, as philosophers, the greatest possible service to education. It is true, as the saying goes, that a person may wear more than one hat. People who are concerned with basic issues in education may, depending on the circumstances, become involved in the behavioral and social sciences as well as in the practical aspects of the craft of teaching. *But* when they are wearing their philosophical hats, they should behave like philosophers.[18]

## A PLAN FOR ANALYSIS

Philosophy of education can be conceived in different senses to serve various purposes, and it can be conducted in differing ways. Our pursuit of the philosophy of education involves three basic theses. These theses are fundamental in the design of the analysis that is to follow. They are:

1. The primary subject matter of philosophy of education is education itself. Philosophy, it has often been observed, has to be philosophy of *something*. If there were not schools and teachers and curricula and students and social ends to be served, there could not be anything called philosophy of education.
2. Education always takes place within a certain constellation of cultural conditions and therefore it cannot be studied as a set of universal and independent phenomena. Some set of relations among education, politics, and social institutions is inevitable and cannot be ignored in any useful analysis.
3. The basic purpose of philosophy of education applies to the ends and means of education and their interrelationships. This is not a simple matter and in considering it a great many things have to be taken into account.

The American tradition in education has developed over a period of about a century and a half of our social and political experience. The tradition is not static and has changed in response to social conditions. This process of change, however, has generally been slow and a marked lag between educational processes and cultural conditions has been

---

[18] Examples of books on philosophy of education conceived in the analytic fashion are Philip G. Smith, *Philosophy of Education: Introductory Studies* (New York: Harper & Row, 1965); and a more recent work, John B. Magee, *Philosophical Analysis in Education* (New York: Harper & Row, 1971).

common. Many observers have often used the school as a classic example of the sociological phenomenon known as cultural lag.

The purposes the American school has generally served are those of preserving and transmitting the so-called essentials of Western culture and of acting as a conserving, civilizing force in society. This conception of purpose is reflected accurately in the way in which schools are organized, the kind of curricula established, and the teaching methods employed.

Other ways of conceiving the aims and means of education exist in addition to those espoused by the conservative tradition. Progressivism, perennialism, Marxism, and existentialism are traditions in philosophy of education that have some currency in the educational scene. Each of these is, in its own way, a protest against not only the existing set of educational arrangements but also the kind of society that perpetuates these arrangements.

This is not to say that there are not fundamental differences both of a philosophical and of an educational nature among these traditions: many differences run deep and controversies are bitter. The thing that they have in common is disavowal of existing American education, and this is the role they currently play. It is essentially a protest role.

An analysis of these traditions, all of which have some degree of influence in American life today, will indicate to us some important things about American education and its potentialities and prospects. These traditions embrace much more than educational ideas. They must be thought of as proposals for ways of life in which all important elements of human culture are represented. Significant for our own purposes is that all these traditions take education seriously. All of them, save perhaps one, embrace a distinct doctrine about the aims, content, and modes of education. The proponents of these traditions earnestly attempt to persuade others that their particular doctrines are right and should be accepted. Most of the knowledgeable proponents of these traditions know that their educational ideas do not stand alone, and that they have an organic connection with other elements in the tradition. They believe that a consistent educational doctrine is not achieved by picking and choosing from various philosophical systems, the way one assembles lunch in a cafeteria line.

All of the traditions have specific proposals for educational objectives, curriculum, and method. If we can understand these proposals, we shall have a background for judgments about our primary interest—the operation of the schools. Analysis of the proposals about educational practices is a beginning in analyzing the tradition as a whole. An important dimension of an idea is the way it relates to other ideas. Since beliefs about educational practice are related to other kinds of beliefs, an important part of our analysis is to trace as far as we can the interrelated beliefs and concepts that form the total body of ideas about education.

Our second conception of philosophy of education, namely, that the central problem is determination of the ends and means of education and all the ramifications thereof, is going to dominate our thinking. Our emphasis is partly historical and therefore descriptive. Where analysis of concepts or of language seems called for, it is used. We shall place considerable emphasis on the normative aspects of the various educational philosophies considered.

The intent of what follows is not to persuade or indoctrinate anyone in any particular position. Obviously, nobody can believe that everything presented here is true, unless he is able to change his mind with about every chapter. It is to be hoped that the reader will analyze and judge for himself and in so doing will enter into the spirit of philosophy.

We are not the first to be concerned with the basic questions of education. Others in this century, some still living and some not, many of them people of very considerable intellectual talents, have already contributed to our understanding. There seems no good reason why each generation has to invent civilization over again. The purpose of this book is to provide a beginning for those who wish to take up the work where others have left off. It is well that they should know where the starting places are.

## SUMMARY

The general plan for our inquiry may now be summarized. The remainder of the book is concerned with a detailed analysis of five traditions, all of which, it is thought, have important things to say about education. These traditions are more than educational theories; most represent comprehensive views of the nature of man and human society, and in every case the specific educational proposals contained in these traditions are related to other social institutions such as politics, economics, religion, and philosophy. In our analysis, we shall begin with the specific educational proposals involved in the tradition being studied. Once we have grasped the general nature of its practical educational thought, we shall inquire into the relation of these practical ideas to other kinds of ideas important in the tradition.

# chapter TWO

# THE
# CONSERVATIVE
# TRADITION

Believe me, Sir, those who attempt to level,
never equalize. In all societies, consisting of
various degrees of citizens, some description
must be uppermost. The levelers, therefore, only
change and pervert the natural order of things;
they load the edifice of society by setting up
in the air what the solidity of the structure
requires to be on the ground.

—EDMUND BURKE

A principal tradition in American education is best known under the name *essentialism*. This term is thought to have been used first by Michael Demiashkevich in a 1935 study of philosophy of education.[1] The name got its widest currency in an article in 1938 that presented a platform for a conservative reform movement in education.[2] Since that time, the term has been adopted by many conservative educational theorists and it has been used widely in writings about the conservative tradition in American education. Conservatives apparently agree that the word expresses particularly well their basic attitude towards education and their conception of the role of the school in society.

Conservatism as a tradition stems from the eighteenth century and it is universally acknowledged that the founder was Edmund Burke, the British statesman and political philosopher. In the United States, the tradition was expressed through such illustrious early Americans as John Adams, Alexander Hamilton, and James Madison. The *Federalist* papers are considered to be perhaps the purest American expression of political and social conservatism. The two-volume work *Democracy in America*, by Alexis de Tocqueville, the noted French political observer and philosopher, is viewed by conservatives to be the most penetrating study of early American society; it is often credited along with Burke's work as being an unusually fertile source for the understanding of conservatism in America.

An unfortunate tendency exists among Americans to identify conservatism exclusively with politics. Conservative intellectuals deplore this tendency; they are always quick to point out that such a limited view effectively obscures the tradition. Conservatism is not merely political doctrine—and anyway conservatives typically look on bodies of doctrine with grave suspicion. Conservatism is more an attitude toward life— a certain view of the world. The conservative's interpretation of the great matters of society in any generation is influenced by his regard for the continuity of tradition, his resistance to uncontrolled social change, and his profound distrust of all utopian reform movements allegedly based on reason.

The conservative tradition is expressed most clearly in the great areas of political and social life, to be sure. It is expressed in ideas about politics, religion, education, economics; as a tradition it is more than any of these and more than their sum total. Our present concern is with the way the conservative tradition is expressed in educational practice in America, but this cannot be our sole concern. The conservative himself believes that

---

[1] Michael Demiashkevich, *An Introduction to the Philosophy of Education* (New York: American Book Co., 1935).

[2] See William C. Bagley, "An Essentialist's Platform for the Advancement of American Education," *Educational Administration and Supervision* 24 (April 1938): 241–56.

education is never independent of other institutions and that it is inseparably linked to political, economic, and religious tradition.

## CLASSIC CONSERVATISM

Since modern conservatism has a history stretching back nearly two centuries, it is only to be expected that various changes, modifications, and reinterpretations should have occurred during these years. One of the great sources of strength this tradition has displayed over the years has been its flexibility, its adaptability, and its power to absorb change from liberal and radical sources and transform them into elements of its own. Following Burke's dictum that change is the basic law of life, something that nonconservatives often overlook or find it convenient to forget, the conservative on occasion will seek change in order to preserve what is, and under different circumstances, he will resist change for about the same reason. The conservative insists, however, that his actions are not expedient but instead that particular decisions he makes are based on fundamental considerations. Burke said, for example, that while he might change his front, he never changed his ground.

American education is interwoven with Western conservatism. The fountainhead of modern conservatism is British but the influence of this tradition has been felt in the United States for nearly two centuries. Because of various factors, not the least of which has been differences in historical and environmental circumstances, the basic ideas of conservatism have been altered to some extent by the American experience. It will be important for our purpose to delineate the basic character of the American version of conservatism, but this can be done more clearly if we consider first some of the principal tenets of classic conservatism. There are various American spokesmen for classic conservatism. We consider the classic form through their writings for the most part.

### SUPERNATURALISM, RELIGION, AND HUMAN NATURE

The classic conservative tradition rests ultimately on the belief in a supernatural creator who is responsible for the world and the events that make up its history. Although there are various sectarian and doctrinal differences about the details of this cosmology, the thesis of an ultimate source of power and authority that transcends nature is central to this tradition. Russell Kirk, one of the most noted spokesmen for classical conservatives, has indicated that this belief is fundamental in the conservative mind.[3]

---

[3] Russell Kirk, *Prospects for Conservatives* (Chicago: Henry Regnery Co., 1956), p. 37.

The conservative links ethics and morality closely to religion and the idea is very common within the tradition that any system of ethics worthy of the name ultimately must be anchored in religious sanctions. Politics, as the conservative understands the meaning of the word, is ultimately concerned with value, and therefore, in the conservative mind there is an indissoluble relation between religion and politics.[4]

The conservative finds a close relation also between the ultimate supernatural creator and the nature of man. The conservative view of human nature reveals a curious combination of outright pessimism and a carefully guarded optimism. The pessimism derives from the conservative acceptance of the Christian doctrine of original sin, which Peter Viereck has said all conservatives accept, either in the literal sense or metaphorically.[5] The concern of the conservative is to disown the doctrine of human perfectibility, historically associated with the liberal tradition, and to emphasize the need for control through tradition of a human nature that is wayward, capricious, and often given to evil thoughts and deeds. This sharp strain of pessimism about human nature runs as a principal theme through the conservative tradition. Traditional institutions of religion and society, we are assured, are not intolerable curbs to the free development of human nature nor are they, as Rousseau called them, the chains that bind men. Rather these products of tradition are what makes human nature possible. They make us men rather than beasts, and they must be preserved.

The guarded optimism of the conservative stems from his belief that if the continuity of tradition can be maintained, every generation will have a source of wisdom to which it can turn for guidance. As a tradition, conservatism insists that in the ordinary affairs of life men should be free to exercise their own judgment and to profit from their own initiative and energy. But beyond the ordinary matters of daily life, the conservative has little faith in either the wisdom or judgment of an individual—or even of a whole generation. Kirk has said, echoing Edmund Burke, that "in matters beyond the scope of material endeavor and the present moment, the individual tends to be foolish, but the species is wise; therefore, we rely in great matters upon the wisdom of our ancestors."[6] The optimism of the conservative, therefore, derives not from his faith in human nature, but from his faith in the accumulated wisdom of all the generations that is available to guide men of any generation through their own perplexities and crises if they will only take advantage of it.

---

[4]  Ibid., p. 37.

[5]  Peter Viereck, *Conservatism from John Adams to Churchill* (Princeton, N.J.: D. Van Nostrand Co., 1956), pp. 13–14.

[6]  Kirk, *Prospects for Conservatives*, p. 38.

The ultimate thesis of the modern conservative (at least of those conservatives who understand conservatism) is identical with that originally propounded by Edmund Burke, the greatest of them all.[7] Burke's conservatism stems from his belief that a great *compact* exists among the generations. Under this compact, no single generation has the right to uproot and destroy the existing pattern of society, whether this be done by revolution or by nonviolent doctrinaire social reform movements. To uproot institutions and ways of life is a breach of faith both with the generations that are gone and those that are yet to come. This is the ultimate immorality and the road to social chaos.

Small wonder, then, that conservatives have reserved some of their strongest wrath and most bitter language for the progressive movement in American education, for as the conservative sees it, this doctrinaire reform movement almost succeeded in less than half a century in destroying our historic conceptions of the school and the very purpose of education itself.

To the conservative mind the great fact of life is the existence of an ultimate power that transcends nature and is responsible for the existence and operations of the natural world. The workings of this ultimate power are made manifest in history, and history itself is, as Kirk has said, "the record of Providential purpose." This same Providence has created human nature in such a fashion that men display elements of both good and evil in their common nature. To the extent that this human nature can be improved (the conservative rejects the idea that it can be perfected), this improvement must stem from within the individual himself as an act of his own will.[8]

The conservative reserves his undying enmity for any idea that advances social reform as a means for betterment or perfection of man's nature. As he sees it, the chance we have for improving the human prospect is to maintain tradition, to keep inviolate the great contract among the generations, to rely for guidance on the wisdom of our ancestors, and to avoid doctrinaire reform proposals in any form. To the conservative, education, when it is conceived as intellectual and moral discipline, and when it is dedicated to preserving and transmitting the essential core of tradition, has an important part to play. The conservative would have us understand that the purpose of education is to preserve and transmit, and as William Buckley has said:

---

[7] The modern conservative always cites Burke as the founder of the tradition and regards Burke's *Reflections on the Revolution in France* as the seminal source of conservative ideals. Viereck has observed that any person can tell whether his own instincts are conservative or liberal by his reactions to the great debate between Burke and Tom Paine. See Viereck's *Conservatism*, p. 13.

[8] See, for example, Kirk, *Prospects for Conservatives*, p. 37.

Conservatism is the tacit acknowledgement that all that is finally important in human experience is behind us; that the crucial explorations have been undertaken, and that it is given to men to know what are the great truths that emerged from them. Whatever is to come cannot outweigh the importance to man of what has gone before.[9]

## CAPITALISM, INDUSTRIALISM, AND THE CONSERVATIVE TRADITION

The conservative mind as it has developed in America tends to identify capitalism as one of the main components of the conservative tradition. Capitalism is all but synonymous with the ideas called free enterprise, individual initiative, sanctity of property, and freedom. Americans typically do not discriminate among American capitalistic economics, American nationalism, and American interpretations of democracy. Apparently to the majority of us, any one of these great traditions could not be maintained in the absence of the others.

The failure to discriminate between genuine conservatism and what Peter Viereck has called "a petrified right wing of atomistic *laissez faire* liberalism" has been the subject of considerable dismayed comment by the intellectuals of conservative thought. To be sure, the conservative regards the sanctity of the "right of property" as of preeminent importance because he maintains that it is property that makes individual freedom possible. Similarly, both the intellectual and the common garden variety of conservative defend private economic enterprise staunchly because in their judgment it is the only workable system for satisfying economic needs. More than this, the conservative holds free enterprise to be the only system of economic life under which men can be truly free.[10] It is with the profit motive and the unrestrained desire for accumulation of wealth that the conservative sometimes finds difficulty. Conservatism has always regarded inherited wealth and the state of mind it fosters as one of the bulwarks of tradition and cultural stability, but it often views with

---

[9]  William F. Buckley, Jr., *Up from Liberalism* (New York: Hillman Periodicals, 1959), p. 172.

[10]  See, for example, Kirk, *Prospects for Conservatives*, p. 35; also in the same volume, chap. 6. In this chapter, Mr. Kirk writes eloquently against the idea that production, consumption, and profit making are the ends of human life. He says that the purpose of production is rather to provide enough goods so that men may have leisure for intellectual and other truly human pursuits. Profit making, therefore, under this view, is a means, not an end. But in free-enterprise capitalism, profit making *must* be the prime motive for economic activity because without profits there is no opportunity for leisure or any kind of good works.

A briefer treatment of the same subject by an economist will be found in Harold B. Wess, "We Can't Have Freedom Without Capitalism," in A. G. Heinsohn, Jr., ed., *Anthology of Conservative Writing in the United States, 1932–1960* (Chicago: Henry Regnery Co., 1962), pp. 374–77.

grave suspicion the influence of new wealth and the cultural rootlessness of those who possess it. To most conservatives, plutocracy is not the most desirable form of government—though they may think it no worse, and perhaps even better, than many liberal interpretations of democracy. Part of the disenchantment with capitalism that sometimes crops up in conservative writing may be owed to the indissoluble relation between capitalism and the industrial revolution.

The classic conservative is amply aware of the disruptive effect that industrialism has had on the traditional pattern of Western culture. As a conservative, he is dedicated to preserving cultural stability and the ethical ideals of honor and responsibility and justice as he conceives these. But the task in these days has become enormous. The urbanization of the population, the decline of agriculture, always a strong conservative influence, the growth of a great culturally rootless proletariat, the constant proliferation of a "new rich" class, and increasing demands for all kinds of social services at state expense combine to disrupt the continuity of tradition, to alter the settled order of society, and ultimately, in the conservative's opinion, to promote the rule of the mob. The task of the modern conservative is to find ways to preserve the traditional ideas in a society grown more corporate and integrated.

And yet, though there are certain nagging doubts among conservatives over economics and the character of capitalism in modern life, underneath these differences runs a common agreement. Viereck, after considering the differences, concludes:

> The diversity of conservative attitudes is shown by the fact that popular parlance in America calls two opposite groups "conservative": (1) The efficient modernism, cash-nexus selfishness, and atomistic society of the plutocrats; (2) The inefficient medievalism, anti-plutocratic idealism, and organic society of Coleridge, Carlyle, Newman, Ruskin. Yet both usages of "conservatism" have a partly unifying common denominator: both distrust the masses, prefer an established elitist authority, and distrust the abstract radical blueprints of utopians and of statists.[11]

## NATIONALISM AND CLASSIC CONSERVATISM

Nationalism, the principle that the primary allegiance of men belongs to the national state, is the most potent political force in the world today. By and large, the conservative tradition in the United States is dedicated to the preservation of American nationalism, and conservative educational doctrine conceives an important responsibility of the school to be to foster

---

[11]  Viereck, *Conservatism*, p. 41.

patriotism. However, conservatives are not completely in accord in their attitudes toward nationalism and the part it should play in modern life. Present-day conservative thought in this respect ranges from an intense insistence on retaining jealously every aspect of national sovereignty—an attitude that approaches the pre–World War II "isolationism"—to an acceptance of internationalism embracing membership in the United Nations, aid to friendly foreign nations, and even participation in such international agencies as UNESCO. About every shade of opinion is represented along the continuum, and the strains that these differences generate within the tradition are often critical.

Part of the reason for these differences, as Viereck has observed, are undoubtedly historical.[12] Throughout its history, the tradition has vacillated between nationalism and internationalism, depending on events at hand. Conservatives, following Burke, regarded nationalism as a tradition that should be preserved, but many of them were aware that other revered traditions—especially Christianity—in the end are not in complete harmony with nationalism and stand the chance of being sacrificed on the altar of chauvinism.[13]

Another reason for differences among conservatives in this area stems from the conservative's deep-dyed suspicion of all doctrinaire reform movements and "social blueprints." To the conservative, far too many of the proposals for mitigating and controlling nationalism in today's world have about them an aura of reform and doctrinaire utopianism. Some conservatives have professed disenchantment with the United Nations, partly on grounds of its alleged ineffectiveness and partly because of the fear of loss of national sovereignty.

Even when these differences of opinions and emphasis are taken into account, the general picture that remains is one in which the conservative tradition today staunchly upholds American nationalism, resists the infringement on national sovereignty by any kind of supranational organization, and lays on the schools the obligation to support national loyalties first of all.

In the schools, dominated as they are by conservative ideas, some of the same uncertainty prevails over the question of American nationalism that was noted among conservatives as a group. Community attitudes vary widely. Some communities actively support, for example, teaching in the schools about the United Nations, the study of materials supplied by UNESCO, and an emphasis on internationalism in the teaching of history. Other communities merely tolerate such activity by the schools, and a smaller number have flatly banned it. Constant pressure for a nationalistic

---

[12]  Viereck, *Conservatism*, p. 22.
[13]  Viereck points out that conservatives historically tended toward internationalism from 1789 to 1848 and toward nationalism after 1870. The end of World War II

and patriotic slant in the teaching of the social studies comes from various patriotic societies. It is likely that no school system in the country is free from this pressure, though it is stronger in some than in others and varies somewhat with events on the national and international scene and on the character of leadership in the various societies themselves.[14]

In the long run, the activities of these groups are probably superfluous because the programs of American schools have always been geared to the propagation of nationalism and there can be little doubt that the schools have met the expectations of Americans in this respect. Various studies of the content of American textbooks show that these books strongly support the idea of unlimited national sovereignty, the superiority of the "American way," and the essential rightness of American foreign policy. These texts also embrace the close relation between capitalism, nationalism, and democracy of conservative belief, and the effort to mend the breach between nationalism and religion by identifying the destiny of the nation with the will of the Creator.

Thus, although various groups periodically conduct vigilante investigations of textbooks and make extravagant charges about the deviation of the schools from nationalistic norms, there is no trustworthy evidence that the schools have ever subverted what is almost surely the will of the populace in this regard. The same thing can be said about the allegiance of teachers. In spite of allegations about the national loyalties of teachers, nobody has ever turned up more than a handful of professional teachers who could be classed as subversive of American nationalism.

## DEMOCRACY AND CLASSIC CONSERVATISM

The third great tradition in American society is democracy. The term *democracy* has manifold meaning, and one that various groups interpret to fit their own purposes. Many bitter doctrinal differences between modern conservatives and liberals can be traced to differing interpretations of this strategic term. Even within the conservative tradition itself grave differences of opinion about its meaning exist.[15]

There appears to be agreement among conservatives that the fundamental significance of the word *democracy* is a moral one and that this moral conception is rooted in traditional religion, particularly the Hebraic-Christian tradition. Belief in the intrinsic worth of the human being and

---

brought a return of internationalism—particularly to European conservatives. The prime motive is the desire for mutual protection against communism, which originally, at least, was international in its appeal.

[14] · For a summary of the activities of superpatriotic groups, see Richard Schmuck and Mark Chesler, "On Super-Patriotism: A Definition and Analysis," *Journal of Social Issues* 19 (April 1963): 31–50.

[15] For a summary of the historical development of these differences among conservatives, see Viereck, *Conservatism*, chaps. 14, 15, and 16.

the equality of all men before their Maker is in harmony with the basic conservative view.[16] The difficulty the conservative finds is that these sentiments have often been exploited by doctrinaire reformers in the effort to achieve social results that are clearly out of harmony with conservative ideals. Further, those ideals of inherent personal worth have often been transformed in American society, lacking as it does the feudal background of European countries, into a kind of primitive egalitarianism that conservatives have warned against since the very beginnings of our national history.[17] One of the main charges in conservative criticism of today's education is that this misconceived egalitarianism has so infected our schools that the superior student is condemned to an unending mediocrity in education and this in the name of equality.

The conservative will argue that all men have the right to live in freedom and justice and that this right, being given by God, is inalienable. But at the same time, he warns sternly that most of us, particularly those of liberal persuasions, talk too much of "rights" and too little of *duty.* Part of the reason for modern decadence, in the opinion of the conservative, lies in the failure of men today to uphold duty and to recognize that only as men understand and accept the responsibilities that go with their station in life and their obligation to tradition will they realize the right to freedom and justice. Many conservatives today have the profound conviction that public education has all but failed to instill a sense of duty and obligation in the young. These young people, products of the social atomism of doctrinaire liberalism that stresses rights and ignores obligation, are rootless, wayward, and committed to nothing but their own desires. Out of this infection grow the ugly sores of juvenile delinquency, counterculture, and adult irresponsibility, improvidence, and crime.

In the field of politics, the conservative is at pains to make clear his interpretation of the word *democracy. Democracy* means literally rule by the people as distinct from rule by an elite class based on wealth, blood, or power. The conservative holds the deepest suspicion of the implications of *democracy* when that term is interpreted as the mere counting of noses to determine which way the winds of passion are blowing the mob on any particular issue of the moment.[18] Historically, conservatives simply did not believe that political democracy would work, and they opposed the extension of the suffrage at every turn. Perhaps in no other area (with the possible

---

[16] Clinton Rossiter, *Conservatism in America: The Thankless Persuasion,* 2nd ed. (New York: Random House, Vintage Books, 1962), pp. 23–24.

[17] Important among these are John Adams, Hamilton, Madison, and Alexis de Tocqueville.

[18] William Buckley has reserved some of his sharpest barbs for those who identify democracy with egalitarian nose counting. See his section "The Liberal: His Root Assumptions," *Up from Liberalism,* pp. 132 ff.

exception of educational theory) is the conservative's distrust of the masses seen more clearly than in politics. Conservatives are prone to remind us as often as possible that our form of government is a *republic*, not a democracy.[19] They are often critical of the schools for not making this distinction clear to students and for promoting a kind of mindless egalitarianism in the classroom.

To the conservative the maintenance of social order and tranquillity is possible only when tradition is maintained and transmitted. The obligation for this is held to rest always on the superior class in society, that is, the social class whose status is based on inherited wealth, superior education, and superior breeding. This is the stratum in society from which wise leadership must come, for except in unusual cases, only in this level of society is to be found that respect for tradition and social order that are the ingredients of wise and competent leadership.

The American conservative is not apologetic about the idea of "aristocracy," though for strategic reasons he may sometimes avoid use of the term. This tradition frankly holds that society should be governed by its wisest and best men—John Adams's "natural and actual aristocracy." Burke's eloquence on the "unbought grace of life" is quoted frequently by modern conservatives as they argue against the domination of political life by the rootless masses, the degradation of morals, taste, and manners in modern society, and the lack of a sense of obligation that characterizes a large portion of the American population.[20]

Thus to the conservative mind, democracy, when its meaning is a regard for justice and order in society, when it indicates the opportunity for men to exercise their natural talents and enjoy the fruits of their efforts, when it protects all men in their right to property, and when it avoids the social leveling based on the idea that "all men are equal," which the conservative says they manifestly are not, then the concept is one of the precious elements in the tradition of the West. But when conjurers of radicalism and liberalism use the term *democracy* to create such illusions

---

[19] This has been a favorite theme of Barry Goldwater. See his *Conscience of a Conservative*, Victor Publishing Co., chap. 2. Buckley has also attacked the glorification of democracy by liberals, saying among other things that "the persistent misuse of the word *democracy* reflects either an ignorance of its ontological emptiness; or . . . the pathetic attempt to endow it with substantive meaning." Buckley, *Up from Liberalism*, p. 135. But the classic statement of this attitude is to be found in Irving Babbitt, *Democracy and Leadership* (Boston: Houghton Mifflin Co., 1924), pp. 243–47.

[20] Edmund Burke, *Reflections on the Revolution in France* (Indianapolis: Bobbs-Merrill Co., Liberal Arts Press, 1955), pp. 85 ff. Burke did not believe in the "natural aristocracy" advocated by Adams, Jefferson, and other Americans. Viereck points out that this is a fundamental difference between American and European conservatism. Certainly the idea of an aristocracy of nature—rather than of blood and wealth—has an important connection with ideas about occupational and social mobility, and hence with ideas about education.

as the elimination of social classes and distinctions in society, the cheap egalitarian doctrine that one man's opinions (and hence his vote) are as good as any other's, the perverse educational doctrine that all men have the same right to education and therefore should have the same kind of education, the advocacy that "human rights" supersede property rights— then the conservative rebels, as indeed many have, against the unending ritualistic recitation of the word.

To the conservative, the tradition of democracy, properly conceived, is one of the foundation stones of modern culture, along with the accompanying historical developments of nationalism and capitalism. Just as the conservative may reject nationalism in its exaggerated chauvinistic form, and the excesses of laissez faire capitalism, so he rejects the libertarian interpretation of democracy that at the very best, he thinks, can mean only rule by the mob and at the very worst, social dissolution, chaos, and ultimately tyranny.

## SCIENCE, SCIENTIFIC METHOD, AND CLASSIC CONSERVATISM

Experimental science is the cultural element that most clearly differentiates the modern mind from the medieval mind. The acceleration of cultural transition in our time owes more to the development of science than to any other single event or class of events. It is commonplace to say that science has served to question the older traditions at virtually every turn. This condition has posed the most severe challenge to the conservatism of our time because conservatism needs to cement into one synthesis modern experimental science, with its tremendous intellectual achievements, and the traditional religious transcendentalism that we have inherited from antiquity and that the conservative regards as the most precious part of tradition.

That this has always been an important problem in the post-medieval world is well known, and the questions involved grow more crucial with each generation. One way in which the conservative tradition seeks to deal with the problem is to insist that the alleged conflict between the naturalism of science and the supernaturalism of religion is not genuine and that no informed person will waste his time any longer arguing about the incompatibility of the two.

A classic example occurred when Sir Julian Huxley spoke at a convocation at the University of Chicago, a centennial celebration of Darwin's *Origin of Species*. Huxley observed that in the evolutionary pattern of thought, there is no place for ideas about supernatural forces affecting events in nature.[21] This observation promptly evoked indignant

---

[21]   See the *Chicago Tribune* for November 28, 1959, part 1, p. 10.

protests from various clergymen and theologians. A common theme in these protests was that Sir Julian was hopelessly out of fashion in his ideas, which were judged more appropriate for a village atheist than a distinguished biologist. The egregious error on Huxley's part lay, according to these spokesmen, in his failure to perceive that God can create through evolution and therefore that there is no necessary contradiction between religious and evolutionary theory. The approach of the spokesmen differs significantly from other beliefs of a more fundamentalist character, which are based largely on a literal interpretation of the Bible, particularly the first chapter of Genesis with its account of a specific and deliberate act of creation.

So long as the mechanical model of the universe furnished by the Newtonian hypothesis obtained, the task of accommodating physics to theology, while not simple, seemed at least possible. In terms of this model, it is possible to speak of a "first cause" in the guise of a "Master Mechanic" who designs the great mechanism of nature and sets it going to run forever in strict harmony with natural law. But as is well known, this conception has been outmoded by the newer physics, and although the fact may be distasteful even to some physicists, the universe that is presented to us now exhibits basic traits of contingency and apparent unpredictability that cannot be ignored.[22] Manifestly, it is not a simple matter to synthesize a cosmology of this character with the supernaturalism that so many conservatives feel is necessary, not only to their tradition but to the very survival of Western culture.

Nor is it a simple affair to harmonize the empirical, experimental conception of the knowledge process, which is the essence of science, with the supernaturalism of religion. Science is built on a method of inquiry that involves a radical empiricism—the principle that the limits of human knowledge are the limits of human experience. Though science is becoming increasingly sophisticated—which is to say it is becoming increasingly precise in its treatment of data and steadily more rational in its theoretical structure—the fact remains that the ultimate appeal of science is in its method of controlled observation and experimentation.

Propositions in metaphysics and theology do not lend themselves to this mode of inquiry because by definition these propositions lie outside

---

[22] It is true that statements appear from time to time in the public press by scientists, some of them distinguished in their fields, about the "ultimate mystery" or "that unknown region which lies beyond physics." These statements are often heralded as evidence that "modern scientists believe in God." Whether one accepts this as genuine evidence or not, it must be admitted that there is a yawning gulf between these vague assertions and the well-defined and widely accepted anthropomorphic conceptions of a Creator and a universe designed for man, which are central to the conservative tradition.

experience and cannot be tested experimentally. The conservative—who cannot maintain his traditional acceptance of supernaturalism if he admits only to an empirical theory of knowledge—must by necessity postulate other modes of knowledge and inquiry than the scientific. He is most apt to advance variations on one or both of the ancient conceptions that the highest truth comes through revelation or through reason.

The strains within the conservative tradition occasioned by the phenomenal advances of the physical sciences, the changes in modern cosmology, and the increasing domination of the curriculum by scientific studies, as opposed to the older humanities, are severe enough. To these there is added a threat that conservatives apparently fear more than any other, and yet this development has originated, in part at least, within the tradition and is closely related to some important aspects of conservative educational doctrine. The condition referred to here is the application of scientific method and scientific modes of inquiry to the study of human behavior in the form of the "social sciences."

Historically, conservatism has been built on a certain conception of human nature and the analysis of this nature has been considered the proper subject matter of philosophy and theology. It is well known, for example, that until comparatively recent times psychology, which has become one of the most aggressive of the behavioral sciences, was a branch of philosophy proper and its methods of inquiry were mainly speculative. Present-day social scientists—psychologists in particular—are not interested in studying some vague human nature but in studying the varied phenomena of *human behavior*. Modern psychology is built on the conviction that human behavior, complex though it may be, is capable of being investigated, analyzed, and understood through scientific method in the same sense that any natural phenomenon can be studied and understood. Sociology, anthropology, and economics rest on the same principle.

The course of cultural transition being what it is, this attitude has penetrated to some extent into conservative quarters, and it is not necessarily inconsistent with many deeply conservative ideas about education. To say that this scientific realism is an entering wedge that may very well split the whole conservative tradition is to underestimate the case. The conservative is going to find it difficult in this affair both to have his cake and eat it. Trite though the phrase may be, in this case it is exactly descriptive of what most conservatives would like to do—embrace both supernaturalism and science in some kind of acceptable synthesis.

A fundamental element in scientific method is the principle of uniformity—whenever the same causal conditions are given, the same results will occur. So if human behavior is a natural phenomenon, it must be assumed that it too is subject to the principle of uniformity and is explainable in terms of the same cause-effect relationship on which all science by necessity depends. If this is accepted, we find ourselves compelled to acknowledge that certain ideas about "freedom of the will" may have to be abandoned or at the very least reinterpreted. Much of the conservative tradition's conception of human nature is built around the presumption that man is free to direct his own behavior and hence is a responsible moral agent. That is to say, man can choose consciously among alternatives, and his behavior is guided by his own volition rather than determined by forces outside himself. And the conservative not only sees this as the basic element in human nature but also hangs his whole case for personal and social morality on it.

One does not have to be an unfriendly critic of the conservative tradition to admit the crucial nature of this situation. Conservatives themselves are amply aware of it and devote careful attention to it. For example, Joseph Wood Krutch has argued eloquently against the determinism inherent in the social sciences. An important part of his argument is based on the reality of consciousness and the awareness of self as the primary fact of consciousness: the only thing we have evidence for is our own consciousness; all of our understanding proceeds from this elemental fact.[23]

Krutch, following the sentiment of many conservatives, attacks the ideas that human nature can be understood in purely scientific terms and that ethical analysis can be nothing but scientific inquiry. He asks whether "we should again believe that what a Shakespeare has to say about human nature and conduct is likely to be as true as, and rather more important than, what the summarizer of ten thousand questionnaires can tell us." [24] Krutch, along with many conservatives, considers such a question strictly rhetorical.

Probably the strongest objection most people have to determinism applied to human behavior is the fatal effect such an idea is believed to have for moral responsibility and the very idea of a system of ethics. Manifestly, if behavior in any human being is determined by antecedent events over which he has no control, it seems idle to talk about his being responsible for what he does. And it would follow that all criminal law— as well as all moral exhortation in home, school and church—is based on impossible premises. This is what Krutch battles against in the book we have referred to, and it is indeed a matter of gravest concern to the whole tradition of conservatism.

Two other objections to determinism are often found in the literature of conservatism. (1) Physics, often thought of as the most deterministic

---

[23]  Joseph Wood Krutch, *The Measure of Man* (New York: Grosset & Dunlap, Grosset's Universal Library Series, 1953). See particularly chap. 6: "The Stubborn Fact of Consciousness."

[24]  Ibid., pp. 231–32.

of the sciences, has found the behavior of subatomic particles to be indeterminate, random, and hence unpredictable. Therefore, at least at present, it is nòt possible to postulate any strict cause-effect relation throughout nature. (2) We cannot ignore the persistent and compelling feeling within ourselves that we do have freedom to choose among alternatives. The objector to determinism argues that we cannot rightfully ignore either the scientific evidence or the conviction of common sense and personal experience.[25] Thus, the conservative tradition faces a severe problem in a world in which scientific modes of thought are advancing steadily—and often at the expense of the older beliefs.

## THE EMPHASIS ON COMMUNITY

When the classic conservative surveys the contemporary world and man's place in it, and when he seeks the source of the malaise that he thinks infests society, his attention is apt to be riveted on the loss of a sense of community among us. We have already remarked the conservative attitude towards nationalism, which despite vacillation over the years is important in the outlook of the conservative. But to be a citizen of a great nation-state is not the same as being a functioning member of a community, with the intimate ties and relationships that this implies. It is no exaggeration to say that the conservative regards the community as the very basis of social solidarity and well-being and that he traces many of the evils that plague us to its disintegration. Much of the blame for this he has usually attributed to liberalism, charging that its doctrinaire rationalism has produced the social atomism that characterizes our society and is in danger of bringing it to the point of dissolution.

The conservative is no egalitarian. He does not believe that men are equal, except in the moral sense; he believes that there must be orders and degrees that are recognized and respected in society. On the other hand, he believes in the integrity and inviolability of the individual, and he believes that the realization of this can come only as the individual is a functioning member of a true community. This means that the individual can realize himself and his own potential only as he is an integral part of community life and that the community can prosper only as its members contribute, each in accord with his own particular talents and abilities. Thus, the conservative believes in a class society, but he does not believe in a *stratified* society. The distinction is important.

There is something of the Greek ideal here, although the classical conservative is leery of pushing it as far as Plato did in *The Republic*.

---

[25] Stimulating discussions on both sides of the determinism question are presented in Sidney Hook, ed., *Determinism and Freedom in the Age of Modern Science* (New York: Crowell-Collier Publishing Co., Collier Books, 1961).

The Greeks did not set the individual and his interests against those of the state, and the Greeks, particularly the Athenians, subscribed to a conception of individual freedom that is still celebrated. But the Greeks emphasized that the individual realized his freedom and individuality through his membership and participation in the polis, the Greek city-state.

In one sense, the conservative's view of the good society is pluralistic. Men, he thinks, live best and most fully when they have strong organic ties with other men, ties that come from association and joint effort within the myriad groups that compose society. The conservative views intrinsic groups like the family and the church of supreme importance here. He also recognizes other kinds of associations into which men enter—schools, labor groups, fraternal organizations of various kinds, and many others. The very presence of these diverse forms of association makes real community possible and acts as a bulwark against the evolution of what the conservative fears most—the monolithic state.

A note of irony creeps into these considerations. It is a risky thing to make too much of something that may be only a temporary and fleeting phenomenon. The fads of one decade have a way of disappearing and being replaced by something quite different in the next. At any rate, it is interesting to note that much, though by no means all, of what the classical conservative has been maintaining for years about the importance of community now has become a principal article of faith of that diverse and heterogeneous movement known, among other things, as the New Left. The New Left, which would consider itself about as far removed from classical conservatism as imagination will permit, is arguing for the re-establishment in American society of a sense and feeling of community, of the participation of all in the diversity of community life, and of a plurality of association into which men may enter.

Moreover, there is to be found among those of the New Left a profound strain of antiintellectualism that is strangely reminiscent of conservatism. The conservative has a strong sense of history and a reverence for the past, elements that are conspicuously missing in the literature of the New Left, but even so there is still something in common. This something is a profound distrust of centralized power, the feeling that there is a mystery about human life and destiny into which reason cannot penetrate, and above all a distrust of liberal, doctrinaire attitudes towards social reform, which both groups believe is not only dangerous but has shown itself a total failure.

Obviously, the comparison can be pushed too far. There is too much in the New Left to put the conservative off: disavowal of conventional sex mores, bizarre forms of dress and grooming, the resort to drugs, the defiance of established authority, and the unending stream of scatological language. But it is possible to imagine that if the shade of Edmund Burke does witness these events, there must occasionally be an ironic smile about his lips when he considers that this group, depraved as it may appear by common conservative standards, has intuitively grasped an important principle of human society.

The conservative maintains that society, if it is to be a true community, must be pluralistic, but this is only half the story. A true community is organic. It is not a collection of individuals each concerned only with "doing his own thing." The myriad forms of association into which men enter can be effective only if they constitute an organic unity in which each institution has its own place and each individual plays the role that is best suited to him.[26]

The analogy that conservatives have turned to most often is that society is a living thing, not a mechanism. A mechanical contraption can be disassembled, its parts replaced, its structure altered. But if a living thing is disassembled it dies and nobody can restore it to its original form or nature. And, the conservative says, so it is with society. An organism is healthy when its various organs and processes operate in harmony, each playing its proper role. When one part fails, the whole organism is affected. And so a healthy society, like a healthy organism, is one in which the component parts act in harmony. Any tampering with one part inevitably affects all. Education is an important component of the social organism that we cannot tamper with and not affect the whole society.

## SUMMARY OF THE BASIC PRINCIPLES OF CLASSIC CONSERVATISM

To summarize the basic ideas inherent in classic conservatism, the following propositions are offered. This list is not intended to be exhaustive but rather to express the general outlook of the classical conservative.[27]

1. A divine intent rules society. History itself is the objective manifestation of a transcendental force.
2. There are universal and unchanging standards of value and these are the measure of goodness.

---

[26] For a more complete account of the classical conservative's view of the nature of society, see Clinton Rossiter, *Conservatism in America: The Thankless Persuasion*, 2nd ed. (New York: Random House, Vintage Books, 1962), especially pp. 24–46. Rossiter's book is one of the most comprehensive and useful sources on Western conservatism available today.

[27] For a more extensive summary, see Rossiter, *Conservatism in America*, pp. 64–66. Rossiter acknowledges the difficulties involved in attempting to delineate in this fashion a tradition as complex as classic conservatism. The present writer shares his misgivings. Russell Kirk presents a shorter list in his *Conservative Mind*, 3d ed. (Chicago: Henry Regnery Co., 1960), pp. 6–8.

3.   Conservatives have affection and veneration for the mystery of traditional life. Reason cannot penetrate all the reaches of human experience.

4.   Private property and freedom are inseparable.

5.   Tradition and established custom provide a rein on man's primitive and impulsive nature, which is itself a compound of good and evil.

6.   Change and reform, when reform is considered improvement, are not identical. Doctrinaire, atomistic liberalism and various forms of radicalism lead ultimately to chaos and tyranny.

7.   The greatest social danger we face is the presence of a great, culturally rootless mass of people who are in danger of falling prey to various forms of alien political and social doctrine. At the root of this situation lies the loss of a sense of community.

8.   Inequality is natural among men. And therefore society should be governed by its wisest and most just men—a natural aristocracy of wisdom and talent.

## CONSERVATISM—AMERICAN STYLE

At the beginning of this discussion, it was suggested that although the seminal source of American conservatism was British, the character of the tradition as it has developed in this country varies in some important respects from its pure Burkean ancestry. In general, most Americans have not thought of themselves as conservatives, certainly not in the classic sense. If as a people we have thought of ourselves as having a continuing, indigenous political and social tradition, that tradition probably has to be liberalism—interpreted more often than not with strong overtones of populism.

There are reasons for this. A fundamental one is that our national life emerged from a background that was nonfeudal and therefore nonaristocratic. This condition has been complicated by the influence of democracy in politics and by industrialism. Clinton Rossiter has said, and here he is referring to classic conservatism, which he denotes with a capital C:

> The reason the American Right is not Conservative today is that it has not been Conservative for more than a hundred years. The reason it first abandoned Conservatism, even the characteristically American version proclaimed by John Adams, may be summed in two words: democracy and industrialism.[28]

---

[28]   Rossiter, *Conservatism in America*, p. 201.

The classic conservative, in spite of his insistence on the free enterprise system and the sanctity of property, has harbored deep uncertainties about the disruptive effects that industrialism has had on Western society, particularly in advancing materialism. The American conservative has been disturbed but very little in this respect. It is paradoxical, as Rossiter has observed, that the great captains of industrialism, those we should consider conservative and who undoubtedly considered themselves in the same way, were the great innovators and architects of social change in America. Whether these industrialists were naive enough to think, for example, that they could introduce into American society such a revolutionary device as the cheap automobile and keep the rest of the social pattern intact—and traditional—or whether they never considered the matter at all is hard to know. That it did happen is more important here than the reason for its happening.[29]

In America, the conservative reflects the attitude of the classic conservative towards misapplication of the term *democracy*. However, conservatism in America, in Rossiter's words, has "had to . . . accept the ground rules of democracy or be thrown out of the game for disloyalty and perversity."[30] Rossiter observes further that the American conservative has learned to play the game with very considerable skill.

The plain truth is that American conservatives have not been good social philosophers, and our native literature on conservative political philosophy that is worth reading has been produced by conservatives whose posture is close to classic European conservatism if not identical with it. Examples of these are Russell Kirk and Peter Viereck. This means that if we were to come up here with any accurate delineation of the American conservative credo, we should have to sift through an appalling amount of literature, if it can be called that, consisting mainly of shopworn homilies, slogans, bitter invective, and simple-minded preaching.[31] Rossiter's analysis of the contrast between classic and American conservatism is an adequate reference. Briefly, there are some principles on which the two forms are in substantial agreement. There are some principles to which the American conservative pays no attention. There are some with which he disagrees for the most part. And there is one, and

---

[29] Rossiter cites Henry Ford as a classic example of the American, conservative to the marrow of his bones in religion, politics, education, and social customs and with a profound nostalgia for the past, and yet in another sense one of the great revolutionaries of this century. For a more extensive discussion of these matters, see Rossiter, *Conservatism in America*, pp. 202–7.

[30] Ibid., p. 202.

[31] The reader who doubts this is invited to browse through *Anthology of Conservative Writing in the United States 1932–1960*, compiled and edited with commentary by A. G. Heinsohn, Jr.

it is a significant one, with which he flatly disagrees—the primacy of community.[32] Rossiter concludes that three main issues distinguish American from classic conservatism. They may be paraphrased as follows:

1.   The American conservative is more optimistic. He has less of the notion of human frailty and the component of evil in human nature, at least he places less emphasis on these. He is more sanguine about the potentialities of human reason and the possibilities of social progress. Even so, he agrees substantially with the classic conservative emphasis on supernatural religion and its importance to man and society.

2.   The American conservative is more materialistic. His political theory has more to do with economics than with ethics and there is often a tinge of Manchestrian economic liberalism in his utterances. When he thinks of progress, he usually tends to equate it with economic progress, or at least economic growth.

3.   The American conservative is more individualistic. The principle of classic conservatism that the American has rejected flatly is the primacy of the community. It well may be that he has never grasped the classic concept that the freedom of the individual is not one of splendid isolation, whether this is called rugged individualism or something else, but depends on association in diverse groups and identification with them, they themselves being functional parts of an encompassing whole. Whether this rejection of community has been conscious or unconscious is unimportant when it is compared with the actual occurrence.[33]

## SUMMARY

Original classic conservatism is seen as an emergent of postmedieval Western culture. Many of its roots are aristocratic and the tradition still shows evidence of this origin. In the American experience, the classic tradition has been altered in certain ways, some of them strategic. The conservative tradition strongly supports the idea of universal education. This is true both of classical and American conservatives.[34] Historically, this has not always been the case. In the nineteenth century, conservatives moved cautiously, as they usually do, and in the face of mounting pressure

---

[32]   Rossiter, *Conservatism in America*, pp. 199–200. The list is too long to be repeated here but the reader who is interested in this strategic aspect of American conservatism should study Rossiter's analysis with care.

[33]   Ibid., p. 201.

[34]   For a discussion of the attitude of classical conservatives toward education, see Rossiter, *Conservatism in America*, pp. 26–27.

for popular education they gave in only a little at a time. Consequently, a large part of the history of American education in the nineteenth century is concerned with the struggle for the establishment and support for free, universal education.

But these events are far behind us now. The modern conservative recognizes the importance of education, and indeed the necessity for it. He sees the school as one of the important bastions of our society. Naturally, the conservative has considered it of the utmost importance to have the schools serve conservative purposes. His success in this respect has been impressive. Conservative education has had its times of troubles in this century and the road ahead is far from smooth. But in the long view, the American school has shown itself remarkably resistant to any fundamental change, and needless to say, the conservative intends to do all he can to keep it that way.

chapter THREE

# ESSENTIALISM: THE CONSERVATIVE TRADITION IN EDUCATION

*Human nature with all its infirmities and depravities is still capable of great things. . . . Education makes a greater difference between man and man, than nature has made between man and brute. The virtues and powers to which men may be trained, by early education and constant discipline, are truly sublime and astonishing.*

—JOHN ADAMS

Ever since the end of World War II there has been increasing evidence of a resurgence of conservative sentiment in the United States. This sentiment has been expressed in varying degrees in every important facet of social life. One area in which there is unmistakable evidence of a great resurgence of conservative doctrine is education.

The conservative mind has its own perceptions of the nature and importance of education. The conservative believes that the schools exist to perform certain functions in society and that there are others they should not perform. He believes that certain subject matters are worthy to be taught in the schools and some are not. He believes that the school should cherish and transmit certain traditional values, and he does not believe that the school should attempt to maintain neutrality about questions of value. He believes further that the school plays a certain role in society, and that certain traditional relations exist between the school and other institutions. Needless to say, he believes these relations should be retained in substantially unaltered form. The conservative tradition is an old tradition and in its development certain differences of opinion and emphasis have developed. It is not possible to show that all conservatives agree exactly on all issues concerning educational policy, nor would conservatives think such complete agreement necessarily desirable. What we can show is that conservatives agree on certain strategic ideas in educational theory. This agreement has been sufficient to bind conservatives together in a united front on educational principles, although they differ significantly on certain detailed issues.

The resurgence of orthodoxy in conservative educational thought began with a polemical movement of awesome proportions. This reaction was in large measure against the alleged excesses of the progressive doctrine that, in the judgment of conservatives, had perverted the American educational system almost beyond hope of recovery. The polemic was directed primarily against the acknowledged leaders of the progressive movement, institutions for the preparation of teachers, and state agencies for the certification of teachers. As is usually the case with polemic, much of the language was not only bitter but vituperative.[1]

While conservative critics were all but unanimous in placing the blame for what they consider the dire state of education on the shoulders

---

[1] The volume of polemical literature by conservative critics is so great that even a listing of it is far beyond the possible scope of this book. For an interesting sample of a biting critique of American education by a leading figure of the new conservatism, see Russell Kirk, *Prospects for Conservatives* (Chicago: Henry Regnery Co., 1956), chap. 3. One of the earlier polemical articles that attracted wide attention and seems to have set the general tone for the many that were yet to come is Harry J. Fuller, "The Emperor's New Clothes, or Prius Dementat," *Scientific Monthly*, January 1951, pp. 32–41.

of schools and colleges of education and professors of education, their attitudes toward the teachers in the schools were mixed. Some held forthrightly that much of the fault could be attributed to classroom teachers who themselves had abdicated their historic duties, lowered standards in the classroom, and substituted for rigorous education a program of juvenile entertainment.[2]

There were others, however, who portrayed teachers as captives of school administrators and certification authorities, aided and abetted by professors of education, who forced them against their will and better judgment to cheapen and degrade the educational process. Those who argued from this position maintained that the salvation of the school system depended on breaking the stranglehold the "educationists" had maintained on American education for nearly half a century. Once the great conspiracy was broken, teachers could feel themselves free once again to give their students a genuine education.[3]

It would be possible to prolong indefinitely this presentation of the conservative's objections to the state of things in contemporary American education as he saw it. In the interests of economy, a few propositions are stated here that summarize passably well the conservative view of education in the 1950s.

1.   Americans have largely lost sight of the true purpose of education, which is intellectual training. We tend to confuse education with all kinds of social, psychological, and vocational services that are often lumped together under the rubric "life adjustment."

2.   The rigor of our educational programs and teaching methods has been declining steadily for several decades. This is true in some measure of every level of the school system from the kindergarten to the university, but the condition is particularly acute in the elementary and secondary schools.

3.   We have failed to provide for the education of our brightest children because instruction has been pitched at the level of the mediocre student and the ablest have been systematically deprived in the name of "equality" and "democracy."

4.   The curricula of our schools have been diluted by the introduction of courses consisting largely of "life adjustment" trivia, and these worthless substitutes have crowded out the historic disciplines that are the core of a true education. Even the brightest students, seeking an easy way out, elect the easy courses and neglect the basic intellectual program.

---

[2]  See, for example, Bernard Iddings Bell, *Crisis in Education* (New York: McGraw-Hill Book Co., 1949), chap. 3 and passim.

[3]  See Albert Lynd, *Quackery in the Public Schools* (Boston: Little, Brown and Co., 1950).

5. Intellectual achievement has declined steadily among American students. Not only is their achievement inferior to that of American students of two or three generations ago; it is also inferior to that of students in every large European country.[4]

6. The schools are failing to meet their obligations to American youth and to American society. They are not only failing in the intellectual task, they are also failing in their responsibility to transmit those values that are the basis of the American tradition. The ancient norms for personal morality are systematically ignored in our classrooms, and teachers no longer transmit the basic American virtues of self-sufficiency, free enterprise, self-direction, and respect for tradition.

The resurgence of conservatism in educational theory, which had its greatest thrust in the 1950s, was an important episode in the philosophy of American education, but it should be seen for what it was—one historical episode in the development of the conservative tradition. The events that combined to make up this episode were patterned primarily around the threat posed by another tradition in the earlier decades of the century. Thus, much that was written about education in the fifties by conservatives was directed against the influence of progressivism.

However interesting this great educational controversy may have been, the important matter for consideration here is not so much what conservatives are against as the basic principles they espouse so firmly and defend so resolutely. What, we may ask ourselves, is it that characterizes the conservative mind so far as educational theory is concerned? What distinguishes the conservative from followers of other persuasions?

## THE THESIS OF ESSENTIALISM

The educational ideology of essentialism is based on four propositions, each concerned with one of the elements found in any educational theory: the purpose of formal education; the nature of the curriculum; the function of teaching and the role of the teacher; and the purposes of the school in society. The convictions of the essentialist on these matters, taken together, define accurately the character of this tradition. Each proposition will be examined in some detail and illustrative examples will be cited from the writings of essentialists and from school practices.

---

[4] The actual number of generations since the golden age of American education is uncertain, although it is possible to infer the existence of such a period from some conservative writing. See, for example, Hyman G. Rickover, *Swiss Schools and Ours: Why Theirs Are Better* (Boston: Atlantic–Little, Brown, 1962).

Many who read what follows will recognize what is really a brief description of the kind of educational experience they themselves have had since first entering school. Many may feel that the account is only a repetition of what "everybody" knows and believes about what schools should do. Reactions of this kind simply testify to the enormous influence this tradition has—and always has had—on American conceptions of formal education.

## THE PURPOSES OF EDUCATION

According to essentialists, the purpose of education is the transmission of certain elements of the cultural heritage whose importance is so great that they cannot be neglected. From the standpoint of the individual, the purpose of education is to help him achieve intellectual discipline. Stated briefly, the essentialist thesis about the aims of education is intellectual training for the individual through rigorous application of the mind to the historic subject matters. This process, the essentialist maintains, and *only* this, is worthy to be called the purpose of education.

The purpose of the school as intellectual discipline is a thesis all essentialists accept. There is, however, some difference of opinion among them about whether the school has any other responsibilities for children and youth. One group maintains that the school's responsibility is for intellectual training and for nothing else. They insist that while children and youth need other kinds of services, these matters, important as they may be, are not the concern of the school and the school should not dissipate its energies in attempting tasks that historically have belonged with the family, the church, and the community at large. The school as an institution is concerned with the life of the mind, and the program of the school should be devoted to cultivating intellectual life. Plainly this cannot be done if the high purposes of education are diluted with all kinds of social services and other diversionary activities.[5]

Another group of conservatives, probably much larger than the first group, takes a somewhat more extended view of the school's responsibility. Members of this group would concede that the school has some stake in the physical and emotional well-being of the young child and that child guidance in such areas is a valid responsibility of the teacher as well as of the school as an institution. They would concede further

---

[5] For an authoritative statement of the conservative thesis about the purpose of education, together with a blistering criticism of variant views, see Arthur E. Bestor, Jr., "Life Adjustment Education: A Critique," *Bulletin of the American Association of University Professors* 38 (Autumn 1952): 413–41. See also the same author, *Educational Wastelands* (Urbana, Ill.: University of Illinois Press, 1953); and *The Restoration of Learning* (New York: Alfred A. Knopf, 1955).

that the secondary school has some proper responsibility for guidance of adolescents toward worthy personal and vocational goals. Similarly, they would allow the school some share in the social life of the adolescent and therefore permit such "extracurricular" enterprises as athletics, musical activities, and journalistic and social events. At the level of higher education, a continuation and perhaps a widening of similar kinds of extracurricular activities would be permitted and even encouraged.

It should be noted, however, that these are *concessions* in the strict sense of the word. These concessions are agreed to only so long as they are regarded and treated strictly as peripheral to the real purpose of the school. There is wide agreement among essentialists that when any subsidiary service or activity begins to interfere with the intellectual purpose of the school it should be relegated immediately to its proper subordinate place.[6]

## THE NATURE OF THE CURRICULUM

The essentialist thesis is further reflected in the curriculum proposed for the school. It should be remembered that the conservative makes a careful distinction between curricular and extracurricular aspects of the school program. He has no time for and little patience with such statements as, "The curriculum is the sum total of all the experiences the school provides for students." To the conservative the curriculum is that part of the school's program that nurtures intellectual discipline.

So far as the nature of the curriculum is concerned, conservatives unite on the stand that it consists of a common core of subject matters, intellectual skills, and accepted values that are so essential they must be transmitted to all who come to school. As the conservative sees it, it is through this kind of program that the school can make its chief contribution to preserving and transmitting the essential heritage of culture. Conservatives typically insist that while the transmission of knowledge, together with the resulting intellectual discipline, constitutes a prime responsibility of the school, the responsibility for transmission does not end with knowledge and skill. The school must also play a large role in transmitting to succeeding generations that body of accepted values that are the core of Western civilization.[7] Conservatives have often seen the upsurge in juvenile delinquency and the alleged increase in moral laxity in the population at large as evidence of what happens when the school neglects its historic role.

---

[6] For a brief and explicit statement of the conservative view on this matter, see James D. Koerner, "Basic Education," *Education* 79 (February 1959): 372–74.

[7] A spokesman for the Council for Basic Education refers to development of mind, will, and conscience as constituting the basic purposes of education. See ibid., p. 372.

In the opinion of the conservative, the education of a child begins when he first enters school and first applies himself to the basic subject matter. In the elementary school, he receives instruction in reading, writing, spelling, and use of the number system. These subjects are taught largely as separate subjects, or disciplines, and thorough mastery is insisted on. Most conservatives agree that progress of the child from one grade to another should depend on his mastery of the "essentials" for a given grade. As the child moves up through the grades he is introduced gradually to the substantive subjects in the curriculum: history, geography (these two often presented together as "social studies"), natural sciences, and perhaps foreign languages. Music and the fine and applied arts find a place in the curriculum but the conservative tends to regard them, along with physical education, as more peripheral than essential.[8]

In the secondary school the organization and rigor of instruction should be increased, according to conservative doctrine. The elementary school, if it has functioned as it should, has been a place of preparation so that the high school student may be equipped for serious application to the essential subject matters. At the high school level, teaching is departmentalized according to subject matter and teachers of the various subjects should be required to have extensive preparation in the subjects they teach.

There is wide agreement among conservatives that all high school students should study a common core of subject matter organized in terms of the traditional disciplines: English, mathematics, history, science, and foreign languages.[9] Although he is willing that the high school should make certain differentiations in curriculum for students of varying abilities, Dr. James B. Conant, one of the best known conservative educational theorists, insists that every student in the high school must study the common core of four years of English, three or four years of social studies (to include American history), a senior course in American government, either algebra or general mathematics, and one year in natural science.[10] Beyond this common essential core, Dr. Conant would permit the election of other subjects—rigorous academic courses for the intellectually able, and vocational or quasivocational courses for the less talented.

---

[8] For a brief and pungent statement of the conservative's conception of the education of young children, see Bernard Iddings Bell, *Crisis in Education* (New York: McGraw-Hill Book Co., Whittlesey House, 1949), chap. 3, "Civilizing the Common Man's Children."

[9] See Arthur E. Bestor, "Education for Intellectual Discipline," in *Philosophies of Education*, ed. Philip H. Phenix (New York: John Wiley & Sons, 1961), pp. 36 ff.

[10] James B. Conant, *The American High School Today* (New York: McGraw-Hill Book Co., 1959), pp. 47–48.

Other conservatives think Conant has conceded too much and would insist that *all* students attending the high school should study the same subjects and that a substantial number not be shunted off into vocational work. These conservatives would make no more concessions in curriculum structure than those necessitated by the range of differences in intelligence among high school students.[11]

The conservative advocates for the level of higher education a continued program of organized subject matters, organized in terms both of breadth and of specialization. Typically, an American college student, particularly in his first two years, continues a program of study that is in some ways very similar to the academic pattern of the high school. Requirements are set up to make certain that the college freshman and sophomore will take courses in all the essential subject matters. These requirements are often spoken of as group requirements, distribution requirements, or general education.[12] After the period of general studies, and perhaps overlapping it somewhat, comes a period of specialization, in which the student concentrates in ("majors in") a single field, sometimes with another less concentrated study in a second ("minor") field. Thus, according to conservative doctrine, when the student has completed his college course he should have mastered the common core of essential knowledge and gained expertness, relatively speaking, in a single discipline.

The conservative's basic conception of the curriculum may be summarized by saying that from the beginning of school to the end the curriculum is an ordered series of subject matters drawn from the total heritage and designed to be transmitted to all who attend school. The ideal scope and range of this common core is summarized succinctly in an excerpt from the writings of a distinguished philosopher and educational conservative:

> There is certainly a basic core of knowledge that every human person ought to know in order to live a genuinely human life as a member of the world community, of his own nation, and of the family. This should be studied by every student and should be presented at levels of increasing complexity and discipline throughout the entire curriculum. First of all, (a) the student should learn to use the basic instruments of knowledge, especially his own language. In order to understand it more

---

[11]   Among these advocates are Arthur Bestor and the Council for Basic Education. See, as an example, Arthur E. Bestor, "Education and Its Proper Relationship to the Forces of American Society," *Daedalus* 88 (Winter 1959): 75–90.

[12]   The term *general education* makes many conservatives uneasy. The term is difficult to define, but probably no more so than *liberal education*, which is a favorite word in the conservative lexicon. *General education* gained much of its initial respectability as a consequence of the famous "Harvard Report," *General Education in a Free Society*, published in 1945 by the Harvard University Press.

clearly and objectively, he should gain some knowledge of at least one foreign language as well. In addition, he should be taught the essentials of humane logic and elementary mathematics. Then (b), he should become acquainted with the methods of physics, chemistry, and biology and the basic facts so far revealed by these sciences. In the third place (c), he should study history and the sciences of man. Then (d), he should gain some familiarity with the great classics of his own and of world literature and art. Finally (e), in the later stages of this basic training, he should be introduced to philosophy and to those basic problems which arise from the attempt to integrate knowledge and practice. Here he should be shown that the world we inhabit is not pure chaos but possesses some stable structure on which certain moral principles at least may be solidly grounded. Of course there should be room for the choice of additional, peripheral subjects to train exceptional capacities, to realize special interests, and to prepare for the professions. But this central core, based on the nature of our human world, should be given to everyone.[13]

## THE ROLE OF TEACHING

To the conservative, education is in essence the transmission of an essential core of subject matters, skills, and values to all who come to school. The art of teaching, therefore, is above all the art of transmitting. Society's agent for this transmitting process is the teacher. It is the teacher who stands between the essential portion of the cultural heritage and the uninformed child, and the function of teaching is to bring the two together. The joining of the two is accomplished by transmitting to the student and instilling into him the essential portion of the accumulated heritage. The teacher, therefore, is the efficient cause of the educational process. It is his activity that brings it about.[14]

Teachers have at their disposal various means for transmitting. The oldest of these ways, and therefore the most respected among conservatives, are lecturing, that is, oral transmission, and transmission through the printed word, particularly by means of books.[15] The textbook has long

---

[13]   John Wild, "Education and Human Society: A Realistic View," in *Modern Philosophies and Education*, ed. John S. Brubacher, 54th Yearbook of the National Society for the Study of Education (Chicago: University of Chicago Press, 1955), pp. 34–35.

[14]   "The teacher as an authority exercises a mediating, communicating function. His first duty is to gain firm ground, to have something sound and true to communicate. But this does not exhaust the matter. His next duty is really to communicate it, to see that it is presented in such a way as to take possession of the student. Even though the truth is known, if it cannot be transmitted and maintained, culture will die." Ibid., p. 30.

[15]   It has been said for many years that lecturing as a method of teaching has been outmoded since the invention of printing. The fact is it still is the single most widely used approach to teaching method. This is very likely true even in the elementary grades.

been the instrument for transmission most used by American teachers at all levels below the graduate school, and it is by no means unknown at the graduate level. In recent years, however, many other media for transmitting have become available and teachers are no longer bound by necessity to the spoken and written word. The development of a technology that originally appeared in the form of audiovisual aids has made many new approaches to transmission possible. Among the best known of the new devices are motion-picture photography, transparencies made from still photographs and designed for projection, sound recordings, video tapes, elaborate graphic materials in the form of diagrams, charts, drawings, and so forth, three-dimensional models, mock-ups, and dioramas. Later developments in educational media include the use of television for instructional purposes and the invention of the "teaching machine," "programmed learning," and computer-assisted instruction.

In order to understand the movement as it has developed and gained in complexity a number of distinctions in terms have to be noted. The key term now is *educational technology*. Educational technology is to be understood as a form of systems approach based on models that have been used in other fields of productive activity. It involves establishing specific objectives whose attainment can be measured in objective terms, which is to say, quantitatively. Also involved is the setting of specific performance requirements—for example, that a student must attain a certain level of achievement in terms of the stated objectives. If it is necessary to alter curriculum materials or modes of communication, then the system is modified until it is capable of producing the desired results.

Thus, there are important distinctions among the terms *technology* (the systems approach), *media,* and *hardware.* A complete system will involve media, the means by which information is transmitted to the learner. The term *media* refers primarily to the methods of communication, whereas *hardware* refers to the devices that are used in communication.[16]

There is no particular point in discussing here the complicated technical questions presented by educational technology. The body of literature in this field is already voluminous and increasing rapidly. A primary point of interest, however, for the philosophy of education is the relation of these new techniques to the conservative tradition and particularly to the conservative's conception of teaching.

A favorite idea of many educators is that programmed learning and the technical devices that use learning programs are creating a "revolution"

---

[16] The state of the art is reviewed by Lawrence P. Grayson in "Costs, Benefits, Effectiveness: Challenge to Educational Technology," *Science* 175 (March 17, 1972): 1216–22. In this article, Mr. Grayson comments on the reluctance of teachers to incorporate educational technology into the educative process.

in American education.[17] This idea has been eagerly taken up by the public press and others of the mass media. At one time, the teaching machine was acclaimed widely as the first big innovation in teaching since the invention of printing. While some resistance to programmed learning and educational technology in general as pedagogical devices is raised by conservatives, the principal attitude seems to be enthusiasm, ranging from the carefully restrained to the ebullient.

Actually, little or nothing involved in educational technology seems to pose any fundamental threat to the conservative tradition. The governing idea about education in this tradition is that it is the transmission of essential subject matter, skill, and values. Anything that will improve the effectiveness of transmission ought to be welcomed by the educational conservative, or so it would appear.

This promise of efficiency is precisely the argument advanced by most advocates of technology. There is little or no hint or promise in the literature of programmed learning that proposes any different objectives for the educational process, or suggests that any alteration in the basic conservative thesis is indicated. In effect, what is promised is that technology will do the tasks that teachers have always done only it will do them more effectively and more economically. It has been difficult to get objective data that show genuine and significant differences in achievement between machine teaching and traditional teaching, but data have already been published that purport to show a difference in economy of time in favor of programmed teaching.

According to conservative doctrine, the teacher not only has the task of transmitting the ordered sequences of subject matters; he also has the responsibility for transmitting values and building these into the behavior of the young. So far as transmitting value is concerned, conservatives expect the teacher to accomplish this through precept and example. Numerous references throughout the literature of educational conservatism indicate the attributes of character teachers should possess. The conservative lays much stress on the academic scholarship of the teacher, particularly for secondary and higher education, but to most conservatives scholarship is not sufficient. The teacher should embody in his own character and behavior such attributes as moral integrity, a profound sense of justice, hatred of evil in all its forms, and commitment to human betterment—as the conservative understands its meaning.[18]

---

[17]  See, for example, Ronald Gross and Judith Murphy, *The Revolution in the School* (New York: Harcourt, Brace & World, 1964).

[18]  For a typical example of the conservative view of the school's role in the value enterprise, see Bernard Iddings Bell, *Crisis in Education,* chap. 5. See also Theodore M. Greene, "A Liberal Christian Idealist Philosophy of Education," in *Modern Philosophies and Education,* pp. 111–12.

An idea common among conservatives is that a close relation always obtains among rigorous intellectual discipline, moral discipline, and character development. They hold that these processes, far from being discrete and isolated from each other, are actually different facets of the same general process. A familiar argument is that relaxation of intellectual training inevitably brings with it relaxation of ethical discipline. In the opinion of some conservatives, this can account for the slack standards of behavior they profess to find among youth today.

The conservative thesis about the role of teaching can be summed up by saying that teaching is essentially the transmission of a body of knowledge and values, accompanied by certain intellectual skills, to children and young people. Although the modern teacher has at his disposal a variety of communication methods, whatever of these he may find it appropriate to use, his task is the same as it has always been—to transmit the essential elements of the cultural heritage to his students. The teacher is the mediator between the historic accumulation of culture, and the generation that must perpetuate that accumulation.

## THE SCHOOL IN SOCIETY

Essentialism holds that the school is one of the most important institutions in modern society. American educational conservatives have small disposition to belittle the importance of the school or the institution of free public education.[19] The conservative sees the school as an institution in society whose purpose is preservation and appraisal of the heritage of culture and whose mission is to give intellectual training to the young. In the judgment of the essentialist, the school has no mission to change or reform the social order but rather to preserve and refine that which exists. Conservatives as a group strongly resist ideas that would alter the historic character and role of the school and they have called on the school to resist all efforts to change its nature. Arthur Bestor has argued that the school occupies a relatively autonomous role in culture and can preserve its own essential historic pattern in the face of cultural change. He has maintained further that the school has the power to alter society without the school itself being changed significantly in the process.[20]

The conservative is particularly apt to react violently to a thesis that educational progressivism once succeeded in advocating widely, namely, that the school should take a prominent role in reforming society and its

---

[19]  Certain exceptions exist but they are not numerous. Reference will be found to some exceptions in the section on problems of essentialism.

[20]  Arthur Bestor, "Education and Its Proper Relationship to the Forces of American Society," *Daedalus* 88 (Winter 1959): 75–90.

institutions. This thesis attracted most notice in the 1930s, when the attention of Americans was directed to the internal economic and social problems attendant on the Great Depression. A leading educational conservative reflected the reaction of contemporary conservatives when he wrote:

> The school is the instrument for maintaining existing social orders and for helping to build new social orders when the public has decided on them; but it does not create them. In the same sense that society is prior to the individual, the social order is prior to the school. As a profession, we may have ambitions to do more than this—to criticize the existing order, to help build a better future, but the fact is inescapable that the school is the servant of society.[21]

Although the thesis of the school as a leader in social reform is not so prevalent as it once was, conservatives have not forgotten the threat that once was posed; some see it again as a cause for heightened concern.[22] As might be expected, the conservative is inclined to see the school as an institution for stability and order; and the more upset and disorganized social life may become in any period, the more he ascribes a need for the school to exert its stabilizing influence.[23] In short, the essentialist finds repugnant the idea that the school actually need mirror the chief characteristics of the society in which it exists. He thinks rather that the school should conserve and cherish the best that a culture has produced and transmit this essential heritage to succeeding generations.

The thesis of essentialism, therefore, can be summed up in four propositions that all conservatives accept with a minimum of qualification:

1.   From the standpoint of the individual, the purpose of education is intellectual discipline and moral discipline and these two are intimately related. From the standpoint of society, the purpose is to transmit the essential portion of the total heritage to all who come to school.

2.   The curriculum of the school is an ordered series of subject matters, intellectual skills, and essential values that are to be transmitted to all who come to school.

---

[21]   Isaac L. Kandel, "Can the School Build a New Social Order?" *Kadelpian Review* 12 (January 1933): 147–52. If Professor Kandel had inserted in the second sentence an additional phrase, "knowledge is prior to the knower," he would have produced the best nutshell definition of essentialism in the English language.

[22]   See, for example, Russell Kirk, *Prospects for Conservatives*, chap. 3. Whether Kirk overestimates the influence of progressivism is not the point here. The point is that he is still reacting violently to the idea of the school as an agent of social reform, even though there is scant evidence that it plays any such role today or ever did.

[23]   See William Bagley, *Education and Emergent Man* (New York: Ronald Press Co., 1934), pp. 154–56.

3.   Teaching is, in essence, transmitting. The art of teaching is the art of transmitting effectively and efficiently. The teacher is the active agent in the transmitting process.

4.   The role of the school in society is preserving and transmitting the essential core of culture. As an institution, the school has no call for reforming or altering the historic character of society, except as it is the function of the school to contribute incidentally to the ordered evolutionary process of change.

## PRACTICAL PROBLEMS OF ESSENTIALISM

The chief elements in the conservative's view of education have now become apparent. The point of view presented here is that those ideas taken together describe accurately the character of existing American educational practice. This is not to say that conservative ideas have enjoyed complete domination of the practical aspects of American education, for other forces have been at work. However, if one considers, from his own experience, any of the ideas conservative doctrine embodies, he will discover that they describe very accurately the school he attended and the education he experienced. There will be some exceptions to this since American education is pluralistic in certain respects, but these exceptions will not be numerous and they will not involve much deviation from the established conservative position.

Essentialism is the dominant *educational* tradition in America and it always has been; certainly this is true in the practical matters of operating our schools. This means that essentialism is more than a related group of abstract ideas about education; it is a *living body of school practices*. Whenever any tradition is operative, that is, when it actively affects what happens in society, certain consequences ensue as the result of the practices. Over a period of time certain difficulties arise to plague adherents of the governing tradition. These difficulties may arise because of original defects in the traditional ideas themselves; they may stem from a certain lag caused by rapid cultural change; or they may stem from lack of competence on the part of people to apply the ideas correctly. More often than not, the practical difficulties encountered by a tradition are the result of a combination of these causal factors.

So long as a body of educational doctrine remains purely conceptual —or nearly so—about the only problems involved are theoretical problems, that is, those concerned largely with coherence and consistency. Any effort to assess the practical significance of these ideas must be speculative. This manifestly is not the case with essentialism. This tradition is faced with practical problems of the utmost gravity and this fact is known to the essentialists quite as much as to the opponents of that tradition. It is our purpose to consider both practical and conceptual problems in various educational traditions.

The memorable days for the resurgent conservative movement in education were the 1950s. That was the time when conservative educational theorists sent barrage after barrage of criticism against American schools. Many people commonly date the main thrust of this great offensive from the time the Soviet Union succeeded in putting a satellite in orbit around the earth. Certainly this event exerted enormous influence, but in reality the offensive had already begun. At this time, conservatives reiterated their ideas about the conduct of education, and they were listened to attentively—not only by school people, who often felt threatened by the criticism, but what's more important, by the general public. The national mood was ripe for more rigor in the schools, and there was but little difficulty in creating a wide popular demand on its behalf.

Viewed in retrospect, much of this criticism appears superfluous, although probably it was inevitable. The schools had not strayed far from educational orthodoxy, if they had strayed at all. It is not unusual for teachers to talk one game and play another, and perhaps this had been the case. If so, even the talk for the most part had subsided to a moderate level.

True, there was evidence that in many respects the schools had not succeeded in discharging the obligation society had laid on them. Not all students were mastering the essentials; some had not even mastered the simple skills of literacy. Actually this situation was not very different from what it had been ever since compulsory education was first legalized. But the sense of urgency was such that the popular outcries for excellence and rigor in public education increased in volume. Essentialism had reasserted itself. Public support was visible—and vocal. The way ahead was assured, or so it appeared as the decade moved to its close.

As the decade turned, so also did the national temper. The years that had been forecast to be a time of progress, tranquillity, achievement, and excellence in education assured by a reestablishment of essentialism turned out to be among the most revolutionary, or at least the most disruptive, periods in the twentieth century. Something went sour in American life; to some people, particularly those of conservative bent, everything seemed to go sour. As is usual in periods of great social unrest, the school is the institution that seems always to bear the greatest attack.

There are many ways to interpret the events of the 1960s. In one sense, the rebellion against formal education, which meant essentialism, originated in the schools themselves and can be interpreted as a reaction to the "pour-it-on" policies of educational conservatives of the fifties. This interpretation is probably valid, but it is by no means sufficient to explain the upheavals that occurred.

The protests and rebellion that occurred were largely centered in the schools and were conducted by students, or at least by those of college and high school ages. On the surface, much of the protest was against organized education, but even the most superficial observer knows that the protest went much deeper. These events are very close to us still and we shall have to leave it to time and future historians to unravel the tangled skein. One thing that seems clear even now is that this was primarily a protest against a way of life and consequently against the schools as supported by that way of life. In some respects but not all, the general course of events recalls the social unrest and revolutionary temper that produced, among other things, the original progressive protest against conservative education at the turn of the century. How it will all come out, if history can be said ever to "come out," we cannot see with any certainty now. The basic practical problems with which essentialism has always had to deal have now reached critical proportions.

## THE PROBLEM OF WHAT IS ESSENTIAL

Essentialism is committed to the idea of a basic and irreducible core of tradition that must be transmitted by the school. To this much, all conservatives in education agree. The term *essential core*, however, is not self-defining. The question that one can always ask essentialists is, What is essential and how can we tell? This is a simple question to ask, but essentialists have not always found it easy to answer.

The first impulse of the conservative is to appeal to tradition and to insist that what is essential are those subject matters that have always, in the words of the Yale Report of 1828, supplied "the discipline and furniture of the mind." [24] Present-day conservatives have attempted to echo these sentiments; for example, Clifton Fadiman, writing for the Council for Basic Education, referred to the essentials as those subjects that have "generative power," and these sentiments are repeated in turn by other essentialists. [25]

Only a rudimentary knowledge of the history of education suffices

---

[24] The Yale Report of 1828 is one of the classics of American essentialism. The air of certainty with which its pronouncements have been made, the open and frank acceptance of faculty psychology and mental discipline, and the advocacy of humanistic studies, particularly ancient languages, as the core of the curriculum differentiate it from the current essentialism, which must by necessity try to find a place for the *experimental* sciences and the spirit of scientific method without sacrificing the humanities. The Yale Report has been reprinted substantially intact in Richard Hofstadter and Wilson Smith, eds., *American Higher Education: A Documentary History*, vol. 1 (Chicago: University of Chicago Press, 1961), pp. 275 ff.

[25] Council for Basic Education, James D. Koerner, ed., *The Case for Basic Education* (Boston: Little, Brown and Co., 1959), p. 6.

to show, however, that ideas about what the "generative subjects" are seem to change with time and circumstance. The authors of the Yale Report of 1828 had no doubt that the superior subjects in this respect were classical languages, and there is no disputing that they thought modern languages definitely inferior in their "generative power."

Modern essentialists are more apt, however, to recommend the study of modern languages, and more often than not, they argue for modern languages largely from utilitarian premises. This kind of utilitarian argument was profoundly distasteful to the essentialists of 1828. Arthur Bestor, for example, has indicated that debate over the relative merits of ancient and modern languages is legitimate, but he does not indicate how we can find a basis for deciding the issue.[26] In this case, the appeal to tradition is not very helpful in assisting us with an important practical matter of curriculum design.

Nor does simple appeal to tradition assist us very well with a problem whose ramifications far outrun the ancient-versus-modern-language controversy. This problem concerns the relative merits of the scientific as opposed to the humanistic studies in the essential curriculum. A real appeal to tradition—if by that is meant an examination of the curriculum content of the nineteenth or some earlier century—will indicate that the humanistic studies, particularly philosophy, languages, and literatures, should be the dominant elements in the curriculum. This means that the experimental sciences must necessarily play a smaller role in the educational program, which indeed they did through most of the last century.

The struggle of the natural sciences, first for recognition in the curriculum, and now for domination of it, began over a century ago. It is not really much of an exaggeration to say that in the academic world of America the humanistic studies and the sciences are locked in a final struggle for supremacy. Some aspects of this struggle are perfectly obvious to any observer; other aspects are often concealed in the cloistered recesses where curriculum committees meet to effect some workable compromise for the schools.

Naturally, a common response is to say that in the modern world the sciences also are essential and therefore must have a place in the common core. This is the notion on which most curriculum innovators in secondary

---

[26] See Arthur E. Bestor, Jr., "Life Adjustment Education: A Critique," *Bulletin of the American Association of University Professors* 38 (Autumn 1952): 413–41, esp. p. 437. Mr. Bestor's writings appear to favor modern languages over classical, and his argument is typical of the utilitarian arguments common in much of today's conservatism. On the other hand, Samuel Eliot Morison, like Bestor a historian, prefers classical languages to modern for the education of youth. The reason he gives for his belief is in essence the superior "generative power" of Latin and Greek. See Samuel Eliot Morison, *The Scholar in America* (New York: Oxford University Press, 1961), pp. 30–31.

and higher education seem to proceed. It may appear simple to add to the humanities already in the essential core the physical, biological, and social sciences. But if these newer subjects are to have a place, something will have to give. Either the period of general education will have to be lengthened at the expense of the period of specialization, or the total time devoted to secondary and higher education will have to be increased beyond the time now allotted to them. Another possibility is that substantial portions of the humanities, considered by tradition to be essential, will have to be reclassified as nonessential. This has already happened to classical languages in United States schools to the sorrow of many conservatives.

The practical problem of compressing an increasing volume of factual material into the essential core has become staggering. One clear example of this is in the field of history. Arthur S. Bolster, discussing the problem in this field, emphasizes the issue.[27] In 1899, a committee of the American Historical Association produced a document on the content of the high school curriculum in history. This report proposed a four-block sequence and recommended essential historical content to go into it. The report was influential in its day and had nine printings. Sixty-one years later, a distinguished historian, Carlton J. H. Hayes, insisted in effect that all of the content recommended as essential in 1899 be covered and in addition the *major historical developments that have occurred since then.*[28] In the years since 1910, there have been two big world wars, a worldwide depression, the rise of revolutionary socialism, the virtual end of colonialism, the consolidation of industrial society, the struggle of minority groups for equality, and the beginnings of the conquest of space—to name only some of the important events.

How can the conservative handle this problem of the vast increase in material—which certainly is not unique to the subject of history? He can for one thing insist that more time be spent in the study of history in the secondary school so that the additional material can be covered. But when he suggests this, he finds quickly that there are proponents of other subject matters who are also jealous of the time of high school students; the conceptual load in other fields is increasing also, and the need for more time is felt here as well as in history. And what will we do in another sixty years when the historical load will be much greater?

It has long since occurred to some people that firm decisions simply will have to be made about what historical material is essential to the

---

[27] Arthur S. Bolster, "History, Historians, and the Secondary School Curriculum," *Harvard Educational Review* 32 (Winter 1962): 39–65.

[28] See Carlton J. H. Hayes, "European and World History," and also Ray Allen Billington, "American History," Council for Basic Education, Koerner, *Case for Basic Education*, pp. 27–61.

curriculum and what is not. This decision ought to be made by historians, or so it would appear, but there is a long history of efforts of this kind among historians and little has been accomplished in defining an irreducible core of material of workable proportions for the secondary curriculum. The difficulty of the curriculum problem is magnified by the pressures from other social sciences for more adequate representation in the curriculum: economics, sociology, geography, and anthropology, for example. Advocates of these fields of study are increasingly aggressive in their claims, and it appears they are out to end the domination that historians have maintained over the social studies in our schools.[29] Meantime, historians generally resist the pruning job that is necessary for producing a tenable essential core.

Another possibility is to compress material more and more into generalizations so that these generalized ideas may be transmitted without the attendant bulk of factual detail. This proposal is viewed with suspicion and often with hostility by the conservative, who tends toward a deep antipathy for "survey" courses, watered-down content, and overblown generalities. There will be great difficulty in persuading many essentialists that this is any solution.

It may be true that the new technological devices will be effective in processing information and ordering it in useful form. Yet the avowed purpose of education in the conservative tradition is to transmit essential knowledge to the learner's nervous system (many essentialists would rather say his intellect), not to record it on microfilm. While there is some evidence that certain devices can transmit some kinds of material more quickly than ordinary teachers can, it does not seem very likely that even use of these devices can keep up with the increase in knowledge, even if their use were thought desirable.

Also, it may be that development of information-retrieval systems could eventually influence the design for teaching in a direction that conservatives in recent years have not been very friendly towards—namely, teaching designs that are built primarily around method (in the case of history, for example, historical method) rather than around the transmission of content. The proposal to use these systems is controversial, particularly because in the twentieth century conservatives have been at a loss to know how to handle the idea of mental discipline. In earlier times the tradition frankly embraced the idea of "mental gymnastics" and developed much of its program on the belief that the mind could be "strength-

---

[29] See, for example, Leonard S. Kenworthy, "Ferment in the Social Studies," *Phi Delta Kappan* 44 (October 1962): 12–16. See also Richard E. Gross and Dwight W. Allen, "Time for a National Effort to Develop the Social Studies Curriculum," *Phi Delta Kappan* 44 (May 1963): 360–65.

ened" through intellectual exercise. The *Yale Report* is a good example of this attitude.

This classic notion has been so discredited by present-day psychology that many conservatives have felt compelled to give it up—although not without regret. Others adhere to it in the face of all evidence to the contrary. However, at least two historians of conservative persuasions have advanced ideas relating to the use of historical method in intellectual discipline.[30] The argument is that even at the level of secondary education the student can be expected to do more than merely absorb the factual material transmitted to him. While the high school student cannot be expected to engage fully in the real historical analysis that is done at the college level, he can be introduced to the elements of historical method in both its analytic and synthetic phases. It may well be that if this direction is followed, some of the emphasis on transmission of subject matter will have to be given up. A real adoption of procedures of this kind might furnish the conservative with a criterion for deciding what is essential in the field of history. Not enough has been done with this idea for us to know what promise it holds for the solution of the essentialist's problem.[31]

Any other of the common branches in the curriculum would do as well for illustrating the difficulty of the situation for the conservative tradition. We have examined history as an example of the problem essentialism faces in maintaining the thesis of an irreducible core of essential material against today's rapid accumulation of knowledge. History furnishes a good example because it is easy to see that the constant accumulation of material in that area is as inevitable as the progress of time itself.

The examples of modern languages versus classical languages and the content of the curriculum in history illustrate one kind of practical problem for the conservative tradition, but they deal only with selecting essential material *within fields that all conservatives find essential*. There may be plenty of controversy among conservatives about whether modern languages are more essential than classical and vice versa, but there is no controversy over the need for foreign languages. There may be wide differences of opinion about what content of history is essential, but there surely are no great differences among conservatives about history itself as an essential of the common curriculum.

Another class of problems derives from the question, What is essential? These problems are concerned with whether certain *areas of knowledge*

---

[30] See W. Burlie Brown, *United States History: A Bridge to the World of Ideas*, a pamphlet published by the American Historical Service Center for Teachers of History. See also Bestor, *Restoration of Learning*, p. 437.

[31] Bolster's judgment is that neither Brown nor Bestor has as yet developed a tenable analysis. See Bolster, "History, Historians, and the Secondary School Curriculum."

are themselves essential. Certainly one of the most difficult of these for the conservative is whether religion is an essential element of the curriculum.[32] To the conservative mind, supernatural religion is one of the most important forces in the direction of cultural stability and the maintenance of tradition. The classical conservative is inclined to think that all the important kinds of problems that face men—politics, education, ethics, and so forth—are at bottom religious problems. Some conservatives even take this view of economic problems, for according to them, the natural laws of the market represent in the last analysis the will of God in the economic sphere.[33]

In the light of these sentiments, it is not surprising that many conservatives regard religion as essential in the program of the school. Burke himself, the great progenitor of the conservative tradition, considered much of the strength of British education—and consequently much of the strength of British society—as stemming from the close relation between education and religion that obtained in his day.[34] Burke's sentiments in this matter still have their original validity, in the opinion of many contemporary conservatives.

The basic tenet of conservatives is that since transmission of ethical values is an essential function of education and since ethics apart from religion are meaningless, it does not seem reasonable for the school arbitrarily to eliminate religious instruction from the curriculum. Bernard Iddings Bell has insisted that religion is of the utmost importance in education at all levels of the school. Similar declarations have been made by William F. Buckley and Russell Kirk. Since many classical conservatives often profess to prefer European ideas of education to American, it is not surprising that there has been favorable comment on the widespread European practice of incorporating religious instruction in the public school curriculum and using public tax monies to support private sectarian schools.

But the conservative, whose primary appeal is to tradition, is faced with the incontrovertible fact that one of the oldest elements in American tradition is the separation of church and state and the encouragement of religious pluralism. These sentiments antedate even our national history. A long series of court decisions has been necessary to interpret the meaning

---

[32] Another question is whether various vocational subjects are essential. American conservatives are well agreed that for the academically talented, vocational subjects are neither essential nor desirable. There are marked differences of opinion over the essential quality of these subjects for slower learners.

[33] See, for example, Frank Chodorov, "The Penalty of Disregarding Natural Law," in A. G. Heinsohn, Jr., ed., *Anthology of Conservative Writing in the United States, 1932–1960* (Chicago: Henry Regnery Co., 1962), pp. 392–96.

[34] Edmund Burke, *Reflections on the Revolution in France* (Indianapolis: Bobbs-Merrill Co., Liberal Arts Press, 1955), pp. 113 ff.

inherent in the First Amendment to the Constitution. While conservatives have not always been pleased with the judgments of the courts, they have themselves been signally unsuccessful in developing a policy of religious instruction in the public schools that would satisfy sectarian interests and conform to legal requirements of the Constitution.[35]

There are conservative educational spokesmen who have expressed grave doubts even about the effect of private schools in American society. James B. Conant, for example, has urged support for public schools, and particularly for the comprehensive high school, as against public assistance for private schools, a majority of which are church-related. In his view, much of our success in assimilating the diverse populations that emigrated to the United States in the nineteenth century is owed to the American public school system. He still sees this system as an important stabilizing and conserving force in American society.[36] To be sure, numerous conservatives do not concur in this judgment and evidence shows that the split within conservative ranks on this issue is growing wider. Apparently, it is one thing to appeal to the wisdom of our forefathers and quite another to know which of these forefathers to heed.[37] This is a pressing practical problem for educational conservatism because this tradition insists that by an appeal to tradition we can know what is essential for the curriculum of our schools.

In view of all these considerations, two general observations seem to be warranted. First, it is of great strategic importance to the conservative tradition to find some tenable method for determining what is essential in the curriculum and what is not. Granted that the problem has not always been as great as it is today, conservatism has never really had a trustworthy means for making these important discriminations. Too often conservatives have been seduced by the charm of easy answers: "tradition," "what everybody knows," "what the scholarly world knows." In a period of enormously accelerated cultural transition, characterized by overwhelming advances in natural science, tradition and the opinions of the scholarly world have not proved definitive guides in the search for what is essential.

---

[35] For example, there was an outpouring of protest, mostly from conservative quarters, when a 1962 decision of the United States Supreme Court made unconstitutional the reading of a "nondenominational" prayer in the public schools of New York. The prayer had been officially approved by the Regents of the State of New York. See *Engle vs. Vitale*, 82 S. Ct. 1261 (1962).

[36] James B. Conant, *Education and Liberty* (New York: Random House, Vintage Books, 1953), pp. 81 ff.

[37] For example, should the conservative heed James Madison on the religious issue? Madison was one of the great original conservatives in America but he was also one of the doughtiest fighters for the separation of church and state. See his famous "Memorial and Remonstrance Against Religious Assessments" (1785).

The second observation is that the challenge of the sciences for domination of the curricula of the schools cannot be shrugged off or wished away. Influential conservatives admit that the humanistic studies are in retreat and have been for a substantial length of time.[38] And yet as far as education is concerned, the humanities have always been the lifeblood of the conservative tradition. It is possible that the old conservatism is dying— a lingering death to be sure, but one that increasingly hastens to the end. It is conceivable that out of this may develop a new social and educational conservatism that substitutes a new authority built on scientific certainties for the older authority of religious and humanistic knowledge. Meantime, in America the conservative tradition in education seeks to preserve itself by a series of tactical compromises, and increasingly these compromises are made on the grounds of the sciences, not on the grounds of the humanities as once was true.[39] The ideal of Burkean conservatism is the *gentleman*, urbane, aristocratic, immersed in the humanistic studies, religious by nature, and always mindful of tradition. But if what is emerging is a new conservatism built on physical science and technology, the ideal must be that of the scientist (or perhaps the engineer) possessed by the rigors of scientific method, whose quest for certainty is not in the superstitions of religion and the vagaries of literature but in reason and experiment and control.[40] If the conservative humanist does not always rest well at night, it is small wonder.[41]

---

[38] See, for example, Kirk, *Prospects for Conservatives*, pp. 53 ff.

[39] One of the best descriptions of this tactical situation has been supplied by Gordon Keith Chalmers: "The central fact about the compromise of curriculum committees ... is a gigantic intellectualist illusion which has characterized American academics for four decades: The illusion that almost every specialty which has managed to make space for itself in the catalog has philosophical rights and claims comparable to every other ... almost every subject has a vote, and what comes out of the committee is a kind of philosophical congress in which all disciplines are represented." Gordon Keith Chalmers, "The Diverse Responsibilities of Liberal and General Education," *Current Issues in Higher Education, 1953*, Proceedings of the Eighth Annual National Conference on Higher Education, Washington, D.C.: Association for Higher Education, a department of the National Education Association, 1953. The quotation is from pp. 34–35.

[40] It is interesting to speculate that such a "new" conservatism, though certainly different from the Burkean variety, could still come close to the criteria suggested by Peter Viereck, *Conservatism from John Adams to Churchill* (Princeton, N.J.: D. Van Nostrand Co., 1956), p. 15, namely, a distrust of human nature; opposition to untested innovations; and a traditional framework to tame human nature. In such a new conservatism the fulfillment of these criteria would derive from scientific not religious-humanistic origins.

[41] Particularly if he reflects on such sentiments as the following: "After the rigors of training in science, the subject content of the humanities seems hardly more difficult than a good novel." Editorial, "Science and the Humanities," *Science* 138 (December 28, 1962): 1367.

In recent years, the definition of what is essential has taken on a new urgency. Essentialism has been trying to cope with this problem for many years and the difficulties it has encountered are manifold. However, this tradition now finds itself faced with another aspect of the problem. This, as is well known, is outright rejection by substantial numbers of students themselves of not only any particular formulation of essentials but also the very idea that *anything* is essential.

In a sense there is nothing new about this. Historically, there has always been a certain resistance among students to academic requirements, lack of choice among subject matters, and other aspects of the academic folkways. Schools at all levels have generally been able to contain this dissatisfaction and keep it underground. But suddenly, and indeed it did seem sudden, the whole thing exploded. This was an integral part of the disruption that originated in the sixties. It seems only fair to say that it caught the traditionalists flat-footed.

They were already at loggerheads with each other over their differences. But these differences and debates at least were within the establishment itself. It is not a part of the conservative credo in education that students should have anything of consequence to say about the curriculum or other important academic matters. Student riots are nothing new. They can be traced back at least as far as the thirteenth century. But to the modern conservative it is one thing for students to riot over the quality of the food in the cafeteria, regrettable as that dissension may be, and quite another for them to riot about the curriculum or the teaching or the administration.

The watchword that became popular very quickly among the students was *relevance*. When the argument they advanced was stripped of its verbiage, it seemed to contend that most if not all of what is taught in schools, particularly in high schools, colleges, and universities, was not "relevant to the lives of students." Further, the whole academic organization has been condemned for its inflexible requirements for degrees, its arbitrary grading system, and its repression of student creativity, and similar charges. The charges are well known, having received wide attention in the popular media as well as in academic circles.

The perplexity and dismay of essentialists over these developments is not difficult to understand. Over and over, in different ways, they have asked themselves, If the historic intellectual disciplines that represent the accumulated wisdom of the race are not relevant to the lives of people, then what is? The question seems a fair one, or at least it seems so to the conservatives, and it must be admitted that the answers given to it appear far from clear, at least in most cases. So far as many conservatives can see, the young proponents of the nonrelevance argument have exhibited a great deal of moral fervor and indignation but not much in the way of reasoned argument or clear alternatives. To the conservatives, the student rhetoric reveals a profound strain of anti-intellectualism with which they find it exceedingly difficult to cope.

To those who are familiar with the conservative mind and the history of conservative strategy, the reaction was predictable. Basically, the strategy has always been and still is to give when the pressure builds beyond toleration, but give as little as possible and always retain the greatest amount of control that is feasible under the circumstances. In the short run, such strategy may often seem uncertain and vacillating, but history suggests that in the long run it has been successful; and it is not a completely reckless prediction to say that it may very well be successful again.

One way to interpret the situation confronting the conservative tradition is to consider that this tradition has been forced by historical necessity to provide for mass education. One may observe further that at most if not all levels of the educational system, the basic organization, and the conception of curriculum, teaching methodologies, and so on, simply are not well adapted to the requirements of mass education. From the historical standpoint, much of our basic organization and teaching theory derive from a time that antedates the mass educational situation confronting us today. Essentialism has always been plagued by various practical difficulties, and the revolt of students against the essentials is simply one more of the practical problems of mass education.

## THE PRACTICAL PROBLEM OF MASS EDUCATION

Almost any teacher or administrator in American schools will agree that the most persistent and baffling problems of education may be traced ultimately to individual differences among students. The area of these differences that is most significant involves ability to achieve. School achievement is known to be a function of many factors, but there is no denying that intelligence is one of the crucial elements in ability to master the curriculum of studies.

American education, dominated as it is by the conservative thesis, has always proceeded on the assumption that there is an irreducible core of essential material that must be transmitted to all. Despite certain differences of opinion among conservatives over what should be in this core, we have not been able to find evidence that essentialists are willing to give up the idea of a basic core for all students.

On the other hand, the United States is committed, and has been committed for a long time, to the principle of universal education. All states in the Union have compulsory attendance laws and all states provide opportunity for twelve years of public schooling. Virtually all children of elementary school age who are capable of profiting at all from formal instruction are in school. The American high school has never succeeded in enrolling all adolescent youth, and though estimates vary, it is certain that less than three-quarters of those who begin school actually finish twelve years. This condition, however, is viewed with grave concern and both educational and political leaders are constantly searching for an answer to the dropout problem. The common ideal is at least twelve years of schooling for every American child.

When universal education is achieved or very nearly achieved, the school population is always highly heterogeneous. All social strata in society are represented and the distribution of intelligence in the school population approximates closely the distribution of intelligence in the general population. This is to say that in our schools the range in ability extends from those who are barely educable to those whose capabilities are rated "genius" on such a scale as the Stanford-Binet test of intelligence. The distribution of intelligence in the schools assumes the general shape of the well-known probability curve.

These two factors taken together generate the most perplexing problems of policy and practice in American public education. On the one hand, there is the essentialist's insistence on a common core of essential subjects; on the other hand, there is the brute fact that people differ greatly in their ability to learn abstract material. Since nobody at present knows how to alter significantly the genetic equipment of individuals and thus narrow the range in learning ability, and since essentialism is unwilling to make any significant compromise in the thesis of a common core, the schools are full of what is known in the trade as low achievers together with a considerable number of "nonachievers." [42] The first group consists of those who do not learn very much, and the second group consists of those who learn little or nothing. The complaints of upper elementary teachers about the poor achievement in the primary grades, the complaints of high school teachers about the lack of preparation in the elementary schools, the complaints of college teachers about the lack of quality in high school graduates, the complaints of graduate schools about the lack of preparation of candidates for graduate study are all legendary.

The conservative tradition has sought to work out these problems within an administrative structure known as the graded system. The graded system dates from about the middle of the nineteenth century and thus has been the prevailing mode of organization throughout most of the American period of universal public education. The graded system of organization involves classifying pupils into grades or classes. These grades correspond to chronological age—at least in the beginning—since children enter the first year of schooling at about the same age. As the theory goes,

---

[42] The trade also recognizes two groups known respectively as underachievers and overachievers. These represent special problems that will not be treated formally in this volume.

a basic core of essential material is set for each grade level, and minimum standards for mastery are also established.[43] If a child is able to master the essential material in the first grade, he is transferred (that is, "promoted") to the second grade, and so on up through the school system. Theoretically, those who fail to achieve the essential core in one year will be retained in that grade until they show evidence of sufficient mastery. Promotion thus becomes the reward for achieving the minimum essentials and retention becomes a penalty for not doing so.

Implementation of this policy is more theoretical than real, however. Teachers and administrators, particularly in the elementary schools, resist filling their classrooms with overage pupils who learn slowly, achieve little, and are constant sources of disturbance. At least some administrators are aware that high scholastic standards in a school cannot be achieved by systematically saving the most backward pupils and keeping them year after year. For reasons such as these, the policy of promotion based on achievement—a policy that numerous present-day conservatives call for loudly—is seldom followed strictly in practice and very likely never will be. Therefore, a great deal of administrative ingenuity has been expended in finding ways to circumvent this aspect of the graded system.

Conservatives are amply aware of the practical problems and they have been diligent in their efforts to find a means of coping with them. The material related to these efforts is vast and thoroughly scattered through the literature. However, it is possible to discern in all this mass of material three general kinds of policy that are being advocated by conservatives today.

The first recommended policy for dealing with the manifold problems of individual differences and mass education goes somewhat as follows: The lack of achievement that is so apparent today at every level of our school system is caused by the poor quality of teaching, the preoccupation of teachers with services and activities that do not contribute to intellectual training, and a lack of high standards of expectation: in short, soft pedagogy. The way out of our difficulties will be found if we will restore to instruction the rigor and thoroughness it once had and now has mostly lost. We also need to return to a curriculum designed for intellectual training and composed of those subjects that tradition has shown to have real intellectual value. But more than this, we need to reorient our basic attitudes about education. We need, in the words of Arthur Bestor, to

> reaffirm our belief in the value of intellectual training to all men,
> whatever their occupation, whatever their background, whatever their

---

[43] American elementary teachers invariably speak of school achievement in terms of "first-grade reading," "third-grade arithmetic," "sixth-grade spelling," and so forth.

income or their position in society. This is to retrace our steps, I grant.
It is to retrace them back to that period when professional educators
really believed in education and when public school leaders really believed in democracy.[44]

On one occasion, Bestor vouchsafed that if we would only reconstruct
our educational procedures and revitalize our curricula and our teaching
processes, we should find that 90 percent of the pupils in the schools would
profit from this rigorous educational program. This proved too much for
Russell Kirk, who has often quoted Bestor's writings with obvious approval. Kirk is sure that the percentage is too high, though he hastens to
agree that many more students would receive a real liberal education than
are receiving it today.[45]

Be this as it may, many people undoubtedly find the ideas embodied
in this policy persuasive. It probably is more widely accepted among
parents of students than among the teachers of these students. Teachers
usually have somewhat more psychological sophistication than parents,
and in any event they have all faced the stark reality that there is a limit
to what teaching skill and rigorous educational programs can achieve. On
the other hand, it is certainly more comfortable for the patrons of schools
to believe that the poor achievement of their children is the fault of the
school and the teacher rather than poor genetic inheritance. Anyone whose
duty it has been to listen to the complaints of school patrons will recognize
the argument, "He can get it all right if you will only *make* him learn!"
and the clear implication that "the reason he doesn't learn is because he
hasn't been taught right."

There are conservatives, however, who doubt that such a policy can
really be adequate to solve the problem of individual differences in a mass
education design. The belief that such a high proportion of the population
as 90 percent can cope with the abstractions of the typical essentialist core
without any modification seems unduly optimistic. Accordingly, a second
kind of policy has been advocated that goes as follows: Let us recognize
that differences in learning ability are large and cannot be ignored. Let us
therefore adjust the organization of our school system to meet these
differences. This can be done through ability grouping at all levels of the
system, differentiated curricula in the high school, and programs of
guidance, particularly in secondary education, that will help individuals
find the programs that are suited to their particular ability and interest.

---

[44] Bestor, "Life Adjustment Education," p. 440.

[45] See Kirk, *Prospects for Conservatives*, p. 69. Though Bestor's essentialism is classic
and entirely beyond reproach, in this instance at least, he betrays an odor of egalitarian
dogma for which any old-line conservative such as Russell Kirk has a very sharp nose.
To suppose that nine-tenths of the population could ever hope to savor any of the
unbought grace of life is a patent absurdity to a Burkean conservative.

This is the general position taken by such a well-known and influential conservative as James B. Conant. It is also the policy advocated by Paul Woodring, who has been influential in conservative circles. The key to Conant's proposal is the establishment of "comprehensive secondary schools," which would offer under one roof a variety of courses and curricula and a program of guidance that would help students find a program of study suitable to their talents.[46] A common core of essentials would be maintained but it would be scaled down considerably from the core recommended by Wild (see p. 56) or by Bestor and the Council for Basic Education. Beyond this common core, students would enroll in courses appropriate to their abilities. Opportunities in the comprehensive high school would range from rigorous academic courses to various kinds of strictly vocational work. Ability grouping would be used for the basic subjects to a degree seldom found in American secondary schools and admission to the academic program would be carefully controlled.[47]

Conant has urged that beyond the comprehensive high school two-year colleges should offer terminal programs for those who desire education beyond the high school but who are not equipped for the rigors of a regular four-year college course. He has suggested that instead of expanding the enrollments and programs of four-year colleges and universities, we retract enrollment in those institutions and admit only applicants who clearly can profit by attendance and who ultimately can engage in graduate study.[48]

Another plan, similar in certain respects to the Conant plan, has been devised by Paul Woodring. This plan would involve a complete reorganization of the American school system. The number of years devoted to elementary schooling would be shortened, pupils would be permitted to advance through the grades at varying rates, and ability grouping would be used extensively. After high school, the academically talented would find their way to liberal arts colleges and ultimately to graduate and professional schools. The average run of students would go to junior colleges, to trade schools, or to work.[49]

---

[46] Conant, *American High School Today.*

[47] Conservatives, by and large, are greatly taken with the idea of grouping by ability. Bestor has advocated it as an important part of his policy. From the reading of the current literature of essentialism one might conclude that ability grouping has just been invented. Actually it has a long history and extensive studies of it have been made.

[48] James B. Conant, *Education and Liberty* (New York: Random House, Vintage Books, 1958), p. 57. This policy would restore the four-year college approximately to the position it held prior to World War I.

[49] For the details of Woodring's proposed reorganization see his *Fourth of a Nation* (New York: McGraw-Hill Book Co., 1957), pp. 143 ff.

Both these policies have been given a favorable hearing, but the ideas advocated by Dr. Conant have been more influential in practice. For one thing, Conant's plan would disrupt the traditional organization of the school system far less than the Woodring proposals. Another factor is the unparalleled personal prestige enjoyed by Conant among citizens at large and among professional teachers and administrators. Although serious objections have come from other conservatives about certain aspects of the Conant policy, Conant has probably been more influential about practical educational policy than any other single individual.[50] After all, he has assured the American people that our basic educational tradition is sound, and that we need no upheaval in organization nor any untested innovations. He has shown us that all we really need do is correct certain details in our present system. Such assurances as these appeal strongly to the basic conservative strain in the American mind.

There is, however, a hard core of essentialists who find untenable both kinds of policy outlined above. Their approach to the problem posed by individual differences is fundamentally different and is what most liberals and possibly many American conservatives would call "undemocratic." The difference in this approach to policy lies in challenging the very idea of universal education—at least beyond a bare minimum of common schooling. The argument goes somewhat as follows: Why do we not admit that a substantial part of the population is simply uneducable in any real sense of the word *educate* and shape our plans accordingly? This would mean giving up the peculiarly American sentiment of egalitarianism and all the havoc it has created in American education. As Albert J. Nock observed a generation ago, our educational system rests on three false premises: equality, democracy, and the belief that the literate society is the good society.[51] It follows that any theory of education derived from these false ideas is itself bound by logical necessity to be false.

Conservatives who follow this line of thought are apparently convinced that humanity is composed of three groups: a relatively small group of the talented, a larger middle stratum of moderately intelligent people who are able and willing to accept leadership by the elite, and at the lowest level a great mass of people who may with great effort be capable of simple literacy but of very little beyond that. The great error of egalitarian educational ideals lies in failing to acknowledge these ineradicable differ-

---

50 For instance, the Council for Basic Education has objected to including vocational courses in the high school curriculum, and Russell Kirk has criticized the consolidation of school districts to create large comprehensive high schools.

51 The classic quality of Nock's book on education is being rediscovered by today's conservatives. It surely is one of the most remarkable treatises on educational theory written in this century. See Albert J. Nock, *The Theory of Education in the United States* (New York: Harcourt, Brace, 1932).

ences. Under the spell of "democratic" ideas, we try to educate all men as if they were all equal in ability. The only way this can be done is to keep everybody at the same level of mediocrity or worse, and this, in the view of these conservatives, is what has been done in the United States. We have failed to educate our talent; we have not even provided a decent education for the middle group. It is held that in trying to educate the masses—who can't be educated anyway—we wind up educating nobody.

There is, say the proponents of this position, only one thing to do. This is to design a school system that will be increasingly selective. Perhaps we must begin with a common school to which everybody will be admitted at first.[52] But, the conservative maintains, though everybody may come in the beginning, everybody does not have to stay in school long after he has learned all he can. What should happen to a person when he ceases to learn? The answer, though it can be expressed in various ways, is simply that he should leave the school forthwith.

Whether these conservatives believe individuals should be put out of school before they have completed the common schooling of the elementary grades is mostly a matter for speculation. But there is no room for doubt about their position on secondary education. The secondary school should be selective. It should admit only those who have demonstrated their ability and willingness to do high-level work. The curriculum of the high school should be uniform and academically rigorous, and the highest standards of achievement should be maintained. With arrangements such as these, we could give a good education to those who are capable of being educated.[53]

Those who advocate this policy are unimpressed by such arguments as the lack of opportunity for gainful employment for youth who would be forced to terminate their schooling at an early age. A common reply to such an argument is that while the plight of many uneducable—and perhaps unemployable—youths is a difficult one, it is not really an educational problem and the school should not be called on to deal with economic and social difficulties that are not its business. To do so is only to continue the debasement of our educational system.

This third policy is accepted by only a minority of American conservatives today and it is all but certain that the mass of the population rejects it as public policy. Its proposals run too much counter to the ingrained doctrine of equality in the American mind. Though proponents

---

[52] Conservatives are not always clear on this point, but in view of the inexorable demands of industrial society, it appears likely that all must agree to a common school that will supply at least the elements of literacy.

[53] See, for example, J. N. D. Bush, "My Credo: Humanist Critic," *Kenyon Review* 13 (Winter 1951): 81–92; and Harold L. Clapp, "Some Lessons from Swiss Education," *Modern Age* 2 (Winter 1957–58): 10–17.

of selective schooling may fulminate against misapplication of egalitarian doctrine in deciding who shall be educated, their message is not really given a sympathetic hearing by the masses. In spite of all the talk about European models for our school system, there is as yet scant evidence that Americans are ready to move in the direction of a truly selective secondary school.[54]

And yet, it may be premature to discount completely the chances of the third policy. Egalitarianism, as commonly understood, may be workable in public education under conditions of early industrialism, but this is not to say that it is necessarily workable under a truly integrated technological society, in which the need for semiskilled human labor is not very great and the real demand is for intensive, specialized scientific and technological training. In spite of egalitarian doctrine, nobody knows today how to transmit specialized, sophisticated scientific and technological knowledge and skill to the mass of people, no matter how they may be grouped for instruction in the school. It can be argued that the real need of a mature technological society is a relatively small group of scientists and technologists—a scientific and technological elite.[55] It is the primary business of education to sort out potential members of this elite and educate them for their responsibilities. The schooling of the rest of a generation may be a troublesome necessity, but it is not the real educational problem, and the rudimentary schooling of the masses should never be permitted to interfere with the *education* of those who are capable of being *educated*.

These three ways of dealing with individual differences and mass education in present-day society illustrate the practical difficulties essentialism faces in translating its basic conservative principles into workable policies for conducting our schools. Adherents of the tradition of conservatism are badly split over this question, and it is not possible to

---

54  Advocacy of a policy of rigorous selection of students for secondary schools has already created dissension in the ranks of the Council for Basic Education. According to an Associated Press release for October 26, 1963, Admiral Hyman G. Rickover, as a featured speaker at the annual meeting of the Council, advocated substantially the policy outlined here. In a discussion that followed, his ideas were criticized, in some respects quite severely, by such stalwarts of essentialism as Arthur Bestor and Carl F. Hansen.

55  Paul Woodring, in commenting on certain ideas of Admiral Hyman G. Rickover, has said that such a policy would not result in an elite, since everybody has the same chance in the beginning. If this is so, it involves an unusual sense of the term *elite*. Under this view, Plato's philosopher-kings would not constitute an elite either, since Plato was careful to point out that every child in the Republic had a chance *in the beginning*. See *Saturday Review* 45 (October 20, 1962): 86–87. For a summary of Rickover's views on educational matters, see "Admiral Rickover on American Education," *Journal of Teacher Education* 10 (September 1959): 3–27.

discern with clarity which if any of the three policies will become the dominant mode of organization in our public schools.

## THE PRACTICAL PROBLEMS OF RETENTION AND TRANSFER

There is one other significant practical problem conservatives must face. This practical question is posed by two considerations known to psychologists as retention, and transfer of learning. The first term refers to the *perpetuation* in subsequent experience of material learned at some prior time. The second term refers to the *application* of learned material in subsequent experience. The processes of remembering and using learned material are generally thought of as psychological rather than philosophical matters of concern. However, the phenomena of retention and transfer of knowledge underlie certain difficult problems facing the conservative tradition in education, and hence they merit some attention.

The conservative tradition in education is built on the belief that the true purpose of education is transmission of selected portions of certain organized subject matters. Much of the teacher's work, according to essentialist doctrine, must be devoted to transmission of facts. This fundamental principle is also expressed in the essentialist idea of the curriculum as an ordered series of subject matters to be transmitted by teachers and "absorbed" by pupils.

To be sure, essentialists regularly point out that students should be expected to do more with factual material than merely commit it to memory. In the last analysis, however, it is always the fact-learning aspect of education that gets the emphasis in essentialist writing. For example, the Council for Basic Education once compared young children and factual learning to a squirrel who gathers nuts and stores them away against the coming winter.[56] Thus, the child in his early years at school gathers and stores away nuggets of factual material against the day that he will need them in his affairs. In this sense, elementary schooling is a preparation for and an anticipation of secondary education and beyond that, adulthood.

In the secondary school the transmission of organized facts becomes more inclusive and more rigorous. The conceptual load becomes greater and greater as the student is expected to study a wider variety of subject matters and some of these subjects in greater depth. At the college level, the same process determines the general character of the teaching design —the transmission of subject matters in increasing scope and depth. In the mind of the conservative, the purpose at every level is for something

---

[56] *CBE Bulletin*, vol. 2, no. 7, Washington, D.C.: Council for Basic Education (February 1958).

that is to come later. Elementary school is preparatory for secondary education; the secondary school prepares for college; the college prepares for graduate school; and the graduate school prepares for adult life. Since very few survive the process through the graduate school, each educational level in the system prepares both for "life" and for the next school level above. One thing is certain: To the conservative, education is first of all a *process of preparation.*

Against this conception of education as transmission and preparation are certain facts that are known both to common sense and to psychology. One of these facts is that a great deal of what is learned under the formal conditions provided in schools is forgotten very quickly. Anyone who has had formal schooling can test this for himself. All one needs to do is consider what his chances would be of passing an examination over some material he had studied even as short a time as six months previously. Unless he had kept practicing on the material in the interim, the chances are not very good for a satisfactory performance on an examination.[57] Students simply assume that they will forget the major part of the factual content of any course they take. Their instructors apparently make the same assumption.

When an essentialist is asked about this state of affairs, he is constrained to admit that a great deal of factual material is lost—he can hardly maintain anything else. But a typical reply to the question, What is left after the transmitted material is lost in such large amount? is typically, What is left is intellectual discipline! Before we analyze this answer, it will be useful to consider briefly another dimension of the problem.

A fundamental presumption of essentialist educational doctrine is that what is learned at one time in school will be available at some future time —either in subsequent school experience or in the broader affairs of life. Clearly, this availability will depend on whether the learning is retained. If the learner forgets it, it will not be available to him. But there is even more to the presumption than this, for apparently there is also the belief that if the material is retained *it will necessarily be transferable to novel situations.*

Modern psychological investigations do not lend much comfort to this presumption. The phenomena involved in the transfer of learning are complicated and some of them obscure, but our present state of understanding is sufficient to show that merely having learned some fact or principle by no means guarantees that this learning will function in some situation that is greatly unlike the conditions under which the original

---

[57] Almost any text in general psychology or educational psychology contains material on remembering and forgetting, theoretical explanations for these phenomena, and so on. A psychological discussion of these matters is outside the scope of this book.

learning took place. If the conservative seeks to hang his case on this presumption, he may well find it a slender thread.

Now we consider the question, What is left over? The conservative answers, "What is left over is intellectual discipline." What does this mean? It is really very hard to know what it means. What the essentialist is apparently saying is that by virtue of "applying the mind" to the essential subject matters something happens to the processes of the mind. They become in some fashion more rigorous and effective. It is said, for example, that a disciplined mind is one that can operate efficiently in any situation and this by virtue of intellectual training.[58]

This explanation could be taken as an application of the classic Aristotelian conception of mind, in which the intellect is conceived as an aggregate of specific powers. Or by a real stretch of the imagination, it could be construed to mean development of the kind of processes of inquiry advocated by John Dewey and the progressivists.[59] What the essentialist really means remains enigmatic. If the intent is to attach Aristotelian psychology to conservative pedagogy, that is one thing. But it is difficult to adopt Aristotle's psychology in isolation from his biology and metaphysics, and probably there are few conservatives today who care to be counted as full-fledged Aristotelians. It is even more difficult to believe that what essentialists intend is something of what Dewey spoke of when he advocated an educational program directed towards developing in pupils the scientific attitude and increasing skill in problem solving, and emphasizing functional use of factual material in inquiry. For one thing, conservatives consistently deplore Dewey's emphasis on method instead of formal teaching of content; for another, Dewey's name is not very popular among present-day conservatives.

It is fair to say that retention and transfer remain among the most difficult practical problems of modern essentialism. This tradition typically has sought to solve its basic problems by organizational means: ability grouping, multiple curricula, acceleration for the gifted, and more recently, various forms of educational technology. The problem of retaining and applying learning, however, does not appear to be capable of resolution by organizational manipulation. The conservative will have to look for other

---

[58]   See, for example, Arthur Bestor, "Education for Intellectual Discipline," in Philip H. Phenix, ed., *Philosophies of Education* (New York: John Wiley & Sons, 1961), pp. 37 ff. When he comes down to explaining this idea, Bestor mentions only that a disciplined mind will "analyze" a situation, not "merely adjust to it." *Analysis* is the only mental function he mentions specifically in this discussion. Since this idea is such an important one in essentialist educational theory—and in all educational theory—it seems a pity that we cannot have a more searching and definitive analysis than this.

[59]   Both these interpretations are complex and will be discussed at length in their proper places in subsequent chapters.

means than changes in administrative policies, but as yet he has accomplished very little in this respect.

Other practical problems of essentialism could well be discussed, but those that have received attention are perhaps sufficient to show the crucial character these problems have for this tradition. It does not seem rash to say that in considerable measure the future of the tradition depends on the ability of its adherents to find workable solutions to these problems. The analyses presented here indicate that essentialism, at least as yet, has not been able to develop such policies.

## SUMMARY

This chapter has been about essentialism as the conservative view of education. Its purpose has been to describe the principal tenets of conservative doctrine in education, to examine important recommendations for educational practice advocated by conservatives, and to consider certain important practical problems that face this tradition. The design throughout this chapter has been practical, and yet as we close we can anticipate certain questions that go far beyond the confines of educational practice. This is inevitable for if we are obstinate in our efforts to think clearly about the problems of education, we shall find ourselves thinking about many things in addition to the practical side of educational affairs.

# chapter FOUR

# PHILOSOPHY
# AND EDUCATIONAL
# ESSENTIALISM

Mind is in itself free; but, if it does not
actualize this possibility, it is in no true sense
free, either for itself or for another. Education
is the influencing of man by man, himself
through his own efforts. The attainment of
perfect manhood as the actualization of the
freedom essential to mind constitutes the nature
of education in general.

—JOHANN KARL FRIEDRICH ROSENKRANZ

The hypothesis that man is not free is essential
to the application of scientific method to the
study of human behavior.

—B. F. SKINNER

Essentialism is a body of doctrine about the purposes and means of education. Essentialism has a close organic relation with the general tradition of political and social conservatism. We come now to evaluating whether essentialism as a body of ideas about education can properly be considered a *philosophy* of education. Whatever conception of philosophy one may accept for himself, it has to meet certain fundamental requirements.

One requirement is internal coherence. This means that the ideas that make up our beliefs in any field must be in harmony with each other. For example, the ideas we hold about teaching method should be consonant with our ideas about curriculum. These ideas, in turn, should be harmonious with the way the purposes of education are conceived. Much of the popular thinking about education that goes on in any historical period fails to meet the criteria of coherence and consistency. Since most folk wisdom about educational matters is based on rule of thumb and on uncritical acceptance of previous experience, it should be no surprise that much of this folk wisdom is based on questionable premises and that often it is shot through with incoherences and logical contradictions.

It goes without saying that the thoughtful conservative does not want his position on educational matters to be considered little if anything more than an aggregate of miscellaneous notions about schools and teaching. The conservative not only believes his ideas are the right ideas and that they should guide our educational efforts; he also believes that his ideas form a coherent and consistent way of looking at education. A great many modern essentialists also like to believe that their ideas on education are consistent with the important elements in the general conservative tradition. Our business is to ascertain whether this is true, and on what grounds the essentialist argues his case.

## ESSENTIALISM AS PHILOSOPHY

There are at least three principal elements in the tradition of essentialism that must be investigated. These matters are not primarily educational in character, but they are closely allied with the essentialist position on educational principles. The position taken here is that a clear and convincing explanation must be forthcoming from conservatives if their educational doctrines are to meet the criteria of coherence and consistency. These issues, whose satisfactory resolution must be accomplished if essentialism is to be regarded as a coherent and consistent body of ideas about education, are certainty in knowledge and truth, certainty in values, and relation of the individual and society.

CERTAINTY IN KNOWLEDGE AND TRUTH

One cannot read the literature of modern educational conservatism without being impressed with the air of certainty that customarily attends its pronouncements. The essentialist rarely is tentative in his argument. One almost never finds him saying that there are different ways of looking at a problem or a situation, or entertaining the notion that there are possible alternative answers to important questions. This air of certainty seems often to have bred a kind of arrogance among conservatives and it is only fair to point this out. Any person can test this statement for himself by reading such diverse works as Albert Lynd's *Quackery in the Public Schools*,[1] or the *Monthly Bulletin* of the Council for Basic Education, or such a scholarly philosophic essay on education as John Wild's "Education and Human Society: A Realistic View."[2]

Whether the conservative is entitled to the superior attitude he displays so frequently in contemporary writing is a tangential question. However, a question of superior concern is this: *What is the source of this air of certainty that pervades essentialist thinking on educational issues?* What makes the conservative so sure that he is right?

Let it be remembered that a basic proposition of all conservative thought on education is the existence of a central body of essential knowledge that must be transmitted to all who come to school. Surely this must be a body of *truth*, for it is exceedingly difficult to think of the essentialist upholding the wholesale transmission of error. Involved also in this position is the belief that education is a preparation for adult life, and it apparently follows that the essentialist knows, or thinks he knows, what essential truths are necessary for such preparation.[3] Moreover, the essentialist must believe that truth has some kind of constancy sufficient to ensure that what is taught in childhood and adolescence will be both true and usable in adulthood.

When an educational theorist talks this way he is talking about more than educational theory. Underneath his statements about the curriculum and the processes of schooling, we may properly suspect, there is a

---

[1]   Boston: Little, Brown and Co., 1953.

[2]   John S. Brubacher, ed., *Modern Philosophies and Education*, Fifty-fourth Yearbook of the National Society for the Study of Education (Chicago: University of Chicago Press), pp. 17–56.

[3]   Arthur Bestor's attempts to handle this issue are interesting because he seems not quite sure whether to argue from the intrinsic or the instrumental values of essential knowledge. In a source cited earlier (Philip H. Phenix, ed., *Philosophies of Education* (New York: John Wiley & Sons, 1961), p. 39), Bestor insists that nine-tenths of what is essential "will always be relatively unchanging." The term *relatively* perhaps provides a convenient escape hatch.

conviction concerning some ultimate source of certainty and dependability for our knowledge. This is to say that the conservative apparently subscribes to some conception of knowledge that assures him that our judgments can be true, that the certainty of truth is possible, and that some objective and trustworthy criterion for truth exists. If the conservative can make a strong case for such a conception of knowledge, we are constrained to admit that he has strengthened the support for his tradition. If, on the other hand, he fails to develop a convincing demonstration, his cause will necessarily suffer considerably. This situation must be studied in depth.

## CERTAINTY IN VALUES

The question of value is the second crucial element in the conservative case. One of the most important functions of the school, according to educational conservatives, is the transmission of certain traditional values to the young. The conservative is certain that there is a body of value and that the school has a proper role in conserving and transmitting this body of truth. One does not have to search far in the literature of conservatism to find that these values are permanent, that they do not change with time or circumstance, and that they can be known to be ultimate in their importance.

The air of certainty with which the conservative presents this view leads us to speculate that he believes in some principle that gives his conception of value standards and value judgments the character—or at least the potential character—of certainty. Such a principle surely would eliminate various kinds of relativism, that is, ideas that standards for value change with changes in culture and therefore any given set of standards can apply only in a certain cultural context. Conservative writing strongly implies that some *source* exists that can provide authoritative answers for our value problems. If such a source does exist, we can see why the conservative does not feel apologetic about transmitting value concepts to children and youth, or even on occasion imposing them. The conservative finds it difficult to understand why, when the truth is known, it should not be transmitted to the uninformed.

We can say again, therefore, that if conservatism can sustain its case for a source of immutable values, its position on the ethical aspects of education is strong. If a case cannot be made to stand, the tradition will suffer accordingly.

## THE INDIVIDUAL AND SOCIETY

The third philosophical requirement for a systematic and coherent conservatism is somewhat different from the two already indicated. It concerns the very old problem of the relation of the individual to society. This question is important to conservatism because in this tradition there are two strains of thought that sometimes seem incompatible. As we know, conservatism has always stressed the importance of conserving existing institutions and patterns in society. The conservative insists that we must maintain a slow and gradual rate of social change. A basic belief of this tradition is that the individual owes his primary allegiance to the existing order and its institutions, and the conservative shows bitter hostility to those who would institute abrupt change through revolution or doctrinaire reform movements.

When we consider this primary theme of conservatism, we may be tempted to believe that to the conservative, society itself is the main consideration and the individual must fit himself without serious protest to the requirements of the social pattern. If so, this would seem to be primarily a process of individual conformity and adjustment.

There is, however, another important theme in the conservative tradition. This is the idea that the integrity and self-identification of the individual must be maintained. Modern conservatives have given much attention to this aspect of their tradition. A great deal of their antistatism has been argued from the point of view that the modern collectivistic state, with all its promises of social welfare, ultimately will engulf the individual and he will become lost in the faceless crowd. Similarly, essentialists have bitterly criticized today's schools. These schools, critics say, are designed only for adjustment of the individual to the group. The net effect of such schooling is to destroy or even prevent the development of individualism and self-identity.

Admittedly, there seems to be some paradox involved in these two main themes of conservative tradition but we do not at this point know whether this apparent paradox is genuine. We need, therefore, to explore the conservative theory of society in which the individual can maintain his own identity and selfhood and at the same time render his primary respect and allegiance to a pattern of society that is built on tradition and a scarcely perceptible rate of change. An account that will successfully reconcile the individual and society—at the expense of neither—will be a strategic success for this tradition, provided that such an account is possible.

## THE SCHISM WIDENS

In the development of essentialism in this century, its nature has gradually changed, and on certain strategic issues this tradition now finds itself a house divided. The schism is partly educational but, more significant, it is philosophic. The achievements of experimental science have affected the basic outlook of conservatism. One of the main issues is the conflict between the empiricism and naturalism inherent in science and the traditional orientation of conservatives towards theological, or at least transcendental, interpretations of man and nature. In the second half of this century, basic differences have developed within essentialism that serve to weaken the unity of its outlook and the united front that must be preserved if the tradition is to endure.

The principal elements in the schism fall into four categories. First, differences in intellectual orientation have taken the form of the humanistic outlook on the one hand and the scientific outlook on the other. Second is the division over the interpretation we place on human nature. Science has had an important effect on this interpretation. Third, grave differences have appeared concerning ethical theory, and the traditional absolutistic position of conservatism on ethics has been jeopardized by some who, by any common definition, are educational conservatives. And last are the conflicting attitudes towards experimental science itself, as well as towards the social and educational effects of modern science.

Historically, the intellectual orientation of educational conservatism has been chiefly humanistic. *Humanism* is a term of varied meanings, but intended here is the idea that the most important achievements of the human mind should constitute the essentials of a true education. Further, it is maintained that these achievements are primarily literary and artistic works as opposed, for example, to utilitarian and practical, or even scientific, studies. Consequently, the humanities may be thought of as embracing languages (both ancient and modern), literature, philosophy, the several fine arts, including music, and perhaps mathematics in the classic sense. The roots of this conception lie in the Renaissance revival of learning, in which there was a concerted effort to supplant ecclesiastical learning, which had dominated education in the medieval world, with the classic learning of the ancient world.

Over a long time, the humanists were able to root Scholasticism out of the control of the universities, a development that led not only to reformulation of the curriculum of the university but also to a new conception of secondary education. Since these events occurred long before the advent of popular education, their influence on elementary education in the beginning was negligible. Since the hold of the humanists on education was so strong, the curricula of higher and secondary education were largely humanistic, and this slant persisted, not only through the nineteenth century but well into the twentieth. Consequently, experimental science had to develop outside the universities for the most part. It is true that work in medicine was offered in some American institutions of higher learning in the eighteenth century and that chemistry was taught as a subject in some places at the beginning of the nineteenth century. But this was "book science," usually taught in the best humanistic fashion. Of significance was the first *laboratory* for instructing students in chemistry, opened at Harvard in 1846; that evidently was regarded as a questionable, if not a dangerous, innovation.[4]

There is more to the story than simply domination of the curriculum by the humanists even after education became much more widespread and public. What is perhaps more significant is the philosophy of human nature implicit in the humanistic tradition and the close relationship of this conception to classical conservatism. Humanists tend to see man not through some framework of Darwinian naturalism but rather through a transcendental, and more often than not a religious, frame of reference. The humanist thinks of the inward urge, the reality of conscience, and the freedom of will. He regards man as set off from other living things by such attributes as these, and typically he exhibits a profound distaste for philosophies and for systems of education that ignore or pervert what he holds to be supremely human—spirit, or mind, or whatever it may be called.[5]

The humanist's view of ethics is closely related to the conception of human nature typical of that tradition, and in many respects to the basic views of conservatism, particularly classical conservatism. There is, the humanist thinks, a higher law to which all men ultimately in one way or another must answer. There are ethical norms that are universal in their application and permanent in their being. Man himself possesses a modicum of good and also a substantial component of evil. These questions of the origin and nature of ethical norms and the way they function in conduct are among the most important in philosophy, and indeed they have been treated exhaustively by the great traditional philosophers. But the humanist also believes that these principles may well have received their most dramatic and compelling portrayal in the great masterpieces of literature and art. And for this reason, as well as perhaps others, the humanist regards it the mission of education to bring to each generation a realization of the importance of our repository of the humanities, in which the human drama is shown in all its marvelous complexity and its tragedy, conveying whatever possibility of hope for man there may be. Thus, as conservative educational theorists have long told us, the purpose of education is not simply scholarship and training of the intellect, important as these may be, but also transmission of the values of a civilization. And these tasks are not separate but part of a total unity. It is the humanities that are essential.

---

[4] Ellwood P. Cubberley, *Public Education in the United States* (Boston: Houghton Mifflin Co., 1934), p. 276.

[5] For an excellent discussion of the conservative tradition, particularly as it has been expressed in American literature, see Allen Guttman, *The Conservative Tradition in America* (New York: Oxford University Press, 1967). Chapter 5, "The Revival of Conservative Ideas," is particularly pertinent to the point discussed here.

And this brings us to the relation between the humanistic approach to education and modern science. Conservatism has had difficulties in its confrontation with experimental science. The concept of determinism, based on the principle of uniformity, has disturbed the conservative's dedication to the idea of free will and personal responsibility for one's actions. The humanist perceives that an assumption of a thoroughgoing determinism leaves any form of ethics meaningless and education then becomes simply animal training, whether this is known as operant conditioning or behavior modification, or by some other fancy name.

Further, the humanities have been in retreat in American education for several decades and the humanist knows it. But what to do? Science is here. It will not be made to go away simply by wishing. Its aggressiveness is such that it cannot be contained. A difficult situation has arisen, and even when the humanist tries to be optimistic about it an unmistakable note of melancholy seems to creep in. "One might say," observed Joseph Wood Krutch, "that the most important of all the functions of literature is to be a part of that whole discourse whose function it is to prevent our understanding of the meaning of human life from degenerating into that 'nothing but' to which all the sciences, because of the simplicity of their conceptions and the crudity of their instruments, tend to reduce it." [6] The main thesis Krutch developed is in essence that the modern "science of human behavior" has steadily lowered human nature to such a point that we have all but lost the chance to restore it to its rightful position of honor and dignity. We have about lost our sense of what the measure of man really is, and it may be said parenthetically, the status of the curricula in our schools shows this plainly. The great literary heritage is more the measure of man than anything else can ever be.

Humanism as we have defined it is one aspect of the conservative tradition in education. It is no longer dominant, as it once was, but it is still alive and still an eloquent expression of educational conservatism. We have suggested that the educational conservative ultimately is confronted with three basic considerations: (1) the source of truth; (2) the certainty of values; and (3) the relation of the individual and society. Although these are not primarily educational considerations, they lie at the base of educational theory, and further they are problems with which traditional educational humanism is concerned.

We propose that the philosophical tradition that best supports the position of the humanistic conservative is idealism, particularly the objective idealism of Hegel—more precisely, certain interpretations placed on various aspects of Hegelian philosophy in the late nineteenth century.

[6] Joseph Wood Krutch, *The Measure of Man* (New York: Grosset & Dunlap, 1954), p. 244.

There is no contention that every humanistic teacher as education theorist is a Hegelian, or that every one of them has worked out his position consciously in terms of idealistic philosophy. The point that is maintained is that the ancient Western tradition of idealism in philosophy is more congenial to the ideas of the humanistic conservatives and is better fitted than any of our other approaches to philosophy for providing a theoretical base for their contentions. For this reason we shall consider some aspects of idealistic philosophy, particularly those related to issues we have raised.

## IDEALISM AS PHILOSOPHY

Idealism as a general tradition is one of the oldest and most respected traditions in Western philosophy. The influence of absolute idealism in the nineteenth century was far greater than that of any other philosophical tradition. Its influence extended beyond the confines of academic philosophy into the broader fields of theology, social and political theory, literature and the other arts, and educational theory. The influence of idealism among philosophers began to diminish near the end of the last century, and in the first half of the present century its influence in this group declined precipitously. There are not many—although there are a few—great representatives of this tradition left in departments of philosophy in American universities.

Several factors have influenced the decline of philosophical idealism. One of them is science and the concomitant development of approaches to philosophy that are influenced by scientific method and that involve problems with which idealism is ordinarily not concerned. A second factor is that there is very little current interest among philosophers in system building. The essence of such a great speculative tradition in philosophy as idealism is its effort to develop an all-encompassing theoretical structure in which the whole of reality is patterned according to some cosmic design. Philosophy today, however, is mainly concerned with analyses and criticism. While, in the eyes of idealists and other system builders, this must give philosophy a more mundane role than it has had traditionally, most present-day philosophers insist that the critical and analytical function is the most important contribution philosophy has to offer. In their judgment, idealism is really of interest only in the history of philosophy.

It is reasonable to ask, therefore, why we should give so much attention to idealism here if it actually is a matter of little interest among modern philosophers. The answer is that although this tradition has lost much of its influence among philosophers, it is far from being without effect in certain other quarters. The stronghold of idealism in higher education today is undoubtedly in various departments of the humanistic studies. The scholars and teachers in these departments are not primarily philosophers, but important aspects of the studies they pursue are closely related to philosophic ideas. For one thing, there are many humanistic scholars who are profoundly disturbed by the concepts of human nature that are emerging from the work of behavioral scientists. There are also many of them who take exception to ideas about knowledge, truth, and value that have been influenced by scientific method.

These scholars and teachers believe that there is more to the nature of reality and more to human nature and destiny than has been or ever will be revealed by the scientific approach. Many of them believe that the road to complete cultural dissolution is paved with the positivism, ethical relativism, and psychological behaviorism that have been fostered by science—and also in no small measure by much of today's philosophy. It is natural, therefore, that persons with this attitude should continue to hold with philosophic ideas that stress the transcendent character of human selfhood, the objectivity of truth—particularly ethical truth—and the fundamental regularity and rationality of the cosmos. To them it is only in a world of the kind portrayed by idealism that the human drama has meaning, and only in this kind of world that the highest aspirations of man can have any chance of being realized. Since idealism is still influential in affecting the perceptions of many people in the field of education, it is important that certain specific aspects of this tradition and their relation to the educational enterprise be understood clearly.

## BASIC THESIS OF IDEALISM

It has often been maintained that all the great systems of philosophical thought that have come into existence are at heart developments and elaborations of certain common elements of human experience. In idealism, the common experience that has been expanded into a philosophical system is the awareness of self. This awareness of the irreducibility of our own consciousness is a universal experience among human beings, and according to idealists at least, it is the most significant fact of individual experience.

The great French philosopher Descartes (1596–1650) pointed out in his *Meditations on the First Philosophy* that a man may doubt everything that he has hitherto accepted as a matter of course. A man may doubt that the elements of physical nature exist; he may doubt that God is divinely good or that He has created the world; a man may doubt that his own body—his own arms and legs—exist. But there is one thing that no man can doubt, no matter what effort he makes. *He cannot doubt that he himself exists.* Awareness of his own existence is the irreducible element in the experience of every man. As Descartes pointed out, "I am" is a true proposition every time I express it or conceive it in my mind. And although

I may succeed in doubting the existence of everything else, one thing is certain: every time I think, *I exist*. The primary and ultimate fact of my experience is mind and consciousness. It is not my physical body of members and organs that is necessarily real, for it is possible to believe that my body does not exist. The ultimate reality in my experience is my *mind*. It alone can be known to be real. The famous Cartesian argument was summed up in the sentence *Cogito, ergo sum*—"I think, therefore I am."

Now the argument is that idealism, as a systematic philosophy, is the elaboration and systematization of this basic proposition that mind is the primary and irreducible fact of individual experience. One part of the basic thesis of all idealism is that mind is prior; that when we seek what is ultimate in the world, when we push back behind the veil of immediate sense experience, we shall find that what is ultimate in the whole universe is of the nature of mind or spirit (the two words are interchangeable in most discussions of idealism)—just as it is mind that is ultimate in the inner world of personal experience. This idea may be expressed in the conception that is central to idealism: *the principle of the priority of consciousness.*

From this central principle of idealism we may come to certain conclusions that are important to understanding the tradition. First, we may conclude that if mind is prior in the sense that it is the ultimate reality, then material things either do not exist at all, or if they do exist, they in some way depend for their existence on mind. Given the basic postulate of the priority of consciousness, we can infer properly that if mind is prior then it is in some sense the *cause* for the existence of other things and for the character of that world of things and events that we meet in our ordinary experience.

This first inference serves to illustrate the function that idealism as a philosophical tradition has had in the intellectual history of Western culture. Idealism has always been conceived as the ancient and implacable enemy of all forms of materialism. There are various forms of philosophical materialism but the basic tenet of all these is that what is ultimately and irreducibly real in the universe is *matter*. Idealists flatly reject this materialistic thesis. For one thing, they are fond of saying, "How can we conceive that mind, which is active and dynamic and creative, could have come from mere material stuff, which is inert and lifeless?" Another question idealists often ask is how a universe that is nothing but matter in motion could possibly have a place in it for value and for those concerns that have always engaged the highest efforts of mankind.

A second important inference that may be drawn from the principle of the priority of consciousness concerns the character of the ultimately real. We know from our own experience that the fact of consciousness gives us certain powers or functions. We know for one thing that as conscious beings, we are capable of *rational thought and knowledge*. We know that one of the attributes of self is rationality, and since ultimate reality is of the nature of mind, we can say with logical certainty that one of the traits of the ultimate Reality must be reason—the powers of cognition and of logical thought.

We can also know from an examination of our own self-experience that as conscious beings we have the power of *volition*. One of the facts of individual experience is the fundamental realization that we are free to choose among alternatives. Our behavior is self-directed and is not merely a response to pressures of a material environment. We have the distinct impression that through the effort of our will we can rise above pressures of the environment and seek the good, even when this seeking is the hard path to follow. Therefore, in view of these convictions, which every person has or can gain from an examination of his own experience, we can know that one of the fundamental attributes of reality is *will*—the power of volition.

Beyond this, our personal experience also reveals that we are endowed with the potential of creativity. We know that, potentially at least, we are creatures of imagination and vision. The strongest drive to action that we experience in our own lives is the urge to self-realization—the drive not only to preserve ourselves, but *to realize ourselves*. This creative dynamic activity of self-realization, even though it may be realized imperfectly, is a fundamental aspect of personal experience, and no man can deny this honestly.[7]

The priority of consciousness is the thesis on which many variant forms of idealism are based. However, there are different ways in which this principle can be interpreted. These ways range from interpretations that are extremely subjective and border on pure solipsism to various forms of objective idealism that incorporate the principle of a transcendental, or cosmic, mind that objectifies itself in a world of things and events—in other words, in the world in which we live and have our experience.[8]

In the history of philosophy, the subjective forms of idealism are interesting for technical reasons, and solipsism is extremely difficult to refute on logical grounds. Very few if any philosophers have, however, accepted the extreme forms of subjectivism, and the really influential philosophic systems built on the priority of consciousness have been objective.

That aspect of metaphysical idealism pertinent to our purposes de-

---

[7] An important discussion of what idealists consider *grounds* for accepting idealism will be found in Herman H. Horne, "An Idealistic Philosophy of Education," in John S. Brubacher, ed., *Philosophies of Education*, Forty-first Yearbook of the National Society for the Study of Education (Bloomington, Ill.: Public School Publishing Co., 1942), pp. 141 ff.

[8] Solipsism is the doctrine that only the individual self exists and that the experience of the self is its own projection.

rives from the German philosopher Hegel, whose influence was one of the great intellectual forces of the last century. Hegel's philosophical system, together with the variations that were developed on it, is usually known as *Absolute idealism*.

## ABSOLUTE IDEALISM

We are ready now to consider certain of the leading ideas involved in Absolute idealism and to investigate their relationship to the conservative tradition in education. The great names in the history of Absolute idealism are Johann Gottlieb Fichte (1762–1814), Friedrich Wilhelm von Schelling (1775–1854), and Georg Wilhelm Friedrich Hegel (1780–1831), all German philosophers and all in part the intellectual heirs of the great Immanuel Kant (1724–1804). There is wide agreement that Kant is the greatest name in the history of modern Western philosophy, but his critical and somewhat eclectic approach to philosophy is of less direct importance to our purpose than the great system builders Fichte, Schelling, and Hegel.[9]

Our purpose is not that of examining in detail the philosophical systems of these three men. It is rather to survey the general architecture of Absolute idealism as an important tradition in philosophy and to examine the effects it often has on men's minds as they consider the problems of education. Accordingly, we give some attention to the metaphysical, the epistemological, and the ethical dimensions of this approach to philosophy.

Absolute idealism is built around the idea that mind is prior in the cosmic sense. In Absolute idealism, reality is one unified whole and this whole is of the nature of mind or spirit. The attributes that characterize this Absolute Mind are those that we know intimately in our own experience: reason, volition, and creativity. The "objective" world that we know in our own experience—the world of things and events—is itself a concrete manifestation of the Absolute Mind as it develops to higher and higher (and endless) levels of self-realization.

Mind is not a static, finished substance. Mind is in a real sense a process. And in that Mind that is ultimate in its perfection, the processes move in accordance with a dynamic and logically perfect pattern. With Hegel, this logic was that of the dialectic in which the resolution of opposites is achieved by their transformation in a synthesis that is novel and yet is a product of that out of which it emerged. The famous Hegelian triad of thesis, antithesis, and synthesis is complex, and to many students of

---

[9] Kant's connection with Absolute idealism lies largely in his derivation of the forms or "categories" of thought that made knowledge possible. Some writers on the relation of idealism and education take Kant as their chief example. The thesis of this book is that the conservative educator owes far more directly to the Hegelians and other Absolute idealists than to Kant.

philosophy it is an impenetrable metaphysical thicket. Whatever other purpose it may serve, it is one way of accounting for a basic belief of idealists that everything that exists is part of an ultimate Unity and that what may appear on the partial view to be contraries (in the logical sense) are actually in process of being transformed into a higher synthesis. This synthesis then becomes a new thesis, is amalgamated with its own contrary (antithesis), and a new synthesis emerges, and so on and on forever in this Great Consciousness that is all-inclusive.

The world as we know it is one concrete manifestation of this cosmic logical process. And what we call history is the objective process of self-realization of the Absolute. In this sense, reality (which is itself a process) is *rational and orderly*. The events that make up the world in which we live are not the product of some fortuitous set of circumstances. Every event that occurs must occur. Every event has a purpose because it is a part of a vast logical system, and every event, no matter how inconsequential it may appear, has meaning because it is a part of this vast process whose innermost character is regularity and logical order. Within the conscious process of the Absolute, there is no internal contradiction. Just as is true for all genuine logical systems, mathematics for example, all propositions are coherent with each other and all have meaning because of their membership in the system.

In Absolute idealism, we are not talking merely of analytical systems such as mathematics; we are talking about the whole process of the cosmos. History in its development displays the same characteristics as geometry. Everything follows necessarily, every event has meaning because every event is related to every other event, and the whole process moves towards higher and higher levels of realization. This is Hegel's theory of history: the theory that history is a concrete manifestation of an all-including Conscious Process that had no beginning and will have no end, and which proceeds for no other purpose outside itself.

Thus, in its metaphysical thesis, Absolute idealism interprets the principle of the priority of consciousness as meaning that the concrete world of things and events is a product of the conscious processes of the Absolute Mind. The process we call history is rational and orderly because it is the product of a Supreme Reason, in which rationality and orderliness function in complete perfection. Even before we examine other dimensions of Absolute idealism, we can anticipate the moral dictum that is implicit in this metaphysics: *"Whatever is, is right!"* For if history is the unfolding of a Great Idea, and if every event in this process follows as a matter of logical necessity, then whatever is at any moment must be right—*in the ethical sense.*

This outline of metaphysics is more Hegelian than anything else. In it, reality is conceived as a process of consciousness that incorporates all existence within itself. In this sense it may seem impersonal, even aloof, from the temporal order of things. Many idealists—particularly Americans —have sought to endow the Absolute with a more personalistic character. Idealism can be thought of as the magnification and elaboration of the individual's conviction that the ultimate in personal experience is the reality of self. All we need do to personalize the Absolute is to conceive it not as an aloof process of logical development, but as a Self with all the attributes of selfhood that we know in our own experience. Those qualities that can be attributed only to self—never to matter—are thought, will, and creativity. Thus we can project our own consciousness of self and conceive that what is the ultimately Real is a great Self—an Absolute Self, the cause and ground for all existence.

And having said this, we now realize that we as individuals and as finite selves bear a special relationship to the Ultimate Reality, for we as human selves share with the Absolute Self those attributes that make It what It is. We are, as idealists rarely tire of saying, "the universe writ small." The universe is a self—an all-inclusive self. It is *macrocosm*, reality in its totality. The human self is in a sense a miniature, though a necessarily imperfect counterpart of this Ultimate Self. The human self is the universe in *microcosm*, and this relation gives man a unique and exalted position in the scheme of things.

The Absolute Self is the embodiment of perfection in every conceivable sense of that word, and its perfection inheres in its complete unity. In our own finite existence, we are impelled to strive for apprehension of those supreme values of Truth, Goodness, and Beauty; and in some measure we are able to apprehend these, though always partially and therefore imperfectly. Through reason we can expect that what is only partial and incomplete with us is complete and perfect in the Absolute. In the Mind of the Ultimate, there exist in pure essential form those universal conceptions of Truth and Goodness and Beauty. In the Absolute, there is no trace of error, no evil, no ugliness. Value has objective reference—it is real, for it exists in pure conceptual form in the Absolute Mind. But disvalue has no objective reality. Error, evil, ugliness have no ideational counterpart in the mind of the Ultimate Self, and hence these have no real character.

If we take all these ideas and combine them into a general scheme, we come out with the kind of cosmology that profoundly influenced the American intellectual climate of the nineteenth century and that still has substantial influence in this century. If we were to make a diagram of this cosmic scheme of things, it would look somewhat like Figure 4.1. This diagram portrays the Absolute as mind or spirit, characterized by the ultimate perfection embodied in the great essences of value, making itself manifest through cognition, volition, and its creative powers in a historical process that unifies all persons, all things, and all events in an unending stream of history. In this historical process, man is the highest manifestation of the Absolute Mind.

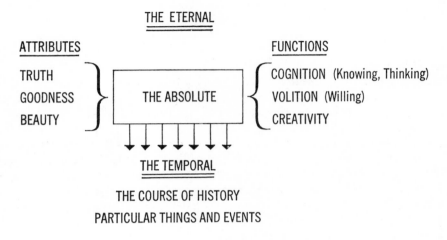

Figure 4.1

*ABSOLUTE IDEALISM AND RELIGION*

One who meets these ideas for the first time feels an element of strangeness, and yet usually something that has a familiar ring. Idealism is a tradition in philosophy, and the doctrines that make up this tradition can be argued on purely philosophical grounds. If idealism is a tenable philosophical position, it can be advanced and defended entirely on metaphysical, epistemological, and axiological grounds. And yet in the history of idealism, few of its advocates have cared to confine themselves to purely philosophical ideas and arguments.

Much of the enormous influence that idealism exerted in its heyday was undoubtedly owed to its close affiliation with Christian religious doctrine, particularly Protestant doctrine. Without exception every great American exponent of Absolute idealism has found an organic connection between the philosophy of idealism and the basic tenets of the Hebraic-Christian view of the world and of man. The amalgamation with religious doctrine gives this philosophy the ring of familiarity to its primary ideas.

In such a cosmology, we need only change a few terms to convert the metaphysical to the theological. The Absolute becomes God, the eternal Spirit. God is not material, but all material things are manifestations of His will, His intelligence, and His creative power. The mind of God encompasses all creation—all that is or has been or ever will be. God is omniscient; He is omnipotent; and He is rational. He has made Himself manifest in a world of things and events and the processes of this world reflect the rational nature of their Author. History is, as religious idealists point out, a record of Providential purpose, and the whole of reality is rational, orderly, and unified.

The religious conception of human nature is all but synonymous with that which idealism presents. Man is the highest expression of the creative power of God. Man was deliberately created in the image of his Maker and he shares some of the same attributes that characterize God himself. Like God, man is a spiritual being, though unlike Him man is also a creature of flesh and this aspect of his being is in time, while God's entire being is outside time. The universe that God created was formed with man's life and destiny foremost in mind. The created world, which is a manifestation of the Divine Intelligence, is a kind of stage on which the human drama of self-realization takes place and in which man seeks to unite himself with the Ultimate. There is nothing fixed in the nature of things that stands between man and his realization of his highest desires. The world itself is friendly to man, and ideals have an objective reality in the nature of things.

There is little need to go further in this recital because most of us have been taught these ideas from earliest childhood. They illustrate the close connection that exists between Absolute idealism and many versions of the Hebraic-Christian cosmology.

## CERTAINTY OF TRUTH AND VALUE

At this point we should perhaps remind ourselves that the object of our search is to find the sources of certainty that are important in the conservative tradition. For an important segment of modern conservatism, the source of certainty is in Absolute idealism, and the key to it is the idealistic doctrine of the priority of consciousness.

In the first place, we are assured by the idealist that the reality we encounter in our own experience is the product of an Ultimate Intelligence, and that the world in its essential character is rational and orderly. This, the idealist thinks, means that our knowledge of the world has the potential of being certain, at least in some respects. The certainty qualification has to be made because idealists have to admit that there is a certain "slippage" between the ideal and the actual. Nevertheless, the idealist assures us that there is an objective body of Truth, and that even finite minds are capable of apprehending it, though not in its entirety.

For the idealist, knowing is always a creative, constructive act. The data that originate in sense experience are combined and interpreted and formed into intelligible ideas. In this sense, what the mind actually does is to construct the object of its own knowledge. The question now becomes one of knowing what the criterion for Truth is: Granted that it is the creative power of mind that accounts for our knowledge, how are we to know when the ideas we hold are true and when they are not true? How are we able to distinguish between truth and error?

To this question, the idealist has a considered answer. We know our ideas are true, he says, *when they are in harmony with the already existing and accepted body of truth.* In other words, the criterion for truth is *consistency,* and idealists often point out that consistency, since it is a logical criterion, is the most rigorous standard possible.[10] Idealists may point out that the most rigorous body of truth in existence is mathematics and that the criterion of truth for any mathematical proposition is its consistency with the whole body of mathematical knowledge. What, the idealist asks, can be more certain than truth established through logical coherence?

Critics of idealism have pointed out that while it is true that coherence is the criterion for truth *in an analytic system such as mathematics,* it is a criterion only for formal validity—since that is the only form of validity possible in an analytic system. If all knowledge were like pure mathematics, then coherence would be the only necessary criterion (and the only possible one). But much of our concern with knowledge is not with those forms that are purely analytical, as in mathematical and logical systems. Our main concerns are those that involve facts, as in common sense and scientific experience. It is in these areas that critics find coherence an insufficient criterion.

However, the idealist can point out that what is overlooked by these critics is the principle that all existence is itself rational and orderly—that the world of experience, being itself a rational product of an Ultimate Reason, does exhibit in macrocosm the formal properties of a logical system, and hence the criterion of coherence is entirely proper. It must be admitted that error does sometimes occur in human knowledge. Knowledge does have to be revised periodically. Theories in science, once accepted as true, have had to be abandoned. Historians find it necessary to "correct" history, and so on. What this shows, according to idealism, is that finite human nature is on occasion fallible and so, even with the rigor of logical coherence, we sometimes mistake error for truth. When we drop one idea for another, it is because the latter meets better the criterion of consistency. Our efforts are in the direction of closer and closer approximations to the Truth. Though we may never reach the ultimate apprehension of all Truth, we can come nearer and nearer to it.

---

[10] Kant and some contemporary idealists have spoken of two criteria: correspondence and coherence. The term *correspondence* in this respect refers to the correspondence of an idea *with the accepted body of truth.* The term *coherence* used in the body of the text in this book includes both correspondence as just defined and coherence in the logical sense. *Correspondence* is an important term in realistic epistemologies and should not be confused with the way idealists use it in their discussions of truth.

We are now in a position to state in propositional form the thesis of idealism concerning knowledge and truth:

1.  The universe is rational and orderly and therefore intelligible.
2.  There is an objective body of Truth that has its origin and existence in the Absolute Mind and that can be known, at least in part, by the human mind.
3.  The act of knowing is essentially an act of reconstructing the data of awareness into intelligible ideas and systems of ideas.
4.  The criterion for the truth of an idea is coherence; that is, an idea is true when it is consistent with the existing and accepted body of truth.

We can see now that idealism has an answer for the first question that motivated our search: There *is* a source of certainty for our knowledge. The universe *is* rational and orderly. There *is* an objective body of Truth. The human mind *is* capable of knowing this Truth; though finite minds can never grasp all Truth in its entirety, they are capable of closer and closer approximations to it. There *is* a criterion that enables us to distinguish truth from falsity. Thus, we can say that if one of the requirements of a consistent essentialism is the assurance that there is a body of objective Truth and that it is capable of being known, then the tradition of idealism can fulfill this requirement.

The next question is whether idealism can extend the same assurance of certainty concerning our value judgments. Essentialism sees the role of education as involving not only transmission of knowledge, but also transmission of value. Surely no more cogent question can be asked than whether there are objective values that hold for all men in all times and that can be transmitted by the teacher with full confidence in their certainty.

Various strains in the idealistic tradition converge to form the ethical thesis, which many idealists think is the single greatest element in their philosophical tradition. First of all, we should remember that' in the eyes of idealists human behavior is inherently purposive. As they see it, behavior is not merely responses to external stimuli, as psychological behaviorists would have it. Rather, there is within the human self an inherent urge for self-realization; the basic motivation for behavior, therefore, lies within the self and is not external to it. That man is a purposive creature means also that he is a *valuing* creature. He cannot escape the necessity of placing value (or disvalue) on the things and events he experiences. The whole of history portrays the continuing efforts of man to gain a firmer and more valid grasp of the Good.

Secondly, if men are to make judgments about value, they must have some standards by which particular things can be judged as good or not good. These norms should be comprehensive and they should be dependable. The idealist is certain that such norms do exist and that they characterize Reality itself. There are ultimate essences of the supreme values of Truth, Goodness, and Beauty. In our world of experience we see these great Ideas embodied in concrete form in things and events. Though it must be admitted that these values are never perfectly expressed in this world, nevertheless we can through reason know that in what is ultimate they exist in pure essential form and they serve as the ideals toward which we strive, even though our best efforts may only be approximations.

In the third place, we have a rigorous criterion for assessing the truth of our value judgments. This criterion is coherence, which is the criterion by which we assess the validity of all our judgments. If those judgments we make that have value significance are consistent with our own most reliable value experience, and if they are coherent with the body of value judgments that are the collective product of human experience, then we can rest assured of their truth and their dependability.

It follows that the good life for man is the life in which value concepts are apprehended intellectually and in which they are expressed in personal conduct. Hence, both understanding and acting are involved, but the essence of goodness in our conduct is that actions be guided by knowledge. So in response to the second question, we can say that from the standpoint of idealism there *is* a source of certainty for value standards. There *is* a criterion for distinguishing good from evil. There *is* a way of knowing what the good life is for man. And all these taken together can give assurance that education must be concerned with transmitting tried and tested values both as standards in conceptual form, and as expressions of these concepts in behavior.

## THE INDIVIDUAL AND SOCIETY

We turn now to the third requirement of a consistent and coherent conservative position in educational philosophy. This requirement involves the relation of the individual to society, and it is an important question in essentialism because the conservative tradition emphasizes the necessity both for individuals to support and conform to the existing social order and for personal freedom and self-realization. On the surface, at least, there appears to be an element of paradox in the conservative position on these matters. Are these two aspects of conservative thought capable of harmonious resolution?

The relation of the individual to society has always been an important issue in social and political philosophy. It is also important in educational theory because the school has a responsibility for establishing whatever relation is to be established between individuals and the greater social group. Sometimes schools are criticized for promoting an excessive conformity in students and thereby teaching them that adjustment to existing society is the greatest good. On the other hand, schools are also criticized for permitting excessive individual freedom, which, it is said, amounts to little more than social anarchy and permits a generation to grow up without restraint or direction.[11] The problem is often stated in such terms as these: Which comes first (or should come first), the interests of the individual or the interests of society? Which has priority, the rights of society or the rights of individuals? Should education find its orientation around the needs of the individual or the needs of society?

To the idealist, these distinctions between the individual and society are unwarranted and the key to understanding idealism's position on this problem is the idea of *unity*, a fundamental element in the idealistic tradition. The point is that every particular thing that exists (and this includes human selves) is part of a total, all-embracing unity. The meaning that anything has is a consequence of its membership in a total system. This is in the same sense that the meaning of any proposition in a logical system depends on the system of which it is a part. Away from this context, a proposition has no function or meaning at all.

Something similar can be said about individual persons. Realization of self is the most important thing in human life; it is literally a sacred right. But this realization can be achieved and selfhood realized only as the individual is able to relate himself progressively to that which is greater than he. If man isolates himself from the greater unity, if he is unwilling or unable to amalgamate himself with it, then like a proposition stripped of its context, he has no real identity. His life has no point to it—it is nothing.

Our thinking about the individual and society involves the so-called *organic conception of society*, basic to classic conservatism. There are various ways of conceiving society. One way is to see it as an aggregation of individuals who live and work together on the basis of an agreement, or contract. If the agreement becomes undesirable for some reason, individuals have the right to abrogate or modify it. This conception of the state is extremely distasteful to idealists, who often speak of it as atomistic. The true nature of society is seen by idealists as being *organic*. This is to say that a society displays the same kind of internal unity that characterizes a living organism. Living things are composed of various parts—arms, legs, head, torso, and so forth. Ultimately a living thing is composed of chemical elements arranged in various combinations. But, the idealist points out, a living thing is far more than a collection of discrete bodily members. Surely it is far more than an aggregation of chemical elements. The idealist's point is often expressed in the familiar saying that "the whole is greater than the sum of its parts."

For example, the human body is a vastly complex organization of

---

[11] Conservatives have from time to time launched both kinds of criticism against the progressive school.

physiological members, but each of these members has identity and function only because it is a part of a larger system. If through some circumstance any member of the body is separated from the total organic unity, it immediately loses both its character and its function, and in a short time, its very existence. Similarly when one organ of the body is diseased, the whole organism is affected adversely. When a man has a "sick" liver, we have more on our hands than a sick liver; we have a sick man.

Now, as the idealist sees it, the organic unity of society is exactly analogous to the unity of an organism. Society in the large sense is composed of lesser unities—which may be compared with the various members of the body. Among these are such institutions as family, community, school, church, nation, and so on. Each of these units of society has its meaning and its function because it is part of a larger unity, which ultimately is the complete unity of the Absolute. If one part of the social body becomes "sick," the total organism suffers. Whenever an institution, the church or the school, for example, malfunctions, the totality of society suffers. In this way societies become sick in the same sense that individual organisms become sick. The only way by which the social organism can regain its health is through the restoration of a harmonious relationship among its parts.

Another dimension to these matters is very important to our present purpose. As idealists commonly see it, society not only exhibits attributes of organic unity, *it also exhibits attributes of personality, or selfhood.* Even common speech is shot through with the belief that personal attributes are possessed by social organisms. For example, we often speak of school spirit, and most schools employ various methods of stimulating it. What is "school spirit"? Is it simply the sum total of the individual "spirits" of the persons who make up the school? Or does it mean that the school is an entity that has the power to possess spirit? It seems likely that if the term *school spirit* has any real meaning, it can be only in this second sense. Now, what kind of things are capable of exhibiting spirit? Certainly inanimate things are not, and just as surely, things that are without consciousness are not. The idealist's conclusion is that the school as an institution is a self and like any self it is possible to predicate spirit of it. A school, it is true, is composed of individual teachers and students, but as an institution it is more than a mere collection of people, just as an organism is more than the arithmetical sum of its various parts.

We now see that the school as a self is a greater and more inclusive unity than the individual student in the school. But, the idealist may ask, what sense does it make to set the student against the school? How can we speak meaningfully of the welfare of the student as opposed in some way to the welfare of the school? If the school did not exist, students would not exist, because to be a student means to be a part of a school, in the same sense that a finger is a finger only when it is part of a hand—

and ultimately a part of a total organism. Schools exist, in part at least, to enable students to realize the potential of their own selfhood, but an individual achieves this only when he identifies himself and his interests with the self that is greater than he is. Only as the individual is able to achieve this self-transcendence and identification with higher and more inclusive levels of unity can he achieve his own self-realization. The interests of the school are the interests of the individual and one cannot be set off separately against the other. The process of self-realization, then, involves the progressive identification of the individual with more and more inclusive levels of unity. This process is illustrated in Figure 4.2.

Figure 4.2

Figure 4.2 Note: There is some variation in the interpretation of the progression of unity. This diagram shows the church as more inclusive than the school. This interpretation would be agreeable to some idealists and not to others. The diagram is intended to be illustrative and not definitive of every possible position.

The realization of self is a continuous process that begins with the birth of the individual. The innermost of the concentric circles in the diagram represents the individual, who at birth is completely self-centered, interested only in his own needs and desires and their fulfillment. His first encounter with an entity greater than himself occurs in his earliest experiences in the family. The family is a self and this selfhood is greater and more inclusive than the members who make up the institution. Consequently, the first necessary act of self-transcendence and identification of the young child is in the family. Modern psychologists agree on the crucial nature of this early experience. Those individuals who through some unfortunate circumstances are unable to achieve this first identification are sorely hampered throughout their lives and may well find it difficult if not impossible to make subsequent adjustments.

As a child grows and matures and his environment broadens, he is called on to identify himself with greater levels of unity. After the family comes the school and the church and the community, each more inclusive of reality and each institution a self. Beyond these institutions is the nation, which in the modern world encompasses all of them and in which the individual realizes his own selfhood through the identification process. Beyond the nation lies the greater unity of humanity and beyond that the all-embracing unity of the Absolute Mind, which to most idealists is the mind of God. Thus, the end toward which the whole process of self-realization moves is the identification of the individual with the totality of all existence. In this process he finds his own selfhood.

Thus, the paradox we spoke of earlier turns out, according to idealists, to be an illusion. The doctrine of the interest of the individual in opposition to the interest of society involves an untenable separation. The individual owes his respect and allegiance to the existing order—to existing and accepted institutions and values and social patterns. In the very act of incorporating his own consciousness and will in the greater consciousness and will, he realizes his own destiny.

## CERTAINTY OF TRUTH

To the educational conservative, the school is an institution whose purpose is the preservation, refinement, and transmission of a body of essential truth. The conservative has never been able to understand the diffidence some teachers exhibit over the question of teaching the truth as if it were *the truth*. This applies particularly to the conservative whose views are tempered by philosophical idealism. The idealist is committed to the belief that there is a body of truth, that this truth can be known, and that it must be transmitted to the young. As an idealist, he is inclined to think that the most important repository of the eternal verities, as they are known to man, are to be found in great literary and other humanistic sources. And the idealist holds the humanistic studies to be the most important of the essentials, for the truth that is portrayed in these sources is superior to any to be found anywhere and more complete.

The conservative has mixed feelings about the ability of the individual to mind his own affairs. He is inclined to think that in the ordinary affairs of life the individual ought to be free to act on his own initiative and responsibility. The conservative believes it is in the important matters that the individual is incompetent to make unguided decisions. And the conservative believes that in matters of great importance we must be guided by tradition—by the wisdom of our ancestors. Here is one point on which the general conservative tradition and the philosophical tradition of idealism coincide. The conservative tells us that our ideas and actions should always be judged in the light of tradition, which is another way of saying that our ideas are worthy *if they are in harmony with the accumulated wisdom of all the generations.* The idealist tells us that the test for the truth of an idea is *its coherence with the body of existing and accepted truth.* Now this body of existing and accepted truth can be nothing else but the wisdom of our ancestors, about which social conservatives say so much.

It seems clear therefore (at least to conservatives), that the responsibility of the school must be to transmit the essential portions of this heritage of tradition to all who come to school. There must be no exceptions because every individual must regulate his conduct in accordance with tradition and the wisdom of our ancestors. Unless he knows what the enduring truths are, and unless he has grasped the essential truths, a man is adrift and without any landmarks to guide him. The idealist believes that the truth exists and that it has objective reality. He also believes that the human mind can distinguish between truth and error, and since tradition furnishes the basis for evaluation of our own ideas, tradition must be perpetuated and passed unblemished from one generation to another. This is the responsibility of education.

## PRIMACY OF VALUE

It has been said that the real purpose of philosophical idealism is to make the world safe for value. To the idealist, the value enterprise is the most important quest in human life—and in philosophy. There is agreement among idealists that, with the possible exception of religion, education is more intimately involved in the value enterprise than any other activity of social life. The teacher is a moral agent in the most fundamental sense of that term, for he is the transmitter of truth, and truth always has moral dimensions. In one sense, any scheme for education is a moral enterprise because the effort to educate is the effort to help an individual become what he would not otherwise be. To the idealist there are objective and well-defined criteria for value and these criteria define the moral dimensions of education. If there were not objective criteria for value in the ultimate sense, then men would not encounter manifestations of value in their individual experience.

This is one point at which the idealist thinks the insufficiencies of science are readily apparent. Science, he points out, may in many instances indicate to us ways of realizing our objectives, but it is entirely outside possibility for science to tell us what objectives we *ought* to seek to realize. Moreover, although there is an ultimate reference for value, the manifestation of value in human life is not automatic. If men are to apprehend values and incorporate them in their own lives, they must make an effort. As in the case of any idea, value concepts must be recreated by the individual and become a part of his own self. In the last analysis, only the individual can do this for himself, but he can be helped in the process—or hindered. This process comes about through the progressive self-identification of the individual with greater dimensions of unity and ultimately with the Absolute Spirit, which is God.

The role of the school is to assist the individual in the apprehension and incorporation of value in his life. The school is not alone in this responsibility, for clearly the family and the church and ultimately the total human community also share in the process. The thing that distinguishes the school's responsibility is that it is the only institution in society whose primary purpose is intellectual development of the individual. Other institutions have some responsibility for the intellectual development of the young, but only in the school is this a primary responsibility.[12]

The intellectual enterprise, however, is not distinct from the moral. Man is a unity—a spiritual unity. Both intellect and will are aspects of his nature. The school as curator of the great intellectual heritage of mankind is thereby also a potent force in the moral life of man, for the school preserves and transmits the great literary heritage whose very essence is ethical.

To the idealist the highest things in life are those of the spirit—the intellectual and moral achievements of man. As he sees it, human life can have meaning only in a world that is itself meaningful, that is itself a product of an Ultimate Reason, and that is ethical in its very nature.

## SCIENTIFIC REALISM, MATERIALISM, AND BEHAVIORISM

The proponents of essentialism now find themselves divided on certain issues. Although these issues are philosophic, they will eventually be

---

[12] See, for example, Theodore M. Greene, "A Liberal Christian Idealist Philosophy of Education," in John S. Brubacher, ed., *Modern Philosophies and Education*, Fifty-fourth Yearbook of the National Society for the Study of Education (Chicago: University of Chicago Press, 1955), pp. 115–17.

expressed in educational theory and policy. Since the issues are divisive, the disunity that is emerging probably bodes no good for the conservative approach to educational practice. We have now examined some of the ideas that undergird the older, more orthodox form of essentialist doctrine, and have seen how philosophic idealism furnishes powerful support for social and educational conservatism. Anyone who is at all conversant with events in the American educational scene knows full well that the whole story has not been told thus far. The humanistic tradition is not dead but it has been weakened gravely in the past few decades. Other ideas have challenged the domination of the humanistic tradition—ideas that are scientific in the broad sense, materialistic in some senses, and behavioristic as we refer to psychology and the philosophy of human nature.

## RESURGENCE OF REALISTIC PHILOSOPHY

In his account of the development of realism in American philosophy, William P. Montague describes the confrontation of the dominant idealism with a resurgent realism.[13]

In essence, the issue around which this battle developed was the speculative, system-building character of idealism as opposed to the emphasis on common sense and the belief in science that had been in many ways characteristic of realism even in antiquity. As might be expected the insurgents against philosophical idealism were younger men, and their interests lay more in the direction of logic, science, and scientific method than in the familiar idealistic direction of metaphysical speculation. They had many bones to pick with the idealists, but were mainly dissatisfied with the cavalier attitude idealism had taken toward science and the achievements of scientific method. As they saw it, a new realism was to lead the way to a return to common sense and to a realization of the importance of science in the modern world and in modern philosophy.

In 1910, six of the insurgents formed an alliance to which they gave the name "The New Realists." [14] The philosophic program they advocated is usually referred to as neorealism, or the new realism. Their philosophic position was most fully presented in a book published in 1912, to which they gave the title *The New Realism*.[15]

There was an important area of agreement among the new realists, but perhaps since they were philosophers, they did not always remain

---

13  William P. Montague, "The Story of American Realism," in Dagobert D. Runes, ed., *Living Schools of Philosophy* (Ames, Iowa: Littlefield, Adams & Co., 1958).

14  The original six of the New Realists were R. B. Perry, E. B. Holt, W. T. Marvin, E. G. Spaulding, W. B. Pitkin, and W. P. Montague.

15  Edwin B. Holt and associates, *The New Realism, Cooperative Studies in Philosophy* (New York: Macmillan Co., 1912).

within that area and many differences of opinion consequently developed among them. In the preparation of their position, they agreed on several matters that they called postulates. These postulates show evidence of the temper of the new realism and are worth noting here. One of these was the idea that, following the example of scientists, philosophers should work together rather than in splendid isolation (as idealists were often wont to do).[16] In the second place, philosophers should behave like scientists by dividing the problems and working on them one at a time rather than trying to wrap up everything in one grand synthesis (as idealists also had often tried to do). Thus, in the first two postulates, the new realists were proposing to model their philosophical inquiries along the same general lines scientists use in their investigations. This was quite in accord with the intellectual outlook of this group.

The remaining three postulates were really propositions in ontology and epistemology and formed the basis of the brand of realism advocated by this group. One of these postulates was to the effect that at least some of the particular things we encounter in experience exist apart from our consciousness. This clearly is a denial of the priority of consciousness and hence of idealism, for idealism holds that the existence of any object presupposes the existence of a subject (knower).

Another postulate stated that at least some of the essences (that is, universal ideas) that we encounter in our experiences also exist when we are not aware of them. This principle of the independent reality of universal ideas came from Plato and his theory of the independent existence of the forms.

The last of the postulates was that at least some of the particular things and some of the universal ideas are known directly by the mind and not through some intervening mental state or other construction of the mind. This proposition also is a denial of idealism, for idealistic philosophy maintains that the object of knowledge is idea and therefore what is known is in some sense a construct of consciousness.

## BASIC THESES OF REALISM

We are now in a position to state the two fundamental propositions of realistic philosophy. These propositions have the same importance in realism that the principle of the priority of consciousness has in modern idealism. The first of these propositions is usually called the principle of independence. This is primarily a proposition about ontology, but it has close relation with a theory of knowledge. *The principle of independence is that there exists a world of things and events and relations among these*

---

[16] According to Montague, the new realists did not live up to this very fully.

*things and events, and this world is not dependent for its existence and character on its being known.* This belief in an independently existing reality, whose character is not affected by its being known, squares both with common sense and with science—at least in the opinion of the realist.

Like idealism, realism is a very old tradition with its main roots in certain portions of the classic tradition. Typically, realists like to claim Aristotle as the great progenitor of their tradition, and they tend to interpret at least part of Plato's doctrine as being realistic (that is, the independent reality of forms). As we have already observed for idealism, when a philosophical tradition is old, and when it has attracted many great minds to its doctrines, then we can expect that there will be areas of disagreement, differences in emphasis, variant interpretations of the same questions, and different conclusions from the same evidence. These conditions are as descriptive of realism as they are of idealism. And yet for all these manifold differences, there is a common rallying point for realists— the principle of independence. It is difficult to see how anyone could profess philosophical realism without accepting the principle of a world that exists apart from consciousness and does not owe its essential character to its being known.

The second basic thesis of realism concerns our knowledge of this independent world and the processes by which we gain knowledge of it. This thesis may be stated somewhat as follows: *The world is capable of being known, at least in part, as it is in itself.* This epistemological principle was partly stated and partly implied in the last-mentioned postulate of the new realists. Here again the realist emphasizes that this doctrine is consonant with common sense. Our fundamental common-sense conviction is that what we know is something outside of our own conscious processes and that we know it directly.

It is one thing to insist that we can know the world as it is in itself, even when this statement includes the qualifications "at least in part," and quite another thing to demonstrate how it is accomplished. This question about the nature of the knowledge process is crucial in modern realism and it is a question over which much controversy has developed among the realists of the present century.[17] Realists have interpreted the knowledge process in various ways.

The new realists, who were the original group of insurgents, maintained that there is no fundamental dualism of mind *and* matter. They insisted that in any act of knowing, the objects of our knowledge are *presented directly in consciousness* and there is no intervening mental construct or mental state and none is needed to account for our knowledge

---

[17]   The classical Aristotelian and the Thomistic analysis of the problem is discussed in the context of the perennial philosophy. See Chapter Eight.

of the external world. We can know this world directly and as it is in its real character. This idea may be interpreted to mean that when any object is present to my consciousness, the qualities that are a part of this object are identical with the qualities that are in my consciousness. This kind of direct realism presupposes a conception of mind that is different in important respects from those we have encountered heretofore.

For example, a common view of mind is that it is in some sense within the organism. Our sense organs convey stimuli from objects to our minds, and these sense data then furnish the raw material for the cognitive processes of the mind. A theory of knowledge of this kind involves a basic dualism: There are some things called minds and some things that are matter, and these two kinds of things are absolutely different in character. Both common sense and much philosophy simply assume that the mind is within the knower and the object of his knowing is external to his mind.

The new realists, however, were opposed to a dualism of this kind. As they saw it, what this kind of interpretation leads to is a "copy" theory of cognition. Thus, under this view, when any object is present to my consciousness there is in my mind a more or less perfect copy or representation of it. This the new realists saw as a chief pitfall of idealism, for how are we ever to break out of the "pictures" that are in our minds and know that they really represent objects in the real world? The new realists thought that the worst that can come from this is subjectivism and about the best we can hope from it is scepticism.

To escape the dualistic pitfall the new realists developed another theory of mind. This theory for many people is not easy to grasp. The reason for this difficulty is not so much in the complexity of the idea but in the common-sense acceptance of the mind as being *in* the organism and the object of knowledge *in* the external environment. To grasp the essential notions of mind as the new realism developed them, we have to make a kind of reorientation of our common-sense beliefs about mind.

For one thing, according to the new realists, mind is not located in the body in the sense that it is *in* the cerebral cortex or the central nervous system or any other specific physiological system. To be sure, mind requires some structure—a nervous system, for example—in order to function, just as walking requires some structure (legs). But just as walking is not the same thing as legs, neither is mind the same thing as the central nervous system. This analogy may also illustrate the new realist's idea that consciousness is a *process* (in this sense walking is also a process). It is one of the processes that go on in nature and the essence of it is the establishment of a certain kind of *relation* between an organism and various objects in its environment. Sensory organs operating at any given time reveal a kind of cross section of reality, and the particular cross section that is revealed is the result of the selection made by the central nervous system of the perceiving organism. Now, as is frequently pointed out, this conception is the view that mind is not simply within the organism, it is also out in the environment with the objects of its awareness.[18] This conception of the unity of mind and object has led to the often quoted observation that idealism had reduced everything to mind but the new realism had reduced mind to everything!

What has been set down here is only the barest statement of a theory of knowledge developed within the new realism and accepted by some —but not all—of the original founders of the movement. However, even in this scanty treatment, there are implicit certain ideas that can be of great importance to our investigation of the relation between modern realism and the conservative theory of education. In the first place, the cross-sectional theory of consciousness eliminates the dualism between subject and object that has haunted philosophy virtually since its beginning. If the epistemological monism advocated by this theory can be made to stick, we are relieved of dealing with a number of problems that history has shown to be extremely resistant to solution. In the second place, under this theory it can be explained how it is that our awareness is of an independently existing reality and not merely of the self-made furniture of our own minds. In the third place—and this is the point of greatest immediate significance for our purpose—it is possible to interpret this presentative realism in behavioristic terms and relate it to certain important developments in scientific psychology that were going on simultaneously with the development of the new realism.

One member of the new realists besides Holt who advocated a behavioristic interpretation of consciousness was Ralph Barton Perry. The general position Holt and Perry took was that in any instance of awareness one's actual consciousness of an object *is a specific response that he makes to that object.*[19] This idea of knowing as responding, while familiar to all today who have the slightest acquaintance with modern psychology, throws on the theory of knowledge a light that is very different from the usual philosophical treatment of this problem.

We have portrayed the knowledge situation by a simple diagram:

$$\text{Subject (Knower)} \leftarrow \text{Cognitive Relationship} \rightarrow \text{Object (Known)}$$

The problem of knowledge is to describe the kind of relation that is established between subject and object in the cognitive relation. We now know from our previous analysis that according to idealism the relations

---

[18] Edwin B. Holt is credited with the original formulation of the "cross-sectional" theory of mind.

[19] For an exposition of Perry's argument, see the chapter "A Realistic Theory of Mind," in his *Present Philosophical Tendencies* (New York: Longmans, Green and Co., 1912).

between subject and object are *internal* and therefore unified. By this means, idealism ultimately is able to explain the unity of subject and object. But we also know that such an explanation cannot do for the realist. The principle of independence indicates that at least some relations are external.[20] This means that objects can enter into new kinds of relations without losing their original character. We know also, in terms of the idea of the new realists, that objects are *presented* in consciousness and there is no intervening mental state needed to account for awareness.

Now suppose we should take the same diagram and merely alter the names given to the two elements. We need only refer to the object as the stimulus and the subject as the response and we have $S \rightarrow R$, which will be recognized immediately as the basic pattern of all behavioristic psychology—granted that different variations can be developed on this original theme. This conception may be summed up by an excerpt from Perry's presentation.

> We . . . find that consciousness is a species of function, exercised by an organism. The organism is correlated with an environment, from which it evolved, and on which it acts. Consciousness is a selective response to a preexisting and independently existing environment. There must be something to be responded to if there is to be any response. The spatial and temporal distribution of bodies in its field of action, and the more abstract logical and mathematical relationships which this field contains, determine the possible objects of consciousness. The actual objects of consciousness are selected from this manifold of possibilities in obedience to the various exigencies of life.[21]

Not all the new realists found this form of behaviorism acceptable. Various rifts continued to occur, not only within the new realist group but also among other realists who had not allied themselves with the original new realists. The various controversies that developed and the varying interpretations and reinterpretations of the epistemological problems of realism are important in the history of philosophy in this century, but they are not of direct significance to our purpose.

Our main concern now is the development in this century of what may be called scientific realism, and an assessment of the influence this philosophic position has on educational theory. Our thesis is that the new realism of the earlier part of the century played an important part in subsequent development of a realistic philosophic doctrine that finds much of its substance in the physical sciences. Some evidence in support of this

---

20  Ibid., pp. 319 ff.
21  Ibid., pp. 322–23.

has already been presented, particularly in the behavioristic interpretation of cognition advanced by some of the new realists. Before we pass to the connection between scientific realism and psychological behaviorism, we should make certain additional observations about the scientific realism of the present century.[22]

In the first place, scientific realism tends to be naturalistic in its ontology. In this sense, naturalism means that the cosmos exists in and of itself and that no supernatural power or force of any kind is necessary to account for either the existence of the natural world or its operation. Reality, then, means the sum total of all things and events that exist in space and time and implies that whatever the regularities that occur, they are parts of the system and not imposed from without. The term *naturalism*, however, is not synonymous with *materialism*, although the two terms are sometimes used interchangeably in common speech. As a doctrine, materialism represents the effort to reduce everything to matter and to posit some ultimate irreducible substance as the basis for all reality. It is perhaps possible to say that all materialists are naturalists, but it is not necessarily true that all naturalists are materialists.

In the second place, scientific realism holds that the most dependable knowledge is scientific knowledge—that is, knowledge established by the techniques and processes of scientific method. The purpose of inquiry is to uncover the real character of the processes of nature, the laws that govern the relations of things and events. In this sense, facts exist prior to and independent of their being known. To know the truth means literally to *dis*cover it, that is, to reveal something that is already there.

## PSYCHOLOGICAL BEHAVIORISM

The first great achievements of science were largely in the area of the physical sciences. Sophisticated application of empirical observation and experimentation to the phenomena of human behavior did not occur in

---

[22] Another kind of development in realism has occurred in this century. This is the movement in which John Wild of Harvard University took the primary leadership. The most definite statement by the group participating in this movement is to be found in Wild, ed., *The Return to Reason* (Chicago: Henry Regnery Co., 1953). A full discussion of this form of realism will be postponed until the chapter on perennialism. Wild has had considerable to say that indicates his agreement with essentialism on various practical matters of education (see pp. 56–57). But Wild's interpretation of realistic philosophy, which presumably is related to his theories of education, represents a return to a more orthodox Aristotelian realism, which seems to the present author, at least, to be better discussed along with other theories that take their direction from classical sources. Substantially the same thing may be said for a more recent book, William O. Martin, *Realism in Education* (New York: Harper & Row, 1969).

any significant degree until the latter part of the nineteenth century. Many of the controversies in educational theory, and much of the internal stress in the conservative tradition itself, may be traced to the development of such behavioral sciences as psychology and sociology. The important developments in these fields have occurred mostly in the present century.

Historically, psychology has been regarded as one of the branches of philosophy. The methods employed by various philosophers who have concerned themselves with human nature and human conduct (this includes most of the important ones) involved mostly speculation and introspection, usually combined with common-sense observations that sometimes were acute. Since speculative thought necessarily starts with some *a priori* principles, much that went on under the name of psychology was really a product of deductive logical analysis. Another approach was the effort to arrive at certain general principles through introspection and logical induction. The familiar philosophic terms of *reason, mind, will, cognition,* and so forth, provided the basic categories of psychological investigation. The dominance of Absolute idealism in the nineteenth century determined in large measure the character of psychological investigation.[23]

Our concern here is not with the history of psychology and it will be sufficient to note that at the same time the new realists were busily clearing away the metaphysical and epistemological lumber left by idealism, some psychologists were engaged in a similar task in their domain. One of the most noted of these psychologists was Edward L. Thorndike.[24]

Thorndike's interests lay in experimental work and were conditioned by the changing climate in psychology. Traditionally, the subject matter of psychology was considered to be *mind,* its structure and functions, but under the influence of scientific methodology psychologists more and more were coming to think that the real subject matter of psychology must

---

[23] An interesting example of this may be found in Josiah Royce's *Outlines of Psychology* (New York: Macmillan Co., 1904). Royce was one of the greatest of American idealists. In the editor's introduction to Royce's book, Nicholas Murray Butler listed what he conceived to be noteworthy problems in psychology: "How and by what warrant do I pass from a knowledge of my own mental states to a knowledge and interpretation of the mental states of others? What are the primary evidences of mind? Into what and how few simplest units can my own complex mental states be broken up? What are the processes of mental growth and development, and what laws govern them?" (p. xxvi).

[24] Thorndike is chosen as the example here partly because of his eminence as a psychologist and partly because of his influence on educational theory and practice in America. It can perhaps be argued that there were other psychologists equal in stature to Thorndike during the early decades of the century. It is, however, difficult to argue that any of them had the impact on education that he has had.

be *behavior*.[25] So long as psychologists deal with "mind" they are practically driven to introspection as their basic method. Mind cannot be observed—some say it cannot even be defined. The "contents" of mind, by definition, are private and subjective. On the other hand, *behavior* is objective and observable. If it is both public and observable it may perhaps be capable of measurement, perhaps predictable, and ultimately even controllable. At least, it is capable of being studied objectively and experimentally. Ideas of this kind were stimulating psychologists in their experimental work with animal and human subjects. Thorndike's early work was with animal subjects and his invention of the "puzzle box" to study animal behavior is regarded as one of the important contributions to psychological technique.

At this point we may note certain agreements—or at least similarities —between leading ideas in the philosophy of the new realists and in the developing behavioristic psychology. A passage from one of Thorndike's books in which he summarized his position will serve as a point of departure:

> All human activity is *reactivity*. For every action there is a definite incentive or cause. Activity is not the result of a sort of spontaneous combustion; it is the response to stimulation. The total state of affairs by which a man is at any time influenced is called the *stimulus* or *situation* and whatever action results—attention, perception, thought, feeling, emotion, glandular secretion, or muscular movement—is called the *reaction* or the *response*.[26]

If we compare Thorndike's statement with that of Ralph Barton Perry, making some allowance for the differences of vocabulary among philosophers and psychologists, we find similarities on the following points:

1. Behavior is a process of reacting to stimuli. (Those functions called consciousness, awareness, and so on are behaviors.)
2. The presence of a stimulus presupposes the existence of some objective environmental state of affairs.
3. Behavior is always caused; it is never spontaneous (that is, "uncaused").

---

[25] For an excellent discussion of the development and status of behaviorism, see B. F. Skinner, "Behaviorism at Fifty," *Science* 140 (May 31, 1963): 951–58. In this article Skinner identifies behaviorism as a *philosophy of science* concerned with psychological method and subject matter.

[26] Edward L. Thorndike and A. I. Gates, *Elementary Principles of Education* (New York: Macmillan Co., 1930), p. 62. Italics are in the original.

4.   The character of the response is a function of the nature of the stimulus field (the "situation").

Now in consideration of these ideas, we see that what the psychologist calls *learning* and what the philosopher calls *knowing* are held to be *responses* of the organism to an objective environmental condition. One of the concerns of the new realism was to emphasize the independence of this external reality from any of the processes of consciousness, while to the psychologists this principle was more or less axiomatic. Whether we adopt the psychological or the philosophical term, the process of learning or the process of knowing is a process of reacting to stimulation. Every mental act from the most primitive and elementary to the most complex and sophisticated can be explained in terms of the basic $S \rightarrow R$ pattern. Learning (knowing) is the formation of bonds or connections between specific stimuli and specific responses. This theory is summed up by Thorndike in the following passage:

> I read the facts which psychologists report about adjustment, configurations, drives, integrations, purposes, tensions, and the like, and all of these facts seem to me to be reducible, so far as concerns their powers to influence the course of thought or feeling or action, to connections and readiness. Learning is connecting. The mind is man's connection system. Purposes are as mechanical in their nature and action as anything else is.[27]

Other examples of the similarity between behaviorism in psychology and in the new realism could be cited; however, we have perhaps seen enough for our present purpose. We are not attempting to show that the resurgence of realistic philosophy was the *cause* of the development of psychological behaviorism, nor that such developments in psychology were the *cause* of the revival of interest in philosophical realism. The most defensible thesis would seem to be that both these developments in intellectual life were the result of the increasing and diversified influence of science on cultural life. In view of the progress science had made in the physical realm and the far-reaching changes in outlook it had engendered, it was all but inevitable that sooner or later its influence would be felt with full force in the fields that deal with human behavior. Though formidable roadblocks were thrown up periodically by idealistic philosophers and by theology, in retrospect it seems clear that none of these barriers could have been sufficient to keep scientific method out of a consideration of the nature of man.

We have seen some evidence of a close resemblance between psychological behaviorism and that interpretation of neorealism advocated by Holt

---

27   Edward L. Thorndike, *Human Learning* (New York: Century Co., 1931), p. 122.

and Perry. Not all the new realists agreed, however, with the behavioristic interpretation of consciousness, and some of the early twentieth-century realists did not agree with the epistemological monism that the new realists advocated. However, it can be argued that the whole intellectual climate of a resurgent realism really worked in favor of the development of scientific philosophy. All approaches to psychology that use scientific method are in some measure behavioristic—at least in their methodology. This is not to say that there are no real differences among the various "schools" of present-day psychology for assuredly there are. All these schools, however, find agreement that the subject matter of psychological investigation is *behavior* and that the methods used in studying behavior should be empirical. It is submitted that such an approach to human behavior will not flourish in a cultural setting that is dominated by idealistic conceptions of mind and self. We have historical evidence that when the cultural focus is on the transcendent and supernatural, psychology—if it can be said to exist at all under such conditions—will find its area of interest in those aspects of human nature that are alleged to be transcendent and supernatural. Certainly this was the case with idealism in the nineteenth century.

One of the fundamental presuppositions of science is the principle of uniformity; that is, whenever the same antecedent conditions are given, the same results will occur. In the present time it is widely acknowledged that such a presupposition is fundamental in the natural sciences. If human psychology is to be a natural science, it must operate within the general canons of scientific method. It must be naturalistic in orientation; it must be empirical in methodology; and it must subscribe to the principle of uniformity.

It is submitted that the resurgence of realism in philosophy was generally beneficent to these developments. The principle of independence does not necessarily imply naturalism, although it certainly can be consistent with a naturalistic outlook. A presentative theory of knowledge does not necessarily imply behaviorism, though this theory can be (and was) interpreted in behavioristic terms by some realists. In addition, there is another strain in realistic philosophy that can be traced far back into its history and that is important to our analysis. This is the emphasis that realism places on regularity and lawfulness.

## EMPHASIS ON REGULARITY AND LAWFULNESS

Men have always been impressed by the regularity that nature exhibits in its working. The earth always moves in the same direction on its axis; the sun always rises in the east and disappears in the west; water always flows downhill; unsupported objects always fall toward the center of the earth; and so on and on for all the observed regularities that even ordinary experience reveals. This awareness of the lawfulness of nature is common to all men, whatever philosophy they may profess, or for that matter, whether they profess any at all.

At least two kinds of intellectual challenge are inherent in the observed regularities of nature. One of these challenges is scientific—the challenge to observe, and classify, and express these regularities in unequivocal (preferably mathematical) terms. When this has been done we can speak of them as the *laws of nature*. These laws are very powerful intellectual tools because they enable us to predict events before these events actually occur. If we can predict, we may well be in a position to exert control over events—at least in some measure. And so, we can list the primary concerns of science as observing, analyzing, classifying, quantifying, predicting, experimenting.

The intellectual enterprise we call science depends on the principle of uniformity. Unless this principle holds, it seems idle to speak of the possibility of accurate prediction of future events—which must always be done on the basis of what has been learned from past experience. We may take passing note that the uniformities of nature have always tended to impress those with a predilection for philosophical realism. This was true even with the classic realism of Aristotle in a time when scientific method, as we understand that term, was unknown. Aristotle himself was a great observer and classifier of natural phenomena and his studies in natural science ranged from astronomy to zoology. The working scientist today is apt to take the principle of uniformity as an axiom and to spend very little time speculating on its ultimate significance in cosmology.

The second challenge inherent in our awareness of the regularities of nature is philosophical. Men are inclined to speculate on what the meaning of natural regularity is for our total grasp of the cosmos. They consider such questions as, Is nature in and of itself characterized by uniformity, regularity, and dependability? Do the orderliness and regularity that characterize events in physical nature also extend to other kinds of phenomena, as for example, individual human behavior and the behavior of men living in social groups? Are there universal laws that govern human behavior in the same sense that the laws of physics govern physical bodies or economic laws govern the market? Behaviorists in psychology are inclined to answer such questions in the affirmative, although they may differ with each other over many details. Under this view, the purpose of psychological science is to discover the laws that govern human behavior and to state them in the same general terms as physicists state physical laws. Although psychology is a young science, compared with physics, for example, it will become a mature science as it uncovers and quantifies the laws of human behavior. When this has been achieved to a reasonable degree, we can expect to develop a technology for behavior control and utilization comparable to the technology we have already achieved for using physical forces for cultural ends. This will be educational technology in the broadest sense.

As we have already indicated, there are people today who find sufficient evidence to believe that we are now in a position to construct an educational technology based on the achievements of scientific psychology. Many people maintain that achievements already accomplished— the systems approach, for example—are significant. This is often held to presage a great revolutionary movement in educational practice. It is also often pointed out that similar advances in the understanding of emotional behavior are being made and that the control of these processes by chemical and other means is a certainty. For the first time in human history, it is said, men see the possibility (as distinguished from the desirability) of a society in which wrongdoing need not exist and in which truth and justice can prevail. Men have always dreamed of such a utopia, but only in recent years has the possibility of achieving it seemed reasonable. Thorndike himself foresaw the possibility in the first decade of the century:

> A complete science of psychology would tell every fact about everyone's intellect and character and behavior, would tell the cause of every change in human nature, would tell the result which every educational force . . . would have. It would aid us to use human beings for the world's welfare with the same surety of result that we now have when we use falling bodies or chemical elements. In proportion as we get such a science we shall become masters of our own souls as we are now masters of heat and light. Progress towards such a science is being made.[28]

A few years later another famous behaviorist proclaimed:

> Give me a dozen healthy infants, well-formed, and my own specified world to bring them up in and I'll guarantee to take anyone at random and train him to become any type of specialist I might select—doctor, lawyer, artist, merchant-chief, and yes, even begger-man and thief, regardless of his talents, penchants, tendencies, abilities, vocations, and race of his ancestors. I am going beyond my facts and I admit it, but so have the advocates of the contrary and they have been doing it for many thousands of years. Please note that when this experiment is made I am to be allowed to specify the way the children are to be brought up and the type of world they have to live in.[29]

With the continued development of psychological science, the conviction has become stronger that the good society, brought about by

---

[28]   Edward L. Thorndike, "The Contribution of Psychology to Education," *Journal of Educational Psychology* 1 (January 1910): 6.

[29]   John B. Watson, *Behaviorism* (New York: W. W. Norton and Co., 1924), p. 82. In his article "Behaviorism at Fifty," B. F. Skinner credits Watson with the first statement that psychology should be viewed as a science of behavior. Skinner acknowledges the importance of Thorndike's contributions but insists that he remained a "mentalist."

psychological science and technology, can be a reality any time we are willing to give the behavioral scientist the degree of control he needs. The most famous contemporary exponent of this idea is B. F. Skinner, whose novel *Walden Two* describes a utopia that has been achieved by scientific management of children's behavior from a very early age.[30] This book has excited the most diverse reactions in its readers, ranging from complete acceptance to what can only be described as utter revulsion.

In a subsequent book, Skinner consolidated and elaborated further the concepts developed in his previous work.[31] Once again he dismissed what he regards as the prescientific notion of the autonomy of the individual, which in turn is based on the ancient belief that man is unique in his possession of an internal entity of some kind (soul, spirit, mind, or whatever it may be called) that enables him to direct his behavior and determine his own destiny. The idea of "freedom of the will," he argues, is a leftover from an age of superstition about human nature, and (as he had written some years before) we are not likely to make real progress in the application of scientific method to the understanding of human behavior until we divest ourselves of it completely.[32]

Skinner's psychology, usually known as operant conditioning, is different in important respects from the earlier behaviorism of Watson and Thorndike, but it is a lineal descendant of the earlier behavioristic movement. It is important to our purpose to note one thing about Skinner's psychological system. Skinner has long since gone beyond psychology, and in this respect he is reminiscent of Thorndike. His technical experimental work is generally regarded as extremely influential in twentieth-century psychology even by those who do not agree with him. But he has turned from psychology to philosophy, particularly the philosophy of human nature, and in *Beyond Freedom and Dignity*, to what may be called in the broad sense social and moral philosophy. Moreover, for many years he has been identified with education and the reform of educational method. As is well known, he developed one of the earliest teaching machines, was a pioneer in educational programming, and employed various new techniques in his own teaching at Harvard. His recommendations concerning the reform of educational method are organically related to his basic philosophy of human nature.[33] His philosophy of human nature is central

---

[30]  B. F. Skinner, *Walden Two* (New York: Macmillan Co., 1948). This book was the main target of Joseph Wood Krutch's *The Measure of Man*, see p. 92.

[31]  *Beyond Freedom and Dignity* (New York: Alfred A. Knopf, 1971).

[32]  *Science and Human Behavior* (New York: Macmillan Co., 1953), p. 449.

[33]  Various important contributions of Skinner to the theory of educational method have been brought together in *The Technology of Teaching* (New York: Appleton-Century-Crofts, 1968).

to his ideas about change in social organization, education, and ethics. Skinner is today's leading spokesman for a concept of human nature that has developed out of the scientific realism and the psychological behaviorism of this century.

## HUMAN NATURE

There is nothing new about the idea that the original nature of man needs to be altered and shaped in desirable directions by external forces. Certainly most systems of formal education, if not all, and most child-rearing practices are designed on the assumption that the behavior of human beings can be managed by exerting certain causal forces on the behavior of children.[34] Although many people insist that there is more to education than training, there are not many who would argue that education does not involve training in some form. To train a child means to alter his "natural" behavior by causing him to react in certain ways to given stimuli and by fixing these responses through appropriate reinforcement.

Against this doctrine is another, also well known in the history of education, that holds that education is fundamentally the unfolding of a design inherent in the organism. The most famous advocate of this position was Rousseau, who held that education should be "negative" in the sense that the growing child should be shielded from unfavorable environmental influences and left to develop "according to nature." Another famous advocate of these sentiments was Froebel, who conceived the development of the child to be analogous to the growth of a plant, which needs no "training" but only a favorable environment in which to unfold its nature. Hence, Froebel called his institution "Kindergarten." Both Rousseau and Froebel maintained that human nature is inherently good, at least in the beginning, and the evil that enters into man's nature is the result of evil environmental influences of various kinds.

We have already seen enough to know that this conception of human nature is not acceptable in the general tradition of social conservatism, that it is rejected by modern educational essentialism, and that it is out of harmony with behavioristic psychology and scientific realism. There are some differences, however, over the basic reasons for the common objections.

Social conservatives in the original tradition of Burke are more apt to object on theological and metaphysical grounds than on scientific grounds, believing as they do that a total conception of human nature is

---

[34] A comprehensive work on the problem of determinism is Sidney Hook, ed., *Determinism and Freedom in the Age of Modern Science* (New York: Collier Books, 1961). See also Sidney Hook, "Moral Freedom in a Determined World," in his *The Quest for Being* (New York: Dell Publishing Co., 1963), pp. 26 ff.

revealed by theology and philosophy. The literature of modern essentialism contains both philosophical-theological and scientific arguments. Those essentialists who are affected by scientific realism advance scientific arguments against the doctrines of the original goodness of human nature, human development as unfolding of an inherent pattern, and the behavioral autonomy of the individual.

Behaviorists in psychology generally agree that the "original nature of man" is insufficient and must be developed along desirable lines that ultimately are determined by society. Ideas about the character of this original nature have changed over the years. Thorndike, for example, held the view that original nature is a complex of inherited tendencies, instincts, and capacities that can be investigated and described objectively. Much of his early work was devoted to this effort and he eventually concluded that the purpose of education is modification of this original human nature—to make it better. He wished to be very clear that the original nature of man could not be conceived as right:

> The original tendencies of man have not been right, are not right, and probably never will be right. By them alone few of the best wants in human life would have been felt and fewer still satisfied. . . . Man is thus eternally altering himself to suit himself. His nature is not right in his own eyes. Only one thing in it, indeed, is unreservedly good, the power to make it better. This power, the power of learning or modification in favor of the satisfying, the capacity represented by the law of effect, is the essential principle of reason and right in the world.[35]

Since Thorndike's time, behaviorists have modified their ideas in various ways but they agree, by and large, on the central issue: the alteration of this original nature—however it may be conceived—through environmental means. Obviously, this is in the broadest sense a social and educational problem of utmost importance.

One primary difference between the early behaviorism and the later behaviorism is that the latter conceives human nature to be more plastic, less determined by inherited instinctive patterns, and largely determined by environmental forces. In *Beyond Freedom and Dignity*, Skinner appears to carry this line of thought to its ultimate conclusion. In this position, he is strongly reminiscent of J. B. Watson as cited earlier in this chapter.[36]

---

[35]  Edward L. Thorndike, *Educational Psychology: Briefer Course* (New York: Teachers College, Columbia University, 1927), pp. 3, 124. Thorndike's views here are reminiscent of an observation by Thomas Hobbes, seventeenth-century materialist philosopher, that in the "natural condition" the life of man is "solitary, poor, nasty, brutish, and short."

[36]  See also Watson, *Behaviorism*, chaps. 5 and 6.

In *Walden Two* (pp. 126–27), Skinner points out that even though the children have all had the same environment since birth, the range of intelligence quotients within the ten-year age group is about the same as in the general population. Thus, environment can work only with the physical structure that nature provides, and the protagonist in the novel is quick to add that "all differences are physical."

Regardless of differences on the nature-nurture question, behavioristic psychologists agree that the original nature of any individual (or of man in general) is not "right" for social life or for the preservation of the species, much less for achievement of the cultural refinements that constitute civilization. This original nature must be modified, and in all cultures this always has been done in some way. Before behavioral science, these ways were generally crude and ineffective, based usually on rule of thumb, folk wisdom, and superstition.

In the *Republic*, Plato proposes that a just society is one in which each person does what he is fitted to do and does not interfere with the work of others. He developed an elaborate plan for modifying the original nature of the citizens of the Republic so that this condition might be achieved. His insight was good enough to indicate that the way to achieve this is through careful environmental control, but there is much about the details of his scheme that today appears crude and unimaginative. There is good reason to think that the Republic would never have worked, even if Plato's scheme had ever been put to action.

It was not until the advent of behavioral science that men claimed to know how to modify the original nature of man with precision and efficiency. We might now be able to create the Republic if scientists could be given the control they would require and provided that we actually wanted something like that utopia. Conservatives have often held the Republic up as a model for what a good society would be. They have admired the Spartan austerity on which it was fashioned; they have agreed with the rigid class structure inherent in it; and they have thought it a supreme example of a state governed by the wisest and best men. Now that something like this is within grasp—or so we are told—many conservatives draw back in consternation.

Apparently, it is one thing to accept application of behavioral science in the form of programmed material for an instructional system (which some essentialists do, but not all) and something else to subscribe to plans for a really comprehensive control and development of human nature through scientific means. Thus, one of the points of real stress for present-day essentialism lies in the competing conceptions of the nature of man. This tradition, that developed originally out of prescientific conceptions of human nature, now finds itself attempting to combine the humanism of the older conservatism with the behaviorism of the scientific realists. In this respect, at least, essentialism is a house divided.

## TRUTH AS CORRESPONDENCE

One of the requirements for a consistent and coherent essentialism is a conception of truth that assures us that our ideas can be judged true or false against some dependable criterion. Such a criterion will enable us to transmit only true ideas in the schools, or at least will assure a minimum of error. Knowledge of such a criterion will also enable us to transmit to students a method for discriminating between truth and error themselves, thus helping to make their own intellectual processes more rigorous.

We have already seen that idealism offers the principle of coherence as such a criterion. Our ideas are true to the extent that they are consistent with the body of truth already existing and accepted. The idealist thinks that coherence is the most rigorous method of proof possible, particularly since it is the method of mathematics, the most rigorous of all systems of knowledge.

The realist, while agreeing that coherence has a part to play in scientific and even in common-sense knowledge, does not think it can be the final criterion for truth. If all knowledge were like pure mathematics, in which all relations are internal (within the system) then coherence would be the ultimate and only criterion for truth. But we now know that realists do not agree that all knowledge is like pure mathematics. The principle of independence implies directly that some relations are external. Both common sense and science deal with matters in which external relations predominate. Therefore, coherence is inadequate to help us distinguish between the truth and the falsity of ideas outside of purely logical systems.

Accordingly, realism advocates a criterion for truth that respects the external character of relations and gives our judgments objectivity and precision that, according to realists, is not possible with any other method. The criterion offered by realistic philosophies is *correspondence*. This means that any idea (proposition) we may hold is true to the extent *that it corresponds with the reality to which it refers*. Thus, an idea *A*, which I hold to be true and which is about some fact *B*, is true if the idea *A* corresponds to the fact *B*. The realist insists that this is what our common sense tells us anyway.

For example, some scientists may accept the hypothesis that living organisms exist on Mars and this hypothesis may be consistent with certain data that are believed reliable. Thus, coherence lends credibility to the hypothesis, but it does not establish it as true or false. The only way the hypothesis can be validated is to determine whether it squares with the reality on Mars. If it is *a fact* that organic life exists on Mars, then the hypothesis is true; if it is not a fact, then the hypothesis lacks correspondence with the reality to which it refers and is therefore false. Knowing, then, is the uncovering of the realities (facts) that exist independently of their being known, and truth is a property that ideas have when they correspond to the realities to which they refer.

In thinking about this, we must understand the following: (1) *Facts* are not true or false. They are what they are, and what they are has nothing to do with whether anybody knows what they are. (2) Truth can only be a property of judgments (propositions, ideas). (3) The correspondence is established between the judgment and the fact. The realist is generally willing to let the argument rest at this point. As he sees it, correspondence is a rigorous, objective criterion that squares with common sense and scientific experience. It is applicable in any intellectual enterprise in which the rigorous testing of propositions is involved. It enables us to know what is true and what is false, and to act accordingly.

Thus, in this way the essentialist, whose outlook is conditioned by these views of knowledge and truth we have just considered, is able to meet the criterion of certainty and dependability of knowledge, a condition of strategic importance to educational conservatism.

## SCIENTIFIC REALISM AND THE VALUE PROBLEM

We come now to value, which is one of the most important considerations so far as essentialism is concerned. We have already considered the way in which the value problem is approached by objective idealists and how this approach is related to the humanistic wing of essentialists. We may recognize in the beginning that the kind of analysis characteristic of idealism must be unacceptable to the kind of scientific realism we have been considering. There are various realistic approaches to value theory. From what we have already seen of the basic postulates of realism, we can foresee that any realistic approach to the theory of value must incorporate the following principles: (1) The existence of a world independent of any consciousness; this is the principle of independence. (2) The assumption that the world can be known in its essential nature. The acceptance of these principles supports the realistic view that there is some objective reference for value norms and that values are not subjective and purely relative.

One of the oldest, and certainly one of the most important realist conceptions of the source of value is the view that goes somewhat as follows: Just as the processes of nature are governed by universal laws, so is there also a lawfulness inherent in human nature. The law that governs the development of man demands that certain conditions be supplied so that the common human nature in which we all share may be realized. Now the conditions that are necessary for the completion of human nature are the same for all men, and in the words of a distinguished advocate of this view:

> The invariable, universal pattern of action, individual as well as social, required for the completion of human nature is called *the moral law* or *natural law*. By self-observation every individual has some minimal knowledge of it. By disciplined study of human nature and the events

of history, this knowledge may be increased and clarified. Such knowledge is the only trustworthy guide for human action.[37]

Under this view, ethics, which is the philosophy of value applied to human conduct, is built on objective foundations. What is right for man and what man needs in order to realize his nature is not a matter of vague speculation or opinion. By the use of our powers of observation and reason, we can know what human nature is and what is needed to complete it. We can *know* that there is a natural (moral) law in the same sense that there are laws of physics. And just as physics is the only reliable knowledge for guiding human action in its dealings with physical nature, so knowledge of the moral law is the only dependable guide for action in dealing with human nature.

It is important to note that such a view as this can be held only by those who accept the basic realistic theses stated above. In this respect Wild's ethical theory is as consistent with his realism as anything can be. The natural law is a *moral imperative*. It tells us what must be. But it is an imperative that is grounded in objective existence, and although idealists (Kant is the leading example) may also speak of a moral imperative, they are unable to demonstrate that such an imperative is grounded on objective knowledge of the nature of things, or so the realist thinks.

However, Wild's realism—and hence his ethical theory—represents, as we observed earlier, a return to the orthodox realism of Aristotle and the classic tradition. Ultimately, it rests on a view of nature that is essentially teleological in character. This means that all existences move toward some final fulfillment that is inherent in their natures, and it is in this way that the regularities of the laws of nature operate. The teleological aspect of Wild's realism puts it out of harmony with much of modern science and with those varieties of realism that are closely related to modern science. Scientists attempt resolutely to eliminate teleological concepts from their inquiries and particularly to eliminate any trace of the notion that the processes of nature are explained by some predetermined final end.[38]

---

[37] John Wild, "Education and Human Society: A Realistic View," in Brubacher, *Modern Philosophies of Education*, p. 18. Wild's views are elaborated more fully in his *Introduction to Realistic Philosophy* (New York: Harper & Brothers, 1948).

[38] Wild has specifically denied that the theory of natural law depends on a teleological conception of nature. See his *Plato's Modern Enemies and the Theory of Natural Law* (Chicago: University of Chicago Press, 1953), chap. 3, and specifically pp. 72 ff. We leave it to the reader to make his own judgment on the merits of opposing views. A common meaning of the term *teleological* is that events in nature are explained in terms of their results, not of their antecedent causes. The difference between mechanism and teleology is that the former explains events in terms of "efficient causes" and the latter explains them in terms of "final causes."

We shall return to this classical conception of nature and ethics in the chapter on the

One approach realists take to the theory of ethics is built around the idea that *value is a function of desire or interest*. This means simply that if I desire a thing, that is, have need of it, that thing thereby acquires value. What invests it with value is my desire for it. This principle is often stated concisely as follows: "Value is any object of interest." One of the chief American proponents of this theory is the realist Ralph Barton Perry. The analysis presented here is derived primarily from his work.

In the first place, Perry reminds us, two basic doctrines of realistic philosophy must be taken into account in thinking about value theory. These realistic principles are: (1) Consciousness is a relation into which objects can enter without losing their independence or their essential character. This indicates that something can be desired by me without having its original nature altered, but the new relationship it acquires by being an object of my conscious interest or desire invests it with value. Hence, says Perry, it is correct to suppose that the nature of a thing is independent of its possessing value, but it is not correct to suppose that the value any given thing possesses is independent of consciousness.[39] (2) Realism maintains that a proposition is independent of its being judged. If I desire some particular thing, the proposition "I desire *A*" is, according to Perry, independent of any judgment I or anybody else may make about it. The upshot of the matter is that whenever values exist it is because they stand in relation to some interest.[40]

These considerations of realistic philosophy point to the character of *moral* value. Problems of moral value occur because the relations of interest are complex and often conflicting. In analyzing moral values two ideas must be introduced. These are (1) rightness, and (2) comparative goodness.[41]

When it is necessary to act to fulfill an interest, the action that is *right* in these circumstances is that action that is *appropriate*—that is, the action that secures the desired results. Rightness in this sense refers to intelligent apprehension of the relation of ends and means, but a right action in this sense is not necessarily a moral action. The moral question arises when there is a conflict of interest.

According to Perry, an act may be right when it helps to fulfill one interest, but it may also be wrong if it detracts from the realization of another interest, and so we have the theory of comparative goodness, which is outlined in Perry's own words as follows:

---

perennial philosophy, a body of thought in which it plays a leading part. In the meantime we shall consider some other approaches of realists to the theory of ethics.

39 Perry, *Present Philosophical Tendencies*, p. 332.

40 Ibid., p. 333.

41 Ibid., pp. 333–34.

Now just as an act may be both right and wrong in that it conduces to the fulfillment of one interest and the detriment of another; so it may be doubly right in that it conduces to the fulfillment of two interests. . . . If the fulfillment of one interest is good, the fulfillment of two is better; and the fulfillment of all interests is best. Similarly, if the act which conduces to goodness is right, the act that conduces to more goodness is more right, and the act which conduces to most goodness is most right. Morality, then, is *such performance as under the circumstances, and in view of all the interests affected, conduces to most goodness.*[42]

Beyond this, Perry points out that it is possible that various acts may all contribute to the same maximum goodness, and when this is the case, they are all morally right. In addition, and Perry calls this the most important single conclusion, *all values are absolute.* By this is meant that all values are completely independent of any opinion. If I desire something, my desiring it is *a fact* that cannot be changed by any amount of opinion about the matter. In that sense it is objective and absolute.

Thus there is a difference between Perry's radical assertion that a value is any object of interest and the comparatively conservative conception of valuation as the determination of comparative goodness. Perry's value theory is a slashing attack on traditional conceptions of value—particularly those of idealism. And while the relativism inherent in Perry's position has often been excoriated by moral idealists, Perry is able in the end to assure us that values are absolute in character because they are what they are in themselves and independent of any judgment about them. Thus, Perry's position can satisfy the social conservative who insists that values are objective and absolute but who at the same time is unable to accept either the metaphysical account furnished by Absolute idealism or the teleological character of the classic tradition.

To conclude this discussion of value theory from the standpoint of scientific realism, we give some attention to the treatment B. F. Skinner has accorded it. It may come as a surprise to some people to find Skinner mentioned in a discussion of value theory when his reputation rests on his work as an experimental, behavioristic psychologist and not as a philosopher. The reason is that Skinner has moved beyond psychology into matters that are still regarded as being in the purview of philosophy. Ethical theory is one of these areas.

Although his treatment of ethics is most specific in *Beyond Freedom and Dignity*, the development his argument would take, indeed the development it would necessarily take, was foreshadowed in certain of his earlier important works, particularly *Walden Two* and *Science and Human Behavior*. The problem is to interpret from Skinner's philosophy of human

---

[42] Ibid., p. 334.

nature that men place value on some things and events and disvalue on others. In other words, Skinner knows as well as anyone else that man is a "valuing animal." The problem is how to interpret this in the context of the determinism and behaviorism that underlie Skinner's philosophy.

His view of the nature of man eliminates any notion that man is autonomous or that his behavior is "self-directed," or can be. Now most Western value theory in some way involves, either implicitly or explicitly, the notion that man can to some extent, through some inner force or power, direct his behavior. The boundaries of the area of choice may vary from one philosopher to another but there seems little doubt that the common view is that man is free in some measure to choose between good and evil or among competing goods.

Obviously, this view is inconsistent with Skinner's views of human behavior and cannot be admitted in his theory of value. In his development of the application of the science of behavior to human social affairs, as in *Beyond Freedom and Dignity*, Skinner has been forced to deal with the value question, partly because of its importance in the logical development of his own position and partly because some of the most acid criticism of his work has centered around this question.

His treatment of value is ingenious and appears consistent with the rest of his system. Identifying a few of the basic propositions involved in it will indicate the general direction of his argument. Those who are interested in the value question in a highly deterministic system will do well to study Skinner's development further in careful detail.

The first proposition has to do with a question that is central to all value theory, that is, What do we mean by *good*, and what do we mean by *bad*, or *evil*? For Skinner, the answer to this question follows directly from his basic premises and therefore may be answered simply: "Good things" are those that reinforce us positively; those whose reinforcement is negative are "bad things." Since as natural organisms we seek positive reinforcement and try to avoid negative, we seek the good and avoid the evil.[43]

A certain similarity exists between this conception of good and the one advanced earlier in the century by Ralph Barton Perry, which we have already considered.[44] When Perry says that "a value is any object of interest," he is not saying the same thing that Skinner says, namely that good things are positive reinforcers. However, it can be argued that there is a certain important similarity and that this similarity derives from the basic behavioristic positions of these two. Skinner's operant conditioning is a more thoroughgoing behaviorism than Perry's and it is likely that

---

[43]   *Beyond Freedom and Dignity*, pp. 103–4.
[44]   See p. 131.

Skinner would characterize Perry in the same way he did Thorndike—a mentalist. Nevertheless, it is perhaps not too long a leap to consider that an "object of interest" is a "positive reinforcer." It is an object of interest *because* it offers positive reinforcement.

A second important question in value theory is that concerned with justification. If we grant, at least for the sake of the argument, that goods are positive reinforcers, then the question is, How do we know that those things that reinforce us positively are really good—that is, that they are desirable and worthy of being prized and sought after? A correlative question concerns the grounds on which judgment is made.

Skinner's answer to this question is drawn from scientific, not philosophical sources. He has observed that behavioral science is itself in part a *science of values*. Things are good or bad, he says, because of the part they have played in helping the species evolve and survive in the face of the numerous contingencies encountered. Briefly, Skinner's point is that "it is part of the genetic endowment called 'human nature' to be reinforced in particular ways by particular things." [45]

Since people have lived and developed their societies under different kinds of conditions, which is to say that people have had to cope with different kinds of contingencies, it is only to be expected that there would be differences in the moral and ethical codes of different societies. What one "ought" to do in one society may be different from what one "ought" to in another. Thus, in Skinner's words, "value is to be found in the social contingencies maintained for purposes of control. It is an ethical or moral judgment in the sense that *ethos* and *mores* refer to the customary practices of a group." [46] A culture will survive or perish according to the degree of control it has over the behavior of people, or rather the generations of people, who make it up, and according to Skinner, survival is the ultimate value by which a culture must be judged.[47]

It can be seen in the light of these considerations that Skinner's approach to value theory is in part relativistic, that is, what is regarded as right and wrong in a given society is relative to the experience of that society. But his approach is also objective in the sense that it is concerned with the contingencies that control behavior and these are objective, observable, and controllable. This is one aspect of Skinner's work in which his realism shows through most clearly. He cautions us to understand the distinction between facts and how people feel about them. Through reinforcement we learn our feelings towards things, and anyway there is no important causal connection between the reinforcement of a stimulus

---

[45] *Beyond Freedom and Dignity*, p. 104.
[46] Ibid., pp. 112–13.
[47] Ibid., p. 136.

and the feelings it engenders. "It is the glass that feels smooth," he says, "not a 'feeling of smoothness.' It is the reinforcer that feels good, not the good feeling." In the long run it is things that are good or bad, not feelings.[48]

It may well be that this short discussion has served to raise more questions than it has answered. If so, then its objective has been achieved. Skinner's excursion into value theory is an important contribution to a trend that has been developing throughout this century. He has worked his ideas out carefully in the context of his psychological theory and they deserve careful attention. It is hoped that those who seek a clear understanding of social and educational conservatism will be mindful of Skinner's contributions and that they will be the subject for serious study.[49]

## SUMMARY

This chapter has been concerned with the relation of certain philosophical concepts to social conservatism and to conservative educational philosophy. In this century a schism has developed in American essentialism, and the division is becoming wider and deeper, producing increasing stress and strain in this tradition. Conservative modes of education, both in the sense of theory and of practice, in this country are in a position of very strong dominance. The question is whether essentialism can continue its hegemony indefinitely in the face of the basic philosophic differences within its structure. Experimental science has been identified as the main influence responsible for the ideological rift, which in various ways has set the older humanistic tradition in education in opposition to the behaviorism and determinism inherent in scientific approaches to educational policy and practice. Primary differences in philosophical outlook have been engendered by science. These differences involve basic intellectual orientations, that is, the humanistic as opposed to the scientific outlook, interpretations of human nature, and theories of value, particularly in moral philosophy.

The relation of certain philosophical traditions to these two competing views has been identified. Various ideas that stem primarily from certain forms of idealistic philosophy support the humanistic orientation, whereas

---

48 Ibid., p. 107.

49 The reviews and articles on Skinner's *Beyond Freedom and Dignity* seem to be almost without number. Two perceptive reviews representing different points of view and contained in one convenient source are to be found in "Skinner Pro and Con," *Contemporary Sociology* 1 (January 1972): 19–29. One article is by Gerald Marwell, the other by Robert Boguslaw.

the scientific realism of this century is congenial to those approaches to theory and practice that are based on behavioristic psychology.

Little doubt exists that the ties that bind today's essentialism are not primarily philosophic. This tradition no longer enjoys the secure ideological unity that was such an important element in its rise to power and its continued dominance of education. It is submitted that what still unites American educational conservatism is a set of beliefs that include:

1. The existence of objective truth that can be known, together with a dependable criterion for distinguishing truth from error.
2. A common core of essential knowledge that must be transmitted.
3. A common core of values that are crucial to cultural survival and must therefore be perpetuated in succeeding generations.
4. The school as a conserving, civilizing force in society, designed to prepare the young for adulthood, vocation, and responsible citizenship.
5. The necessity for an elite, based on talent and achievement, that will provide wise leadership, guidance, and control of the masses, together with the educational arrangements necessary to achieve this objective.

These are powerful ideas and there is every reason to believe that they are widely accepted by American citizens. Perhaps these ideas will be sufficient to hold this approach to education intact for a long time to come. They can be supported by philosophic views that are themselves very far apart.

And yet, a lingering doubt remains, for history shows that fundamental changes in the intellectual climate of a society inevitably bring with it changes in conceptions and practices in education. The process is slow and often imperceptible but we know it is real. For this reason, then, there is occasion to wonder whether social conservatism, and the educational institutions and processes associated with it, has the vitality to adapt itself to an increasingly corporate society. Obviously, no one knows for sure, but the odds seem far from impossible.

*chapter FIVE*

# EDUCATIONAL PROGRESSIVISM: THE LIBERAL PROTEST

*Let us admit the case of the conservative: if we once start thinking no one can guarantee where we shall come out, except that many objects, ends and institutions are doomed. Every thinker puts some portion of an apparently stable world in peril and no one can wholly predict what will emerge in its place.*

—JOHN DEWEY

Certain traditions in educational theory are in some way protests against the fundamental character of educational conservatism and its domination of practical educational affairs in America. Essentialism, the conservative tradition in education, has dominated educational practice in this country throughout our national history. The character of the conservative tradition has changed in certain important respects, largely because of the acceleration of cultural change in the present century. That there are severe stresses within conservatism is no secret. Our conclusion is, however, that in spite of numerous disruptive conditions, the conservative tradition in education has been able to consolidate its position into one of great strength.

In the course of its history, essentialism has had to withstand the impact of certain protest movements, some of which have been potent enough to pose severe threats to educational conservatism. There is not much doubt that the most severe threat to which essentialism has been subjected thus far was posed by a tradition in education commonly called *progressivism*. Much of the literature of essentialism published since the end of World War II has been devoted to continuing violent reactions against the threat progressivism once posed. It is our contention, however, that in spite of the great strength the progressive tradition was able to muster at an earlier time in this century, the conservative tradition in education has emerged substantially intact. Whether progressivism or something akin to it may again in some future time pose a new threat is an interesting speculative matter. Our immediate concern is to analyze the progressive tradition, giving attention to its general social orientation, its principal educational ideas, and the relation of these ideas to underlying philosophical issues.

## THE LIBERAL TRADITION IN AMERICA

Liberalism as a social and political tradition resists any rigorous definition and none will be attempted here. Rather we shall attempt to describe various aspects of this tradition and at strategic points contrast it with social conservatism. Like all historical traditions, liberalism has changed with the years and in response to the pressures of cultural transition.

The origins of liberalism lie mainly in the eighteenth century and the development of this tradition is closely related to the rise of the middle class. Even before the beginning of the eighteenth century, John Locke, the great English philosopher, had advanced the basic theses of political liberalism. In brief, these theses deny the divine right of kings to govern as they see fit; they substitute instead the idea that society is in reality a contract between citizens and their government. The terms of this contract are that the government is delegated certain power and authority and in return government must protect the natural rights of citizens. These natural rights, according to Locke and numerous political liberals since his time, are life, liberty, and property.

Originally, liberalism was a protest against the arbitrary interference of institutions, particularly church and state, in the affairs of citizens. Liberalism was a call for men to be free to pursue their own affairs unmolested and to enjoy the civil liberties that are the rights of all. Early in its history, however, the mainstream of liberalism split into two branches. One branch was that form of liberal thought whose main emphasis was on freedom in economic activity. In essence, the doctrines of laissez faire capitalism formed the basic core around which economic liberalism formed itself. The chief ideas here were the existence of natural economic law, the basic motives in human nature as the desire for personal gain, and the belief that individuals are capable of managing their own affairs and should be left alone.

This stream of liberal thought had more influence in England than on the continent and the rugged individualism that is inherent in it has had a great effect on the American character. The classic intellectual work of this early economic liberalism was Adam Smith's *The Wealth of Nations*. This branch of liberalism became closely related to the development of industrial capitalism and therefore is associated historically with the various social and political problems that have emerged from industrial society.

The other branch into which the mainstream of liberal thought divided is often spoken of as social and humanitarian liberalism. This branch of the liberal tradition owes more to the political philosophy of the French than it does to the British. Inherent in the social and humanitarian liberalism of the eighteenth century is a concern for the welfare of the common people, expressed, for example, by Rousseau in his idea that the state rests on the general will of all the people, not merely on that of property owners. This tradition emphasized the idea of natural rights but insisted that the rights to life, liberty, and property do not exhaust the list of natural rights. To these must be added the right of the individual to the pursuit of happiness—a phrase that ultimately was to be incorporated in the American *Declaration of Independence*. Even in its earliest period, the weight of this stream of liberalism was thrown in the direction of social and political reform that would better the condition of the mass of people.

Although the two components of liberal thought had a common historical source, the differences between them grew constantly greater and by the early decades of the nineteenth century grave conflicts had developed between them. These conflicts were primarily associated with the poor condition of the common people under the early factory system. Humanitarian liberals launched bitter protests against the exploitation of human beings in factories, the employment of young children and women in the most onerous and dangerous occupations, and the cancerous growth of urban slums. These liberals denied the thesis that human labor is an economic commodity, subject only to the laws of the market, and their demands for social reform grew in volume.

We are here concerned with humanitarian liberalism. The protest movement in education we call progressivism was one of the historical emergents of the tradition of humanitarian liberalism. Our first task in developing this thesis will be to examine some distinguishing characteristics of this tradition and to contrast them at certain points with the ideas of conservatism.

In considering the general character of the American liberal tradition, we should first note the emphasis on experience and on an experimental attitude toward social institutions and social ideals. In part, at least, contemporary liberals are in this respect heirs of the rationalism of the eighteenth century. Briefly, the liberal attitude is that no set of ideals, no constellation of institutions, is so hallowed by tradition that it should stand outside the possibility of critical scrutiny and, if necessary, substantial alteration. Institutions exist to serve human welfare, and when they fail to do so they should be changed or abolished. Tradition is not the only criterion of value for assessing the worth of institutions. The real test of their worth is how they serve human beings.

This experimental attitude is linked to an abiding faith in the potential power of human intelligence. The call of social liberalism is for men resolutely to face the problems of their own times and to use intelligence, the most powerful means at their disposal, to build a better society and a better life for all of a generation. There are differing attitudes towards religion to be found among liberals, but even among those who are devout adherents to some religious body, this same orientation to the here and now keeps breaking through. As in the old "Wobbly" song, there may be "pie in the sky by and by," but, the liberal believes typically, our business is here in this world, with the problems and injustices that infest it. And if the Creator did endow every man with certain inalienable rights, the business of society is to see that in every generation men secure the full enjoyment of these rights. The liberal is therefore more concerned with human rights than with property rights. He is generally in agreement that the right to hold property is an important matter, but when the case comes down to whether the rights of property or the rights of men shall prevail, the liberal typically casts his lot with man and insists that human welfare must come first.

It is not difficult to see that sentiments of this kind imply in some respects a very different attitude towards human nature from that which we discovered in the conservative tradition. Throughout its history, the liberal tradition has been noted for the essentially optimistic view it has of the nature of man. It is perhaps unnecessary to say that this has always been one of the sore points between conservatives and liberals. Whereas the conservative has maintained that, except in the common affairs of life, the judgment of the individual is not to be trusted, the liberal has insisted that intelligence is sufficiently distributed in the population so that all men, when sufficiently nurtured by education, can make the wise decisions necessary to self-government. The conservative has never been very sanguine about popular rule, preferring to think that society should be governed by its wisest and most able men, and more often than not arguing for the education of an elite governing class.

Although the belief of Condorcet and other liberals of the eighteenth century that the possible extent of human progress is unlimited has been tempered somewhat in present-day liberalism, still there is more than a little of this attitude left. The modern liberal still tends toward Rousseau's belief that human nature in its original state is essentially good (or at the very least, is not contaminated by original evil).[1] If evil is not inherent in human nature, then it must stem from the environment, particularly the social environment. Immoral society produces immoral men, and the elimination of evil from human nature must involve the reform and recon-struction of social institutions.

These considerations provide the grounds for the deepest controversies between liberal and conservative forces. The conservative rejects any notion of the perfectibility of human nature. To the extent that he believes that human nature is capable of any improvement, he believes this must come largely from within the individual. Thus, religion, moral exhortation, and perhaps the influence of great literature can bring about the necessary "inner working." So, from the standpoint of classic conservatism, the focus of morality is within man, and a man with the will to raise the quality of his own life above that of the environment can do it. We have already seen how idealism can be employed to contribute strong philosophical support to this view of man and his nature.

There is a far different view of man implicit in the liberal's approach to human society and the problems of bettering human life. Under this view, human behavior is a product of both internal and external factors. The quality of human life is partly a product of what is within man, but it is also a product of the social environment in which men live. The liberal cannot agree with the basic conservative presumption of an inherent evil in man. To liberalism, human nature is originally good (or at least neutral). It may be that we can do little to change the inherited part of human nature but *we can control the environment in which this nature develops.*

Now this leads to the ground that liberals and conservatives have

---

[1] It will be remembered that Viereck has said that the idea of original sin, taken either figuratively or literally, is one criterion for distinguishing the conservative from the liberal.

contested for years—the need for consciously designed liberal reform movements. We have already seen the general contempt a thoroughgoing conservative has for what he usually refers to as doctrinaire liberal reform. To him, "do-gooding" reforms sponsored by private groups are bad enough; the real tragedy comes when liberals call for government to intervene on the side of social reform. Essentialists even today are reacting violently to the idea that the school itself should be a force for effecting far-reaching social changes.

To these basic differences over the nature of man and the efficacy of social reform in improving human life, we may add some lesser but still important issues. For one thing, liberalism customarily has viewed cultural pluralism as the condition of a healthy society. This means that a good society will not only *tolerate* differences of opinion and belief, it will actually *encourage* them. Liberalism historically has opposed resolutely various authoritarian schemes for enforcing conformity in personal and political life.

The liberal, moreover, is not impressed with conservative claims that it is the conservative tradition that promotes individual freedom and variety in social life. No tradition, the liberal is inclined to think, that stresses the individual's adherence to the existing order and that conceives the realization of self as coming through identification of the individual with the greater unity of society is in any position to talk seriously about promoting individuality and social pluralism. In the estimation of some liberals, the basic educational doctrines of the conservative tradition are plain evidence for this conclusion. The typical curriculum with its essential core that all must study, the inflexible requirements and standards that are always involved, and a methodology that is designed for transmitting subject matter appear to the liberal unlikely to do much besides promote intellectual and social conformity.

Another source of difference between the two traditions lies in the area of civil liberties and their preservation. The differences here are not of the stark black and white character they are sometimes taken to be for, after all, the liberal has no private option on the idea of inalienable rights. Liberals, however, may point out that the real issue is not the acceptance of high-level abstractions but the concrete support of individual rights when these are threatened in specific cases. Thus, the liberal will submit that it is one thing to talk in lofty generalizations about intellectual freedom and another thing to defend the schools of a given community against book banning by a group that justifies its actions in the name of social morality and protection of children against subversion.

There are considerable practical differences among conservatives on the question of civil liberties and there are also differences among liberals. Historical evidence does seem sufficient to support the generalization that liberalism, as a tradition, has supported the idea of basic civil liberties and the guarantee of these liberties in law. Let us examine relations to the great cultural components of supernaturalism, capitalism, nationalism, democracy, and science for the liberal tradition as we have done for the conservative tradition.

## SUPERNATURALISM AND HUMAN NATURE

Liberal attitudes toward organized religion and religious doctrines vary considerably, and it is by no means possible to point to *the* liberal position in this area. There are still traces of the eighteenth-century age of reason left in the liberal mind and not a little of the deism that colored the philosophy of a man like Jefferson. The range of religious belief within the tradition is from the reasonably orthodox acceptance of the supernatural basis of religion to out-and-out naturalism. The effects of cultural transition have left their marks on the liberal tradition as well as the conservative tradition in this respect.

There have been efforts within the liberal tradition to reconcile supernaturalism and naturalism. Conservatives have tried the same thing. Liberals have more often than not stressed the ethic of the Hebraic-Christian tradition more than they have the supernatural basis of that ethic, and many of them believe there is a close connection between the Hebraic-Christian tradition and the ethical ideals of modern democracy.

Thus, some of the same doubts and confusions concerning supernatural religion that beset the conservative tradition also are present in modern liberalism. There are, however, certain differences between the two traditions about supernaturalism and the nature of man that are important. In the first place, the liberal tends to be more tolerant in matters of religion than his conservative counterpart does. This means that the liberal typically will hold that the right *not* to adhere to any religion is as firmly grounded as the right to preference among religious creeds. Secondly, the liberal defends that part of the First Amendment to the Constitution that provides for separation of church and state, and while this may be true of some conservatives also, they are more apt to be the exception than the rule. Liberals generally have applauded decisions of the Supreme Court that have upheld the division between state and church. In the third place, liberals have not insisted that adherence to some form of supernaturalism is a necessity for personal and social ethics—although in their own personal lives many liberals may agree with this principle.

The significant thing, it would seem, is that liberalism has shown more concern for the condition of man here in this world. Liberals have believed that the earthly lot of man can, and should, be improved; and by and large, they have maintained that the reform of certain aspects of the social structure is the way to get it. Liberalism has always seen popular education as an important means for the improvement of human society and human life, but it has not supported the union of public school and religious sectarianism in the process. Perhaps the outstanding characteristic of the liberal mind in its conception of human nature is its faith in the power of human intelligence and the underlying optimism about the possibility of improving the lot of mankind.

*CAPITALISM*

Many of the fierce struggles between liberals and conservatives have occurred in the economic sphere of social life. American liberalism has in general accepted capitalism as the basic economic pattern and has not advocated the overthrow of that system, even though on occasion such effort has been alleged by conservatives. However, in large measure the history of liberalism in America is the history of the struggle for economic reform and the betterment of the conditions of the working class. Humanitarian liberals have often found historic institutions and processes of capitalism to be laden with weaknesses and injustice, and they have insisted that there is nothing so sacred about tradition that these conditions should be allowed to persist.

The liberal approach to economic reform has, however, been piecemeal and atomistic. This tradition has often displayed a nostalgic longing for an economy based on small-scale enterprise and a chance for the small businessman and the individual farmer to compete successfully in the market. Similarly, liberalism has had a close relation to the growth of trade unionism and has been involved in the struggle to have the rights of trade unions established in law. Yet another approach to economic reform has been the manipulation of money and credit—inflation, deflation, or stabilization, depending on the nature of conditions at a particular time. To this may be added the periodic crusades of liberals against the trusts and monopolies and their efforts to invoke the power of government against these hindrances to a free economy and the interests of common citizens.

In summation of liberals' attitudes toward capitalism, it may be said that they accept the system but with considerable reservation about many aspects of it. This tradition has always been in the forefront of campaigns to reform the institutions and processes of capitalism, but no comprehensive program has been advocated or instituted. The liberal approach to economic reform has not only been gradualistic; it has also in many respects been opportunistic.[2] Liberalism has seldom hesitated to invoke the power

---

[2] Perhaps the most concerted effort at economic reform through the power of government occurred during the New Deal under President Franklin D. Roosevelt. For a discussion of the essentially opportunistic character of the New Deal economic reform movement, see Richard Hofstadter, *The Age of Reform* (New York: Vintage Books, 1960), chap. 7 and particularly pp. 302 ff.

of government on the side of reform whenever this could be achieved. So far as the school is concerned in these matters, liberals have seen it as a chief means of social mobility, enabling an individual to rise, by means of superior education, to a higher social and economic status. In the depths of the Great Depression that began in 1929, liberal educational theorists moved to make the school itself an instrument of political and economic reform.

## NATIONALISM

The sentiments of modern liberalism concerning nationalism are often as mixed as those of conservatism. Liberalism accepts a world whose basic political unit is the national state. The liberal would like to see these nation-states liberal and democratic in their basic internal character and in their relations with each other. There does not seem to be much question that modern liberals accept the idea of national self-determination and that their vision of a world community is one of a plurality of nation-states, liberal and democratic in their orientation, and actively engaged in cooperative effort for the good of all concerned. Liberalism has tried to keep chauvinism out of American national life and usually has been suspicious of the activities of aggressively patriotic groups and societies. Liberals have often come to the defense of schools when these institutions have felt undue pressure from nationalistic groups.[3]

On the other hand, liberalism has not agitated notably for a true cosmopolitanism and has not supported the teaching of such a doctrine in the schools. In the earlier part of the century, liberals supported the League of Nations as a means to international peace and security. Modern liberals typically support the United Nations for about the same reasons. We have pointed out before, however, that the opposite of nationalism is not internationalism because, by definition, the latter presupposes the existence of nation-states. Modern liberalism has been staunch in its advocacy of international sentiments and support for the United Nations. On occasion it has appeared to favor some relinquishing of national sovereignty (at least many conservatives think it has) in order that the power of the United Nations might be increased. While liberals are certainly more willing to discuss the need and advisability of such relinquishment, there is little evidence to indicate that such policies have made significant headway.

There can be little doubt, however, that liberalism has supported the

---

[3] Although John Dewey's estimation of the strengths and weaknesses of modern nationalism was written a decade before World War II, today's liberals are in general agreement with it. See his *Characters and Events* (New York: Henry Holt and Co., 1929), pp. 798–803.

idea that the schools should foster internationalist ideas and propagate them among students. They have sought to temper the irrationalism and chauvinism that are apparently inherent in much of modern nationalism and to interpret to the young the idea that patriotism is devotion to the good of the total community and not the paranoid intolerance of everything that lies outside the immediate interest of the national state.

## DEMOCRACY

There is no concept in American thought today that has a closer relation to modern liberalism than the idea of democracy. Conceptually, at least, liberals agree that at heart democracy is an ethical concept and that when the equality of all men is asserted, the assertion concerns their moral equality. It must be admitted that in making decisions about what moral equality means in particular and concrete cases, the contemporary liberal finds problems as thorny as those of his conservative counterpart. An example is the question of what equality of opportunity means in the educational sense. We have already seen that this problem causes severe strains and disruptions in modern educational conservatism. It often serves the same purpose among those of liberal persuasion. Typically, the liberal has worked for legislation and other formal guarantees for free schooling— tax support for education, free schooling for all for at least twelve years, racial integration, compulsory attendance laws, free textbooks, and so on. More often than not, liberals have been in the forefront of the battle to extend the scope of the curriculum so that the needs and interests of a diversified school population might be served, but it is more difficult to make broad generalizations here. The presence of various kinds of practical and vocational subjects in the curriculum is far from being altogether the work of educational liberals, and many of them do not view highly vocational courses with approval.

On the broad social and political scale, the contemporary liberal approaches the problems of society in much the same fashion as he approaches educational problems. This is to say he is apt to stress its formal, political phases, particularly universal suffrage, representative government, legal protection of civil liberties, and the rights of minority groups. There is no question that these are necessary ingredients for the realization of a democratic way of life. There is some question, however, whether these outward forms are sufficient for the purpose. Such an important spokesman for the liberal tradition as John Dewey often pointed this out and attempted to infuse a deeper understanding of the democratic ethic into his liberal associates. Even though liberalism has often found the problems of realizing political democracy in an age of industrial society exceedingly difficult, this tradition has battled resolutely to retain and improve the basic parliamentary institutions of popular government, to encourage pluralism and diversity in social life, to emphasize individual freedom in social action, and to put the needs of men above the sanctity of tradition.

To the adherents of every tradition with which this book deals, save perhaps one, education is an important enterprise, but to American liberalism it comes close to being a sacred word. Much of the battle in the nineteenth century to establish a system of free, universal education was fought under the banners of political liberalism and the leaders of the forces were middle-class intellectuals, perhaps best typified in that era by Horace Mann. It was out of the great resurgence of political and social liberalism that began in the last decade of the nineteenth century that the progressive protest against the domination of essentialism emerged. Before we consider the conditions out of which this protest movement developed, we must give some attention to the relation of experimental science to modern liberalism.

## SCIENCE, SCIENTIFIC METHOD, AND THE LIBERAL MIND

Since the attitudes of modern liberals toward supernatural religious doctrines display considerable variation, this tradition has not escaped the effects of the impact of scientific achievement on the traditions of religion. In many cases the effects of the contradictory influence of science has troubled the liberal in the same way it has troubled his conservative counterpart. But when this has been said, the fact remains that the liberal tradition has often been more hospitable to the scientific enterprise, has been more willing to accept the deeper implications of science for various areas of experience, and more than any other tradition, has recognized the possibilities for educational method that are inherent in scientific method.

It may well be that an important reason for these attitudes is historical, and that the effects of the eighteenth-century Enlightenment still have a potent influence in this tradition. We have already observed that one characteristic that distinguishes the liberal from the conservative is the effort of the former to maintain an experimental attitude toward social institutions and modes of social life. The liberal, often to the disgust of conservatives, is more apt to appeal to empirical evidence and to evaluate social policies on the basis of objective evidence rather than on the basis of tradition. At its best, this approach has been a conscious effort to apply the canons of scientific method to the study of social problems and the formulation of social policy.

Adherents to the liberal tradition have often echoed Francis Bacon's famous dictum that "knowledge is power." And they have believed, as Bacon believed, that the knowledge that yields power is scientific knowledge. It is true that there has developed a considerable disenchantment among liberal elements about the power of military destruction that the scientific enterprise has made possible, but much of this disenchantment is with technology and social policy and not with experimental science itself. The liberal would hold that the threat of total annihilation is of our own making and that it results from our own misuse of modern technology and our own failure to apply the method of intelligence to political affairs with the same dedication we have employed it in creating the engines of military destruction.

Progressivism in education, as a facet of American liberalism, represented the effort to achieve a new humanism built on the achievements and potentialities of experimental science and the power inherent in scientific method. At a time when the program of the schools was dominated by the conservative tradition, liberals were agitating in favor of a larger place for the scientific studies in the curriculum and John Dewey, as an outstanding example, was experimenting with a scientific program for children in the Laboratory School at the University of Chicago.

While some liberals have been troubled by the radical naturalism that is inherent in experimental science, this tradition, certainly more than conservatism, has been willing to face the consequences of an out-and-out naturalistic interpretation of human nature. John Dewey, who is recognized above all others as the philosopher of modern liberalism and of educational progressivism, built his whole philosophical structure on a thoroughgoing naturalism.

## RESURGENCE OF AMERICAN LIBERALISM AND THE DEVELOPMENT OF PROGRESSIVISM IN EDUCATION

Progressivism in education developed as a protest movement against essentialism and its domination of American education. The protest lodged against the conservative tradition in education was part of a larger liberal reform movement that had powerful effects on events in America from the turn of the century to the beginning of World War II. We shall not recount the twists and turns that the progressive movement in education took in its development but shall confine our attention to the systematic theoretical aspect of the liberal protest in educational theory. It should be understood that many times there was a great, and often a complete, gap between the actions of educational progressives and the theoretical constructs to which presumably they were dedicated. Progressive education, as a historic reality, was a movement of vast and untidy proportions. It was eclectic in its origins, in some of its aspects incurably romantic and even sentimental about childhood, and self-contradictory on numerous theoretical points. The thing the progressives had in common, which was sufficient to hold them together for four decades, was a profound distaste for the traditional school and for many aspects of the society that supported that school. Sometimes—and this is often the case with protest movements—it was easier to tell what the progressives were against than what they were for. Fortunately, we now have available an admirable study of the historical reality of the progressive protest and the many variant forms it took. Any student who seriously wishes to grasp the historic character of the liberal protest should apply himself to Lawrence A. Cremin's *The Transformation of the School*.[4]

In the present context, we can make only the briefest comments about the origins of the progressive protest. Perhaps it will be sufficient to observe that the reform movement of the earlier part of the present century was essentially a revolt of humanitarian liberals against some very unfavorable aspects of industrial culture. Among these were the appalling conditions of urban living in the earlier part of the industrial era, the submersion of humanity in the emerging factory system, the increasingly arbitrary division of labor and leisure, and all the tawdriness and uniformity that flowed from it. This revolt of the liberals was in considerable part the effort to reestablish under different cultural conditions the ideals of moral equality and individual worth that Americans have held as an important part of their heritage.

Much of the energy of the liberal reformers was directed toward economic and political reform. The familiar liberal thesis that the improvement of the human prospect inevitably involves social reforms of far-reaching significance was everywhere to be heard. These reformers were a motley lot, ranging from "free-silverites" and "greenbackers" to trade unionists, settlement-house workers, and agitators for female suffrage. The battles they fought were many and varied and their total forces were never coordinated, but one conviction held them together: there was something rotten in the state of things in America and it needed to be cleaned out. The liberals had nurtured a dream, based in large part on the promises of the eighteenth century, and the gritty reality in which they found themselves revolted them.[5]

One aspect of this gritty reality against which liberal elements revolted was the American system of public education. To the liberal mind of America, *education* comes near to being a sacred word. Liberal elements had battled through most of the nineteenth century to establish and support a system of free schools, a system that was to be the very lifeblood of American democracy. They had fought the tight-fisted burghers of a score of states for a tax on property and they had battled with the "interests." By the last decade of the century they had very nearly achieved at

---

[4] New York: Alfred A. Knopf, 1961. Another briefer but useful source is Oscar Handlin, *John Dewey's Challenge to Education* (New York: Harper & Brothers, 1959).
[5] Hofstadter's *The Age of Reform*, cited above, is a valuable source of information on the general social context out of which educational progressivism developed.

least the outward form of a system of universal schooling, ranging from the primary grades through the high school. These things had been done in large measure under the spell of the eighteenth-century belief that the school is an agent of popular enlightenment and that only an enlightened people can be free. Now as the century drew to its close they looked about them, and what did they see?

In a remarkable series of articles published in a New York magazine, *The Forum*, in 1892 and 1893, Joseph Mayer Rice told them what they would see if they would take the trouble to look at their schools. Rice was a pediatrician who had become interested enough in educational theory to spend two years of study on that subject in German universities. When he returned to the States he agreed to do a study of American schools for *The Forum*.

During this study he toured the country, visiting more than a score of cities, talking with hundreds of teachers and parents, and attending school board meetings wherever he could. What he found in his travels was profoundly shocking to the liberals. In his articles he portrayed a school system shot through with the worst kind of ward-heeling politics, political corruption in appointments of teachers and administrators, and an atmosphere in the schools so deadly to the intellectual enterprise that it was enough to shock even a hardened journalistic muckraker.[6]

Rice found some signs of hope, but they were few and far between. He was most attracted by the work of Col. Francis Parker at the Cook County Normal School in Chicago, where, he reported, an educational program for children could be found that involved a broad curriculum of studies and teachers of competence and enthusiasm. But despite this and a few other places, the picture was uniform and black. The temptation here is to describe the authoritarianism, the mechanical uniformity, and the sterility of method and content as reported by Rice, but in the interests of space a brief summary by Handlin will suffice:

> The realm of the classroom in the 1890's was totally set off from the experience of the child who inhabited it. The teachers' lessons encrusted by habit, the seats arranged in formal rows, and the rigid etiquette of behavior all emphasized the difference between school and life. Hence learning consisted of the tedious memorization of data without a meaning immediately clear to the pupil.[7]

---

[6] For a more complete account of Rice's findings, see Cremin, *Transformation of the School*, chap. 1. The articles in *The Forum* later were published in book form as *The Public School System of the United States* (1893). Those familiar with the history of educational research will remember Rice as the author of the article "The Futility of the Spelling Grind," one of the first empirical studies of the relation of achievement to the amount of time invested in isolated drill.

[7] Handlin, *John Dewey's Challenge*, p. 42.

Even where innovations from European reformers had found their way into the schools, these new approaches had succumbed quickly to the formalism of the prevailing tradition:

> When some years ago a little boy entered the elementary school, he conceived in his heart a curse upon beans and busy work, which had by that time invaded the midlands, even the hinterlands of the United States. . . . Little did the boy suspect as he sat long hours before his simple rows of beans and corn, that in one book there were "62 pages of busy work devices to occupy heads and hands from September to June." [8]

The protest of liberal elements against the prevailing state of education at the turn of the century had a number of facets. These may be summarized somewhat as follows:

1. Liberals had seen education as a necessity for a free people and they had envisioned the school always in the vanguard of social progress, an institution always close to the people and always in the mainstream of social life. But the reality was an institution that had walled itself off from society and become a kind of separate universe in itself. Thus, to the liberal perception, the social role played by the school was essentially negative— a perverse kind of conservatism whose total effect was blind perpetuation of the status quo.

2. The exalted American tradition, and one for which liberalism always had a strong affinity, that the school is the cradle of liberty, the institution in which the young can learn the meaning of democracy and freedom, had been completely abrogated by the prevailing conservatism. Instead of being a place in which children could learn the basic elements of democratic social life, not only by precept *but also by example,* the educational reality was an institution authoritarian to its core and based on the most coercive and even brutal discipline.

3. The ideal of a school as a source of popular enlightenment has always been close to the heart of the American liberal. But as he looked about him, perhaps under the guidance of Dr. Rice's *Forum* articles, he saw an educational process grown dull and mechanical beyond belief. The curriculum was a dreary lockstep of desiccated subject matters. The chief teaching methods were repetitive drill and endless recitation of half-understood facts. Individual differences were ignored as much as possible, and the graded system, which had already received virtually universal acceptance in urban schools, only served to increase the emphasis on uniformity.

---

[8] Thomas Woody in National Society for the Study of Education, Thirty-third Yearbook (Bloomington, Ill.: Public School Publishing Co., 1934), p. 31.

These, then, were the kinds of conditions the liberals were protesting. They were protesting the idea of education as primarily transmission of subject matter; the authoritarian character of an institution whose primary role should be the extension of democratic ideals; and the failure of the school to sponsor social betterment for the masses. Much of this protest was emotional and sometimes ill-informed, at least in the beginning; for many, it was never anything else. But these protests came from the heart of American liberalism and the trend of the times was such that people were disposed to listen.

Meanwhile, as the schoolboy sat over his rows of corn and beans or pursued the "spelling grind" Dr. Rice had excoriated so thoroughly, certain events were shaping themselves so that out of this resurgence of liberal sentiment would grow a protest against the reigning conservatism that would be more than emotional—a philosophical protest that would rock essentialism as it had never been rocked before. This part of the story begins when a young professor of philosophy left his post at the University of Michigan and went to Chicago to assume his duties as chairman of the department of philosophy in the new university there.

## GROWTH OF PROGRESSIVISM

Not all the dissatisfaction and disillusionment over education were centered in New York City, and there were other sources of protest besides the articles of Dr. Rice. The city of Chicago itself was one of the main centers of the reform movement, and representatives of virtually every one of the liberal reform groups were congregated there. This city was already experiencing a storm of protests from liberal elements over the state of the public schools and an ad hoc citizens' committee composed of some of Chicago's most distinguished liberals had been formed to investigate the character of the city's public education.[9]

In one of his *Forum* articles, Rice had made a blistering attack on the Chicago schools and had extolled Col. Parker's work at the Cook County Normal School as being one of the bright spots in an otherwise dreary picture. In so doing, Rice had touched an exposed nerve, for a storm center of the educational controversy in Chicago was Col. Parker himself. Parker, who had been an outstanding school administrator in Quincy, Massachusetts, had come to the Cook County Normal School with the reputation of being a leading educational reformer. He had not been there

---

[9] Among the committee members were Jane Addams and Marshall Field. Various other committees and commissions were formed to deal with educational problems in this reform period. For a panorama of the situation in Chicago in the nineties, see Robert L. McCaul, "Dewey's Chicago," *School Review* 67 (Summer 1959): 258–86.

long before he was locked in mortal combat with the Cook County Board of Commissioners, which controlled the budget of his institution and whose members' views on education were decidedly conservative. The local press was full of intelligence about Parker's annual batterings of the Cook County Board, and the citizens were fairly well divided into two opposing groups: the pro-Parkerites and the anti-Parkerites. It was in this heady atmosphere of controversy and reform that the young professor, lately come from the chairmanship of philosophy at Michigan, was to begin his work of providing the liberal reform movement in America with the means for a systematic philosophic attack on the conservative tradition and all its works, most notably, its educational works.

John Dewey was thirty-five years old when he went to the University of Chicago as chairman of the department of philosophy, psychology, and education. He was born in 1859 in Burlington, Vermont, where he grew up and attended the state university. Subsequently he studied at Johns Hopkins University, where he came under the tutelage of Professor George Sylvester Morris. Morris introduced Dewey to Hegelian idealism, the dominant philosophical influence of that time. At Johns Hopkins, Dewey also heard lectures by G. Stanley Hall, who founded the child-study movement, and Charles Sanders Peirce, who gave pragmatic philosophy its original title.

After he had finished his doctoral studies, Dewey accepted an invitation from Morris, who had gone to the University of Michigan as head of the philosophy department, to come to that institution as an instructor in philosophy. Accordingly, Dewey came to Ann Arbor, where he was to remain for a decade, except for one year, when he was lured away by the University of Minnesota. During his years at Michigan, he did not teach courses in educational theory nor did he publish anything significant in that field.[10]

The situation at Chicago offered unusual opportunity for Dewey to expand his philosophical activities to include systematic work in educational theory. With the whole atmosphere of the city one of protest and reform, there was strong dissatisfaction with the status of the schools.

---

[10] The most recent and comprehensive biography of Dewey is George Dykhuizen's *The Life and Mind of John Dewey* (Carbondale, Ill.: Southern Illinois University Press, 1973). Other important sources of information about his life and career are "Biography of John Dewey" by his daughter Jane M. Dewey, in Paul Schilpp, ed., *The Philosophy of John Dewey* (Chicago and Evanston: Northwestern University, 1939); "From Absolutism to Experimentalism" in G. P. Adams and William P. Montague, eds., *Contemporary American Philosophy*, vol. 2 (New York: Macmillan Co., 1930); Max Eastman, "John Dewey," *Atlantic Monthly* 168 (December 1941): 671–85. An interesting account of his career at the University of Michigan is Willinda Savage, "The Evolution of John Dewey's Philosophy of Experimentalism as Developed at the University of Michigan" (Ph.D. dissertation, University of Michigan, 1950).

More than this, William Rainey Harper, president of the university, was himself deeply interested in public education and the improvement of the schools and was extending the services and facilities of the university for conferences, study groups, and public meetings on educational questions.[11] And Dewey had the opportunity to build a department that would reflect his own ideas on the role of philosophy as an intellectual discipline and its relation to cultural affairs.

There seems to be good reason to think that while Dewey did not teach any courses in education at Michigan, his studies in philosophy and psychology had strongly influenced his ideas about education and the need for reform of the schools. Admittedly, this is partly conjecture, but there is also evidence for it in Dewey's own writings. In one instance, he wrote that the ideas that led to the founding of the Laboratory School at Chicago originated in philosophy and psychology and owed far more to those fields than to "educational experience or precedent."[12]

## FOUNDING OF THE LABORATORY SCHOOL

One of the decisive events in the history of the progressive movement in education was the founding by Dewey and his associates of the Laboratory School at the University of Chicago.[13] This school was founded in 1896, two years after Dewey's arrival at the university, and is important in the history of education for a number of reasons. In the first place, the decision to found an experimental school illustrates the conviction that permeates Dewey's philosophy that ideas, even though they may appear to stand to reason, can be tested and their meaning clarified only as they are given concrete application and the results are noted. Dewey had developed certain ideas about the conduct of the educational process and certain proposals for the reform of the schools, but he believed that these ideas needed to be tested and clarified and that the only way this could be done was by applying them in a school situation.

It obviously was idle to think of testing new ideas in the existing pub-

---

11   See McCaul, "Dewey's Chicago," pp. 262–63.

12   Some important sources of information concerning the Dewey Laboratory School and Dewey's work in Chicago are Katherine C. Mayhew and Anna C. Edwards, *The Dewey School* (New York: D. Appleton-Century Co., 1936); Melvin C. Baker, *Foundations of John Dewey's Educational Theory* (New York: Columbia University, King's Crown Press, 1955); three articles by Robert L. McCaul published in *School and Society*, dated respectively March 25, 1961, April 8, 1961, and April 22, 1961; George Dykhuizen, "John Dewey: The Chicago Years," *Journal of the History of Philosophy*, vol. 2, no. 2 (October 1964): 227–53; "John Dewey in Chicago: Some Biographical Notes," ibid., vol. 3, no. 2:217–33.

13   John Dewey, "The Theory of the Chicago Experiment," Appendix II in Mayhew and Edwards, *The Dewey School*, p. 464.

lic schools and while Col. Parker's school was a vigorous institution, Dewey did not believe it would serve the purpose of testing his own ideas for educational reform. Therefore, the decision was made to found another school, which was to be a laboratory for educational experimentation.

A second reason for the importance of the Laboratory School is that it, far more than any other school bearing the name *progressive*, was a concrete example of what education would be like if Dewey's ideas were faithfully and intelligently applied in practice. The Laboratory School was an institution for young children, and hence through the study of extant documents we can get a fairly clear picture of an elementary school that operated on Dewey's basic principles. What secondary education would be if it had ever felt the real impact of Dewey's philosophy is for the most part purely and simply a speculative matter and will remain such until someone undertakes to put his ideas to work in a secondary school—a possibility that at present seems remote.

A third reason for the historic importance of the Laboratory School was the way in which its founders sought to meet the principal criticisms liberals were making of American public education. The first of these was the allegation by liberal elements that the existing schools were basically undemocratic in their structure and internal relationships. In shaping the organization of the school, Dewey and his associates sought to find a way between the rigid authoritarianism to which liberals were reacting and the loose, laissez faire romanticism, which was an inevitable reaction against the educational lockstep and which was already creeping into the progressive movement. The fundamental idea in the Laboratory School was that the school should itself be a community, simplified and purified, to be sure, to match the developmental stage of its pupils. As a community, it would give children a chance to live and work day by day in a social setting that exemplified the basic tenets of democracy.

## ORGANIZATION AND ADMINISTRATION OF THE LABORATORY SCHOOL

It was recognized from the beginning that a democratic community requires leadership and that social order is a necessity in any satisfactory social life. The problem here was not to react blindly to the excesses of authoritarianism by abandoning social structure and social order, but rather to reinterpret the source and character of these in a genuinely democratic mode of social life.

Accordingly, careful attention was given to the interpersonal relations in the school. The most important of these relations are those among children in the school and between children and their teachers. Apparently, Dewey and his coworkers had already learned that democracy in the life of a school is all of a piece—an institution is either democratic from top to bottom or it is not democratic at all. It is hopeless to suppose that democratic modes of life can exist in the schoolroom while the administration of education remains autocratic and repressive. There was plenty of evidence available for this conclusion even by a cursory examination of the existing system.

A fundamental meaning of the term *community* is "shared effort." In a democratic community, the work of the group and the responsibility for it is shared by all participants, and basic policies and plans are the product of all. It is often overlooked that democracy, more than any other mode of social life, lays the heaviest obligations on its members. In some respects, it is always easier to follow the dictates of authority and thus escape the necessity for making decisions and shouldering the responsibility for them, but as Dewey thought, this is no way to educate the prospective citizens of a society whose cherished belief is political democracy. Since active participation in policymaking is not only crucial in democratic social life but also exceedingly difficult to learn, it seemed to those in the Laboratory School that it is important to start it as early as possible, and this means as soon as the child comes to school.

For such reasons as these, the Dewey school strongly emphasized participation of pupils in planning activities and procedures in their school. Children were encouraged to participate in planning activities and in evaluating the results. It is well to emphasize that the idea was *participation* by pupils in planning, not turning over to pupils the responsibility for curriculum making. The business of the teacher, as Dewey saw it, was to guide the process, exercising the authority he had as a natural consequence of his role as representative of adult society.

To say that this emphasis on pupil participation was a radical departure from accepted practice in 1896 is to understate the case badly. The idea of the participation of pupils in formulating activities is well known today, at least as an idea, and "pupil-teacher planning" has become one of the bromides against which conservatives erupt periodically. But in the Laboratory School the reasons for it were understood clearly and the whole curricular structure depended on it.

The same emphasis that was placed on shared effort among pupils also extended to members of the teaching staff. The most painstaking efforts were made to keep channels of communication open among faculty members and the prevailing practice of dictating content and teaching method from the top of the organizational hierarchy apparently was unknown in this school. There is evidence that Dewey believed that qualified teachers are capable of knowing what needs to be done in the educational enterprise and of knowing how to accomplish it. He saw no need for the kind of supervision of teachers that was common in those days (and by no means unknown in these) and which consisted largely of prescription and inspection.

This is not to say, however, that there were no recognizable lines of responsibility and authority in the school's organization. Dewey had seen how teachers under the prevailing conservatism in the schools misused their authority, but he never questioned the authority of the teacher's role. As he saw it, the business of the teacher, as the representative of the adult culture, was to assist in inducting the immature child into social life. This was not to be accomplished by imposition, as essentialists have always maintained it should be. Rather:

> The teacher is not in the school to impose certain ideas or to form certain habits in the child but is there as a member of the community to select the influences which shall affect the child and to assist him in properly responding to these influences.[14]

Likewise, Dewey never questioned the need for responsibility and authority in administration of the school, though he was bitterly critical of the hierarchical authoritarianism prevalent in the schools of that day. Administrative roles in the Laboratory School were assigned to a general supervisor, a principal, and department heads. Dewey himself was the general head of the school. Each administrative officer was responsible for certain aspects of the school's operation and hence the division was more one of responsibility than of authority. But the contributions of all members of the staff were always solicited and every effort was made to implement the idea that democracy means the participation of all in the making of policy.

It remains to be noted that the parents of children who were enrolled in the school were also considered members of the community, and no effort was spared to involve them in the school's curriculum and the experimental work being carried on. A parents' association of the Laboratory School was formed and members of the association were encouraged to participate in evaluating and developing the school's program. Some of Dewey's early publications on educational theory had their origin in materials he prepared for discussion by the parent group.

So the organization of the school as a community of pupils, teachers, and parents, each with a unique interest and role, and all committed to mutual effort, was Dewey's solution for the increasing tendency of the school to remove itself from the mainstream of social life and to become a world apart, not only apart from the experience of the child but from the living culture itself.

## CURRICULUM AND INSTRUCTION IN THE LABORATORY SCHOOL

From the standpoint of the organization for instruction, two significant innovations were made in the Laboratory School. In the first place, the school was departmentalized, each of the departments being under the

---

[14]  John Dewey, *My Pedagogic Creed* (first published by E. L. Kellogg & Co., 1897), reprinted in *Education Today* (New York: G. P. Putnam's Sons, 1940).

direction of a staff member who had thorough training in the field of knowledge represented in his department. Departmentalization of instruction has never been common in American elementary schools, although it has been the prevailing pattern in secondary and higher education. Elementary teachers in those days as well as these commonly have been expected to teach all the subject matters in the curriculum with the possible exceptions of such "special subjects" as art, music, and physical education. This traditional role of the elementary teacher has dictated a program of teacher education that necessarily stresses breadth at the expense of depth of scholarship. This fact has often provoked criticism from conservative circles, but no one has ever been able to show how elementary teachers can secure the depth of learning in a single field that most essentialists think desirable, have the generality of background necessitated by their role, and still complete their college education in the traditional four years.

Dewey's conviction was that the teacher should be so well grounded in the subject matter with which he deals that his attention should be on the student and his responses to the material. In *Democracy and Education*, written after the Laboratory School had closed, he observed:

> When engaged in the direct act of teaching, the instructor needs to have subject matter at his finger's ends: his attention should be upon the attitude and response of the pupil. To understand the latter in its interplay with subject matter is his task, while the pupil's mind, naturally, should be not on itself but on the topic in hand.[15]

It was thought that one way of ensuring this degree of academic competence lay in departmentalizing the school and putting each department in the charge of a person with the necessary degree of scholarship. The school was divided into the following departments: kindergarten, history (the social sciences), natural science and mathematics, domestic science and industries, manual training, art, music, languages (French and Latin were taught), and physical culture.

Dewey and his associates were aware of the danger of compartmentalization of subject matter inherent in a departmental organization for they had seen its effects in the secondary schools and in higher education. They believed, however, that the usual compartmentalization need not occur if communication among staff members were prevalent and if every member of the staff played his proper role in planning the educational experiences of the various groups of pupils. This, by necessity, involved a high degree of shared effort by staff members, which Dewey thought to be the very essence of social democracy.

---

15 John Dewey, *Democracy and Education* (New York: Macmillan Co., 1916), p. 215.

The second innovation in the instructional organization of the school was that it was ungraded. The graded system of organization of elementary education dates only from the middle of the nineteenth century, but even in the days of the Laboratory School the graded system had already become virtually the only mode of organization for elementary education outside the one-room schools of the rural areas. The problems that the essentialists experienced with the graded system did not exist in the Laboratory School because the school was not graded and there were none of the familiar features of the graded system: minimum essentials for each grade, promotion from grade to grade on the basis of mastering the material deemed essential for a given grade, and the effort to deal with individual differences in achievement by nonpromotion and by acceleration. Children in Dewey's school were grouped for instruction according to interests and abilities, and while these provided a rough correlation with age, there was no effort to construct the groups exclusively along chronological age lines. Flexibility in grouping was the basic principle and there were no problems of grade standards and promotions. This arrangement was in part Dewey's answer to the "educational lockstep," which was receiving bitter criticism from liberals.

Thus, the two primary innovations in the organization of the school were departmentalization and a flexible, nongraded structure. There is one other feature of the school that should be mentioned. This is the character of the school plant. As everybody knows, the conventional school building, which is designed to accommodate the kind of program that essentialists have always advocated, consists mainly of classrooms. Usually, though by no means always, there are certain auxiliary rooms: a gymnasium, an auditorium, a music or art room or both, and so on. Generally, these rooms are for the "special subjects" or for "extracurricular activities." Under the traditional view, the main business of the school goes on in classrooms, which are designed for the traditional methods of lecturing, reciting, and testing.

Since the methodology employed in the Laboratory School did not involve these traditional techniques of instruction, a different kind of school plant had to be arranged. The school was never housed in a proper school building. Instead, it occupied a series of buildings originally designed for other purposes. When the school began, it was quite small; but as the enrollment grew, it was necessary to move to larger quarters. In each instance, the house and its outbuildings were adapted to the needs of the program.

The significant aspect is that all of the rooms in the building were designed for active work, not for lecturing and reciting. They included a gymnasium, manual training rooms (shop), art and textile studios, two laboratories, one for the physical sciences and one for the biological sciences, and a suite of rooms for languages and social sciences. Each of these locations was under the supervision of a staff member with thorough training in the field. Thus the school plant was a place for active work in all fields represented in the curriculum.[16]

These innovations in the design of the school plant were necessitated by the nature of the school's program. We now come to the feature of the Dewey school that effectively differentiates it from the pedagogy of the conservative tradition and that is the most telling aspect of the liberal protest against educational essentialism. This is the conception of the nature of the curriculum. All Dewey's important organizational innovations derive from this basic departure from conservative pedagogical orthodoxy.

In essentialism, the curriculum is always viewed as some organized series of subject matters that are deemed essential and that are to be mastered by all who come to school. Essentialists may disagree about what subjects are essential and must be in the curriculum, but there is no disagreement among them over the principle that curriculum means *some* series of subject matters.

Abandoning this basic conservative principle, Dewey and his co-workers proposed that the curriculum should be conceived as *an ordered series of active occupations.*[17] Admittedly, it is very difficult for most of us to conceive what a school program would be like whose basic conception of curriculum is an organized series of active enterprises carried on by pupils under the guidance and leadership of teachers. In the pedagogy of essentialism, which has always dominated American education, the unit of instruction is "the lesson." There are different patterns of lessons, but they all involve assigning some task to be done and then checking the work of the pupils to see that they have done it. The task may be listening to a lecture by the teacher, reading a portion of a book and "learning" the contents, engaging in drill as in arithmetic or spelling, or writing some kind of assigned composition. The teacher may check the work of the pupils by oral recitation and various kinds of written tests. The pupil is "graded" in terms of his performance. It is the sequence of lessons that constitutes the curriculum of the conservative tradition.

In the Dewey school there were no lessons, no assignments as con-

---

[16] In one of his early books, *The School and Society*, originally published by the University of Chicago Press in 1899, Dewey relates the difficulties he experienced in buying furniture and equipment for the school. After searching the school supply houses of Chicago he finally was told by one dealer that he would never find what he sought because the school furniture of that day was designed for sitting and listening, not for working.

[17] Dewey used the term *occupations* in describing the program of the Laboratory School. I am convinced that the term *enterprise* in some contexts is more descriptive of what actually went on in the school and that it has the further advantage of being relatively free of a vocational connotation. For these reasons, in my own discussion I often use the term *enterprise*.

servatives understand that term, and no examinations. *The unit of instruction was the enterprise.* An enterprise differs from a lesson in important and strategic ways. For one thing, an enterprise is of longer duration. When planned properly it has an inherent unity of organization, and it involves generally the union of thought and action. An enterprise involves some goal or end that those involved in it wish to attain. To attain this goal, certain strategies and plans must be made that promise to bring about the desired consummation. These plans must then be implemented by appropriate actions and judged for their adequacy by the way they work out.

Clearly, enterprises can be of various kinds, depending on the character of the desired end. For example, there are enterprises that involve the production of some physical thing or things, as in the manual arts; there are enterprises that involve inquiry and the effort to find solutions to problems and the answers to questions, as in the various sciences; and there are enterprises that involve the production of objects of beauty, as in literature and the fine arts. There are also enterprises that are of sufficient scope to involve all of these elements.

Curriculum design in the Laboratory School involved the following points: (1) The program had to be one of active work—physical and intellectual—rather than the passive absorption of subject matter. A big effort here was made by abandoning the lesson and substituting the enterprise in its place. (2) The sequence of enterprises that made up the educational experience of pupils had to be planned around a basic unifying theme that would give an underlying unity to experiences that might otherwise be discrete and atomistic. Dewey held that the unifying force should always be the experience of the child, and that the basic problem of education was to ensure that the experience of the child in school built on and illuminated the experience he had in the home and community.

However, an important technical pedagogical problem was determining the content that should be introduced into the experience of the child while he was in school. After extensive experimentation in the early years of the school's history, the staff of the school worked out a plan by which the active enterprises carried on by pupils were developed around certain broad themes of the development of civilization. These themes, according to the report of Mayhew and Edwards, were as follows: (1) Household and social occupations (kindergarten group); (2) Progress through invention and discovery; (3) Progress through exploration and discovery; (4) Local history; (5) European backgrounds.[18]

---

[18] Mayhew and Edwards, *The Dewey School.* The authors give fairly extended reports of how each of these themes was developed.

Part of the rationale for this kind of program may be seen in the following quotation from an early publication by Dewey:

> The primary basis of education is the child's powers at work along the same general constructive lines as those which have brought civilization into being.
>
> The only way to make the child conscious of his social heritage is to enable him to perform those fundamental types of activity which make civilization what it is.
>
> In the so called expressive or constructive activities is the center of correlation.
>
> This gives the standard for the place of cooking, sewing, manual training, etc., in the school.
>
> They are not special studies which are to be introduced over and above a lot of others in the way of relaxation or relief, or as additional accomplishments. I believe rather that they represent, as types, fundamental forms of social activity; and that it is possible and desirable that the child's introduction into the more formal subjects of the curriculum be through the medium of these constructive activities.[19]

We now understand that these departures by the Laboratory School really were necessitated by the conception of curriculum that governed the work of the school. The real challenge that the Laboratory School posed to the conservative tradition was that the curriculum should be viewed as a series of active enterprises conducted by pupils under the guidance of teachers, who themselves possessed superior scholarship and keen psychological insight into the nature of childhood. However, thus far we have considered only certain innovations introduced into educational practice by the Laboratory School staff. We have not as yet given attention to the reasons Dewey and his associates had for developing these innovations that to the conservatives of that day and this have often seemed bizarre and dangerous.

## "MY PEDAGOGIC CREED"

We have already referred to parts of a statement published by Dewey in 1897, the second year of operation of the Laboratory School. This little document is of the greatest importance in the history of progressivism. It is convincing evidence on the one hand that Dewey's ideas on education developed concurrently with his ideas in psychology and the various branches of philosophy, and on the other that his educational theory is not

---

[19]  Dewey, *My Pedagogic Creed.*

merely a series of deductions from a preestablished pragmatic philosophy—
a point that many friendly as well as unfriendly critics of Dewey have
found difficult to understand.

Another reason for the importance of *My Pedagogic Creed* is that in
this early statement Dewey laid down the basic lines of his educational
position, and though the theses stated in this work were developed more
fully and in some respects modified over the years, he never departed
significantly from the basic position revealed in this early work. Only a
careful reading of the original document can reveal all the nuances of the
theoretical position delineated in it. As introduction to a firsthand study,
we shall examine its basic themes.

## "WHAT EDUCATION IS"

The document is composed of five "articles," each of which deals
with a primary aspect of a theory of education. The first of these articles
is concerned with what education is. In Dewey's estimation, "all education
proceeds by the participation of the individual in the social consciousness
of the race." This process begins with the birth of the child and in the
beginning is unconscious but powerful in shaping the primary powers and
dispositions of the developing child. Gradually, the child begins to share
consciously in the funded intellectual and moral resources we call civilization. This developmental process is serial, proceeding from the gross and
undifferentiated impulses of infancy to the increasingly organized responses
of maturity. Thus "the only true education comes through the stimulation
of the child's powers by the demands of the social situations in which he
finds himself."

There are always two sides to the educative process: the psychological
and the sociological, and neither of these can safely be neglected. The
psychological side provides the basis of all education, for it is the child's
instincts and powers that give the starting point for the process. "Save
as the efforts of the educator connect with some activity which the
child is carrying on of his own initiative independent of the educator,
education becomes reduced to a pressure from without."

Consideration of the sociological factor reveals that while the child
has his own instincts and tendencies, the meaning of these is not known
until they are translated into their social equivalents. "In order to know
what a power really is we must know what its end, use, or function is,
and this we cannot know save as we conceive of the individual as active
in social relationships." The only tenable approach to education, particularly under the dynamic conditions of modern industrial society,
consists in helping the child to realize as completely as possible the native
powers he possesses. We cannot know with any certainty what society will
be like even a few years from now, and it is futile to attempt to prepare

the child for a specific set of future conditions. The best we can do for him is "to give him command of himself . . . to train him that he will have the full and ready use of all his capacities; that his eye and ear and hand may be tools ready to command, that his judgment may be capable of grasping the conditions under which he has to work, and the executive forces be trained to act economically and efficiently."

## "WHAT THE SCHOOL IS"

The school is a form of community life in which a concentrated effort is made in "bringing the child to share in the inherited resources of the race, and to use his own powers for social ends." Education must be conceived as a "process of living and not a preparation for future living" and the experience the child has in the school must be as real and vital to him as that of the home or the neighborhood.

The only way to secure continuity in the child's growth is to plan his school experience so that it grows gradually out of his home life and the activities he has become familiar with in the home. This background of previous experience provides the background that will give meaning to the new ideas presented in the school. A main reason for the failure of traditional education is that it does not see the school as a form of community life. The conservative tradition sees the school as a place in which certain information is transmitted and certain habits formed as a means of preparing for the future. "As a result they do not become a part of the life experience of the child and so are not truly educative."

Education has a moral dimension when it is seen as a mode of social life. Effective moral training occurs when the individual relates to others in "a unity of work and thought," and thus the child's behavior is stimulated and controlled through the life of the community. The traditional school fails to give any genuine, regular moral training because it ignores the role of the community and vests the sole responsibility for control in the teacher.

## "THE SUBJECT MATTER OF EDUCATION"

"The social life of the child is the basis of concentration or correlation . . . social life gives the unconscious unity and the background of all his efforts and all his attainments. None of the traditional school subjects, whether taken singly or together, can furnish the true center of correlation. The traditional school errs gravely when it introduces the young child too early and too abruptly to a program of special subjects: reading, writing, geography, etc., for these are presented out of relation to social life and hence have little meaning for the child. The real business of the school is the progressive development and enrichment of the child's experience and the enhancement of his own native powers and therefore: *'Education must be conceived as a continuing reconstruction of experience; that the process and the goal of education are one and the same thing.' "* [20] Subject matters, as we usually think of them in terms of history, mathematics, literature, and so forth, are important as means, but they are not the ends of education and they have meaning only as they enter actively into social life.

## "THE NATURE OF METHOD"

"The question of method is ultimately reducible to the question of the order of development of the child's powers and interest." Thus the order in which material is presented and the way it is treated derive from the child's own nature. In the development of the child, the active side always precedes the passive, "consciousness is essentially motor or impulsive . . . and conscious states tend to project themselves in action."

Ideas result from action and are important as controls of action. It is idle to attempt to develop powers of reason and judgment apart from their role in selecting and arranging means for action. Since traditional education ignores this, the child is continuously presented with arbitrary symbols. Symbols are important means of our intellectual processes but presented in isolation, as in the traditional school, they are only "a mass of meaningless and arbitrary ideas imposed from without."

"Interests are the signs and symptoms of growing processes." A child's interests show the stage of development he has reached and indicate the stage he is about to enter. It is greatly important, therefore, that the teacher give constant attention to the interests of his pupils. The point is not that interests should be indulged or that they should be repressed, for an interest is always the sign of some power and the business of the teacher is to discover this power and arrange for its expression and development.

## "THE SCHOOL AND SOCIAL PROGRESS"

"Education is the fundamental method of social progress and reform." Reforms based on laws and legal threats or superficial modifications in society are futile. The only trustworthy means of social reconstruction lies in the adjustment, through education, of individual actions on the basis of social consciousness. This approach recognizes both the individual and the social factors and it indicates that the ideal school will reconcile individualistic and institutional ideals. ". . . Thru education society can formulate its own purposes, can organize its own means and resources,

---

[20] This sentence is a very famous one in Dewey's educational writings. It is one of his earliest statements that education is a process and as a process it is of far greater importance than any of its products.

and thus shape itself with definiteness and economy in the direction in which it wishes to move."

## SUMMARY

The liberal protest developed against the conservative domination of American society and particularly American education. This protest movement in education grew out of and was an important part of a broad resurgence of liberal sentiment and the resulting liberal reform movement, whose effects were felt in every important aspect of American life.

John Dewey and his associates founded an experimental school at the University of Chicago. This school provided a situation in which certain ideas for the reform of education could be tested experimentally. Dewey developed these ideas, in part at least, concurrently with his work in psychology and philosophy. He regarded the school not only as a place in which practical innovations in education could be tested, but also as a means for testing psychological and philosophical ideas.

Certainly there is far more to the development of the liberal protest movement and the emergence of progressivism in education than what is to be found in the work of the Laboratory School or in such early writings of Dewey as *My Pedagogic Creed*. At the same time the Dewey school was flourishing at Chicago, other schools in various parts of the country were also engaged in testing innovations in education. In many cases, these schools were notably different from the Laboratory School in their programs and their conception of the objectives of education. The historic reality that was progressivism in education was enormously complex, and this makes easy generalizations about it impossible.

However, John Dewey is recognized universally as the chief figure in the development of liberal social and political philosophy, as well as progressivist educational philosophy, in the earlier decades of this century. This recognition has always been given him by those who are friendly to his ideas as well as by those who are not. Most of the salient ideas in the philosophy of educational progressivism can be attributed primarily to Dewey, though some important contributions to the philosophy of progressivism came from other sources.

# chapter SIX

# JOHN DEWEY
# AND THE LIBERAL PROTEST
# IN EDUCATION

*The child comes to the traditional school with
a healthy body and a more or less unwilling
mind, though, in fact, he does not bring both his
body and mind with him; he has to leave his
mind behind, because there is no way to use it
in the school. If he had a purely abstract mind,
he could bring it to school with him, but his
is a concrete one, interested in concrete things,
and unless these things get over into school life
he cannot take his mind with him.*

—JOHN DEWEY

Progressivism in education owes much of its philosophy to Dewey's thoughts on education. *My Pedagogic Creed* and the Laboratory School were products of these thoughts and also expressions of them. Although Dewey was not the sole exponent and developer of progressivism in education, his writings reflected the liberal protest against essentialism, and they are an admirable conveyance of the progressivist philosophy.

## PURPOSES OF EDUCATION

The way an educational tradition conceives the fundamental purposes of education is important in determining its conception of the character of the curriculum, the nature of educational method, and the role of the teacher. Much of the liberal protest against essentialism stems from the conservative view that the foremost purpose of education is perpetuation of tradition and preparation of the immature for adulthood. The essence of Dewey's argument against the conservative thesis became apparent in his early educational writings and is clearly expressed in *My Pedagogic Creed*. In the early chapters of *Democracy and Education*, he gives extended treatment to how the ends of education should be conceived and he criticizes certain variant views.

Dewey's argument begins with his observation that the salient fact of life is the organism's power to grow. The growth of a human being is different in important ways from that of other kinds of organisms, the chief difference being the relatively plastic nature of the child and the prolonged period of dependency that characterizes human infancy. Most animals, for example, come into the world with their potential repertory of behavior patterns already fixed by heredity. Learning in these creatures, then, is essentially that of the progressive developing and maturing of what was already present in potential. The animal learns by responding to environmental situations on the basis of instinct. Thus, experience affects animal learning but not in the same way that it affects the human being.

The human infant at birth is extraordinarily plastic in nature. By this is meant that beyond a bare minimum of apparently reflex (unlearned) behavior patterns, infant behavior is impulsive, that is, unformed by specific hereditary patterns and therefore capable of developing in various ways and in various directions. This initial plasticity of human nature also means that mankind has the capacity of learning from experience, that is, of becoming progressively more able to foresee the probable course of events that will ensue from some action, and thereby regulating behavior.

Dewey applied the term *habit* to the psychological mechanism by which initial native impulsive behavior is molded. This is a common psychological term, but it exhibits many shades of meaning. The use Dewey applied is considerably different from that of many psychologists who use it to denote relatively simple and narrow elements of learned behavior. By *habit*, Dewey meant patterns of behavior that are far more extensive and flexible than rigid responses to specific stimuli. In his use of the word, habits are *arts*, ways of doing things.

> Habits are ways of using and incorporating the environment in which the latter has its say as surely as the former. We may borrow words from a context less technical than that of biology, and convey the same idea by saying that habits are arts. They involve skill of sensory and motor organs, cunning or craft, and objective materials. They assimilate objective energies, and eventuate in a command of environment. They require order, discipline, and manifest technique.[1]

From this, we conclude that habits, as arts or learned ways of using the objects and energies of the environment for conscious purposes, are the ways by which growth takes place and are also indexes of growth in the child. We can say also that since the most important aspect of the human environment is social, habits themselves are significantly social in their origin and character. They are the very stuff on which the continuity of social and individual experience depends. Without this capacity to preserve experience through habit, the human species could not survive. But there is also a danger that lurks always in the background, for habits have a way of becoming stiff and unyielding instead of being flexible and artistic means to furthering experience. When they become rigid, they can constitute an arrest of growth.

The molding of the native, impulsive behavior of the human being into meaningful patterns of habit is what education means in its broadest sense. Education, then, is a continuing process of the reconstruction of experience. This process involves the total experience of the individual and only a part of it takes place in the school. Further, the continuing process of reconstruction of experience is an aspect of growth itself, and as Dewey reasoned:

> Since growth is the characteristic of life, education is all one with growing; it has no end beyond itself. The criterion of the value of school education is the extent in which it creates a desire for continued growth and supplies means for making the desire effective in fact.[2]

This statement, occurring in Dewey's greatest contribution to educational theory, has puzzled and frequently outraged his readers ever since it was first published. There is much in these innocent-appearing few

---

[1] John Dewey, *Human Nature and Conduct* (New York: Henry Holt and Co., 1922), p. 15. This book is the most complete exposition of Dewey's psychology.

[2] *Democracy and Education* (New York: Macmillan Co., 1916), p. 62.

lines that calls into question some of the most cherished convictions in the Western tradition; for example: Does not growth always proceed toward some final end or fulfillment? Growth is a process but a process moves toward some goal. What goal does Dewey see? His answer was always "continued growth," but this never seemed to satisfy his critics or enlighten many of his friends. And so inevitably the questions came about how we can know when growth is in the right direction. The development of cancer is growth, but is *that* desirable? Becoming an increasingly expert swindler is a process of growth. Is that desirable? No, Dewey answered many times, these are not growth.[3] They are developments that stunt or destroy the possibilities for further growth. The advent of cancer heralds the end of continued growth and the death of the organism, precluding further development. A life of crime closes important avenues of experience and stunts and perverts development. We know these things by observing the consequences sickness and crime entail. Education, as a continuing process of growth, frees impulse, keeps habit flexible and adaptable to changed circumstances, and thus provides for future development of experience.

Another criticism often urged against Dewey's conception goes somewhat as follows: Dewey has made growth the characteristic of life, and he has said further that growth has no end beyond itself. This must mean that life has no end beyond itself; in other words, Dewey is really saying that life itself moves toward nothing and thus has no purpose. This kind of objection raises certain fundamental questions in the theory of value that we shall not attempt to consider until we have outlined Dewey's position more fully. But provisionally, we can say that Dewey rejects the notion that there is some *summum bonum* toward which all human striving should proceed and suggests that inflated statements about *the meaning of life* usually have little meaning of their own. Any human life itself has the meaning to it that the experience of the person makes possible. Meaning is not something that stands outside the life process; it is instead a quality of it. The purpose of education, broadly conceived, is to make possible the widening and the deepening of meaning. The end of life is synonymous with the process: to live more fully and more richly.

The process we call education, then, is developing the native powers and tendencies of the child as they exist initially in impulsive form. Growth proceeds as these powers and tendencies are formed into meaningful habits through their expression in an ever social environment. This process has no end outside itself, since growth has no end outside itself.

---

[3] See, for example, Dewey's *Experience and Education* (New York: Macmillan Co., 1938), pp. 28–29.

Dewey criticized contemporary objectives of education, contrasting them with his own view of education as growth. Understanding these objectives he criticized will help us understand the protest Dewey was making against the older traditions of schooling. He first directed attention to the idea that education is preparation for some relatively distant future in the life of the child. We have already paid close attention to this notion because it is the basic working idea of essentialism. Today's conservatism puts the idea of education as preparation central to its educational philosophy and makes everything else subordinate, and this was as true in Dewey's day as it is in this. The purpose of the elementary school is preparation for the secondary school; the secondary school is preparatory for the college; and the college for the graduate school. The whole process (granted that very few ever make their way through the entire gamut) is preparatory for adult life. When a child enters school at the age of five or six, he is embarking on a process of preparation for something that lies in a distant future.

Dewey argued that there are insurmountable difficulties involved in this conception.[4] For one thing, an educational program based on preparation always loses the energy and motive power pupils possess in such abundance. Children live in the present, and a distant future of which they can have little or no awareness provides scant motivation for school tasks. This in turn leads to procrastination and idleness in the classroom. As the child sees it, if the future is so far off, there must be plenty of time to prepare for it, and there are so many things to do in the meantime. Thus, much time spent in school is aimless and barren of desired results.

This condition is aggravated by another element of the conservative tradition. Essentialism has always found it necessary to establish some minimum average standard, "the essentials for the grade," as the prevailing expectation for pupil achievement. And what began as a floor is soon found to be a ceiling. What conservative schools actually do, as Dewey saw it, is to substitute "a conventional average standard of expectation and requirement for a standard which concerns the specific powers of the individual. . . ." And out of this comes the mediocrity that conservatives consistently deplore but that their schools systematically cultivate.

Finally, Dewey pointed out, it is always necessary to use extraneous rewards and punishments wherever the notion of education as preparation exists. The conservative school ignores or suppresses the inborn motive powers of children and for this natural motivation substitutes marks, failures, praise, honor rolls, promotions, retardations, and expulsion from school. The pedagogical pendulum periodically swings from iron rule to

---

[4] See *Democracy and Education*, chap. 5.

sugar coating and back, one as futile as the other. So long as the view prevails that education is preparation for some distant future, these evils are not to be escaped.

Dewey next turned attention to a conception of education as the unfolding of some latent potential in the child. This is one of the oldest systematic views of human growth and development of knowledge in the individual. One form of it is found in Plato in the guise of innate ideas that are brought to consciousness by the ministrations of the teacher. A variant appeared in the nineteenth century as an aspect of Absolute idealism and received its clearest pedagogical development with Froebel. It also was a notion that played a part in the educational progressivism of Dewey's own time and to which he was strongly opposed.

The difficulty that attends the unfolding theory of development is at heart the same as with the preparation theory. While the former recognizes that development is growth, it sees this process as a moving toward some ultimate perfection, or final end. Growth is thus a series of "approximations to a final unchanging goal." Now the theory of preparation really is the same idea; the difference between the two lies in what the ultimate goal is thought to be. With the preparationists, it is conceived usually as practical and vocational, and with the unfolders it is more apt to be spiritual and ethical.

Since the goal towards which the child's nature is said to unfold is so remote, it is not only unattainable, it is also incapable of giving any real guidance to the teacher and therefore something has to be substituted for it. What usually is substituted for it is something *the teacher thinks the child should learn.* So by "expert questioning," the teacher "draws out" of the child the response desired. This may satisfy the teacher, but it contributes little to the education of the child, for he has no way of knowing what the teacher really is after. Continued experience of this kind makes the pupil more and more dependent on the cues that come from the teacher; his own originality and motivation are suppressed or ignored. Dewey observed that less harm is probably done simply by telling the child whatever it is we want him to know; he added wryly, "At least it remains with the child how much will stick."

The real difficulty with the unfolding theory is that it ignores the nature of experience, which as Dewey had already stated in *My Pedagogic Creed*, always involves both the inner nature of the child and the external environment in which the native powers of the child find meaningful expression. The unfolding theory concentrates on the inner nature and ignores the importance of the outer. Consequently, when this theory is acted on in school situations, its effects are found to be as bad as those of the preparation theory.

The third conception of education Dewey criticized is education as the training of faculties, or as it is often called, "mental discipline." This theory is one of the most persuasive pedagogic notions in the history of Western education. It goes back at least as far as Aristotle, and it was restated in classic form by John Locke. It has always been important in the essentialist tradition and still remains so despite its lack of support in experimental psychology.

Dewey began by agreeing that the theory of mental discipline has the proper ideal in mind because it views the end products of education as "specific powers of accomplishment." In this sense, the educated person is one whose original powers are developed to the extent that he is skillful and effective in all aspects of his life and work. This is what Dewey meant when he said that habits, which are the outcomes of educative experience, are ways or arts for dealing with the environment. The difficulty with the mental discipline theory—and it was a big one in Dewey's estimation— is that it is false to the psychological facts. The origin of its greatest error lies in the fundamental dualism that has been characteristic of so much Western philosophy. This dualism, as expressed in Locke, for example, postulates an external world from which stimuli (sensations) impinge on a passive intellect. It also postulates an internal mind possessed of various powers of observation, memory, association, and so forth. Through the operations of these powers of the active intellect, complex ideas are constructed, and these are the objects of our knowledge. In theory then, the task of education is the development of these specific mental powers, or "faculties," through appropriate exercise.

In the first place, Dewey said, the existence of these original faculties is a pure myth. There simply are no such well-defined powers waiting to be trained. What does exist is a pool of native tendencies and impulses that take on specific and meaningful function as they are expressed in the environment and become habits. The more specific the training, the narrower and less flexible the habits that come from it.

For another thing, this theory is in error in the way it treats subject matter, for what the character of the content used in mental training is makes little difference, so long as it provides specific training. But, Dewey pointed out, we want people to remember and understand and make use of learned material that will contribute to their lives and work. This point is ignored in the theory of mental discipline, since this theory represents a failure to understand that the meaning of any subject matter—broad or narrow—lies in its relation to the social context in which experience goes on. Thus, although there is an important element of truth in the mental discipline approach, it turns out to be untenable because it is based on faulty psychological ideas.

What was Dewey's conception of aims in the educative process? We now know that not only did Dewey not accept the notion of some ultimate aim or purpose for education, which by necessity exists outside the process itself, but he considered such an idea fatal to effective educational procedures. But, many have asked, does this mean that education has no aims, aside from the vague criterion of "continued growth"?

Dewey did not consider continuity of growth a vague criterion. He did agree, however, that the aims that operate *within* the educative process are important and require close attention. He observed that it is meaningless to speak of some abstract process such as education as having aims. Abstractions do not have aims, but people do.[5] Educators, like people in any field of work, have certain things to accomplish, and they must work with the resources they have and in terms of the obstacles they must overcome. A teacher must formulate his aims around the children with whom he is working and the social context in which life goes on, and as Dewey observed, the point is to have "energies work together instead of against one another." The teacher who sets some aim without any reference either to the child's nature or the nature of society is as foolish as a farmer who sets the aim of growing some crop without any attention to the soil or climate.

In view of these matters then, good educational aims will first of all be conceived around the needs, native powers, and previous experience of the person to be educated. In the second place, an aim must be capable of giving guidance to the development of suitable method. It must function as a working idea that will guide the development of day-by-day operations. Dewey is strong in his belief that externally imposed aims not only cannot do these things, they even prevent the teacher's using his own common sense and ingenuity. And the wisest thing a teacher can do is to be forever on his guard against aims that are allegedly general and ultimate.

## NATURE OF THE CURRICULUM

We have examined the program of the Dewey Laboratory School in some detail and we know that the curriculum of that school was built around active enterprises, or active occupations to use Dewey's designation. We know also that in his early writings on education Dewey advocated an active curriculum as opposed to the passive acquisition of subject matters around which the traditional school organizes its program. In *Democracy and Education,* he restated this basic thesis on curriculum organization and elaborated it more fully.

Dewey pointed out that a great many kinds of active occupations had already found their way into the curriculum to some extent in the form of

---

[5] *Democracy and Education,* p. 125. Chapter 8 is an extended treatment of the subject of aims in education.

the fine and applied arts. Usually this work was carried on as something "extra" to the "regular curriculum" of subject matters and more often than not such activities were employed as a means of relief from the tedium of the regular studies. Today's essentialism still views them mainly in this light.

As Dewey saw it:

> The problem of the educator is to engage pupils in these activities in such ways that while manual skill and technical efficiency are gained and immediate satisfaction found in the work, together with preparation for later usefulness, these things shall be subordinated to *education*— that is, to intellectual results and the forming of a socialized disposition.[6]

Therefore, it is not enough to introduce active work into the school. The crucial matter is the way in which activities are used, and therefore certain procedures are ruled out immediately. Active occupations should never be devoted merely to copying some kind of model, for this effectively prevents the pupil from using his own judgment in relating means to ends —which is the intelligent factor in all enterprises. The copying of an assigned model or the meticulous following of prescribed steps is slavish, not liberating, to the child's intelligence. Further, active work should always be organized in *wholes,* and this was done in the Laboratory School in the form of enterprises—interest in achieving some foreseen purpose or outcome, devising plans for doing it, executing the plans, and observing the outcomes. This approach rules out isolated exercises. Whether isolated drill is with manual or with intellectual tools, the results are the same. The processes lack significance for the learner because they are isolated from the purposes that alone can give them meaning.

Active occupations are sound educational devices because they work in with the active, manipulative tendencies of childhood; but their greatest educational strength is that in representing basic modes of social life they provide the necessary context out of which systematic mastery of specialized knowledge can *develop*. It is a fact of history that the great organized bodies of knowledge had their origin in and developed out of the efforts of men to cope with basic social needs. Mathematics began with reckoning, keeping account of things, measuring, and so on, and after that became the rigorous discipline we know today. The natural sciences grew out of efforts to control and use the natural environment for human purposes. Literature and the fine arts developed as means of expression of personal and social feeling and the effort to preserve and interpret experience.

Now in a sense, this genetic development of experience, from the

---

[6] *Democracy and Education,* p. 231.

immediate and practical to the specialized and conceptual, through which the race has gone must be repeated by every individual, and there is no true short cut. This does not mean that the child must re-create the whole of civilization but it does mean that the development of knowledge in the human being is also a genetic process and the growth of meaning in an individual's cognitive structure in this sense is necessarily of the same character as the development of knowledge in a civilization.

In a passage in Chapter 14 of *Democracy and Education,* Dewey described the character of the genetic process of knowledge. This statement is often read over without its significance being appreciated. Actually, it is a significant statement in his philosophy of education.

> In its first estate, knowledge exists as the content of intelligent ability— power to do. This kind of subject matter or known material, is expressed in familiarity or acquaintance with things. Then this material gradually is surcharged and deepened through communicated knowledge or information. Finally, it is enlarged and worked over into rationally or logically organized material—that of the one who, relatively speaking, is expert in the subject.[7]

Concerning the first stage, Dewey pointed out that the knowledge people master first and retain longest is *how to do.* The first evidence we see in the behavior of young people of growth of understanding is their increasing tendency to take materials in the environment and use them to realize foreseen outcomes. The blocks that the child first manipulated at random become materials that are consciously shaped into a house or automobile or some other recognizable object. In this way comes acquaintance with things, their potentialities and their limitations, and this leads to the kind of wisdom that is widely recognized as being associated with the intelligent direction of life activities. "Only in education," said Dewey, "never in the life of farmer, sailor, merchant, physician, or laboratory experimenter, does knowledge mean primarily a store of information aloof from doing."[8]

Therefore, since the natural development of knowledge begins with intelligent doing, and since the manipulative, constructive activities in which children engage are pregnant with educational possibilities, Dewey insisted that arts and occupations should form the first stages of the school curriculum. This idea was followed in the Dewey Laboratory School.

The second stage begins early in the life of the child and overlaps and blends with the first. Learning at the human level is always social. Not only does the child carry on his activities in the presence of others and with

---

[7] *Democracy and Education,* pp. 216–17.
[8] Ibid.

their cooperation; the very materials and ideas with which he works are social products. This social context provides the conditions necessary for communicated experience. He learns from his peers and he also learns particularly from those adults whose business is the welfare and development of children—parents and teachers. The enterprises in which the child is engaged provide a context in which new ideas can be communicated, ideas that illuminate and extend the meaning of knowledge already acquired.

This communication of meaning goes on throughout the life of an individual, but childhood and youth are particularly strategic in this respect. Dewey never doubted that communication is the lifeblood of education, nor did he denigrate the value of the preserved experience we call subject matter. He did insist that certain criteria must be met if communication is to be meaningful to the pupil and thus effective in developing his own awareness and understanding. The point is not how the communicating is done—by oral telling, by printed materials, or by the newer technological devices. There are many ways to communicate; some are old, some are new. The test any item of communicated information must meet is:

> Does it grow naturally out of some question with which the student is concerned? Does it fit into his more direct acquaintance so as to increase its efficacy and deepen its meaning? If it meets these two requirements it is educative. The amount heard or read is of no importance—the more the better, *provided* the student has a need for it and can apply it in some situation of his own.[9]

Thus, according to Dewey, the reason so much of the communication that goes on in school is fruitless is that it is done outside any context that enables the learner to relate the new material to his previous accomplishments.

The third stage in the development of knowledge in the individual *emerges* as a result of his progression through the first two stages. Out of the continuum of experience that begins in childhood with familiarity with things and is expressed as intelligent ability to do, and through the communication of meanings that broaden and illuminate experience, there comes an increasing degree of organization and synthesis that represents mastery of knowledge. But this third stage is reached *only as the conditions of the first two are satisfied.*

This, said Dewey, is the natural, genetic course that the development of knowledge takes. The school can respect it and work with it, or it can ignore it and work against it, *but the school cannot change it.* This point constitutes one of Dewey's chief protests against essentialism. The tradi-

---

9   *Democracy and Education*, p. 219.

tional school begins exactly end around. Instead of beginning with the native powers and tendencies of the child and seeking to shape them into increasing mastery and power, the school begins with a series of subject matters already organized and synthesized by somebody besides the learner. The school sees its function as transmitting these subject matters to the child in as intact a form as possible. External imposition of this kind is never very successful, and it is the source of most of the difficulties the traditional school has to endure and that it has never succeeded in coping with adequately.

Dewey was joined in this protest by William James, another distinguished psychologist and philosopher who played an important role in developing the basic arguments against the conservative tradition.[10] James, speaking to the teachers of Cambridge as a psychologist, advised them:

> Begin with the line of his [the child's] native interests, and offer him objects that have some immediate connection with these.
> Next, step by step, connect with these first objects and experiences the later objects and ideas which you wish to instill. Associate the new with the old in some natural and telling way, so that the interest, being shed along from point to point, finally suffuses the entire system of objects of thought.[11]

Thus, James also inveighed against the formalism of the education of his day and believed that the improvements in pedagogy that were so badly needed could be had by reinterpreting the teaching-learning process in the light of experimental psychology.

A second aspect of the curriculum concerns the part organized subject matter has to play in the educative process. Dewey did not believe that subject matters are to be transmitted directly to the young, or even that they can be. He saw the great organized subject matters as *means* for carrying on enterprises and dealing with problems successfully. As he saw it, this is the function they perform in every other area of life—except in the typical school.

Dewey disputed the belief, one that has always been a principal plank in the essentialist platform, that some subject matters possess an intrinsic worth that makes them desirable regardless of any particular set of circumstances. These subjects, says the conservative, must be taught to everybody because their very nature makes them good for everybody. To deny this, he says, is to denigrate the greatest achievements of the human intellect. Not so, says Dewey:

---

[10] James's contributions to the development of pragmatic philosophy are considered in the next chapter.

[11] William James, *Talks to Teachers on Psychology: and to Students on Some of Life's Ideals* (New York: Henry Holt and Co., 1906), pp. 95–96.

It is no reflection on the nutritive quality of beefsteak that it is not fed to infants. It is not an invidious reflection on trigonometry that we do not teach it in the first or fifth grade of school. It is not the subject *per se* that is educative or that is conducive to growth. There is no subject that is in and of itself, or without regard to the stage of growth attained by the learner, such that inherent educational value can be attributed to it. . . . There is no such thing as educational value in the abstract.[12]

The value that organized subject matter has lies in its instrumental potentialities. It is valuable as it enables us to deal with the perplexities and problems of our own experience for it is a bridge between the past, which is settled and secure, to the present and future, which are contingent and problematic. From the standpoint of the curriculum of formal education, matters must be arranged so that pupils engage in the *use* of ideas to plan and conduct enterprises and to deal with the problems that arise within the content of these activities. In this way, Dewey maintained, the native intellectual potential of the child develops. And this was one of the main ideas underlying the program of the Laboratory School.

Specifically, Dewey regarded history and geography, or what we today call in a somewhat broader sense the social studies, as the important subject matters of elementary education. As he saw it, the value of these studies lies in their enriching and liberating the more direct experience of the child. Since the occupations that are the starting point of the curriculum are themselves social in origin, participation in these activities provides a context for meaningful communication of accomplishments already achieved by the race. The delicate pedagogical problem is to introduce these into the experience of the child so that they connect with his own stock of ideas and form a solid part of them, and thus become resources for understanding and assimilating new ideas.[13]

Dewey himself regarded the economic and industrial phases of history as far superior to political and military history. The economic and industrial aspects are concerned with the increasing control men have achieved over nature, and the growth of power and liberty that have resulted. He recommends also that stress should be placed on intellectual history. The progress of civilization has come about through the use of intelligence, and the great achievements of the race are not military conquests or the rise and fall of dynasties but the inventions and discoveries that have

---

[12] *Experience and Education*, pp. 45–46.

[13] The problem is more delicate than many realize and this is likely true even at the college level, where heed is virtually never given it. William James, one of the most famous of American teachers of philosophy, once observed: "I think I have seen college students unfitted forever for 'philosophy' from having taken that study up a year too soon." James, *Talks to Teachers*, p. 149.

made possible the rise of man from savagery to civilization. Again, this was the general theme around which the curriculum of the Laboratory School was organized.

The other subject matter that Dewey thought important in the curriculum was science. He saw a close connection between intellectual history and the history of scientific development. Dewey proposed that the curriculum be organized around the broad social theme of the development of civilization through progress in inventions and discoveries. The significant episode in this development was the advent and increasing perfection of scientific method. The evolution of modern science, therefore, must be a main concern in the school's program.

Dewey knew that science can be taught in a way as stereotyped as the older subjects are taught in the traditional curriculum. The view that the teaching of science is a process of transmitting information about the concepts and facts established by prior scientific inquiries leads to the same isolation of subject matter from the experience of the learner that Dewey had already criticized in connection with the older subjects in the curriculum. The description he gave of the contemporary situation is strongly reminiscent of our school today:

> Pupils begin their study of science with texts in which the subject is organized into topics according to the order of the specialist. Technical concepts with their definitions, are introduced at the outset. Laws are introduced at a very early stage, with at best a few indications of the way in which they were arrived at. The pupils learn a "science" instead of learning the scientific way of treating the familiar material of ordinary experience. The method of the advanced student dominates college teaching; the approach of the college is transferred into the high school, and so on down the line, with such omissions as may make the subject easier.[14]

Dewey had the highest possible opinion of the power of scientific method. To him the method of science was the method of intelligence *par excellence.* He sought to make scientific method the basis for educational methodology. The power of science derives from the basic activities of observation, reflection, and testing of ideas. The subject matter this method yields is the most dependable and trustworthy knowledge it is possible to achieve. "Both logically and educationally," he said, "science is the perfecting of knowing, its last stage." [15]

Dewey's protest against the way the essentialist approaches the teach-

---

[14] *Democracy and Education,* p. 257. Whether one judges Dewey's conception of the place of science in the curriculum as right or wrong, it is hard to deny that this description is an accurate account of much that exists at the present time.

[15] Ibid., p. 256.

ing of science was a repetition of his protest against all education that was conceived primarily as transmission of information. The rigor of scientific form is what the teaching process works toward, not what it begins with. What it should begin with are the familiar phenomena encountered in the home, the garden, and the fields and woods. Experience of this kind yields the subject matter that increasingly can be treated by the rigorous methods of observation, reflection, and testing. Communicated experience plays the same role here as it does in the development of any subject matter. Out of this continuum of experience come the habits of mind and the methods of approach to problems that characterize the scientific mind.

## PRINCIPLES OF METHOD

Dewey's approach to educational method was formulated during the early years at Chicago. In *My Pedagogic Creed,* he stated the proposition that was to guide the later development of his ideas on pedagogical method: "I believe that the question of method is ultimately reducible to the question of the order of development of the child's powers and interests. The law for presenting and treating material is the law implicit within the child's own nature."

His protest against the methodology of essentialism was directed at the dualism of subject matter *and* learner. The way the essentialist sees the situation is that on the one hand there is certain essential subject matter and on the other hand the prospective learner. The methodological problem is how to bring these together. As Dewey described it:

> Subject matter then becomes a ready-made systematized classification of the facts and principles of the world of nature and man. Method then has for its province a consideration of the ways in which this antecedent subject matter may be best presented to and impressed upon the mind; or, a consideration of the ways in which the mind may be externally brought to bear upon the matter so as to facilitate its acquisition and possession.[16]

This dualism of content *and* method is precisely the starting point of the quarrel between the supporters of methods courses for teacher training and subject-matter specialists, who have a low opinion of any alleged science of method. On the one hand, there is the assumption that methods of teaching anything can be deduced from some psychological or other scientific theories of mind without any consideration for the subject matters these methods may be applied to. On the other hand, there

---

[16]  Ibid., p. 193.

is the assumption that an organized subject matter has a logic inherent in it and a person who is proficient in that subject matter has all he needs to teach it to somebody else. This controversy is particularly bitter today, as the most cursory examination of the literature of essentialism will show, and ironically enough, the blame for the proliferation of isolated methods courses is often laid on progressivism and particularly on Dewey. Actually, as early as the publication of *Democracy and Education*, Dewey protested not only against the pedagogical dualism of subject and method, but against the underlying philosophical dualism inherent in essentialism.[17]

To Dewey, the way out of the impasse was to reconsider the learner's experience and the parts subject matter and method play in it. The developing experience of the child is the central concern of education, but experience is a process involving both internal and external factors. Experience is always *of* something. We can make a distinction between method and the material acted upon, just as we can make a distinction between eating and food, and sometimes for technical purposes it is useful to make such a distinction. The fatal error, however, is to forget that this distinction is conceptual and not existentially real.

When we come down to it, a method is simply an effective way of using material to realize some objective. This is universally recognized, except perhaps for learning in school. Under Dewey's view, method from the standpoint of the teacher meant effective ways of using the native resources of the pupil, including the fruits of his previous experience, together with the material and social forces in the environment, to further his intellectual development. From the standpoint of the learner, method meant the way in which things and ideas are used effectively to realize some desired objective, which in itself leads on to other desired objectives. The key to understanding the true nature of method lies in grasping the nature of experience. "Experience," said Dewey, "is not a combination of mind and world, subject and object, method and subject matter, but is a single continuous interaction of a great diversity . . . of energies."[18] Here is the nub of Dewey's approach to method.

The two working ideas to be used in the formulation of educational method are *interaction and continuity* and both these concepts refer to Dewey's idea of the nature of experience. In *My Pedagogic Creed*, he had insisted that education, which takes place within experience, always involves two factors: the child's own native impulsive behavior and the environment in which these native powers function and which gives them meaning. Experience then, in its most fundamental sense, is the interaction

---

[17] Both objective idealism and realism involve the dualism of mind *and* matter and these are the two philosophical traditions most closely related to essentialism.

[18] *Democracy and Education*, pp. 196–97.

of a living thing with the environment in which it lives and by means of which it lives. Experience is a continuum; it is serial in character. The events that make it up are not discrete and isolated; rather, succeeding events grow out of and are conditioned by antecedent events. Every experience inevitably affects future experiences, sometimes for good and sometimes not.

Now what we often call intelligence develops within this experimental continuum. There are many definitions for this slippery word, and Dewey suggested that it is better viewed as a modifier rather than a substantive. "Intelligent" behavior is that behavior that puts one in control of the environment and hence of his own experience. Our behavior is intelligent when proposed actions are determined in the light of anticipated consequences. Intelligence therefore signifies ability to relate means and ends; to regulate conduct with reference to objectives desired but not yet achieved. Ability to foresee the probable course of events depends on the fruits of previous experience—either the fruits of direct personal experience or the communicated experience of others, and generally both of these. This is the function information (subject matter) has in experience. It represents the funded capital an individual has with which to meet the necessities and perplexities that arise in his own affairs.

Experience is not necessarily educative, although one episode in some way affects subsequent experience. When an experience is educative, it is continuous with previous experience; resources are available for the person to deal with the situation in an intelligent (as opposed to a random) fashion. The person involved in the situation makes forward and backward connections among events; he discerns the relations between means and consequences that are operative in the situation; by reflection he decides on a course of action, and having undertaken it, sees the results of his decision. Out of experience of this kind come changes in attitude, outlook, and behavior, which in Dewey's words is a transformation and reconstruction of experience.

Whatever conditions favor this kind of experience are beneficial; whatever conditions hinder it are miseducative and should be avoided. Here again is Dewey's protest against the methodology of the traditional school. In his view, that school created the separation of content from method, thinking from acting, school experience from life experience. The conservative tradition in education fails to achieve proper results because it fails to see that experience is an interactive continuum in which continuity is the key to meaningful learning. Educational method that truly respects the real nature of experience will lead to a conception of education Dewey described in this way:

> Education takes the individual while he is relatively plastic, before he
> has become so indurated by isolated experiences as to be rendered hope-

lessly empirical in his habit of mind. The attitude of childhood is naïve, wondering, experimental; the world of man and nature is new. Right methods of education preserve and perfect this attitude, and thereby short-circuit for the individual the slow progress of the race, eliminating the waste that comes from inert routine and lazy dependence on the past.[19]

In an earlier publication, Dewey had described the ideal school by comparing the program of such a school with the kind of experience a child has in a good home. An ideal home involves parents who are intelligent enough to understand the nature and needs of childhood, and who involve the child in the activities of the family and use these as a means for furthering the intellectual and social development of the child. This home would have facilities in which the child could engage in active work in constructing and experimenting. It would be situated in a place such that gardens and woods, and open fields would be nearby and these too, would be used for intellectual growth.[20] There are very few homes, of course, that can provide opportunities of this kind. But in Dewey's estimation, an idealized home experience furnished a proper model for what the school would be if it based its work on a correct understanding of experience and grasped the significance of this for educational method.

Educational method is the means through which the teacher arranges the environment so that the experience of the child continuously develops and broadens and the native powers of the child are nurtured and formed into flexible and functional habits. This means that educational methodology must take account of the many-sided nature of human development: intellectual, moral, and esthetic. But it is characteristic of Dewey's educational thought, as well as his general philosophical position, that experience at its best is continuous, and the moral and esthetic aspects of it are pervaded with the intellectual, for in these facets of experience there is always some element of meaning and therefore of thought. When the intellectual is arbitrarily separated from the rest of experience, Dewey said, "practical activity is mechanical and routine, morals are blind and arbitrary, and esthetic appreciation is sentimental gush. . . . We state emphatically *that upon its intellectual side education consists in the formation of wide-awake, careful, thorough habits of thinking.*"[21]

Therefore, in Dewey's opinion, an important problem in educational method was to discover the conditions that stimulate pupils to think. If teachers understand the psychology of thought, they will be in a position to provide the kinds of opportunity needed for the formation of the habits

---

19   John Dewey, *How We Think*, 2nd ed. (Boston: D. C. Heath and Co., 1933), p. 202.
20   See *The School and Society*, pp. 34 ff.
21   *How We Think*, p. 78.

and attitudes involved in reflection. It is true that most theories of education in some way stress the importance of thinking and see an important role of the school as that of "teaching people how to think." Dewey's protest was never against the idea that one purpose of the school is to teach students to think. His protest was against what he considered erroneous conceptions of how reflective thought affects experience.

In most educational traditions, including essentialism, reflective thought appears to be conceived either as a vague kind of psychic energy that the pupil can turn on or off at will, or as some separate faculty or group of faculties that can be brought to bear through will. In Dewey's view, both of these conceptions—and all variations on them—were false to the facts of experience.

Reflective thought is a behavior people exhibit when they meet situations they cannot deal with on the basis of habit. Habit gives continuity to experience and the power to adjust to the environment and control it. But the environment is never completely stable. In the experience of every person, situations develop that are indeterminate and disunified. These situations, because of their existential character, are perplexing and problematic to the person involved. *They are problematic because habit no longer suffices to guide behavior.* In the literal sense, *the person caught up in these circumstances does not know what to do.* Dewey illustrated the "problematic situation" in this way:

> A man traveling in an unfamiliar region comes to a branching of the road. Having no sure knowledge to fall back upon, he is brought to a standstill of hesitation and suspense. Which road is right? And how shall his perplexity be resolved? There are but two alternatives: he must either blindly and arbitrarily take his course, trusting to luck for the outcome, or he must discover grounds for the conclusion that a given road is right.[22]

In the face of the forked road, which for Dewey symbolized all the indeterminate conditions that we experience, we have an option. We can act blindly, trusting to chance, or Providence, that the decision we make will turn out favorably; *or we can act on the basis of intelligence.* That is to say, we can regulate our behavior by reflection. The service that reflective thought offers is making some plan of action that promises best, so far as can be seen, to resolve the problematic and doubtful character of the situation—in terms of Dewey's example, to "choose the right fork of the road."

The data inherent in the situation itself are insufficient to yield an idea; if they were sufficient, the situation would not be problematic because

---

[22] Ibid., p. 13.

habit would be adequate to guide behavior. What a person has to fall back on, therefore, is the fund of relevant knowledge that is the product of previous experience. Here again, the importance of the continuity of experience is stressed. If the person does not have resources adequate for dealing with the situation intelligently, he is forced to some more primitive level of behavior. In Dewey's words, "confusion remains pure confusion."

> Even when a child (or a grown-up) has a problem, it is wholly futile to urge him to think when he has no prior experiences that involve some of the same conditions.[23]

One function of reflective thought, then, is identifying the problematic character of situations that disrupt the even flow of experience and developing possible ideas or plans for some action that will resolve the indeterminate and disunified character of the situation. However, in most instances we think of more than one possible course of action, which is to say that several ideas compete for acceptance and action. A primary difference between impulsive behavior and behavior controlled by thought is that in the latter, overt action is forestalled so that possibilities can be evaluated in terms of relevant data and probable consequences. Our reflective thought processes enable us to choose among the possible alternatives and adopt as a course of action the plan that promises best to change the problematic and indeterminate situation. Ultimately we must act if the situation is to be altered, and if our plan works out we can know that it was adequate for the situation. By putting the idea to action, we have tested it as an idea and we have found it either adequate or inadequate.

This was Dewey's analysis of the role reflective thought plays in experience. In his view, every complete act of thought involved in some measure the following steps:

1. An indeterminate situation arises. This situation disrupts the course of experience because prior experience in the form of habit is inadequate to deal with it. The presence of this situation stimulates reflective behavior. When there is no disturbing state of affairs, there is no thought because habit is sufficient.

2. The person (or persons) involved perceive the situation *in its problematic character.* This is to say, they are able to structure the elements of the situation sufficiently to see what the elements are and what impediments must be overcome if the situation is to be changed.

3. Ideas are evolved that can guide action that must be undertaken if the situation is to be changed. In this sense, *ideas are plans for acting.*

---

[23] Ibid., pp. 15–16.

4. The ideas evolved are subjected to logical elaboration, which in essence is the effort to determine what outcomes can be foreseen as probable if a given idea is acted on. As a result of this operation, some idea is chosen to be acted on.

5. The operations indicated in the idea are performed. The character of these operations depends on the problem. They change the character of the situation, and if they produce the consequences anticipated, *the idea is warranted*. It has "paid off." [24]

There are many connections here between Dewey's analysis of thinking and his conception of educational method. The school is always concerned with the intellectual growth of its students, but it is also concerned with the ethical and esthetic phases of experience. To Dewey, experience was unitary and not fragmented and the ethical and esthetic, since they too involved apprehension of meaning, were pervaded with an intellectual quality, that is to say, with thought.

Accordingly, from the standpoint of the intellectual side, the methodology of education should proceed so as to facilitate activity in school that involves problem solving through inquiry. This should begin with the child's very first experience in school. Ideally, it would have its real beginning in the home, but over this the school has no real control. Within the school itself certain conditions will have to be met:

First, the activities that go on in the school must be such that they stimulate thought and develop in the child habits of acting on thinking. The program must be an active affair, for genuine thinking always involves action of some kind. The activities must be arranged so that pupils encounter problematic situations that arise naturally out of the work itself and are not arbitrarily imposed by the teacher.

Second, the school must respect the continuity of experience. The activities and materials that are introduced must mesh with the experience already had by the pupils but yet lead on to other experience that will challenge without frustrating. This Dewey regarded as one of the most delicate and difficult aspects of educational method.

Third, communicated knowledge (information, facts, subject matter, and so forth) must be given in a relevant context if it is to have any meaning for the learner; note carefully that *the relevance is to the experience of the*

---

[24] This formulation of a complete act of thought is one of Dewey's best-known contributions to psychology and logic. The most complete treatment of it from the psychological and pedagogical standpoint is in his *How We Think*. Chapter 12 in *Democracy and Education* deals with thinking in the educational process. Certain logical aspects will be considered in the next chapter.

*pupil and the situation in which he is involved,* not to the teacher's sense of logic or some organization allegedly inherent in the subject matter itself.

An important emergent of such experience is a constellation of attitudes and abilities that Dewey referred to as critical intelligence. This refers not to an attitude of destructive criticism or to the easy scepticism one sometimes finds among young people; it points rather to an attitude that ideas are plans for considered action and that as ideas they are to be judged not by their origins or their place in tradition, but by their fruits.

Dewey believed that the traditional school did not provide such experiential opportunities and he also believed that the traditional school did not really value critical intelligence. Many followers of the progressive movement joined him in this belief. Essentialists have always extolled the importance of thought and the development of the intellect; Dewey protested that they did not, however, consciously provide for it in their schools. On the other hand, the Laboratory School under his direction sought through a curriculum based on active occupations organized as enterprises to provide the conditions in which the reflective powers of the child were developed through organized inquiry.

## SCHOOL AND SOCIETY

As early as the time *My Pedagogic Creed* was published, Dewey had advanced the thesis that expressed his conception of the relation of the school to society: "I believe that education is the fundamental method of social progress and reform." By this expression, he not only was stating his personal belief but also was restating a fundamental part of the American social tradition. This sentiment cannot be attributed solely to social liberalism for it is so much a part of the American mind that many conservatives agree with it also. We grant that the liberal's interpretation of the idea may be somewhat different from the interpretation by his conservative counterpart.

Be this as it may, in advancing this proposition in 1897 Dewey assuredly was echoing the sentiments of the liberal reform group. The liberals were calling insistently for a reform of the schools that would reinstate the democratic ideal as the ethical basis for education. Dewey knew that certain ideas needed to be reinterpreted to make them meaningful for a society whose character had already been transformed by the industrial revolution.

Individualism has always been a cherished ideal of the American tradition, and this ideal had two sources. One was the economic pattern of life in America in the eighteenth and early part of the nineteenth century. In this agrarian society, a degree of economic equality obtained that had seldom, if ever, existed before. It has been estimated that at the time of the American Revolution more than 90 percent of all heads of family were freeholders, owning and working their own land with the assistance of their immediate families. Wealth and success were achieved largely in proportion to the ingenuity and effort of the individual. It is small wonder that observers of the early American scene were always impressed by the aggressive individualism of the American.

The spirit of capitalism contributed to the spirit of individualism and reinforced it. Capitalism, reinforced as it was by the Protestant ethic, glorified the same qualities of independence, thrift, and individual effort. "Getting ahead" was the credo of American life, and in view of the basic economic pattern, occupational and social mobility were genuine realities. The schools were pervaded with this spirit of individualism, and as the influence of organized education grew, the school became another important means to individual success.

The conditions that produced this "rugged individualism" were transformed by the industrial revolution, and the transition to a culture focused on technology and urban living. But the old sentiments prevailed and the individualism that had found true expression in the economic and social conditions of preindustrial life now was expressed more and more in pressure politics and the activities of myriad groups representing special interests. Out of this condition has grown the universal plaint that has now become an important theme in literature, in psychology, and in some philosophy—"the lost individual."

As Dewey saw it, the trouble stems from the effort to retain in an increasingly corporate and integrated society a conception of individuality that is the product of an age irretrievably gone. Since this effort has proved itself to be in vain, many people find no alternative except to sit in sackcloth and ashes and bewail the fate of man in the modern world.

There is an alternative, Dewey believed, that goes beyond this kind of hopelessness. The solution, he said, is to develop a new individualism that will be to the modern age what the old individualism was in its own proper time.[25] The trouble is not that modern man finds himself involved in numerous associations and relationships—far more than men have ever been involved in before. The real difficulty is that these associations do not function harmoniously and nurture the emotional and imaginative aspects of individuality. The reason they do not is that there is lack of harmony within society itself. The situation appears circular and vicious,

---

[25] This matter is discussed in many of Dewey's writings. The most concentrated and systematic treatment of it will be found in *Individualism Old and New* (New York: Minton, Balch and Co., 1930).

true enough, but Dewey maintained it would yield if intelligence were brought to bear on it. In this, the school has an important role.

The school, as Dewey believed, would contribute to a new individualism by cultivating in children and young people the method of critical intelligence. To employ intelligence in one's life means to face the facts as they are and to grasp the consequences they portend. There is another aspect of acceptance and commitment, which we usually think of in terms of emotions and will. These are not separate and disconnected elements, however; any effective commitment involves intellectual acceptance or denial. The alternative to intelligence, if in truth there is one, can be little other than a kind of abject irrationalism that often becomes pathological. In view of considerations of this kind, Dewey believed that the kind of educational policies he advocated would, if intelligently put to practice in the school, help to cultivate a new individualism that would be as worthy as the older one was in its day.

But this role of the school, as important as it is, cannot be the whole story, for the school does not exist apart from the rest of society and students live in an environment more extensive than the school. This brings us again to the role of the school in social change. Writing in a time when the country was still in the throes of the Great Depression and when the outbreak of the Second World War was only two years in the future, Dewey described three possibilities: One of these was that those responsible for the schools should accede to the prevailing cultural confusion and unsettlement and simply drift with the tide. Such a choice is blind and unintelligent, he pointed out, but it is a choice. A second possibility was to ally the schools with the new developments—scientific, technological and cultural—that were transforming society and help the young to develop the understanding and intellectual power needed in the task of social reconstruction lying ahead. The third alternative was that educators should adopt an intelligent conservatism and seek to make the school an agent in conserving the old order.[26]

Dewey rejected the first possibility completely, seeing in it only the seeds of social dissolution and ultimate disaster. The third he saw as an intelligent choice but one that the progress of events was making more and more untenable. He accepted the second as the role the school should play. He was careful to say, however, that he was not recommending that the schools should enter the political arena and take sides there. "I am not talking about parties," he wrote, "I am talking about social forces and their

---

[26] See "Education and Social Change," *Social Frontier* 3 (May 1937): 237. This has been reprinted in Joseph Ratner, ed., *Intelligence in the Modern World: John Dewey's Philosophy* (New York: Modern Library, 1939), pp. 691 ff.

movements." [27] His conviction was that the school, by developing social intelligence and awareness in individuals, could make its greatest contribution to social reconstruction.

While this proposal appears to have been squarely within the mainstream of American liberalism, Dewey's position was a target for criticism from various quarters because the times were desperate. Some criticism naturally came from the conservatives, who deplored the idea that the school should be other than a conserving, stabilizing force in society.

Dewey's conception of the role of the school in social change was also criticized by others who found his liberalism inadequate for the times. In the 1930s, there was considerable sentiment expressed for teachers' allying themselves with the "class struggle," as that term was understood in the Marxist-Leninist-Stalinist sense. The class concept and the irreconcilability of social classes, it was argued, would furnish the guideline for the work of the schools. Teachers must become conscious of their own class status. They must see themselves as members of the exploited working class and they must throw their weight and the weight of the schools in favor of the destruction of the old order and the establishment of the new.

This proposal obviously originated outside the stream of American liberal thought and is antithetical to basic beliefs of liberalism. But other criticism came from those who were squarely in the liberal camp. George Counts, for example, who was associated with the liberal protest movement, but who was by no means friendly to the "child-centered school" espoused by many progressives, lashed out against the lack of any positive conception of social welfare within the progressive movement. As Counts saw it, the progressive schools of the 'thirties were dominated by upper-middle-class people whose liberalism was at best lukewarm and who had no grasp of the great issues of the day. In his judgment, they were "romantic sentimentalists, but with a sharp eye on the main chance." These people, he said, are not competent to guide the affairs of the schools, particularly in a time of crisis.

Counts's call was for the teachers to use the power they had to influence the attitudes and beliefs of the young in definite conscious fashion and in the directing of far-reaching social reform. The old haggling over whether the school should impose certain beliefs on children and indoctrinate them in these beliefs should be shelved permanently. The child is always imposed on by somebody; the real question should be by whom and for what.[28]

---

[27] Ibid.

[28] See George S. Counts, *Dare the School Build a New Social Order?* (New York: John Day Co., 1932).

This emphasis on social reconstructionism, which was always present in the progressive movement and which received its second big emphasis in the troubled decade before the second great war, called forth conservatism's perhaps most violent reaction to progressivism. This threat was so great to conservatives that conservative literature, particularly of the 1950s, was full of polemics against the idea of the school as an agent of social reconstruction.[29]

Dewey criticized many of the proposals of the social reconstructionists. He did not question the depth or the sincerity of their liberalism, nor did he underestimate the gravity of the situation in which the country found itself. But his conception of society indicated that the school alone could never determine the direction and character of social change. He held that the school is only one of a great number of institutions; that education, while a necessary condition for intelligent social change, is not a sufficient condition; and that schools will help social reconstruction most if they will do what they are really equipped to do—to help the young, through appropriate experience in school, to develop sensitivity to the great problems of the time and to cultivate powers of critical intelligence, which alone can provide a trustworthy guide for the future.

Mention should be made of another important figure in the progressive movement who, like Counts, also found serious weaknesses within it. Boyd H. Bode, who for many years was professor of education at Ohio State University, sought to clarify certain key ideas current in the progressive movement, believing that their popular acceptance and use had obscured their meaning and converted them into empty slogans. On most of the main issues in progressivism, Bode and Dewey found themselves in agreement. Bode's criticism was for the most part leveled against the misinterpretation of such concepts as the doctrine of interest, pupil needs, and continued growth as the purpose of the educative process.

Bode maintained that in the fourth decade of the century progressive education had reached a crossroad and was confronted with a choice. The choice, he said, lay between "becoming the avowed exponent of democracy or becoming a set of ingenious devices for tempering the wind to the shorn lamb."[30] Genuine democracy, he maintained, must have a distinctive educational system and this system must have as its basis a psychology

---

[29] It may seem to many people in retrospect that the clarion call of the social reconstructionists was the ultimate in political naiveté but it was not so regarded at the time. A student reading Counts's *Dare the School Build a New Social Order?* today may well find the title the most radical part of the document, but in its issue for July 17, 1935, *Time* warned against the emergence of a "pedagogic party" that would give Columbia University control of the United States. By far the best account of this fascinating period in the progressive movement is in Cremin, chap. 6.

[30] *Progressive Education at the Crossroads* (New York: Newson and Co., 1938), p. 26.

in which knowledge and truth are seen as functions in controlling experience, and an ethical theory centered around improving human life through shared effort.[31] Democracy, Bode thought, is always in conflict with absolutism in both the social and the philosophical sense. "The center of any educational program which professes to be democratic," he said, "must be the irreconcilable conflict between democracy and absolutism."

Bode's call was for the progressive movement to become more rigorous in its philosophical foundations and to face squarely that the initial successes of the progressive schools were being undermined by lack of awareness of the decisive relation between social liberalism and progressive principles of education. Uncritical acceptance and lack of understanding of "education as growth," "we learn by doing," "the needs of pupils," which by the thirties had become slogans, were corrupting and weakening the progressive protest, he held. Much of the criticism in *Crossroads* is similar to that in Dewey's *Experience and Education*. But Bode's criticism, like that of Dewey, came too late and fell on either deaf or uncomprehending ears. By the time Bode had published his discerning critique, the initial progressive protest had about run its course. World War II was only a year away and with it the beginnings of an era of resurgent conservatism.

## SUMMARY

Dewey advanced certain significant pedagogical doctrines in his voluminous writings on educational theory. His was the most authentic philosophical voice to be heard in the development of the liberal protest. Many others marched under the banners of social and educational liberalism, but overall he was the acknowledged leader of the procession.

Dewey's educational philosophy was an organic element in his whole approach to philosophy. His basic educational views took shape along with his ideas in logic, psychology, and ethics. Certainly the beliefs he held about educational matters cannot be considered simply as logical inferences from some predetermined ideas in logic, ethics or any other field of academic philosophy, though he found his studies in the various branches of philosophy to be fruitful sources for his ideas on education.

The full impact of Dewey's educational philosophy can be sensed only by understanding how it relates to his interpretations of other philosophic questions. The philosophic tradition of pragmatism made important

---

[31]   Bode's major contribution to psychology was *How We Learn* (Boston: D. C. Heath and Co., 1940). This volume was a revision of an earlier work, *Conflicting Psychologies of Learning*. An important contribution to educational philosophy is his *Modern Educational Theories* (New York: Macmillan Co., 1927).

contributions to the progressive protest against essentialism and to Dewey's educational philosophy. The key ideas on which Dewey based his educational philosophy have a larger significance outside of educational theory. These concepts are (1) the nature of experience; (2) the significance of meaning and the pragmatic conception of truth; (3) logic as inquiry and its relation to scientific method, the nature of value, and the process of valuation; (4) the ontology of pragmatism.

# chapter SEVEN

# AMERICAN PRAGMATISM AND THE LIBERAL PROTEST

*I only desire to point out how impossible it is
that we should have an idea in our minds which
relates to anything but conceived sensible effects
of things. Our idea of anything is our idea of
its sensible effects; and if we fancy that we have
any other we deceive ourselves, and mistake a
mere sensation accompanying the thought
for a part of the thought itself.*

— CHARLES SANDERS PEIRCE

As the nineteenth century drew to its close, two protest movements in philosophy developed. Initially, these movements were largely protests against the domination of Absolute idealism over Western philosophy, and indeed its domination over much of the intellectual life of the West. One philosophical protest took the form of a resurgence of philosophical realism and the emergence of a group who called themselves the New Realists. We have already considered the relation of the resurgence of realism in philosophy to the conservative tradition in education. We turn now to the other protest movement, which was to have the most far-reaching effects on philosophy and on the philosophy of education. The name we use for this philosophical tradition is *pragmatism*.

## DEVELOPMENT OF PRAGMATISM

The main contributions to pragmatic philosophy were made by Americans, and although this philosophy is not exclusively American, it is usually thought of here as well as abroad as peculiarly American in its spirit and in its principal doctrines. The great names in this tradition are Charles Sanders Peirce (1839–1914), William James (1842–1910), and John Dewey (1859–1952). We have already considered some of the salient facts in Dewey's long career in philosophy and the contributions he made to the philosophy of American liberalism and to progressivism in educational theory. James, too, had an interest in educational theory and was himself one of the greatest of American teachers. We have not given any attention to Peirce because his effect on the liberal protest in education was indirect, in the form of fundamental contributions to pragmatic philosophy rather than to educational theory. Both James and Dewey acknowledged their profound indebtedness to Peirce and considered him the source of many of their own ideas.

Peirce, himself the son of an eminent mathematical scholar at Harvard, was thoroughly trained not only in mathematics and logic but also in the sciences, particularly the physical sciences. He was also accomplished in philosophy and by his own account had studied Kant so thoroughly that he knew *The Critique of Pure Reason* practically by heart.[1]

In the 1870s, a group of men in Cambridge were in the habit of meeting at frequent intervals to discuss philosophical questions, particularly questions concerning the impact of science and scientific method on philosophy. Peirce was a regular member of this group, as William James was. Also among the members were Oliver Wendell Holmes, who later was to become the famed liberal justice on the United States Supreme Court, and

---

[1] Justus Buchler, ed., *Philosophical Writings of Peirce* (New York: Dover Publications, 1955), chap. 1.

Chauncy Wright, who was a staunch advocate of the liberal philosophy of John Stuart Mill. Members of the group called their association The Metaphysical Club. This was supposed to be ironic because the general spirit of the group was in the direction of scientific considerations and away from metaphysical speculation. It was at meetings of this club that Peirce first presented two papers that were greatly important in the development of pragmatic philosophy.[2]

Many of the same conditions that were responsible for the emergence and development of pragmatism were involved in the resurgence of philosophical realism. A responsible factor was the influence of science and scientific method and, particularly in the case of Dewey, the scientific revolution in biology that was initiated by the publication of Darwin's *Origin of Species*. Some members of The Metaphysical Club were corresponding with Darwin and all of them were greatly interested in the impact evolutionary theory was having on science, religion, and philosophy. As one historian said, "Darwin's *Origin of Species* had come into the theological world like a plough into an anthill. Everywhere those thus rudely awakened from their old comfort and repose had swarmed forth angry and confused."[3] The first great disruption occurred in theology probably because the threat of organic evolutionary theory was most obvious there, but as soon became evident, the "plough" was also creating havoc in the philosophical anthill.

Although the scientific revolution that was set in motion by the *Origin of Species* had a profound effect on all three of the founders of pragmatic philosophy, Dewey has been most explicit about the impact of biology on his own philosophical position, and he more than either Peirce or James consciously incorporated the principles of organic evolution into his effort of what he called the reconstruction of philosophy. Dewey's estimate of the revolutionary impact of Darwinian theory on the intellectual life of the West is revealed in the following quotation:

> Doubtless the greatest dissolvent in contemporary thought of old questions, the greatest precipitant of new methods, new intentions, new problems, is the one effected by the scientific revolution that found its climax in the *Origin of Species*.[4]

---

[2] These two papers will be considered later in this chapter. Peirce's own account of the activities of The Metaphysical Club may be found in his paper "Pragmatism in Retrospect: A Last Formulation." See Buchler, *Peirce*, pp. 269 ff.

[3] Andrew Dickson White, *A History of the Warfare of Science with Theology in Christendom* (first published in 1896), reprinted by Dover Publications, New York, 1960. The quotation here is from vol. 1, p. 70. White's section "The Final Effort of Theology" is a classic summary of the effects of Darwin's work on the intellectual life of the later part of the nineteenth century. See vol. 1, pp. 70–88.

[4] John Dewey, *The Influence of Darwin on Philosophy* (New York: Henry Holt and Co., 1910), p. 9.

Dewey attributed great influence to Darwin, and emphasized the effect his evolutionary theory had on philosophy. One important factor was the awareness that in the light of scientific biology man in his totality was finally brought within the natural order. The ancient dualistic conception of man could no longer hold. Man is seen now as a natural organism, only one of numerous species. He is continuous with the totality of nature and his behavior is a phenomenon of nature in the same sense that any natural event is part of the natural order. Human experience must be understood as the interaction of the human organism and a dynamic natural and social environment. In this sense, experience is a transaction going on in nature. It is simply one among the innumerable transactions that make up the natural world, but qualitatively this form of transaction is different from other forms. The difference lies in certain attributes of human beings, attributes not possessed by other organisms, but also attributes that have originated and evolved through natural processes.

Far more, however, can be attributed to Darwin's influence than merely the reinterpretation of human nature in biological terms. Both Dewey and Peirce saw the need for a transformation of logic—a complete reorientation of philosophy. Before Darwin, the philosophical and scientific world was still very much enveloped in Aristotelian logic. The logic of science rested on the idea of fixed forms or species and ultimately on the existence of a "first cause." Under this view, nature is a progressive realization of an inherent purpose, and knowledge is the apprehension of what holds all change within bounds and thus makes fixed truth possible.

In the view of the pragmatists, Darwin's work constituted the *coup de grace* for this conception of nature. The idea of a "block universe" has to be given up, said James; nature is pluralistic, not monistic. Novelty is inherent in the nature of things. Chance, argued Peirce, is a genuine force in the universe. And perhaps it was all summed up best in James's cry that this is "a universe with the lid off."

Dewey saw two courses open to philosophy. One was to take the direction indicated by the new advances in science. If philosophy took this course, it would concern itself with the objects and methods of inquiry that originate within the natural world; its concern would be the specific conditions and circumstances that generate the problems with which men have to deal and the modes of inquiry and action that make the solution of these problems possible. The alternative he saw was to pursue the course Western philosophy had customarily followed. This was to continue the historic philosophical quest for a certainty embedded in some transcendental and supernatural reality that, by definition, must lie outside human experience. In the judgment of the pragmatists, this whole course of Western philosophy had been wrong, for experience reveals no ultimate certainty, nor any certainty at all.

Peirce and Dewey agreed that philosophy would become intellectually responsible when it concerned itself with problems that can be studied by methods developed within experience and with conclusions that can be verified by an appeal to experience. Said Dewey:

> Once admit that the sole verifiable or fruitful object of knowledge is the particular set of changes that generate the object of study together with the consequences that then flow from it, and no intelligible question can be asked about what, by assumption, lies outside.[5]

Another influence on the development of pragmatic philosophy that deserves some mention here was that of the German schools of idealism. Pragmatism was a protest against idealism, but it was also a kind of offspring of that tradition. Dewey himself had been a more or less orthodox Hegelian in the earlier part of his career, having been introduced to Hegel's philosophy when he was a student of George Sylvester Morris at Johns Hopkins. Dewey never concealed his admiration for Hegel's work and on one occasion attributed to it a "greater insight and richness" than is to be found in any other philosopher, except perhaps Plato.

Hegel's appeal for Dewey lay mainly in the idea of unity, which permeates Absolute idealism and which Dewey thought promised a way out of the familiar philosophical dualisms that apparently had troubled him even in his student days. He has reported his early dissatisfaction with the dualism involved in the prevailing philosophy: the separation of soul from body, self from the world, and God from nature. Dewey evolved the belief that one of the fundamental defects of traditional conceptions of education lay in the dualism inherent in them. The direct influence of Hegelian philosophy on Dewey's work gradually diminished as other forces, particularly scientific method, altered his views, but the campaign against dualism, which he considered the great philosophical fallacy, continued throughout his career as a philosopher.[6]

Peirce also acknowledged his debt to German philosophy, which he has said was the first purely philosophical material he studied seriously. He had little use for the speculative system-building methodology employed in it, preferring the empirical approach of British philosophers, but he found it a "rich mine of philosophical suggestions."[7] He also pointed

---

[5] *Influence of Darwin*, p. 14. Peirce made comments in a similar vein although his language was usually more acerbic than Dewey's. See Buchler, *Peirce*, chap. 1.

[6] Dewey's estimate of Hegelian influence on his own work will be found in G. P. Adams and W. P. Montague, eds., *Contemporary American Philosophy*, vol. 2 (New York: Macmillan Co., 1930), pp. 16–19.

[7] See Buchler, *Peirce*, p. 2.

out the close relation Hegelian idealism had with pragmatism, though he rejected Hegel's effort to reduce the whole of reality to pure thought.[8]

One other influence that had much to do with the character of pragmatic philosophy was exerted by developments in scientific psychology. The chief contributor here was William James. Dewey has said that the psychological influence that contributed most was behaviorism, and he specifically mentions J. B. Watson as the chief advocate of this approach to psychology.[9] But he also maintained that the origins of the psychological position of pragmatism lay in James's great psychological work *Principles of Psychology*.[10]

According to Dewey, two strains of thought are discernible in the *Principles of Psychology*. One is a continuation, but also a reinterpretation, of the introspective approach to psychology. Differing from the atomistic approach of Locke and the other British empiricists, in which ideas are built up from discrete sense data, James substituted a continuum of sensory experience that he called the stream of consciousness.

The other theme developed by James was influenced by biology. This theme is seen clearly, said Dewey, in James's operational theory of mind: "The pursuance of future ends and the choice of means for their attainment are thus the mark and criterion of the presence of mentality in a phenomenon." Dewey's own theory of mind, closely connected with his educational theory, follows this concept from the *Principles of Psychology*.

It may be said in summation that pragmatism, while in a sense developing out of idealism, also constituted a great protest against it. The chief inspiration of the pragmatists was the possibilities they saw inherent in scientific method. They saw the method not only as a means of transforming the physical structure of society, but also as having the power of transforming intellectual life. We now turn to a consideration of the interpretation pragmatism gives to the concepts listed at the end of the last chapter and which are strategic to this philosophical tradition.

## EXPERIENCE, MIND, AND MEANING

Dewey defined experience as the interaction of the human being with its environment. In this interactive process two aspects are discernible: the person acts on some elements in the environment; out of this action certain consequences ensue. The person then undergoes the consequences of his

---

[8]  Ibid., pp. 266–67.

[9]  For Dewey's analysis of the development of pragmatism, including the psychological elements in it, see "The Development of American Pragmatism" in his *Philosophy and Civilization* (New York: Minton, Balch and Co., 1931), pp. 13–35.

[10]  In two volumes. (New York: Henry Holt and Co., 1890.)

action. Thus, experience is a matter of doing and undergoing in which both the individual and the environment are changed in some measure.

Now nature itself is a great complex of interactions of many and diverse kinds and one of these is experience—the interaction of a human being with the environmental media in which and by which it lives. Many of these transactions are among things that in common sense we call physical. Common sense knows that the interactions of living things and environmental conditions are different from the interactions of inanimate things and the environment. They are so different that both common sense and philosophy have often made the distinction absolute. Here is one source of the familiar dualisms we have already had occasion to consider, and here also is a point at which Darwinian theory can be seen affecting pragmatic philosophy.

Darwin's evolutionary theory postulates a continuity that persists throughout nature. Under this view there are no abrupt breaks, and thus no absolute distinctions are possible. The evolution from simple forms to higher and more complex forms is continuous within nature. There are differences between the animate and the inanimate, but there are also similarities. Both kinds of bodies are subject to certain internal tensions set up by external conditions, and they both react so as to achieve a state of equilibrium. But the difference, according to Dewey's interpretation, is not that a plant or other animate thing has something besides physico-chemical energy, which a nugget of iron has also, but that the way in which this energy is interconnected and functions, is different for plant and iron.

We know that the interconnections are different (although we do not as yet know how) since we know the consequences are different. In living things, the readaptive behavior *takes place in terms of the previous history of the organism* and this is not the case with the lump of iron or any other inanimate matter. To distinguish the activities of living things from those of physical things, Dewey adopted the term *psychophysical*. The prefix *psycho*, however, does not represent any mystical ingredient to be added to the *physical* and thus constitute an answer to "the mystery of life." He intended it to mean simply that at this level of nature physical activity has gained additional properties, namely the ability to react selectively in terms of a continuing history. There is no dualism of the psychic and the physical. Empirically, there are certain events marked by distinctive qualities, of which one of these is organization. We may not know now under what conditions this organization of behavior happens nor what all the consequences of it are, though assuredly we are closer to it now than when Dewey was making his naturalistic analysis of experience. But as he saw it, the question of the origin of life is subject matter for a highly complex inquiry of science. In this inquiry, no hypothesis should be ruled out arbitrarily so long as it can be tested by experimental methods, but there is one thing that must be ruled out in the beginning. What must be ruled out is any effort to explain the phenomenon of life in terms of some force from outside nature or to postulate such an outside force as the cause of changes within the evolutionary process.[11]

Thus, "animate bodies" are what they are, not because they possess some transcendental factor variously called life or soul, but because one of the qualities they exhibit is the continuous effort to maintain a serial pattern of behavior in an environment that is always changing. Since environmental conditions are never stable, the organism is subjected to strains, tensions, and dislocations in its relation to the environment, and the organism has to make certain existential changes so that the pattern of behavior may be continued. The effort of the organism is to make readjustments in its relation to the environment, and the readjustment involves changes in the organism and changes in the environment. Life, therefore, is a constant process of readaptation to a dynamic environment and experience, which is the interactive process at the human level, a process of doing and undergoing—a matter of anticipation and consummation.

Thus, this naturalistic interpretation of experience makes possible an explanation of certain key terms without invoking transcendental forces.

> By need is meant a condition of tensional distribution of energies such that the body is in a condition of uneasy or unstable equilibrium. By demand or effort is meant the fact that this state is manifested in movements which modify environing bodies in ways which react upon the body, so that its characteristic pattern of active equilibrium is restored. By satisfaction is meant this recovery of equilibrium pattern, consequent upon the changes of environment due to interactions with the active demands of the organism.[12]

The basis of all motivation is the effort of the organism to maintain adjustment so that its own identity can be maintained. Pleasure or self-satisfaction is not itself the motivating factor in organic activity, as various forms of hedonism maintain. Pleasure or satisfaction is the quality of the event of successful readjustment—it is the result of a process, not the goal of it.[13] Organisms are "biased" toward perpetuation of prior patterns

---

[11] For an extended discussion of these matters, see John Dewey, *Logic: The Theory of Inquiry* (New York: Henry-Holt and Co., 1938), chap. 2. The ruling out of any extranatural causal force in the evolutionary process, it will be recalled, was what got Sir Julian Huxley in trouble with the theologians. See pp. 38–39.

[12] John Dewey, *Experience and Nature* (Chicago: Open Court Publishing Co., 1925), p. 253.

[13] Ibid., pp. 63–64. In this sense, *hedonism* means the theory that all motivation can be explained in terms of desire for pleasure and the avoidance of pain. James along with Dewey criticized psychological hedonism as the explanation of motivation. James's critique will be found in the second volume of *Principles of Psychology*, pp. 549 ff.

of behavior and their readaptive efforts are directed toward that end. Empirically, sensitivity is a quality of behavior exhibited by animate bodies since they do not respond at random to environmental forces but are selective and discriminatory in their responses.

For animals that have organs of locomotion and sensory organs that allow the reception of distant stimuli, interest becomes, along with sensitivity, a realization of feeling. There is evidence for this, because in such organisms two kinds of activity may be observed: activity that may be distinguished as *preparatory* and activity that may be identified as *consummatory*. Anticipatory activities are permeated with the anticipation of the consummation that is to come. The consummation, therefore, is not simply a fortuitous emergent of the preparatory activities; it is in Dewey's words a "funded conservation of them." [14] When consummation comes, the sensitivity of the organism is realized as *feeling*. Below the level of human structure, animals realize feeling in terms of gross states of uneasiness, comfort, vigor, exhaustion, and so on. But it is Dewey's view that even such gross bodily states sum up the history of an event and that they form the threshold of mental life.

The more complex the organism, the more varied and indicative the feeling, but though these animals may have feelings, they do not *know* they have them. Activity is still psychophysical, not mental. Psychophysical feelings provide the threshold of mental life, but only creatures capable of having and using *meanings* are rightly described as having mental life. Thus, meaning is feeling with an added property, objectivity.

Meaning does not inhere in the objects and events in the environment, nor is it a peculiar property of the organism. Meaning is a quality of the interaction of organism and environment; *it is a property of behavior*. Meanings are objective—not private and subjective—because they are natural modes of interaction with objects and energies in the environment. What gives meaning its objectivity, as contrasted with the essentially subjective character of feeling, is language. Meaning, since it is objectified in symbolic fashion, becomes *a sign of operations to be performed*. [15]

Since man alone is known to use language in any significant degree, only the human species displays the capacity to have and use meanings in experience, and hence only human beings are capable of mental life. [16] Meanings are *signs* of events and therefore are capable of being manipu-

---

[14] Ibid., p. 257.

[15] It will be recalled that in the preceding chapter ideas were defined in similar fashion as plans for action.

[16] Dewey maintained that though animals other than man do communicate with each other in various ways, the signaling acts of animals are generically different from human speech. Ibid., p. 179.

lated, arranged, and combined; and it is this behavior that we call reflective thought. The growth of meanings, which according to this account occurs in and through experience, is a genetic process. It begins in the impulsive and relatively gross behavior of infancy and early childhood and grows through the medium of the experiential continuum. Dewey analyzed the genetic development of knowledge in the individual (see Chapter Six). Here we are speaking of the same thing under somewhat different terms. The cognitive structure possessed by any individual is the system of meanings present in his behavior and available to him in his relationships with the social and physical environment.

We can, however, make one additional observation about the essentially biological interpretation Dewey and others in the pragmatic tradition gave to experience. What is meant by *mind* is simply the system of meanings that has developed through experience. Mind, therefore, is an *emergent* of the experiential process and in this sense it is *learned behavior*. Mind is not given; it is achieved. And the term itself does not represent a "substance" either material or immaterial. In part, *mind* is better thought of from the standpoint of language as a modifier rather than a substantive. Mind is behavior with a distinctive property and as a behavior it is instrumental in adaptation to the pressures of the environment. It is the most powerful means to survival yet to emerge from the evolutionary process. From the standpoint of physical structure, man in many ways is inferior to other species of animals, but language and the property of meaning language makes possible have given the human species a far greater power of control over the environment and more flexibility and adaptability than any other species possesses.

A similar observation may be made about the term *self*. Under the view we have been examining here, individuality or selfhood must also be an emergent of experience. Only human beings can achieve selfhood, because they are the only organisms that can share consciously in group life. Some animals, ants and bees for example, live in highly integrated social environments but their behavior is psychophysical, not mental. The kind of self an individual becomes depends on his genetic inheritance and on the environment in which he grows up, because both of these are parts of the transaction we call experience. Society is made by men, to be sure, but men are also made by society. A man who grew up entirely apart from any human society, supposing that this could actually happen, who had never acquired language, and had never seen any of his kind nor been influenced by any human institution, would not be a human self but a brute.[17]

---

[17]  An important contribution to the naturalistic conceptions of the origin of mind and self was made by George Herbert Mead (1863–1931). Mead was a colleague of Dewey at the University of Chicago and was an important figure in the development of

The physiological structure that makes possible development of mind and self is an emergent of the evolutionary process that operates through natural selection, but the actual emergence of selfhood results from the individual's conscious participation in social life.

Thus we can recognize the interpretation pragmatic philosophy puts on such strategic terms as *experience, mind,* and *self.* These concepts, viewed here in their biological and psychological aspects, are completely *naturalistic* in character. The pragmatist takes experience as he finds it and attempts to analyze it as a phenomenon of nature. He does not invoke any supernatural or transcendental entities to account for human motivation, mental life, or the achievement of self, for these, he thinks, are as much a part of nature as the motion of the planets or the fall of rain on a dusty road.

Thus, for the pragmatist, the revolution in biology that Darwin's thesis precipitated points the way not alone to a new philosophy of human nature, but to a reconstruction and a redirection of the whole of philosophy. In Dewey's words:

> To see the organism *in* nature, the nervous system in the organism, the brain in the nervous system, the cortex in the brain is the answer to the problems which haunt philosophy. And when they are thus seen they will be seen *in,* not as marbles are in a box but as events are in history, in a moving, growing never finished process.[18]

## LOGICAL ASPECTS OF MEANING

One of the important concepts that has been mentioned from time to time in our considerations has been the term *meaning.* This term is significant in Dewey's educational theory; and we have just completed an analysis of the psychological dimensions of it as these are viewed in pragmatic philosophy. There is, however, another dimension of this strategic term that is important in rounding out our understanding.

In the introduction to the present chapter, reference was made to two papers Peirce presented at meetings of The Metaphysical Club. The observation was made that these two papers had a profound effect on the development of pragmatic philosophy in this country and that the ideas contained in them greatly influenced the philosophy of Dewey and James.

---

American pragmatism. One of his big works that bears on the discussion above is *Mind, Self, and Society* (Chicago: University of Chicago Press, 1939). A compact anthology compiled from Mead's work is Anselm Strauss, ed., *The Social Psychology of George Herbert Mead* (Chicago: University of Chicago Press, 1956), in which see part 5.

[18] Dewey, *Experience and Nature,* p. 295.

One of these papers bears the title "How to Make Our Ideas Clear" and is concerned with the logical aspects of meaning.[19]

In this paper, Peirce began by demonstrating that classic logic had never succeeded in advancing any trustworthy criterion for distinguishing between clear and unclear concepts. He contended that the first lesson logic should teach is a method of making our ideas clear and it should, moreover, provide a criterion that would enable us to distinguish between the clear conception and the unclear. Briefly, Peirce's argument was that *any idea we might have could be nothing besides our grasp of its sensible effects.* The whole purpose of thought is to guide action and help us form habits, which themselves are modes of action. It appeared to Peirce, therefore, that in light of the function that thought plays and in view of the empirical character of all ideas, a good maxim, or rule, that would define meaning and simultaneously provide a criterion for distinguishing meaningful concepts from those without meaning would be the following:

> Consider what effects, that might conceivably have practical bearings,
> we conceive the object of our conception to have. Then, our conception
> of these effects is the whole of our conception of the object.[20]

For example, if we let *H* stand for any concept, then the meaning of *H*, according to the pragmatic rule, is whatever consequences follow from it. If *a, b, c,* and *d* are effects that are entailed by *H*, then the meaning of *H* is *a, b, c,* and *d*. If we conceive no consequences whatever as arising from *H*, then *H* has no meaning.

In applying the pragmatic rule, we must always use certain operations. In the first place, we must assume hypothetically that *H* is true. Secondly, we must propose that some operation should be performed. Third, we must expect that some consequences must result from the operations. It is these consequences, according to the rule, that constitute the meaning of *H*. In his original essay, Peirce used as examples two terms, *hard* and *weight*. When we say that something is hard, we indicate that it will scratch other objects. When we say that some object has weight, we indicate that if we remove all opposing forces the object will fall. In both these simple cases, an operation is indicated (rubbing one object against another; removing support) and certain consequences ensue (appearance of scratches; falling). Thus, when we predicate hardness of some object *A*, we mean that if *A* is hard, it will produce scratches on other substances when it is rubbed

---

[19]  First published in *Popular Science Monthly* in 1878. Now available in *The Collected Papers of Charles Sanders Peirce*, vol. 5 (Cambridge, Mass.: Harvard University Press, 1931–1935). This paper has been reprinted in Buchler, *Peirce*, chap. 3. My citations are to the latter edition.

[20]  Buchler, *Peirce*, p. 31.

against them and it will not be scratched itself. These consequences are the meaning of the term *hard*, and Peirce observed that there was no difference between a hard thing and a soft thing except as they were brought to the test.

We have seen that according to the pragmatic rule any concept $H$ means whatever consequences ensue when some operations are performed. If it is impossible to conceive of any operations and their ensuing consequences, then the term has no meaning. To this may be added the further observation that if two terms involve the same consequences, they are really the same conception expressed in different ways. Thus, if $H$ involves as consequences $a$, $b$, $c$, and $d$ and if $H'$ also involves $a$, $b$, $c$, and $d$, these being identical, then $H$ and $H'$ are the same conception.

Peirce believed that the pragmatic rule would go a long way toward clearing what he considered the metaphysical rubbish out of the mansions of philosophy. In an essay published some years after "How to Make Our Ideas Clear," he said that the chief advantage to be gained from the pragmatic maxim would be that of demonstrating that most metaphysical propositions are either "meaningless gibberish" or otherwise "downright absurd." Once this rubbish is cleared away, said Peirce, what will remain are problems that can be studied by the methods of the true sciences.[21]

Anyone with the slightest acquaintance with the history of philosophy knows that there are numerous questions or problems that, although they were first stated some two thousand years ago and have been puzzled over by the finest minds Western civilization has produced, still remain unsettled, and show little promise of ever being settled. These problems are mostly metaphysical and theological in character. One reaction to these problems is often called agnostic. This is the attitude that the problems are unsettled because it is impossible to get evidence, either positive or negative, to establish truth or falsity about them. Therefore, propositions about the existence of God, for example, cannot be settled because of the impossibility of gathering evidence to support or deny the statement.

Peirce thought that the pragmatic rule cut at these statements in another direction and in a different way. If the pragmatic rule is applied to such a statement, it is found that the statement itself is *meaningless*. For example, if we consider the proposition "Pixies abound in the fifth dimension," and examine this statement in the light of the pragmatic rule, we find that neither of the operations provided in the rule can be applied. If we put this statement in the hypothetical form that the rule requires and say, "If pixies abound in the fifth dimension, then what conceivable consequences follow?" we are constrained to answer that there are no operations possible that would provide any observable consequences. Therefore, the

---

[21]   See "The Essentials of Pragmatism," in Buchler, *Peirce*, pp. 251 ff.

conclusion must be that this statement is meaningless and any debate about whether it is true or false is idle. It is generally conceded that truth or falsity cannot be affirmed of meaningless statements, of which this is an example. The statement about the pixies is a perfectly proper English sentence, every word of which can be defined, but it does not meet the requirements of the pragmatic rule because it is impossible to conceive of any operations that will yield any observable consequences. And according to the rule, whatever consequences ensue is what the statement means: no consequences—no meaning. This, according to Peirce, is why there are so many "unsolved problems" in theology and metaphysics.

Peirce himself considered the heart of pragmatic philosophy to be a theory about the nature of meaning, which he conceived in operational terms. None of the formulations of the rule made by Peirce says anything about truth or falsity or the process of validation. Manifestly, in terms of the rule, a statement can be meaningful and still be false. If I say that water boils at 115° Fahrenheit at sea level, I am uttering a proposition that is capable of operational interpretation: operations can be conceived and one can foresee the consequences to be observed. These consequences will reveal, as everyone knows, that my statement is false, but it is nevertheless meaningful.

In the same sense, there are propositions that are meaningful but whose validity is still in doubt. If I say that psychosis is caused by chemical imbalance in the body, I am making a statement whose truth or falsity is unknown at the present time. It is, however, a meaningful statement because it is possible to discern possible operations and foresee probable consequences of these operations. For verification of this statement, many complex and delicate scientific inquiries must be conducted. There is always the possibility that its truth or falsity can never be established, but this in no way affects the fact that as a statement it is meaningful. On the other hand, all statements of the kind about the pixies are meaningless now and always will be. Peirce considered most, if not all, metaphysical and theological statements to be of this kind.

Both James and Dewey were profoundly affected by Peirce's theory of meaning and his statement of the pragmatic maxim. James seized on it with his usual enthusiasm and intellectual vigor. Whatever ideas he touched had a way of being transformed, and the pragmatic rule proved to be no exception. He saw pragmatic method as a means of finding a tenable middle ground between the two extremes of philosophical position that he characterized by the now famous dichotomy of "the tough-minded" and "the tender-minded." The tough-minded were the scientific realists, the positivists, the empiricists, who among other things were materialistic, irreligious, fatalistic, and pessimistic, and therefore in many ways unacceptable to James, who was none of these. The tender-minded alternative was idealism, particularly absolute idealism, and James used such terms as *intellectualistic, optimistic, religious, dogmatical,* and *free-willist* to describe this position. He believed that pragmatism offered a middle position that would be philosophically tenable; he also saw that if the new philosophy were to serve this important office, it would have to be enlarged beyond the scope that Peirce, who was himself more than a little tough-minded, had allowed.

What eventually happened to the pragmatic rule in the hands of James was a reinterpretation and extension of the terms *consequences,* or *effects.* Peirce had used the second term in his first statement of the rule. Perhaps even more significant was James's achievement of transforming the pragmatic rule so that it became for him at least a theory of truth as well as a theory of meaning. James's contribution will be considered in connection with the pragmatic conception of truth.

Dewey's philosophical thought also was much influenced by Peirce's analysis. The operationalism and the emphasis on the consequences of action became parts of his own conception of meaning and the knowledge process, particularly concerning the relation of doing and knowing. The logical elements of the pragmatic rule worked in with and illuminated the biological and psychological interpretation of meaning. The influence of the pragmatic rule on pedagogical ideas, particularly those of Dewey, can be summed up in two statements:

First, if a concept is to have meaning for an individual, he must put it to work, that is, he must apply it to some state of affairs. Only in this way can he become acquainted with its consequences and hence with its relationships to other things and events. The structure of the school's curriculum must be deliberately designed to make this possible, and more than that, to encourage it. There is an inherent relation between action and knowledge, and meaning can be communicated only in a context that is itself meaningful to the learner.

Secondly, knowing is the apprehending of meaning. The object of knowledge is, What consequences occur when a concept is put to application? To know means to inquire, to change relationships, and to reveal the connections between means and consequences. If there are no actions and no operations, there are no consequences; and if there are no consequences, there is no object of knowledge.

For the school program, these ideas indicate the necessity for a curriculum built around active enterprises that will stimulate intellectual inquiry. This is one of the main considerations teachers must bear in mind when they make provision for activities in the classroom. In neither the psychological nor the logical sense can mind be correctly perceived as the mere spectator of an antecedent reality, however this reality may be conceived. These ideas were among the most important in Dewey's conception of the educative process, and they played a strategic part in the experimental program of the Laboratory School.

We are now aware that the heart of pragmatism is the theory of meaning. We have not had anything to say about the connection of the pragmatic rule with a theory of truth, except to note that James believed that it denoted not only a conception of meaning but also a means of verification. Conventionally, most Western epistemology has always been concerned with what constitutes truth and with discovering methods by which statements may be judged true or false. We shall now concern ourselves with the position pragmatism takes on this point and the ramifications these matters have for educational theory.

## LOGIC, INQUIRY, AND THE NATURE OF TRUTH

Another essay of Peirce that originally was presented at the Metaphysical Club antedated the one we have already considered and was first published in the *Scientific Monthly* in 1877. Peirce gave this paper the title "The Fixation of Belief." [22] There is no possibility of reproducing the intriguing flavor of Peirce's exposition, but an outline of the argument he advanced will allow us to grasp its important connection with pragmatic philosophy.

The argument begins with the statement that there is a difference between a condition of doubt and a condition of belief. Belief influences our desires and our actions and it establishes in us habits of behavior. These habits are strong or weak according to the strength or weakness of the beliefs that form them. Psychologically, a state of doubt is always irritating and uncomfortable. We resist being in this state and seek to pass beyond it to the relatively complacent and comfortable condition that belief brings. Doubt is the irritant, or the stimulus, that urges us to struggle for belief. Belief, on the other hand, is not an immediate spur to action. Instead it creates in us a habit, so that when the occasion arises we act in a way determined by our belief.

The struggle to pass from a state of doubt to a state of belief Peirce called *inquiry*, noting that it was not a completely satisfactory term. Inquiry begins when doubt begins and it ends when belief is attained. The only function inquiry has, said Peirce, is to settle opinion. To be sure, people often say that merely to reach some opinion is not enough; what we really are after is a "true" opinion. This notion, however, will not stand analysis, for as soon as a firm belief is gained, inquiry ceases and

---

[22] Available in the *Collected Works of Peirce*, vol. 5, pp. 358–87; also reprinted intact in Buchler, *Peirce*, pp. 5–22. Citations here are to Buchler's volume. Any person with a genuine interest in pragmatism will wish to savor Peirce's pungent style directly.

we are satisfied. We like to say we are searching for beliefs that are true, but this turns out to be a tautology because we really think our beliefs are "true" anyway.[23]

Peirce next raised the question of whether under this view belief might not be attained simply by reiterating the answer to some question and resolutely ignoring anything that might be in opposition to it. If inquiry is simply the process of establishing belief, then this would appear to be the most direct method. Assuredly it is a very common way people fix belief, said Peirce, and he called it *the method of tenacity*. He then began the analysis of alternative methods of fixating belief.

When beliefs are fixed on the basis of tenacity, we simply cling to some view. We have no interest in whatever evidence there may be to the contrary, or if we do have any interest, it is in ignoring or suppressing such evidence. There is no doubt, Peirce agreed, that belief maintained by tenacity can often bring peace of mind and what is often admiringly called moral resolution. Nor should we be patronizing about people who go through life on the basis of this method of belief. What point is there in calling this method irrational when the people who use it make no profession of being rational and often express doubt about the very potency of human reason?

The real difficulty with the method of tenacity is that it ultimately breaks down in practice. A person who follows this method will find sooner or later that there are other beliefs that people hold as tenaciously as he holds his own, and it is therefore inevitable that ultimately the seeds of doubt will sprout in the mind of the tenacious believer. It will occur to him that other men's beliefs may be as good as his own. Since all of us cannot go off into the wilderness and become hermits, thereby shielding our cherished beliefs from contamination, another necessity presents itself. This Peirce called the problem of fixing belief in the community.[24]

We come, then, to another method of fixing belief, which Peirce called *the method of authority*. To use this method, it is necessary to create some kind of authoritative institution in society. The function of this authority is to keep the desired beliefs constantly before the people, and of course to teach them to children. All contrary ideas and negative evidence must be suppressed and people kept in ignorance of alternative possibilities. When deviants appear in society and prove to be incapable of righting their beliefs, the only course is the use of force. "A general massacre," Peirce observed, "has proved a very effective means of settling opinion in a country."

---

[23] Buchler, *Peirce*, pp. 10–11.
[24] Ibid., pp. 12–13.

The method of authority has always been a chief means of supporting religious and political doctrines. Wherever there has been a privileged class—priesthood, aristocracy, or any group whose power rests on some body of dogma—this method will be found at work. Ultimately there is no limit to the cruelty and coercion that the authority will use to maintain orthodoxy of belief.

This method, Peirce observed, is in its main effects greatly superior to emotional tenacity. History has shown that many of the works of civilization achieved under it have been impressive beyond measure. The difficulty is that in the long run it fails. It fails because all heresy cannot be kept down. Beliefs do change, though very slowly and imperceptibly, and usually the rate of change is slow enough so that the beliefs of any individual may remain virtually unchanged throughout his lifetime. To this Peirce added the tart observation that perhaps for most people this is the best method. "If it is their highest impulse to be intellectual slaves, then slaves they ought to remain." [25] But there are always a few men who do not wish to be intellectual slaves and, since even the most tyrannous authority cannot regulate opinion on every subject, they become aware that in other places and in other times people have held opinions that are contrary to the prevailing authority. These men begin to wonder whether there is any reason to hold that the authoritative beliefs of their own time really are superior to those of other times and places. So, ultimately, these people give up the idea of fixating belief on the basis of authority and adopt another method.

This brings us to the third method, which Peirce called the *a priori*. The essence of this method is that people fix those beliefs that are in agreement with their own "reason." In a sense, this method involves a much more liberal and pluralistic approach to the formation of belief. There is a free market in ideas. Men are able to analyze and discuss their ideas and develop those beliefs they find that "stand to reason." (Peirce was careful to point out that the concern in this method is that the beliefs *stand to reason, not experience*.) This method Peirce interpreted as being the approach employed by speculative philosophy, which typically has sought to establish beliefs that "rational" men have been inclined to accept —Plato, for example, who found it reasonable to believe "that the distances of the celestial spheres from one another should be proportional to the different lengths of strings which produce harmonious chords." [26] Granted, this method in many ways is more humane and liberal than the method of authority since it allows much more free play of instinct and habit; however, it also displays severe weakness when it is employed fully. In the long

---

25  Ibid., p. 14.
26  Ibid., p. 15.

run, beliefs fixed on the basis of right reason turn out to be as various and subjective as personal tastes. Under this view, I may prefer monogamy over polygamy for about the same reason that I prefer oysters over clams. Is there any reason why everyone should concur in my preferred belief in monogamy any more than they should concur in my preference for oysters? If belief is to be fixed on the basis of what is agreeable to the reason of individuals—then any substantial agreement on beliefs is impossible, and in Peirce's view, the history of metaphysical philosophy is an excellent example of this fact.

What is needed to overcome the deficiencies in the *a priori* method is a basis for fixating belief that appeals to something outside the mind—something that cannot be changed by thinking and therefore something that can direct inquiry so that all men can come to agreement on the basis of evidence. This method of fixing belief, said Peirce, is precisely *the method employed by science*, which ultimately involves an appeal to experience. Experience involves both the inward activity of thought and the real things in the environment that possess the character they do independent of thought and are governed by laws that exist and operate apart from opinion and belief.[27] It is true that these external things affect our senses in different ways but, "any man, if he have sufficient experience and he reason enough about it, will be led to the one true conclusion." [28] Thus, scientific method can lend objectivity to our beliefs—a quality that none of the other methods is capable of yielding. Peirce took care to note that all of the methods of fixating belief have certain advantages, but he held that the most advantageous method was the scientific. The reason scientific method can be judged to be superior is that the results it yields are superior to the results obtained by other methods.

The pragmatic rule is a good starting point for considering some of the formal aspects of the logic of scientific method. The rule states that a conception is meaningful when it is possible to discern certain operations that can be performed and to foresee that consequences will ensue from these operations that can be observed in some way. If we let $H$ stand for any idea (belief) that is to be tested, then according to the rule, we must state $H$ in hypothetical form: If $H$, then $a, b, c, d$ (where $a, b, c, d$ stand for operations and their ensuing consequences): but $a, b, c,$ and $d$ when the operations performed are found to yield the consequences anticipated—that is, when they "check out." Now what can be concluded about $H$? Can it be said that $H$ is true?

In the ordinary sense of the word, we cannot say that $H$ has been shown to be "true." It is a fact that the operations performed have shown

---

[27]   Ibid., pp. 18–19.

[28]   Ibid.

through their consequences that they bear out $H$, but how are we to know that $a$, $b$, $c$, and $d$ exhaust all the possible operations? Even if we were to subject $H$ to a very long sequence of operations, could we ever know that we had exhausted all possibilities and therefore would be warranted in attributing unqualified truth to $H$? Suppose that we one day found that operation $x'$ failed to confirm $H$. What then? Peirce's answer:

> But the scientific spirit requires a man to be at all times ready to dump his whole cartload of beliefs the moment experience is against them. The desire to learn forbids him to be perfectly cocksure that he knows already. Besides positive science can only rest on experience; and experience can never result in absolute certainty, exactitude, necessity, or universality.[29]

Therefore, if we feel it necessary to say something about the *truth* of $H$, the most we can possibly say is that $H$ is *probably true*. The whole scientific enterprise, then, becomes one of increasing the probability of the adequacy of our ideas (hypotheses); and this is done by increasing the number of tested inferences derived from the idea. Now, we may ask, is this true of all cognitive statements? The answer the pragmatist gives is, Yes, except for analytic statements (logical or mathematical), which are tautologies anyway and can have only formal validity. And so if we follow the logic of scientific thought, which pragmatists think is what one should do, we must give up the notion that there are some judgments that have the property of truth in the complete and unalterable sense of the word.

In his own work in pragmatic logic, Dewey followed the general position stated by Peirce. Inquiry was defined by Peirce as activity that mediates between a state of doubt and the fixation of belief. Peirce had demonstrated that there are various methods of fixating belief; the way he considered most effective is that in which inquiry is identical with the method of science. Dewey joined Peirce in this conclusion and he believed, as Peirce believed, that an important need of modern philosophy was a logic of inquiry, a logic concerned with "finding out" rather than demonstrating known fact or deriving tautological statements from axioms by *a priori* methods.[30] Much of Dewey's long career in philosophy was devoted to working out a logic of inquiry, which amounted to generalizing the experimental method of science so that it might be applicable to any meaningful subject matter.

Dewey's work in logic not only paralleled his work in educational theory; it was organically related to it. The five steps of "a complete act of thought" drawn up by Dewey reflected his belief in a logic of inquiry.

---

[29] Ibid., pp. 46–47.

[30] For Dewey's commentary on the needed reform in logic, see *Logic: The Theory of Inquiry*, chap. 5.

He sought to make this method of inquiry the central element in educational method, designing the curriculum in the Laboratory School around it. We can now be aware of the influences that preceded Dewey's formulation of the act of inquiry. Inquiry begins, as Peirce had said, with a state of doubt and the desire to move from doubt to belief. Dewey's interpretation of this idea was biological and behavioral. Inquiry begins when a disunified and confused state of affairs is encountered. This state of affairs blocks and impedes behavior because the habitual behavior of the person involved is inadequate to cope with the situation. The psychological, or affective, response of the person is one of doubt, as Peirce had observed, but feeling on the part of the person is itself a product of the situation in which he finds himself. Doubt is not something we have inside ourselves and then project into the environment. We doubt because we live in an environment that in some of its aspects is contingent and therefore doubtful. Doubt is an uncomfortable, irritating, and anxiety-producing state and we try to pass from it to the comparatively settled, complacent, comfortable state that Peirce has called belief.

If we are to do this, however, something has to be done to the conditions that are responsible for the state of doubt. Peirce's analysis showed various ways that could be used, but the most effective is the general method of science, or as Dewey often called it, the method of intelligence.

A crucial step in resolving an indeterminate situation is to recognize it as a situation requiring inquiry, that is, to recognize it for its problematic character. The presence of an indeterminate situation is a prerequisite for inquiry, but as a situation it is whatever it existentially is, and it does not owe its character to thought or cognition. The first necessary achievement of an inquiry is to transform an indeterminate situation into *a problem*. When a problem is well formulated, it is on its way to solution.

The third stage of inquiry is finding possible solutions to the problem, and this comes about as we are able to grasp the structure of the situation and to see what the relevant facts in it are. The facts represent what must be taken into account in our efforts to deal with the problem. If we are able to determine the salient factual aspects of the problem, we can foresee certain possibilities, and these possibilities are *ideas*. Both Peirce and Dewey conceived ideas as proposed plans of action—possible operations —and in this sense, idea is synonymous with *hypothesis*. Ideas are always hypothetical because they are expectations of possible consequences; their function is pointing ahead and directing action. This stage of inquiry, then, is one of developing possible plans for operations to be performed.

The fourth stage of inquiry is devoted to a logical evaluation of the relative merits of proposed ideas, and this involves determining the meaning of various proposals and their attendant factual connections. The pragmatic rule indicates the hypothetical method of determining the meaning of an idea. If I act on the basis of $H$, where $H$ stands for a possible operation, what consequences can be foreseen? All ideas we have developed are subjected to this logical treatment, and the selection of one course of action, together with the rejection of others, is made in terms of the foreseeable consequences.

The fifth and terminating step is to act on the situation in terms of the idea (hypothesis) chosen to guide the operations. To this point, inquiry has proceeded by means of a series of partial and tentative judgments. In the last stage, a terminal judgment is made, and the object of this judgment is whether or not the situation, which originally was one of indeterminancy and disunity, has been transformed into a unified and determinate set of conditions. If it has been so transformed, our psychological experience is to move from doubt to belief, *but this psychological transformation is itself a product of the transformed situation.* The terminal judgment is therefore not subjective and personal; it is objective and public. Both Peirce and Dewey agreed in this, and it was on this point that an important controversy developed between them and James.

Now what about truth? Is the terminal judgment in an inquiry concerned with establishing truth or falsity? Do the terms *truth* and *falsity* really make any sense in this context? If they do make sense, it is in ways that differ significantly from traditional philosophical conceptions of truth.[31] In one way, it is more useful to use the terms *true* and *false* as modifiers, for it is sensible to think of ideas leading us truly toward our goal, or on the contrary, leading us falsely so that we miss our objective. Or at least, at one time it seemed meaningful to say that ideas are true in the sense that they work, but this phrase has been so misinterpreted and misused that pragmatists have given it up and it is now mostly used as a straw man by unfriendly critics who like to knock it over. From the standpoint of a logical definition, Dewey advocated and used the term *warranted assertibility* to denote the terminal judgment of inquiry, and he expressed agreement with Peirce's statement that truth is "the opinion which is fated to be ultimately agreed to by all who investigate."[32]

The ideas that emerge from the analysis by Peirce and Dewey of scientific inquiry that are most important to our purposes are such as these: (1) Ideas that enable us to transform indeterminate and disunified situations are adequate or warranted, and as emergents of the processes of inquiry, they become the means to help us in subsequent inquiries. The general process of inquiry is continuous and serial in character and this in the same sense that experience in general is continuous and serial. (2) Inquiry is always operational and experimental and is, consequently, objective and

---

[31] A valuable summary of the chief differences between pragmatic and traditional views of truth will be found in Dewey's *Philosophy and Civilization,* pp. 23 ff.

[32] See *Logic: The Theory of Inquiry,* p. 345.

public in the same way that all scientific work is objective and public—in both methods and results. Favorable affective responses follow the successful termination of inquiry, but these favorable feelings are not themselves the test of the hypothesis; the test of the hypothesis is whether or not the indeterminate situation was transformed. This is an objective public matter. (3) Meaning is always relative to the specific operations and consequences that establish it. There is no possibility of attributing universal truth to statements because there is no method by which this can be done. The limits of human knowledge are the limits of human experience, and as Peirce observed, "experience can never result in absolute certainty, exactitude, necessity, or universality."

We come now to the differences that developed in pragmatic philosophy, particularly the different interpretation of the pragmatic rule by William James. James was greatly impressed by Peirce's approach to the problem of meaning and added the pragmatic method to his own radical empiricism. James saw pragmatic method as a means of finding middle ground between the extremes of tough-mindedness and tender-mindedness, neither of which extreme he thought tenable. He made several formulations of the pragmatic rule and agreed with Peirce that the meaning of a concept lies in its practical consequences.[33] But James also believed that pragmatism could be interpreted as a theory of truth and that such an interpretation would make it possible to test some ideas from theology and philosophy that Peirce himself thought were rendered meaningless by the pragmatic rule. James's interpretation involved extending the meaning of the term *consequences* to include consequences that are ethical and psychological and therefore in a measure subjective, whereas Peirce had restricted the meaning to those that are logical and scientific and hence public and objective. Out of James's extension of pragmatic method came the proposal that if a person believes a certain idea to be true, and if his belief in this idea has certain beneficial results in his experience, then on pragmatic grounds this belief may be judged true.

The most celebrated application of this principle occurs in James's essay "What Pragmatism Means." In this paper he argues that if theological ideas—belief in the existence of God, for example—have favorable consequences in the lives of people, then to that extent the hypothesis that God exists must be true on pragmatic grounds. James qualified the statement somewhat by adding that the truth of the idea also would depend on its relations to other truths; but this qualification was not sufficient to stem the protests that were made against what Peirce and others considered

---

[33] See, for example, James, "What Pragmatism Means," in *Essays in Pragmatism* (New York: Hafner Publishing Co., 1948), p. 142. This famous paper was first published in 1907 and has been reprinted many times.

an unwarranted extension of the rule.[34] Peirce, who had originally coined the term *pragmatism*, eventually gave it up and substituted in its place the word *pragmaticism*, which he said "is ugly enough to be safe from kidnappers." [35]

In developing his own philosophical position, Dewey remained much closer to Peirce than to James, particularly on the public and objective character of consequences. He emphasized that James had recognized the instrumental function that ideas have in experience, but he also pointed out that James had not tried to develop any theory of logical forms based on the instrumental view. Much of Dewey's own work in logic was devoted to the effort to demonstrate that the rules of logic are themselves emergents of inquiry. He did not regard the name *pragmatism* as very useful in characterizing his own philosophical position. In the earlier part of his career, he used the term *instrumentalism* to characterize his own work; in the later part of his life, he described it by *experimentalism*. One of Dewey's most noteworthy contributions to the general pragmatic tradition was his relating of experimental method to the chief aspects of value theory. Ethics was always a primary philosophical interest with Dewey and he saw close relationships between value theory and broad social and educational questions.

## VALUE AND VALUATION

One of the areas both in philosophy and in general experience in which a philosophical tradition reveals its power—or lack of it—is the area of value, specifically, ethics. In this aspect of experience, the theories of reality, of knowledge, and of truth of a given philosophical approach converge to throw light on the most important class of problems human beings encounter. One of the great attractions Peirce's pragmatism had for James was the promise it seemed to offer for a middle ground between the extreme apriorism of various absolutist conceptions of value and the extreme relativism of many positivistic and materialistic approaches to philosophy. James's reinterpretation of the pragmatic rule, which extended the idea of consequences to include more than Peirce had intended, was his effort to make pragmatic method available for analyzing ethical questions. Both Peirce and Dewey objected to James's broadening of the rule. Dewey himself agreed with Peirce that truth is public, and when he set out himself to study the relation of experimental logic to value he stuck with the principle that genuine validation is always objective and public.

---

34 Ibid., p. 154.
35 Buchler, *Peirce*, p. 255.

Dewey's work in experimental logic had led him to the conclusion that the method of intelligence, which he equated with the general method of science, is applicable to any meaningful subject matter. This indicated, at least to himself and his followers, that the processes of inquiry need not be limited to the subject matters with which the natural sciences customarily deal. It is true that by far the most impressive accomplishments of controlled inquiry are to be seen in the natural sciences, the reason being that in those fields the method has had its most rigorous and systematic application. But it should also be recalled that at one time— and that time was not so long ago—men derived many of their beliefs about the physical world by other methods than the experimental approach.

The phenomenal advances of the natural sciences in the past four or five centuries is related directly to the development of methods of inquiry that are built around observation, hypothesis, and experiment. A great part of Dewey's philosophy was the call to submit other areas of human concern to the logic of controlled inquiry. Men meet critical problems in other fields besides physics and biology, and the question is whether such areas as politics, education, and religion can also be unified and ordered in the same way that the natural sciences are unified and made rational. Leaving aside for the moment the question of whether scientific inquiry itself involves any value dimensions, when we come to consider problems of human association and endeavor in social life it is clear to us that these matters seem always to involve dimensions of value. In the face of a problematic situation, as for example in education, we are confronted by the question, What can we do? and also by the question, What ought we do? As is well known, the position of much of Western philosophy is that we shall never find the answer to the second kind of question by using scientific method. For as it is often said, science deals with means and cannot deal with ends.

The application of experimental method to ethical questions is one of the most important contributions of American pragmatism to philosophy. It is also one of the most complex areas of pragmatic thought. An outline of Dewey's arguments on ethical theory will show how they apply to other parts of his philosophical position. Two general questions are pertinent: (1) the nature and origin of ethical norms; and (2) the process of valuation.

One of the facts of experience is that we not only interact with the environment in which we live, but also constantly place value on certain aspects of it and disvalue on others. We are seldom "neutral," for we actively desire and seek to possess some objects and ends and also to avoid others. Some objects and events show themselves to be of such importance and desirability that we idealize them; that is, we endow them with the character of ideals. These ideals then become leading ideas that guide our conduct in various ways amidst the contingencies of experience. These ideals function as norms or standards. They provide criteria that enable us to judge the desirability or the undesirability of specific objects and events. One does not have to be a pragmatic philosopher—in fact, he does not have to be any kind of philosopher—to know that human experience is, among other things, an affair of judging and choosing, in which certain general ideas or concepts exert a normative influence.

The philosophical question arises when we attempt to determine where those normative ideas come from and what their character is, particularly whether they are completely dependable or whether they work out only in certain kinds of circumstances. Perhaps, to understand the position taken by Dewey and other experimentalists, it will help if we give some notice to two extreme points of view on ethical norms. If we think of this question in terms of a continuum, we can identify two polar extremes. One of these is occupied by various absolutistic theories about ethical norms and the other by various forms of ethical relativism.

There are different ways of conceiving norms in terms of absolutes, but they all involve certain common characteristics, namely, that (1) norms are universal in their reference, and (2) they do not change with time and circumstance. Whatever character they are alleged to possess and whatever origins they may be thought to have, the important matter is that as values they have this universality and timelessness. We can expect with considerable confidence that the source of these absolute norms will be something other than nature itself because nature, at least as human beings experience it, does not exhibit any character of complete permanence, and everything that exists is subject to the temporal processes of the natural order. Those who think of ethical norms as universal and timeless, therefore, must conceive of the origins of these standards in some transcendental fashion. This must also mean that ethical standards cannot be derived through empirical method because the limits of that method are the limits of experience.

In Western culture, two main accounts for the origin of absolute ethical norms have developed; many variations of these primary themes have appeared in Western philosophy, but in essence norms are alleged to possess their absolute character either because they are truths revealed directly from some transcendental authority, or because they derive from characteristics built into the very nature of reality and are knowable through rational (not empirical) processes. The first of these is exemplified in the Hebraic-Christian tradition; the second in the Greek tradition of ethical rationalism. The point is that whether values are thought to be the direct pronouncements of an almighty god or rational derivations from the very structure of Being, they are absolute and universal in their character and function.

At the other extreme are the relativists. Their central position is that values do not possess a character of universality and permanence because they are always functions of some context. This context may be objective, in the sense of being cultural and historical, or it may be subjective, in the sense of being personal and psychological. Cultural anthropology has been instrumental in demonstrating how wide and varied the structure of systems of practical ethics actually is. What is viewed as valuable—or at least tolerable—in one society or at one time may be viewed as evil and depraved in another society or at another time.

A tendency now exists to scale down the extreme relativism portrayed by some of the earlier anthropologists and to identify a considerably wider community of ethical beliefs, but even when this is done there is still left over a broad spectrum of differences in ethical standards. This appears to be true even of the so-called subcultures within a society. Thus, there are often marked differences in certain value conceptions among social classes in a society, granted also that there is a community of agreement within the society. Cultural relativists therefore believe that there is an overwhelming amount of empirical evidence against the belief that ethical norms actually are independent of particular cultural and historical contexts.

The other form of ethical relativism involves an underlying subjective element. In this case, things take on value because they are objects of some person's interest and desire. In the ethical theory of the new realist Ralph Barton Perry, if "A value is any object of interest," then the fact of value derives from such psychological factors as wanting and desiring. Things take on the property of value when somebody actively needs and wants them. Unless something else is incorporated in the situation, this form of relativism would appear ultimately to reduce all values to the status of personal taste, which is about as relative as anything can get.

Dewey finds a certain amount of validity in both of these positions on the source and character of ethical standards, but he also finds grave defects in them. The absolutists are right, he thinks, in holding that we actually do possess general ideas, or conceptions, about good and that these general ideas are of importance in guiding our behavior and helping us make decisions. In this sense, we do empirically have ideals and these exert on us a sense of obligation; they are imperative. But the great fallacy in all absolutism lies in the effort to give these leading ethical ideas a transcendental and timeless character. The only way we can say that they have such a character is to hold that they originate outside experience, which in turn raises the question of how they then can be said to function within experience as ethical imperatives. We do not have to endow our scientific ideas with a supernatural character to enhance their status; we know that it is the power of these products of experience to guide inquiry that compels us to admire them and cherish them. The absolutist replies that the case with ethical values is different because ethical values—if they really are ethical and values—exert a moral obligation, or claim, on the individual.

The experimentalist has an answer to this. It is true, he says, that ethical values do exert a moral claim on us, and in the same fashion scientific ideas also exert a claim on our behavior. We know that if we want our scientific inquiries to proceed fruitfully, we have to respect and act in accord with certain ideas and rules. If we do not behave in accordance with these rules, our inquiries will be inept and without significant consequences and we stand little chance of reaching any desired objective. In this sense, the general ideas of scientific procedure do exert a claim on us. They demand, as it were, that we behave in such-and-such ways in the presence of certain kinds of situations. Yet, in the view of pragmatism, nobody can claim seriously that these rules for inquiry are anything but the conceptualized products of antecedent inquiries. These rules are imperative because they have emerged from scientific work and have been tested over and over; and in the process, they have been refined and increasingly perfected. The value they possess and the imperative character they have are owing to the consequences they produce, not their origin.

Dewey's point is that ethical generalizations also are the products of human social experience. Why do we have to embalm them in some metaphysical fluid to appreciate the enormous impact they have in human life? Certainly these ideas have an ethical claim—they *are* imperatives— but this is because prior experience has tested and refined them and in so doing has demonstrated their value for application in future experience. The reason man is a "social animal" is because he has language and can share consciously in social life, and the reason he can become an "ethical animal" is that he can regulate his behavior consciously in terms of the shared moral experience of mankind. Ethical ideas exert a moral claim because they assist us in behaving wisely in the presence of problematic situations in which some value conflict is involved.[36] They are not separate from other kinds of ideas and set against them as absolutely different in kind. They are as natural as anything else that functions in social life.

Thus, the function ethical ideas (standards, norms, ideals, and so on) have in experience is acting as *leading ideas;* in this role they help us make the decisions we are called on to make in the presence of confused and problematic situations. In Dewey's experimentalism, valuation is essentially the process of intelligent inquiry, and intelligent inquiry presupposes our possession of ideas that derive from antecedent experience and are relevant in some fashion to the matter in hand.[37] Before we turn to a consideration of the process of ethical inquiry, we shall give attention to some ideas stemming from the relativistic end of the continuum.

It will be recalled that at the other extreme are found those conceptions of ethical standards that involve the relation of ethical norms to some kind

---

[36] See Dewey's discussion of moral claims in John Dewey and James H. Tufts, *Ethics* (New York: Henry Holt and Co., 1932), pp. 236 ff.

[37] Ibid., pp. 304–13.

of specific context. A context may be cultural-historical or psychological. In Dewey's estimation, there was something important to be learned about value theory from these positions. For one thing, whenever we meet some allegedly universal ethical standard, we know that this standard has a history. It has arisen in some kind of social context and it has had certain kinds of consequences. These matters are of great importance to us as we consider the relevance any particular idea may have for our own ethical deliberations.[38]

In the second place, whenever we meet a problematic situation, we do have a stake in the issue. The situation is problematic because the elements in the situation are blocking our efforts to realize some objective that we have an interest in. Thus, interest and desire play a part in the ethical situation, for clearly if nothing is desired and no need must be fulfilled, there is no problem, ethical or otherwise. Need and desire are elements in the situation that generate the ethical problem, but it is one thing to say that and another thing to say that desire and desirability are the same thing. The function of reflection is to guide impulse into reasoned response, that behavior in which account is taken of future consequences. That an object or event is desired is simply an occurrence—a fact—but whether the object is *desirable* is a matter of reflective thought that attempts to estimate what effects will follow if this impulse is acted on.

We come now to the question of how the general method of inquiry can be used in dealing with situations that have value dimensions. Situations of this character have their origins in experience and arise when habit becomes insufficient to guide behavior. We are confronted by a state of affairs in which we do not know what to do. The question that is often asked is how a value situation differs from one that is ethically neutral. What is the difference between a moral act and one in which moral dimensions are lacking? In Dewey's estimation, the difference is mostly one of degree rather than kind, for every act potentially has moral dimensions.[39]

Whenever the road of experience forks, whenever we are faced with the necessity of choosing one way instead of another, the likelihood is that the consequences of our chosen act will affect the lives and interests of other people, and certainly the course of our own conduct and character will be affected. That the effect of some actions is minimal, nobody will deny, but Dewey believed Aristotle was right when he observed of a moral act that not only must a man be aware of what he is doing and be able to choose, *but the act itself must be a true expression of a formed and stable character.*[40] So, the moral quality of any act is, in part at least, owing to the fact that this particular act is continuous with the previous experience

---

[38]  Ibid., pp. 161–63.

[39]  Ibid., pp. 178 ff.

[40]  Ibid., p. 176.

of the person, that it represents a deliberate and considered decision to act in a given way, and that therefore it is neither purely impulsive nor merely the product of routine habit.

Problematic situations that have ethical properties arise in the same way any problematic situation arises. There is an existential state of affairs in which we find ourselves. The situation itself is disunified and indeterminate. The road forks and there is nothing forthcoming from our previous experience that tells us what we should do—and yet, we must do something. At this point it should be emphasized that all ethical situations are specific and unique. What we are required to do is to find a way to act *under those circumstances at this particular time.* We are not called on to solve all problems or to make universal judgments or to find some *summum bonum.* We are called on to find a way to act *now* that promises best to transform the indeterminate character of the events in which we find ourselves to one that is unified and determinate.

The situation that confronts us always is unique. It is unlike any that has ever existed before and also any that will ever exist again. It is problematic because the residue of prior experience is insufficient to guide us under these circumstances, though such previous learning must provide a means for instituting inquiry if we are to deal with the situation intelligently. As a situation, it is not simply a matter of choosing between right and wrong, for if there are these two courses of action and these are plainly labeled in some way, *there is no problem.* It is true that much traditional moral theory proceeds on the assumption that ethical acts are essentially choices between alternatives that represent good or evil. If this is really the case, then ethical actions represent merely the *will* to choose the *right* path, and reflection plays a subservient role if indeed it plays any at all. Dewey used an example of a bank clerk who is considering embezzling money. This clerk knows perfectly well that to embezzle the bank's money is wrong and in this sense there is no ethical problem at all. He may be trying to find some reason why it would not be wrong for him to take the money, but, said Dewey, "He is not really thinking, he is merely permitting his desire to govern his beliefs." [41] It may seem a simple and trustworthy matter to say that to live an ethical life means to "follow the rules," the rules being the Ten Commandments or some other code, but what do we do when we are not clear what a given rule means under a particular set of circumstances? Things do not always come plainly labeled "good" and "evil"; if they did, there would be no need for reflection nor would there be any need for ethical theories.

The reason a genuinely moral act involves reflection is that the choice of action we must make is really a choice among competing goods. It is this

---

[41] Ibid., p. 174.

fact that sets the problem for inquiry and also it is the condition that gives our ethical decisions the poignant quality they have. In demonstrating that moral problems originate when goods come into conflict with each other, Dewey used the example of a man whose country has just declared war.[42] This person is a good and loyal citizen who loves his country and is devoted to its welfare. But he also harbors fundamental convictions that are anchored in his religious beliefs that war is evil and is really nothing but mass murder. But, he is told on good authority, the only way the nation can survive is to wage war resolutely and by any means possible to destroy the enemy. Unless total victory is achieved, the nation will be lost.

A man faced with these circumstances is not presented with the simple choice of good or evil. On the one hand, he is powerfully affected by his concern for the country he loves and wishes to preserve, but he is also torn in another direction by his deep-seated religious and ethical beliefs against killing human beings. Up to this time these values have not been in conflict and in reality have often seemed to reinforce each other. But they are in conflict now, and what is the universal ethical rule that can be invoked to settle this matter?

In ethical inquiry, as in any genuine act of inquiry, we search for a way to act that promises best to change the indeterminate character of the situation. The resources we have to assist us are the fruits of previous experience in the form of ideas. We attempt to foresee the consequences of possible action as best we can and to evaluate and choose on the basis of our foresight. The idea we choose to act on is tested by the way it affects the situation that generated the problem. Can we be sure that in this kind of reflection we shall always foresee all possible consequences? No, there can be no such assurance. If we act on the basis of the most careful reflection we are capable of, can we be sure we shall do the "right" thing? No, not if by the right thing is meant that all situations are capable of being resolved satisfactorily for all concerned or that we are always able to perceive what means will best secure the ends we desire. Given the kind of world we live in, we find the quest for certainty futile, for certainty is no more attainable in the making of judgments about value than it is in making scientific judgments.

The objections to Dewey's approach to ethical theory are numerous and of varied character, stemming as they do both from absolutist and from naturalistic-relativistic sources. The absolutist's fundamental criticism is that Dewey refuses to grant universality and permanence to ethical standards and that he insists that values originate in experience and must be tested in experience. There are many variations on this theme, but the common element in all of them is that ideas cannot have a normative

---

[42] Ibid.

function unless they are in some secure sense absolute and unless there is some ultimate Good to which all other goods are subordinate in the sense of being merely instrumental to the Ultimate. This Good may be the *eudaemonia* of Aristotle or the spiritual salvation of the New Testament, but however it may be conceived, all other goods are subaltern to it.

Although Dewey's own ethical theory is in the naturalistic tradition, he also receives severe criticism from others of that tradition, in large measure because he has refused to accept the belief that unexamined desire or preference is sufficient to determine value—in short, that to be desired means to be desirable. If ethical statements are simply expressions of our own desires and feelings, as some modern analytic philosophy holds, then a cognitive ethics is simply impossible, for statements of this kind are neither true nor false. It is permissible to say that they are meaningful, in the sense that they do communicate our own feelings and desires, but we can no more attribute truth or falsity to the imperative "Love thy neighbor!" than we can to the imperative "Shut the door!" Under this view, ethical norms function as axioms do in logical systems. They can be related logically to certain rules of conduct, but they cannot themselves be proven true.[43]

Dewey's answer—at least one of his answers—is that there is no substitute for knowledge in conducting any inquiry, whether the inquiry is concerned with science, with common sense, or with ethics. The conditions that control inquiry are those inherent in the situation. It is they that determine what is relevant and what is not. To the extent that we understand the factual structure of the situation, we are able to make wise decisions to act. Even if we do not wish to agree that knowledge is virtue, this hardly means that ignorance is the best state of mind for making ethical decisions.[44]

Dewey has maintained that one of the underlying causes for this disjunction between knowledge and values, between fact and worth, is the ancient dualism that sets mind and consciousness against a material environment of brute fact. Under this view, knowledge, science, and inquiry can only deal with primary qualities inherent in the world of things while those qualities men prize for what they are in themselves are secondary and subjective. But a thoroughgoing naturalism recognizes that within nature things and events possess not only instrumental potentialities but also final qualities that are as much a part of their natures as any other qualities they may possess.[45] Once we set man and his experience apart

---

[43] See, for example, Hans Reichenbach, *The Rise of Scientific Philosophy* (Berkeley, Cal.: University of California Press, 1951), chap. 17.

[44] An interesting development of this point is found in Charles S. Stevenson, "The Scientist's Role and the Aims of Education," *Harvard Educational Review* 24:231–38.

[45] *Experience and Nature*, p. 96.

from nature, we inherit all the dualisms that philosophy has to cope with, and so every generation struggles with the problem of being, the problem of knowledge, and the problem of value. But what is held to be a problem here, in the judgment of the naturalist, is a pseudoproblem, for it is an effort to find a way to account for our possession of what we do empirically possess, which is to say it is the effort to rejoin by elaborate means what should never have been put asunder.

## MAN AND NATURE:
## THE ONTOLOGY OF PRAGMATISM

It is often said that pragmatism as a philosophical tradition offers nothing but a method. Some have held that it cannot rightfully be called a philosophy at all because it has refused to be concerned with metaphysical questions except in a destructively critical way. It is true that pragmatists (James is perhaps in some measure an exception here) have declined to deal with the traditional "why" questions: Why are we here? Why do we suffer? Why is there evil in the world? We know that the pragmatic rule eliminates as meaningless those questions that do not lend themselves to the operations of inquiry, and "why" questions are generally of this kind. However, though such questions may be meaningless in the linguistic and scientific sense, they are genuinely expressive of the realities of experience that go on in a world that itself possesses basic attributes of contingency and unpredictability.[46]

In the early part of his career, Dewey foresaw that one of the effects of the theory of organic evolution that would be most difficult for modern man to accept was a new concept of nature that departed radically from the idealized cosmology of the classic tradition, the anthropocentricism of the Hebraic-Christian tradition, and perhaps even the mechanistic determinism of Newtonian physics. Those worlds, each in its own way, displayed a character of completion and fixity. They seemed to provide a secure place for the human drama to be played out because they exhibited a basic character of rationality, lawfulness, and order into which it was possible to read the answers to the "why" questions. But the physics of relativity and the revolution in biology and all that has followed from these have changed our conceptions of the conditions under which we must live and work. There are various possible ways to react to the kind of world portrayed by modern science and in a certain degree today's philosophy has attempted some interpretation of the new cosmology and the place of man in the scheme of things. Pragmatism is one of the tradi-

---

[46] One of Dewey's most important contributions to naturalistic ontology is found in *Experience and Nature*, chaps. 2 and 3.

tions in modern philosophy in which the consequences of a scientific, naturalistic outlook have been developed philosophically.

In the view of this tradition, traditional philosophies have been pre-occupied with putting a sure, finished, complete character on the "world of real existence" and they often have shown themselves capable of going to any extreme to do it. But, says the pragmatist, regardless of what pre-vious philosophizing says about the identity of the Real with what is sure and complete and perfect, empirically we do live in a world in which all is not finished and sure. The world we know in our experience is a mixture of the ordered and the indeterminate.

Even when classic metaphysics identifies the good with the Real, the fact still remains that something is left over that is uncertain, fluid, and changing. This was relegated in the classic tradition to the realm of "be-coming" or "appearance" or the "merely empirical," and yet, the pragma-tist reminds us, the world remains what it is and always was—a suffusion of the indeterminate and the relatively stable. In this arbitrary separation of the seemingly permanent and the obviously transient, philosophy for-sook the very conditions that brought it into being; for it is at the point where the unstable and the regular impinge, where the goods men desire are the most elusive, and where choice demands struggle and action that philosophy was born. If philosophy was indeed born of wonder, as Aristotle said, classic metaphysics converted it from wonder to contemplation.

The very fact that men do experience satisfaction indicates that nature is characterized by both the assured and the perilous. Satisfactions come as the result of difficulties being cleared up and of the consequent relief from tensions. If there were no hindrances, or no blockings in the environ-ment, and if the path were always smooth and assured, there would be no tension and no satisfaction. When a desirable fulfillment does come, it is taken as good because its possession was and continues to be un-certain and because it had to be striven after. Once a desired outcome is achieved and experienced, it becomes ideal. We make it ideal because prior experience has shown it to be worthy of desire and effort. In retrospect, we commemorate its issue from struggle to assurance. Thus, the precarious nature of existence is, in a sense, the source of all trouble, but it also is the condition of all satisfaction and hence of all ideality.

If the world were not in its basic character partly a matter of con-tingency and indeterminacy, what role would intelligence have to play? To Dewey and other pragmatists, the office of thinking is one of clearing up the dubious and making the situation assured—of passing from doubt to belief, in Peirce's terms. Thinking is like any tool or natural energy that may be used to clear up the indeterminate by applying to it the regular and assured. Thinking is not an abrupt transition from a "natural" to a "ra-tional" level; it is reorganizing and reconstructing experience within a world of space and time. The problematic always lies where the unpredictable and the stable intersect, and in this sense every act, idea, and existence is an experiment. Those whose wish it is to act wisely, and to have their actions guided by intelligence, must be cognizant of the nature of the world, for those who do not understand how to use nature to advantage will be continually at its mercy. We may as well face the reality that nothing lasts forever. Any existent thing has its existence in some context and all the forces operating in that context are never entirely compatible with its existence. Change is intelligible only as a relation of events and permanency is comparative, not absolute. An existence may endure for eons, but not forever.

There are always those who lament this and refuse to face it, and in the estimation of pragmatists, there are distinguished representatives of this group to be found in the history of philosophy. But as Dewey has said, there is no occasion to gloat over or to mourn what is so clearly a fact of nature. If the goods we prize are not eternal, neither are the evils that plague us. If the game is not rigged in our favor, neither is it rigged against us. The call is to face the world we know and in which we must live. The way to make secure in the future those things that deliberation shows to be most worthy of preserving is by studying and inquiring into events, assaying their interconnections, and noting the final qualities for which we prize them.

Inquiry is the method of intelligence, and in the estimation of Peirce and Dewey, the method of intelligence is the general method of science. In having said this, we are brought full circle in our study of the liberal protest. In the preface to the first edition of *How We Think,* Dewey wrote:

> This scientific attitude of mind might conceivably be quite irrelevant to teaching children and youth. But this book also represents the conviction that such is not the case; that the native and unspoiled attitude of childhood, marked by ardent curiosity, fertile imagination, and love of experimental inquiry, is near, very near, to the attitude of the scientific mind.

## SUMMARY: IMPACT OF THE LIBERAL PROTEST

What influence, then, has the liberal protest had on American educational philosophy? Our consideration of the progressive protest against essentialism has been concerned mainly with the educational theory developed within this tradition and for which John Dewey took the main responsibility. Some attention has been given to the historic context out of which this philosophy developed but we have made no effort to portray the wide scope and the varied character the progressive movement assumed in the years between the turn of the century and the ending of the

Second World War. For this reason the assessment made here will be confined largely to the impact of the liberal protest as this protest was evidenced in a systematic philosophical position in which educational theory had an organic relation with American pragmatism. In the last chapter of his *Transformation of the School*, Lawrence Cremin advanced a number of reasons for the abrupt decline of the progressive education movement. Those who wish a broader understanding of the decline of progressivism and the resurgence of a militant conservatism should study the concluding chapter of Cremin's book.

Both the friends and the foes of Dewey's progressivism and his experimental naturalism have often found it useful to overstate the impact of this tradition. Conservatives have sometimes proclaimed it the cause of all our social ills, and it is not unusual to find adherents of progressive educational philosophy attributing every significant advance in the status of public education directly to it. For example, it seems reasonable to think that on historical grounds the following achievements may properly be claimed for the American educational system in this century.

1.   Conceptions of the purposes of free public education have been extended and enhanced. The idea that every person should have educational opportunities appropriate to his own needs and abilities is probably more nearly realized in this country than anywhere else on earth. (It is granted that this achievement is incomplete and that the statement means somewhat different things in conservatism and in progressivism.)
2.   The school curriculum has been liberalized and extended. A broader range of educational experiences is now available than ever before in history.
3.   Conceptions of individual and group discipline have become more humane and in some ways more effective.
4.   The importance, as well as the possibility, of enlisting child interest and purpose in the educative process have been demonstrated. (Here again the differing perceptions of conservatives and progressives of the meaning of this statement should be noted.)
5.   The materials of instruction have been improved and many new devices and materials have been developed.
6.   The value of orienting method and curriculum around scientifically established concepts of human development and the psychology of learning has been established.

That the liberal protest movement favored such developments and supported them at virtually every turn appears so well established as to be outside the possibility of serious argument. It is, however, quite another thing to attribute them solely or even mainly to the direct influence of educational progressivism. The extension of the scope of the curriculum, for example, has included many areas that progressives never particularly sanctioned, and certainly in the case of many narrow vocational courses it is fruitless to search for support of these in the educational writings of John Dewey. In the same way, progressives view the products of the "new technology" with mixed feelings, even though they have consistently favored and worked for the improvement of the materials of instruction. It does not appear necessary to go beyond the facts to say that many of these changes probably would have come about anyway, whether a rigorous protest movement in liberal educational philosophy had developed in this century or not.

The purpose of these remarks is not to belittle or denigrate the achievements of educational progressivism. But the causes of cultural change are always complex, and there have been many forces at work in this century besides the experimentalism of John Dewey and the varying interpretations placed on it by his host of followers. The really foundational elements in Dewey's educational philosophy never received widespread testing in the progressive movement, however. Why this was so is a matter best left to the historians, and Cremin for one has already found some cogent things to say about it.

For Dewey, education was a process in which the latent, plastic powers and tendencies of the child were developed through a carefully planned sequence of experience in which experimental method was the basis of educational method. In this view, the purpose of educational effort is the continuous growth of the person in the fullest possible sense. There is nothing that growth can be subordinate to for growth itself is what is "given." Neither can education, which itself is growth, be said to be subordinate to something else—particularly to some distant *summum bonum* that more often than not is endowed with a mystical character. Dewey believed that education is something more—considerably more—than the communication of established knowledge and that the method of education ought to reflect the principle that in the long view what the Greeks used to call "the art of knowledge" is more important than the products of that art, as valuable as they may be. Dewey's contention that the curriculum of the school should be a process of active work was closely related to his studies in psychology and philosophy. It has been suggested in this book that the main difference between the pedagogy of progressivism and that of essentialism is that progressivism viewed the curriculum as an ordered series of active enterprises, whereas essentialism has always seen it as some ordered series of subject matters. It has also been suggested that most of the differences in practical methodology of the two traditions stem from this source.

The idea that knowing and doing are inextricably linked in the cognitive process was never grasped very firmly in progressive practice, and the "activity movement" that reached its highwater mark in the thirties proceeded at the practical level largely without any real psychological or logical foundations. That this lack of understanding by teachers led to much questionable improvisation and playing by ear is well established, and if there was any connection to be found between what Dewey had called the method of intelligence and the cutting, coloring, and pasting that went on in many schools in the 1930s, it was not easy to locate.

What had begun as the "project method" developed by William H. Kilpatrick, one of the most celebrated of the interpreters of Dewey's educational philosophy, grew into the "activity movement" of the 1930s and by the close of that decade had become formalized in a kind of "unit teaching" that often bore about as much resemblance to the active enterprises of the Laboratory School as the formalized Pestalozzian object lesson had to the Old Master's own work at Yverdon.[47]

Probably no reform movement ever really succeeds, if by success is meant that the foundations of its ideology receive faithful translation into action. Certainly if this is the criterion of success, Dewey's long adventure into educational theory was a failure, and by the same token, so were those of Plato and Rousseau and Pestalozzi and all the others who came before him. Whatever else it may or may not have done, progressivism raised the question of what the purposes and means of education must be in an industrial, urban society, whose basic pattern is as different from the early industrialism of the nineteenth century as an Apollo rocket is from a box kite. We have not mastered this question yet.

Viewed in retrospect, Dewey's effort was to find the way to a new humanism, a humanism that would be built on the achievements and potentialities of scientific method and the ethical postulates of democracy. In the evolution of this new humanism, education, he thought, should play a strategic role, but in many respects it should be a new education in which the insights of science would assist us in the fuller realization of our common humanity. With the conditions that existed in American schools of the 1890s, some kind of reform movement probably was inevitable. It may well be that for the progressive movement the historical irony is that Dewey's influence could not have been greater. Perhaps one way to sum it all up is to say that this, the greatest of the protest movements against American essentialism, ultimately was sold out—unconsciously, to be sure—by those who in Sidney Hook's words "thought they could remain progressive while ceasing to be liberal."

---

[47] See William H. Kilpatrick, "The Project Method," *Teachers College Record* 19 (1918): 319–35.

# chapter EIGHT

# THE PROTEST
# OF THE PERENNIAL
# PHILOSOPHY

*. . . We act as if the task of education were to infuse into the child or the adolescent, only abridging and concentrating it, the very science or knowledge of the adult—that is to say, of the philologist, the historian, the grammarian, the scientist, etc., the most specialized experts. So we try to cram young people with a chaos of summarized adult notions which have been either condensed, dogmatized, and textbookishly cut up or else made so easy that they are reduced to the vanishing point. As a result, we run the risk of producing either an instructed, bewildered intellectual dwarf, or an ignorant intellectual dwarf playing at dolls with our science.*

—JACQUES MARITAIN

There are three traditions in philosophy and education that, along with progressivism, constitute significant protests against modern American essentialism in educational theory and practice. One of these three traditions has been given the name *perennialism,* or *the perennial philosophy.* The perennial philosophy was formed from a great synthesis of the Hebraic-Christian tradition in theology and the Hellenic tradition in philosophy. Perennialism, therefore, presents for our consideration a view of the world and of man that in many important respects is very different from other ideas about these matters.

For example, the established, or conservative, tradition in American education is a product primarily of the modern world. We have seen that there are important elements of both the classic and medieval traditions still to be found in conservatism today, yet this tradition in its basic structure exhibits the postmedieval and middle-class nature of its origins. In America, the conservative tradition, differing as it does in certain important respects from European conservatism, has incorporated much of that strain of eighteenth-century liberalism from which emerged the economic "rugged individualism" and "free enterprise" so clearly associated with the American character. Conservatism is also the tradition that has attempted to accommodate the tenets of supernatural religion to the spirit, methodology, and achievements of experimental science. Thus it has tried to fashion a kind of "public philosophy" by which men may live in a culture characterized by science and corporate industrialism but by which they may also regulate their lives according to a tradition, many of whose roots lie in the supernatural. The eclectic character of the conservative tradition is mirrored in the educational theory advanced and supported by that tradition and in the schools of our time.

It is important to understand that perennialism is not simply a kind of conservative philosophy of society and education, although it has on occasion been treated in the literature as if it were, just as some of the leading American spokesmen for the perennialist protest against American essentialism sometimes have been classified as educational conservatives. The protest of the perennial philosophy is not against simply the educational theories of the modern world—whether these are conservative or liberal. Its objections are not merely to miscellaneous ideas in science or philosophy, which for one reason or another it finds untenable. Perennialism is a strong and continuing protest against the pattern of contemporary Western culture with its science and technology, its corporate industrialism, and its political and educational institutions, which in America, at least, have become almost completely secularized. It is, in effect, an invitation—or perhaps better, an insistence—that we turn our backs on the folly we have wrought and return to a pattern of culture that Western man abandoned nearly half a dozen centuries ago. In this sense, perennialism is openly and frankly a proposal for cultural regression, for at the heart of its proposals is the demand that we return to those conceptions of nature, of man, of society, and of the nature of good from which we were tempted by the hollow and arrogant promises of natural science and middle-class economics.

Clearly, a proposal of this kind puts perennialism in opposition to modern conservatism and modern liberalism, for both of these recognize the inevitability of cultural change and social evolution, though the conservative and the liberal differ sharply on the desirable rate of cultural alteration. Even so, both conservatism and liberalism represent efforts to combine the basic elements of modern culture into a workable synthesis. Both these traditions support democracy, capitalism, nationalism, and experimental science, although both of them continue to experience difficulty in accommodating these traditions to each other. Both the conservative and liberal traditions have accepted natural science and the profound alterations it has brought about in Western life, and both of them have found an important place for scientific studies in the curriculum of the schools. The invasion of the traditional humanistic curriculum by the natural sciences has created strains within American essentialism that at times seem almost intolerable, yet there is seldom found in the present-day literature of the conservative tradition any serious proposal to eliminate natural science from the curriculum or to give it a truly subordinate role.

So far as education is concerned, perennialism has always found progressivism a natural and usually a mortal enemy. This is because it is in progressivism that the influence of modern naturalism and empiricism is most clearly seen, and the perennialist believes that the gross ills of modern society may be traced ultimately to these two elements. It is true that on occasion essentialists and perennialists have joined forces against the common enemy, progressivism, particularly in earlier decades of the present century, when the progressive protest was far stronger than it is today. It is likely that this temporary truce was part of the cause for some commentators' listing of prominent American perennialists as educational conservatives. Any truce between essentialism and perennialism, however, is mostly a matter of convenience and is always uneasy. Though it is certain that perennialism has no love for progressivism, the important point is that the main thrust of the perennialist protest is against the established American tradition in education, and the prevailing tradition in American education is essentialism. Robert M. Hutchins, certainly one of the foremost spokesmen for the perennial tradition in America, has for many years engaged progressives in lively combat over educational theory, but he has always been at his best when lambasting existing educational institutions, particularly the American university—that citadel of American essentialism.

If we are to understand the part that perennialism plays in today's educational scene, we must see it as a vigorous and serious protest against the character of American society, and we must also understand that the proposals of perennialism for the righting of the wrongs that infest our system of education necessarily involve profound changes in the pattern of contemporary culture. To understand the proposals for educational reform that perennialists advocate so vigorously, we must analyze a view of the world and man's place in it that originated in classic Greek thought, reached its full flower in the works of Plato and Aristotle, and ultimately became amalgamated with the Hebraic-Christian tradition in the great medieval synthesis. Our first step in this inquiry will be to survey the character of modern perennialism.

## THE CHARACTER OF MODERN PERENNIALISM

In some respects perennialists are more pessimistic about the future of Western man than any other important group in America. The depth and intensity of this attitude vary from one spokesman for the tradition to another, but the roots of their pessimism are the same, and lie in the interpretation of history that often appears in perennialist literature. Under this view, the decline of Western society began in the fourteenth century and the event that precipitated this decadence was the abandonment of the classic belief in the independent existence of universals. This event came about as a consequence of the great medieval debate over the character of universals in which the Platonic, the Aristotelian, and various intermediate positions were argued by some of the greatest philosophic minds in Europe.[1] Briefly, the debate over universals concerned the question whether universal ideas have a real existence and if they do, how the universal is related to the particular. For example, it may be asked whether there is a universal idea of man that has an existence that is independent of individual men and yet is in some way related to the individual natures of different men? Plato took the position that ultimate reality is composed of forms (universals) that exist prior to and independent of any particular things or events. Plato was convinced that particular things owe their natures to participation in these universals, but he never could develop a complete demonstration of this relation. The Platonic position figured strongly in the debate that developed in the medieval world, in which it

---

[1]  This thesis that the alleged decadence of modern culture began with the defeat of logical realism and the ultimate triumph of nominalism has been developed in a brilliant and remarkable book by Richard M. Weaver, *Ideas Have Consequences* (Chicago: University of Chicago Press, 1948). Weaver is often spoken of as a conservative and has contributed to conservative publications. However he may be classified otherwise, the essentially Platonic argument he advances in this book indicates strong leanings toward the perennialist explanation for the sickness of present-day society.

was argued as "Extreme Realism" by such able adherents as Anselm of Canterbury (1033–1109). Anselm's position was that universals exist independent of thought or things; thus there is a universal form of man that exists prior to and independent of any particular person. As a Christian, he went beyond Plato in arguing that universals exist in the mind of God, and therefore when we recognize truth, our minds are in accord with the mind of God.

A serious difference over the status of universals developed between Plato and Aristotle.[2] Where Plato had insisted that the universal exists prior to and independent of particulars, Aristotle maintained that the universal (form) always is found united with matter in substantial entities. This principle of the union of form and matter is known as *hylomorphism*. Aristotle's position on the status of universals is known as *moderate realism*. In the medieval debate, the most distinguished advocate of moderate realism was Thomas Aquinas (1225–1274), and this essentially Aristotelian doctrine was ultimately accepted as the philosophic position of the Church.

Certain intermediate positions on universals developed, but the real challenge to logical realism was offered by a philosophic position usually known as *nominalism*. Nominalism is, in essence, the denial that general terms (that is, universals) actually refer to anything that really exists; it holds instead that universals are simply terms that have been found convenient for denoting objects that are similar. According to this idea therefore, anything that is real is an individual thing. Any universal ideas we may have about individual things consequently are products of our own observation and classification and they have no reality beyond that; they are simply words. An early advocate of this position was Roscellinus (c. 1050–1122) who was forced by the Church to recant. The most celebrated advocate of nominalism, however, was William of Occam, a fourteenth-century philosopher. Occam's nominalism was regarded as dangerous to various aspects of the doctrinal position of the Church, for if nominalism is accepted as a correct explanation of the character of universals, it becomes impossible to demonstrate philosophically certain important tenets of the Christian faith, for example, such important tenets as the existence of God and the immortality of the soul. Therefore, since it is impossible to demonstrate these doctrines rationally, all that remains is the possibility of accepting them purely on the basis of faith. Such a position was rejected by the Church.

Many moderns may well wonder what the debate over these ideas has to do with events in the contemporary world, particularly since this great intellectual controversy occurred over five centuries ago. Perennialists,

---

[2]  Aristotle's criticism of Plato's doctrine of the forms is found in *Metaphysics*, Book I.

however, are of the opinion that the consequences of this debate have a great deal to do with the character of contemporary society and some of those in this tradition, whose pessimism about modern society runs deep, believe that the eventual triumph of nominalism paved the way for modern decadence. Richard Weaver, whom we have identified as a representative of this view, has said that the net effect of nominalism has been to deny the reality known by the mind and to put in its place what we know through the senses. And, he argues, once this profound philosophical reorientation was achieved the West started down the road to modern empiricism.[3] That we have continued to follow this road explains the predicament in which modern man finds himself. This road has led us to rationalism; thence inevitably to materialism; to the arrogance of experimental science; to technology, which is the fruit of scientific materialism; and to industrial society in which man is no longer *Homo sapiens*, but *Homo faber*. Weaver is not very sanguine about the chances of our survival; ours, he points out, would not be the first civilization in history to disappear into oblivion.

If we do have a chance to survive, it will be realized to the extent that we can correct the momentous error that was committed. The road back to the point at which we were betrayed by our ancestors may be a long one, and our hopes of reaching it are by no means assured, but it is the only effort that can be worth while. We must recapture for ourselves the vision of the objectivity of truth, which is possible only if universals have an independent reality of their own. If we can do this, we shall again accept the view of man and nature encompassed in classical and medieval philosophy, and once this view is reinstated as dominant, the school, the church, and other great institutions of society will be purged of their ills and will once again become effective in the lives of men.

Not all of today's proponents of the perennial philosophy profess as profound a pessimism as Weaver's, nor do they always argue that the whole course of Western history has been determined simply by the triumph of nominalistic philosophy. On the other hand, there are few, if any, of this philosophic persuasion who do not believe that profound changes must occur in contemporary society if we are to escape a final disaster, and the model they most often present to us to guide our efforts is one in which the classic and medieval traditions in society and education predominate.

Modern perennialism in America is represented by two main groups. The community of interest between these two groups is extensive but there is also a fundamental difference between them. Both these groups have had a very great deal to say about educational theory and practice,

---

[3] *Ideas Have Consequences*, p. 3.

and there is wide agreement between them concerning the ills that are typical of American education. They often find themselves in close accord on proposals for remedying these ills. One of these groups is made up of men who identify themselves primarily, though not exclusively, with the original classic Greek philosophic tradition, particularly Aristotelianism. Their approach to education, for example, is most often characterized by Aristotelian conceptions of human nature and the nature of society, of science, and of ethics. We refer to this wing of modern American perennialism as *rational humanism*. The other main group comprises those who represent the modern version of scholasticism, which is to say that they are the modern intellectual heirs of Saint Thomas Aquinas and medieval scholasticism. This group will be referred to as neo-Scholastics or neo-Thomists. The fundamental difference between the rational humanists and the neo-Scholastics is that those in the former group are not identified with the Roman Catholic church and do not necessarily subscribe to its theological doctrines; a survey of the literature, however, will reveal a sympathetic attitude on the part of many non-Catholic perennialists toward Roman Catholic theology. On the other hand, the neo-Scholastics are composed partly of lay philosophers, some of whom are scholars of high distinction and who have made distinguished contributions to perennialist educational philosophy. Others of this neo-Scholastic group are members of the Roman Catholic clergy, but they often approach the problems of education from philosophical as well as theological grounds.

We may summarize modern perennialism by saying that (1) it is a strong and continuing protest against much of modern industrial society; (2) it insists that the salvation of Western society depends on our achieving a reorientation of our views of the universe and of man, which will involve a recovery of the classic and scholastic theses; and (3) the tradition today in America is represented by two groups, one secular and proceeding mainly from Aristotelian premises, the other religious and oriented about the Thomistic tradition. Although there are differences between these two groups, these differences being occasioned perhaps more by theology than by philosophy, there is also much common ground. One of the areas in which there is considerable unanimity is educational theory. Both wings of this tradition have often launched bitter criticism against American education. Our next step in the analysis of the perennial philosophy will be to examine the protest this tradition makes against the state of things in American schools.

## PERENNIALIST PROTEST IN EDUCATION

In the first chapter of one of his earlier books, Robert Hutchins said that the confusion in American higher education is caused by three primary conditions in society: the love of money, a misconception of democracy, and a mistaken idea of progress.[4] The university is not free, and hence cannot be a true intellectual center, because it is always pursuing money, either from legislative bodies or private donors, usually from both, and always from students. The practical effect of the love of money is the emergence of the "service station" concept of education, which means, said Hutchins, that a university must make itself "felt in the community." The expectation is that whatever immediate problems face society must be taken up and made the primary business of the university. Since the character of these problems varies from one period of time to another, the university expends its energy and resources variously on everything from agriculture to military weaponry, and the purposes for which the higher learning should exist are honored only in the breach. The American university persists in keeping underclassmen on its rolls because typically they pay more in fees than it costs to teach them (at least in proportion to the cost for upperclassmen and graduate students), since they can be entrusted to graduate students who can be made into teaching fellows and who will work for low wages.[5] Thus, the love of money helps perpetuate the confusion of collegiate education with university education and few Americans can tell the difference.

The scramble for money has increased manyfold in the years since the end of the last World War, primarily because of the vast sums of it that have been poured into universities by the federal government and by private business for various kinds of research. A whole new class of administrators has developed; the purpose these officials serve is to get as many research projects as possible for their institutions. The status of faculty members necessarily is determined more and more by the amount of federal or industrial money they have been able to garner. Hutchins has said, "The universities have demonstrated their willingness to do almost anything for money."[6]

The second source of confusion in American education lies in a misapprehension of what democracy means, particularly when the term is applied to educational theory. The chief effects of the confusion over

---

[4]  *The Higher Learning in America* (New Haven: Yale University Press, 1936), reissued in 1962 as a Yale Paperbound with a new preface by Hutchins. References here are to the later edition. Many changes have occurred in American education since the publication of *The Higher Learning*, but Hutchins's criticisms appear to have about as much relevance as they ever had. It is possible to interpret many of today's events as fulfillments of his predictions.

[5]  Ibid., p. 8.

[6]  Ibid., p. xi.

democracy are several. First, this confusion is responsible for the typical American belief that a young person should be allowed to stay in school as long as he likes, study whatever appeals to him, and be a candidate for any degree he finds attractive.[7] Thus, the typical American belief has developed that everybody has a right to the same amount and the same kind of education as everybody else. Another effect, one closely allied to the two just noted, is that everybody in the country thinks he is an expert on education and rarely forgoes the opportunity to intrude himself into the making of educational policy. And when the citizens set out to tell the authorities how the public schools and colleges or the universities should be run, the confusion is many times compounded.

The other source of the confusion that affects education in our country is our misconceived notion of what constitutes progress. We tend to identify progress with accumulation of information and development of science and technology. In a search for more and more information, the sciences have become increasingly specialized, and one by one they have split off from their original source, which Hutchins, like most perennialists, believes to be philosophy. The final triumph of empiricism came, he said, "when the social sciences, law, and even philosophy and theology themselves became experimental and progressive."[8] Here we see again the theme that runs through perennialist thought: the ultimate source of our troubles lies in our abandonment of logical realism—and therefore in our denial of the power and importance of human reason—and our acceptance of nominalism and hence of empiricism. "And so," Hutchins said, "empiricism having taken the place of thought as the basis of research, took its place, too, as the basis of education. It led by easy stages to vocationalism; because the facts you learn about your environment (particularly if you love money) ought to be as immediate and useful as possible."[9]

Now it is perhaps only to be expected that a society as confused over educational policy as our own is would conceive education as serving fundamentally a vocational purpose, and therefore would not only ignore the importance of liberal education, but indeed would not even be able to define what the term *liberal* means when it is associated with the term *education*. It might also be expected that such a society in its reverence for "facts" would see the process of teaching as essentially one of transmitting as much factual material to students as possibly can be done. Perennialists point out that there are grave difficulties with this idea. One is that facts do not stay current and therefore may not prove to be

---

[7]  Ibid., p. 13.

[8]  Ibid., p. 26.

[9]  Ibid.

very useful, even if they are remembered. Another difficulty is that there is already such a bulk of factual detail, and it appears to be increasing in quantity at a geometric rate of progression, that nobody could possibly learn it all, even if he stayed in school until middle age. The third kind of criticism advanced by perennialists concerning education conceived as the transmission of factual material is that students simply do not have the maturity and experience needed to assimilate in any meaningful way either the kind or the vast amount of material schools try to transmit.[10]

It should be recognized that criticism of this kind necessarily is directed against the essentialist tradition in education, for it is that tradition in which education is considered to be the transmission and absorption of organized factual material. Spokesmen for educational progressivism have also criticized the prevailing tradition on the same grounds; much of the liberal protest is against the effort to prepare students for some distant future by transmitting to them various bodies of "essential subject matters," and progressivists also have paid careful attention to the problem of meaning. As might be expected, progressivism and perennialism find very different kinds of philosophical reasons for their protests against essentialism, yet the protests of the two traditions *at the practical level* are very similar, if not identical. This in itself should be enough to correct the common belief that perennialism is simply a kind of conservative approach to education.

Perennialists find many things to criticize in the prevailing mode of education in America, but some of their strongest protests are against the vocationalism that they believe infests our schools, particularly our secondary schools and our institutions of higher learning. The considered opinion of most perennialists is that the height of our educational folly is to be found in what we have done to the university, which once was the greatest educational institution ever developed in the West. The higher learning, in the judgment of perennialists, has become little else than a glorified training for various occupations. The colleges have long since lost any sight of what is meant by liberal education—even when they try to define it, they attempt to do so by listing an array of subject matters dignified by the word *discipline*. The university has become a collection of professional schools in which a student can learn how to do almost anything except what is important. In the university, research is now the

---

10 Objections of this kind have already been developed at some length in the chapter on essentialism and will not be repeated here in detail. Hutchins's writings contain many variations of these criticisms, one of his most forthright statements being found in *The Conflict in Education* (New York: Harper & Brothers, 1953). A similar criticism will be found in Jacques Maritain, *Education at the Crossroads* (New Haven: Yale University Press, 1943), chap 3. My references are to the paperbound edition of Maritain's book issued in 1960.

great prestige-building activity; in many, if not most, institutions one of the cherished perquisites of the full professor is that he can reduce his teaching, particularly of underclassmen, or perhaps escape it entirely and concentrate on research. Therefore, Hutchins has said, it is small wonder that in America the chief opponent of liberal education is the professor who works in a university that has a reputation for research and professional training.[11] Nor is it surprising that the real commitment of a professor is to his own subject rather than to his university or to the education of students. It used to be said that the university is a community of scholars, but said Hutchins, "This community, if it ever existed has now collapsed."[12]

A conflict exists in American education but fundamentally this conflict is not between teaching and research, for this struggle is simply symptomatic of a greater confusion. The real conflict exists because of differing conceptions of the aim of education. If we take the university, for example, we find that historically the purpose of this institution has been pursuit of truth for its own sake, but gradually the idea has developed among us that the purpose of a university is to prepare people for their life's work. To the perennialist, these two aims of a university education are irreconcilable. Since Americans are practically unanimous on the issue that higher education should prepare students for their chosen vocations, not only have universities become aggregations of professional schools, but the older departments, which formerly considered themselves the curators of the liberal arts and sciences, are as vocationally oriented as the schools of library science, engineering, veterinary medicine, or any of the others that have grown up in this century.[13]

The dead hand of vocationalism is also everywhere to be found in our secondary schools. As a people, we have always thought that universal education could accomplish almost anything, but we really do not know what it can do because we have never tried it out. A very large majority of students in the American high school have simply pursued various

---

[11] "An Appraisal of American Higher Education," School and Society 90 (May 5, 1962): 214–18.

[12] Ibid., p. 216.

[13] See, for example, The Higher Learning in America, chap. 2. A study conducted by the University of Michigan Survey Research Center, Public Concepts of the Costs and Utility of Higher Education, by Angus Campbell and William C. Eckerman (Ann Arbor: University of Michigan Institute for Social Research, 1964), indicates that a preponderant number of the American public think that training for a good job is the most important objective of a college education. To perennialists this is simply one more link in a long chain of evidence that shows the complete inability of Americans to conceive of what liberal education is or what its values are. It is also an example of the typical American inability to distinguish between collegiate and university grade education.

kinds of vocational training courses that will provide them with "marketable skills" but which contribute nothing to their education. Essentialists, to be sure, are in strong accord on the policy that the intellectually gifted student should study only the academic subjects, particularly those that prepare for entrance to college. However, the conservative tradition is badly split on what to do with those students who have no intention of going to college and who cannot cope with the essentials of the academic high school curriculum. Arthur Bestor and others of the Council for Basic Education have been generally in opposition to including vocational courses in the curriculum for non-college-bound students, though in the long run a substantial part of their argument for the essentials turns out to be utilitarian. However, James B. Conant is the conservative voice to which contemporary Americans have attended most closely, and Conant has consistently advocated inclusion of vocational courses in the high school program for students who are not going to college. In his book *Slums and Suburbs* Conant proposes that the plight of slum children can be alleviated by giving them vocational training courses that are tied directly to the current labor market in the local community.[14]

Such a proposal as this is profoundly distasteful to perennialists for at least two important reasons. The more immediate reason they point out is that narrow, excessively practical skills quickly lose relevance in a technology as dynamic as that of contemporary America. Much of the unemployment today is suffered by people who have only a few vocational skills that have been outmoded by automation or other technical advances in industry. On one occasion, Hutchins, addressing himself to the current employment situation, observed that those who have Ph.D.s in physics can usually sell them without difficulty, but those who have only marketable mechanical and manual skills find few takers in the labor market. Since the latter group is composed in large measure of adolescents who got little or nothing in high school but vocational training, the unemployment rate among youth up to age nineteen is twice that of adults and growing constantly larger. Viewing these events in another context, Hutchins said that Conant's proposals to tie vocational education directly to local labor markets will do nothing but make the situation worse.[15]

Perennialists advance a far more serious criticism, however, of vocational education than the one just considered. To train a young person in school, they hold, simply to do some such servile task as cosmetology, automobile mechanics, or television repair, and this at the expense of his

---

14  New York: McGraw-Hill Book Co., 1961.
15  Robert M. Hutchins, "That Candles May Be Brought," *Graduate Comment* 3, Wayne State University (April 1960): 4.

*education,* amounts purely and simply to the debasement of human nature. Hutchins, describing the curriculum in cosmetology pursued by a young girl in a public technical high school, noted after listing the courses she was required to take in driver training, homemaking, physical education, and so on, that "this is the education of a slave . . . not the education of a free citizen of a society that hopes to remain free. It is barbarous." [16] If we are serious about democracy, Hutchins has insisted, either we are going to have to learn how to *educate* all citizens or we shall be forced to change our form of government. If all men are to be rulers, which is what democracy means, then all men must be educated as rulers; nine-tenths of them cannot continue to be trained as slaves. The alternative to educating all men as rulers is to return to a government in which a small elite will rule the great uneducated, slavish masses. This will represent a tacit, if not an explicit, agreement with the ancient Greek conviction that some men are by nature fit only to be slaves. In the judgment of perennialists, we are operating our schools as if most men were fit only for servile occupations, not for the obligations of free citizenship. [17]

How does the American perennialist think the confusion that besets today's society and current educational matters can be cleared up? Knowing what they think will set the stage for considering their position on educational theory and practice. It is difficult to determine from reading the literature of modern perennialists precisely what their position is on this matter. What is involved is the question of the role the school can (and should) play in society. Specifically, can the school right itself, change its program, and purge itself of its ills, even when the society in which the school exists does not change; or if the society does change, when the direction taken is worse instead of better? Much in the perennial tradition indicates the belief that corruption in the school results from corruption in the society in which the school exists. It may be concluded, therefore, that under this view the reform of education can come only after the reform of society has been achieved. Parenthetically, we might remind ourselves again that perennialism represents a protest against the whole character of modern Western society and not simply certain ideas about education that are current in this society. Therefore, we should seem justified in concluding that the needed reform in education cannot occur until a complete reform in society has been achieved. The character the school possesses at any particular time is a function of the social context in which the school exists. Evidence in favor of this view is not difficult to find in perennialist literature.

---

[16] Ibid.

[17] Hutchins, *The Conflict in Education,* p. 66.

For example, Hutchins in his book *Education for Freedom*, raised the question, What is wrong with our educational system? [18] The answer, he says, is *nothing*. "There is never anything wrong with the educational system of a country. What is wrong is the country. The educational system that any country has will be the system that country wants." One does seem justified in concluding from these remarks that the only salvation for education lies in a reform of society and that education can be altered significantly only when such a reformation has been achieved.[19]

On the other hand, there is much to be seen in the behavior of perennialists to indicate that they really believe that organized education has the power to effect desirable changes in society. For a great many years, spokesmen for this tradition have expended their energies and intelligence in promoting reform movements in education, particularly in higher education. The ordinary observer has usually been led to believe that the leaders of this protest movement promise improvements in society as a result of improvements in education. If Hutchins really believes, for example, that sick societies can only have sick schools, why has he devoted his considerable talents to promoting so many reform movements in education, particularly when there seems to be so little evidence that the condition of American society is improving, at least by any criteria he or his associates have offered? According to the initial thesis, these efforts would necessarily have to be viewed as futile. Perhaps the reorganization of Saint John's College, the Great Books movement, and the Hutchins reform efforts at the University of Chicago properly can be viewed as last acts of desperation performed in the face of an impending catastrophe, but for some reason this explanation does not ring true. These do not look like the acts of desperate men; they look much more like the concrete plans of men who believe that the ills of society can be made to yield to the power of education. We cannot resolve this apparent contradiction here, but we recommend it for the reader's consideration for it is an example of the confusion that so often obtains over the question of the relation of the school to society.

Thus far in our inquiry, we have given systematic attention only to the criticisms the perennial philosophy makes of present-day society and education. We are now ready to turn our attention to ideas about education that are advocated by this tradition. We shall consider how such

---

[18] Baton Rouge: Louisiana State University Press, 1943, p. 48.

[19] Jacques Maritain also indicated that it is too much to expect teachers to make up for the evils and insufficiencies in a culture. See *The Education of Man: The Educational Philosophy of Jacques Maritain*, ed. Donald and Idella Gallagher (Garden City, N.Y.: Doubleday & Co., 1962), p. 82.

matters as the objectives of education, the curriculum, and the role of the teacher are conceived by perennialists.

## PERENNIALIST APPROACH
## TO PRACTICAL EDUCATION

The perennial philosophy is an outstanding example of the approach to educational theory that seeks to derive directives for educational practice from certain philosophical statements that serve as initial premises. Where we have already raised serious doubt that the philosophy of education can properly be considered a series of deductions from some set of *a priori* principles, we should contemplate the perennial educational theory against this judgment.

### AIMS AND MEANS OF EDUCATION

In his most celebrated treatise on education, *Education at the Cross-roads*, Jacques Maritain has said, "The chief task of education is above all to shape man, or to guide the evolving dynamism through which man forms himself as a man." [20] He observes also that "nothing is more important for each of us, or more difficult, than *to become a man*." The art of education, therefore, is essentially that of helping individuals to realize the nature that is inherent in them, and what education must be will necessarily depend on what this human nature is. Therefore, to know what human education *must* be, we are required to direct our attention to the nature of man, for here the answers to our most urgent educational questions will be found. Once we know the ultimate ends toward which education should proceed, we shall then, and only then, be in a position to know what means we must employ to realize these ends.

These things being so, it follows that the ultimate ends of education are universal. They do not change with time or culture or any circumstance. The reason for this is that the purpose of education is to actualize a potential nature, and since all men have the same potential nature, the ends pursued in the art of education must always be the same. It is in this sense that perennialists hold the ultimate ends of education to be absolute and universal. [21] What constitutes these ultimate aims, says the

---

[20]   Page 1.

[21]   One of the clearest statements of this position ever made is to be found in Mortimer J. Adler, "In Defense of the Philosophy of Education," *Philosophies of Education*, Forty-first Yearbook of the National Society for the Study of Education, part 1, ed. John S. Brubacher (Bloomington, Ill.: Public School Publishing Co., 1942), pp. 197–249. See particularly pp. 221 ff.

perennialist, is not simply a matter of opinion or prejudice. What they are can be known in absolute fashion; in other words, they can be demonstrated rationally. This means that any person sufficiently intelligent to understand the argument must concur in the judgment of what the ultimate and absolute aims of education are. And further, this means that there can really be only one philosophy of education. Many kinds of opinions about education are circulating in contemporary society and often various combinations of these are advertised as philosophies of education. That these collections of opinion and prejudices are spoken of as philosophies of education is clear evidence of the debasement to which philosophy has been subjected in an age dominated by nominalism and empiricism. To put the matter simply, philosophy of education, as the perennialist sees it, deals with two things—and only two—namely, the ultimate aims of education, which are its first principles, and the general means, which are its secondary principles. These first and secondary principles can be known in an absolute manner, and this is what is properly known as philosophy of education. Anybody who denies the absolute and universal character of these principles or the possibility of their being known in an absolute and universal fashion is simply denying that there can be anything properly called philosophy of education.[22]

If we pause for a moment to take stock of the progress of our inquiry, we find we have two important ideas. We have learned that, according to the perennialist view, the ultimate aims of education are the same for all men in all times and under all circumstances, and the general means for realizing these aims are also universal. We have established, in addition, that perennialists believe that the ultimate aim of education is "to make a man." Now, the next step in understanding this position is to understand that the aims of education, being derived from the nature of man, must always be the same *because human nature is always and everywhere the same.*[23] It is obviously very important in this tradition to be able to demonstrate in complete fashion that human nature itself is universal and unchanging, for on this proposition much of the educational argument necessarily depends.

When we come to consider the question of educational means, we must make certain distinctions. For one thing, the ends of education, while universal, are also plural, and education therefore necessarily deals both with moral development and with intellectual development. Intellectual

---

[22]  Ibid., p. 222.

[23]  This is also the general position of John Wild, whose connection with educational conservatism was noted in Chapter Four. In the chapter on philosophical realism, it was proposed that Wild's position be included in the perennial philosophy since his realism is largely in the orthodox Aristotelian tradition.

development in turn must be subdivided into the speculative and the artistic. Thus, we see that the means employed must be adapted to the educational end being sought, and these means are somewhat different in moral education from what they are in intellectual education. What is important to note here is that education always involves the exercise of a person's own powers, whether he teaches himself or is taught by another. The means of education in general, therefore, are the exercise of the natural powers men have, and since all men have the same natural powers, the means in general are the same for all men. We have already seen that the means will vary depending on the type of education being considered, since the powers involved in moral education are different from the powers involved in intellectual education. Now that we have established the perennialist's belief in the universality of the objectives and general means of education, we are ready to explain in more detail his conception of the educative process.

## THE ART OF TEACHING

The purpose of education is "to make a man," and the means by which this is done is the exercise of the individual's own powers. The art of teaching, therefore, is the art of stimulating and directing the activity of these powers so that they are developed and perfected. One of the most important sources from which perennialists draw their ideas about the art of the teacher is a treatise by Saint Thomas Aquinas, *De Magistro* (*Concerning the Teacher*).[24] Saint Thomas was one of the most important scholars involved in the great medieval synthesis of classic philosophy and Hebraic-Christian theology and his interpretation of Aristotle's realism remains the accepted position of the Catholic church on the question of the status of universals. Aquinas himself was one of the greatest teachers at the University of Paris and it is likely that he drew on his own considered experience as a teacher as well as on philosophy and theology in formulating his views of the educative process.

In the first sentence of his *Metaphysics*, Aristotle said, "All men by nature desire to know." This means that the final end toward which certain natural powers of the intellect tend is grasping truth for its own sake. However, like all natural powers of the organism, the rational powers exist originally only as potencies. Some cause must function to move them from potentiality to increasing degrees of actuality. This process is what

---

[24] *De Magistro* is part of a larger work, *De Veritate*. My citations here are to an edition titled *The Teacher—The Mind*, trans. J. V. McGlynn, S.J. (Chicago: Henry Regnery Co., 1959). A much more complete explanation of Saint Thomas's theory than can be given here will be found in Herbert Johnston, *A Philosophy of Education* (New York: McGraw-Hill Book Co., 1963), chap. 7.

we usually refer to as education—particularly when we wish to differentiate between education and training. The art of teaching, therefore, is the process of converting the natural powers of reason from potential to actuality, and the real question is what the source of causation is that makes this possible. Since Saint Thomas's analysis was Christian as well as Aristotelian, he first demonstrated that the primary cause of human knowledge must be God. God is the primary cause since he created man's nature, which is in part intellectual, and if man's nature were not intellectual—that is, in Aristotle's terms, if men did not by their nature desire to know—there would be no human knowledge. God, then, is the primary cause of knowledge, but he has created man in such a way that man is capable of being the secondary principal cause of his learning, since it is through the use of his own natural powers that man learns.

The Thomistic position on this point involves a distinction between two forms of potency. One of these is the potency that is active and complete in the sense that it has the power to result in a complete act. A well-known example of this is the power of the body to heal itself. The other kind of potency is passive in nature and is exemplified by a pile of sticks that has the potency to become a fire but does not have within itself the power to ignite itself. Thus, if it is to become a fire, an agent external to the wood must ignite it (that is, cause it to burn) because the pile of sticks does not have within itself the power to effect this change. Now, according to Saint Thomas, the potency of the human intellect is of the same kind as the power of the body to heal itself; that is, knowledge exists in the learner in the sense of active potentiality. If this were not true, man would not be able to gain knowledge for himself without the help of another person. It is a fact, however, that men can gain knowledge for themselves without the help of another through the process of natural reason we speak of as *discovery*. The other way of learning is through the process of *instruction*, which is the way most formal instruction proceeds and which involves the activities of a *teacher*. The principal question we are concerned with here is what the function of the teacher is.

The Thomistic answer is that the function of the teacher when he teaches a student is analogous to the function of the physician when he heals a patient. The physician heals the patient by cooperating with and assisting nature, furnishing medicines and other means that nature can use to effect a cure. The physician, therefore, is the *secondary cause* of the patient's recovery; the principal cause is the natural powers of the body to heal itself. This is not to say that the ministrations of the physician are unimportant; it is to say, however, that the physician's efforts are a cause only in the secondary sense. If this were not true, no one would be able to recover his health without the aid of a physician, and everyone knows that sick people sometimes do recover without medical assistance. There is widespread agreement, however, that the services of a physician promote and expedite the recovery of health.

In the process of learning, the teacher plays the same kind of secondary causal role that the physician plays in the healing process. The active cause of the pupil's learning is the operations of his own natural powers of intellect. "Consequently," said Saint Thomas, "one person is said to teach another inasmuch as, by signs, he manifests to that other the reasoning process which he himself goes through by his own natural reason. And thus, through the instrumentality, as it were, of what is told him, the natural reason of the pupil arrives at a knowledge of the things which he did not know." [25] Thus, the intellect is not to be viewed as analogous to a pile of sticks that can be changed into a fire only as an external cause is brought to bear on it, and the teacher's role is not that of a torchbearer who thrusts fire into the dry wood to kindle it and thus is the active cause of the conflagration. Saint Thomas also maintained that teaching is not the communication to the student of knowledge possessed by the teacher. Rather, the knowledge that is in the student's intellect is caused by the student's own intellectual activity. What the teacher does is to present certain signs (words, symbols, and so on) that stand for things that then may be not present to sense, and from these signs the intellect of the student derives the things not present to sense and causes them to exist in his own mind. In this way, the teacher's activity plays a mediating role in the learning process. [26]

These ideas about the self-activity of the learner and the role of the teacher as secondary and ministerial constitute an important source of the perennialist protest against the pedagogy of essentialism. Essentialism as a theory of education is built around the assumption of an irreducible core of subject matters to be transmitted to all and the conception of the teacher as the agent who transfers these subject matters into the mind of the student. The structure and functioning of our entire educational installation in this country derive from this conception of education. In considering this aspect of the American approach to education, Maritain has said bluntly, "Any education which considers the teacher as the principal agent perverts the very nature of the educational task." [27] And he has reserved some of his bitterest criticism for a system of schooling that is devoted to cramming students with predigested, overorganized, synthesized subject matters—usually through the medium of textbooks. This condemnation of the conception of the teacher as a kind of intellectual pumping station is a

---

25  *The Teacher*, p. 17.
26  Ibid., p. 23.
27  *Education at the Crossroads*, p. 32.

primary theme in the educational philosophy of the perennial philosophy, and this is as true in the case of such modern rational humanists as Hutchins, Adler, and Van Doren as it is of neo-Scholastics.

This same element is part of the protest of progressivism. John Dewey denied that education could be (much less, should be) considered primarily as the transmission of organized information. He also insisted that the self-activity of the student is the means by which the educative process goes on, and he conceived the role of the teacher as one of mediator, guide, and perhaps, one might even say, ministerial agent. In the case of progressivism, this conception of the art of teaching makes a great deal of difference in the way the curriculum and organization of instruction are conceived. The way that the perennialist views the art of teaching also makes for profound differences between his conception of the curriculum and that of the prevailing essentialism. In this connection we should not attempt to make more out of this striking similarity between the progressive and perennialist protests than the facts warrant. There are, to be sure, vast differences in the way in which human nature is viewed in these two traditions. The fact remains, however, that both of them view education as a *process* in which the self-activity of the learner is the principal cause of his learning, and they both agree with Aristotle that it is important to know the difference between the art of knowledge and its products. It is possible that Maritain has been more aware of this similarity between the two protest movements than the leading figures among the rational humanists have. Maritain has had kind things to say on occasion about the achievements of progressivism, though he has necessarily deplored the naturalism and pragmatism out of which it developed, and in saying these things he has insisted that a big contribution of the progressive movement has been to reassert that the dynamic factor in education is the self-activity of the student. Even when allowance is made for the differences in underlying philosophical conceptions, one can hardly help being struck by the similarity of this statement to many made by John Dewey and other progressives.[28]

*THE CURRICULUM*

The purpose of education is "to make a man" and the art of teaching, as the perennialist sees it, deals with the processes by which the individual

---

[28] Some sixteen years after Dewey's death, Hutchins acknowledged that what Dewey had said in *My Pedagogic Creed* was correct, namely, that education should help every person gain complete possession of all his powers. Dewey had maintained that this is the only constructive role education can play in a rapidly changing society. Hutchins agreed. See Robert M. Hutchins, "Permanence and Change," *Center Magazine* 1 (September 1968): 2–6.

realizes in actuality the intellectual powers he possesses in potential. We should perhaps remind ourselves again that "making a man" does not mean that human nature can be shaped and molded like a ball of wax, nor does it mean that the role of the teacher is one of pumping pre-processed material into the mind of the student. With these things in mind, we are now ready to consider the program of studies that perennialists believe to be necessary for achieving the objectives of the educational process.

The key to understanding the perennialist curriculum, and the whole perennialist protest against essentialist pedagogy, is the idea of *liberal education*. Although this term is prominent in essentialist writing, it is often difficult—if not impossible—to know with any precision what is meant by conservatives when they talk about liberal learning. The most usual approach is to attempt to define it in terms of organized subject matters in which some subjects are liberal and some are illiberal. Aristotle warned against trying to define liberal education in this way for, he pointed out, some arts may be liberal or illiberal depending on the purpose for which they are learned. We should also recall that the concept of liberal learning, as opposed to illiberal, originated not only in Greek philosophy, but also in the realities of Greek social organization. Given the Greeks' attitude towards productive work and their idea of the deleterious effect of labor on the human personality, we do not find it difficult to understand the difference between liberal and servile learning as it was viewed in the Hellenic world. Nor is it difficult to understand Hutchins's protest that a girl trained in her high school to do little else than drive automobiles, perform household chores, and arrange coiffures is being trained as a slave —a slave in the modern manner, to be sure, but still a slave.

The process that makes a man, and not simply a slave, is liberal education. The end towards which the intellectual activity of the student tends is development and perfection of the natural powers of intellect that all men possess. The model that modern perennialists take is the Greek ideal of liberal learning, particularly as this was conditioned by medieval thought, and the model of collegiate and university education they follow is one that emerged in the flowering of medieval culture in the thirteenth and fourteenth centuries. When classic learning passed into the medieval world, it took the form of the "Seven Liberal Arts." Commentaries on the liberal arts were prepared by various late classical and early Christian scholars including the Romans Varro and Quintilian, and Saint Augustine, who was one of the most influential as well as one of the most learned of the early church fathers. However, the most famous treatise on the liberal arts undoubtedly was an allegory, *The Marriage of Philology and Mercury*, written by Martianus Capella in the fifth century, and containing virtually all the learning of the classic era that survived in the early Middle Ages. There is some reason to think that this may be the dullest book ever written, though any generalization about this dubious honor is admittedly dangerous. However, dull or not, it is said to have been used more widely in the early Middle Ages than any other textbook on the ancient learning.

Capella followed Plato's original example in dividing the liberal arts into two categories: the trivium and the quadrivium. The trivium is made up of grammar, rhetoric, and dialectic. The quadrivium is composed of arithmetic, geometry, astronomy, and music (really harmony, since it was concerned with the mathematical relationships involved in musical harmony). Thus, the arts in the trivium were the literary arts and those of the quadrivium were the mathematical arts. In their recommendations about the content of the curriculum, American rational humanists usually have stayed close to the original medieval model. Hutchins, for example, has maintained that in today's world the liberal arts should be viewed as four: rhetoric, grammar, dialectic, and mathematics. Mastery of the liberal arts, he has said, means mastery of the arts of reading, writing, and reckoning.[29] The liberal arts constitute general education and should be pursued by every student, whether he plans to terminate his education at the secondary level or whether he plans to enter the higher learning and ultimately one of the learned professions. It is the liberal arts that bring out the common human nature in all of us, and since this nature is the same for all men, the liberal arts are for all men. There is no place in the curriculum for "electives"; all students must pursue the same curriculum.

The liberal arts are, in the strict sense of the word, ways of doing things; that is what the word *art* means. Thus, there are the arts of rhetorical analysis, grammatical analysis, and logical analysis. Taken together, they constitute the art of reading. The art of mathematics is the process of quantitative and geometric analysis. Thus, the liberal arts are disciplinary in character; that is, they develop the natural powers of intellect and lead towards the perfection of these powers. In this sense, they are instrumental. In Hutchins's own words, "The liberal arts are, after all, the arts of reducing the intellect from mere potentiality to act." [30] However, an art, being a mode of action, requires something to be acted on. Education proceeds through the activity of the student's intellectual powers, but there must be some material on which these powers may be brought to bear. What, according to perennialists, should this be? A significant answer to this question has been supplied by rational humanists and given such emphasis that almost all Americans have heard of the "Great Books"

---

29  *The Higher Learning in America*, pp. 82 ff. See also his remarks to the first class entering the college at the University of Chicago, reprinted in the *Social Frontier* 5 (January 1939): 98.
30  *The Higher Learning in America*, p. 115.

even if they are innocent of any other knowledge of the perennialist tradition in education.

The content that is appropriate for liberal education, say the perennialists, are the *permanent studies* and these are found in their most universal and therefore in their most valuable form in the great literary products of the West. They are, in short, the *great books*—the classics. A classic, as perennialists are fond of saying, is a book that is contemporary with every age. It is held further that these books must be a part of liberal education because a person cannot understand developments in the modern world and in his own times unless he has studied these classics.[31] Moreover, in liberal education the major portion of the time of the student is to be spent in reading, discussing, and analyzing the great books. "The reading of these books is not for antiquarian purposes," Adler has cautioned: "The intent is not archaeological or philological. . . . Rather the books are to be read because they are as contemporary today as when they were written, and that because *the problems they deal with and the ideas they present are not subject to the law of perpetual and interminable progress.*" [32] The program of Saint John's College in Annapolis, Maryland, which is the purest American example of the rational humanist's ideal of collegiate education, is essentially one of reading and analyzing the great books. Therefore, it is very likely the only college in the country that really provides the opportunity for a liberal education as that term is understood in the perennial philosophy. Meantime, American colleges, dominated as they are by educational essentialism, see their mission as transmitting portions of organized subject matters—largely through the medium of textbooks. And "textbooks," Hutchins has said, "have probably done as much to degrade the American intelligence as any single force." [33]

Liberal education, which is designed to discipline the intellectual faculties of the student, is preparatory to university education and is essential to it. Mastery of the liberal arts, therefore, is prerequisite to admission to the university. We have already seen something of the bitterness with which perennialism attacks the professionalism and the empiricism that pervade the American university. Although no perennialist

---

[31] Ibid., pp. 78–79.

[32] Mortimer J. Adler, "The Crisis in Contemporary Education," *Social Frontier* 5 (February 1939): 140–45, esp. p. 144. Italics are in the original. For another discussion of the actual workings of the curriculum, together with a description of the Saint John's program, see Mark Van Doren, *Liberal Education* (New York: Henry Holt and Co., 1943). My citations are to the edition by the Beacon Press issued in 1959, pp. 144–65.

[33] *The Higher Learning in America*, p. 78.

has ever succeeded in purging an American university of these ills—and Mr. Hutchins must receive credit for having tried the hardest—the ideas of perennialists on this subject are perfectly lucid. The clearest model for the university emanating from contemporary rational humanism is that furnished by Hutchins. Its general outlines briefly are as follows.

First of all, the university is to be considered an *educational institution*, not, we might note, a heterogeneous collection of research institutes in which a little teaching is done on the side. Hutchins, for one, has said that he recognizes the importance of the fact finding and accumulation of data to which the empirical sciences are devoted. But he also has said many times and in many ways that a university is not the place to do these things, the reason being that these activities inevitably obscure the true purpose of a university. The main reason for the confusion and atomism that are characteristic of our university is that there is no unity in it. Every subject matter, every department is fractionated and specialized beyond belief. It is no longer a matter of members of different departments being unable to communicate meaningfully with each other. The malaise of specialization has spread until even faculty members within a department have no common intellectual ground. On the other hand, the medieval university was unified intellectually and what provided the unifying principle was theology. Knowledge, both speculative and practical, was unified and ordered; all scholars had mastered this order and those who aspired to be scholars knew what there was to be mastered.

However, Hutchins, along with others of the rational humanists, has acknowledged that under the conditions of the modern world, there is no possibility of making theology the great synthesizing and unifying discipline it once was in the university.[34] Hutchins has pointed out that if we eliminate from theology the ideas of faith and revelation, we shall find ourselves in about the same philosophical position as the Greeks, which is to say that we shall regard metaphysics as the highest form of knowledge and employ it, as the Greeks did, as the great unifying discipline in the higher learning. Here is one of the big points of difference within modern perennialism. Although neo-Thomists agree with Hutchins and his associates that metaphysics is the highest form of rational knowledge, they insist that unless education is anchored in the revealed truths of theology it remains rootless.[35]

---

[34] See *The Higher Learning in America*, p. 97; and Van Doren's *Liberal Education*, pp. 142–44. This and what follows from it bear out our earlier observation that today's rational humanists are in many respects closer to Aristotle than to Saint Thomas.

[35] For example, see William McGucken, S.J., "The Philosophy of Catholic Education," *Philosophies of Education*, chap. 6, p. 256.

Whereas liberal education is the proper enterprise of elementary and secondary education, the higher learning deals with organized knowledge or the sciences.[36] In the university, as it is envisioned by Hutchins, there would be three divisions or faculties: metaphysics, natural science, and social science. Students in the university would study in all three and emphasis would be placed on the interrelations among them. Since metaphysics is the highest form of knowledge, being speculative in character and dealing with first principles, social and natural science are necessarily inferior to it, and in fact dependent on it for their own first principles. Hutchins would allow a student some degree of specialization in one of the subordinate fields, but this would not be at the expense of study in depth in the other two divisions.

Empirical research and practical training would be banished from the university and organized in a series of technical institutes. Those preparing for the learned professions would be *educated* in the university and given their *practical training* in a technical institute. Thus, a student who aspired to be a physician would not only study natural science, which is the science directly related to the art of medicine, he would also study metaphysics, which is superior to all empirical science, and social science, which is also related to the knowledge required for an educated man and for a physician. The actual practice of the art of medicine would be acquired in a technical institute attached to a hospital. The technical institute would also be the place in which empirical research would be conducted and the results fed back into the university where the new material would be integrated into the existing bodies of knowledge. The primary tasks of the faculties of the university, therefore, are those of organizing, unifying, and teaching.

The general view of an educational organization that emerges from present-day rational humanism is ordered around three levels: elementary education, secondary (collegiate) education, and higher (university) education. We have seen in some detail that collegiate education is concerned with liberal education and the mastery of the liberal arts and that the university is concerned with the sciences and the perfection of the intellectual virtues. There is not much to be said about the rational humanist's ideas concerning elementary education for these have received little attention in the literature of this tradition. Hutchins and Adler have rarely said anything about the education of young children except in brief passing

---

[36] Perennialists use the term *science* in the same sense as the Greeks used it, namely to denote any organized body of knowledge in which principles and conclusions are related. A simple body of factual material is not science even if there are no errors in it and it is eminently useful in the practical sense. Hence, in this view, the data in a telephone directory are not scientific knowledge, but mathematics, metaphysics, and theology are.

remarks, and Van Doren's observations in his *Liberal Education* (pp. 88 ff.) are so random and fragmentary as to furnish little insight or guidance. Apparently, there would first be a level of elementary education extending from entrance to school to about the end of what we now call the sophomore year of high school.[37] The main purpose of elementary schooling would be to introduce the child to the rudiments of the liberal arts, which are reading, writing, and reckoning, and to prepare him for the intellectual work of the college. The years of collegiate education would span the period from the junior year of high school to the end of what we now call the sophomore year of college. When a student could give a demonstration of his mastery of the liberal arts, he would be given the bachelor's degree. By definition and by historical precedent, the A.B. degree means mastery of the trivium and the quadrivium. Only those who had mastered collegiate education would be admitted to the university.

Many questions are often raised about what is to happen to those who are unable to make their way very far up this educational ladder. Many people have held that this proposal is for a highly selective system of education, and it seems certain that relatively few will survive very far beyond the end of elementary schooling. The perennialist will remind us that this organization will enable all individuals to do what most of them are debarred from doing under our existing system—namely, getting as much liberal education as they can profit from. Presumably, once the school has done as much for a student as it can, to the limit of his own potentialities, its obligation ceases. It has no obligation in the matter of unemployment, for instance. Unemployment may be a social problem of great importance and vast dimensions, but in this view it is hardly an educational problem.

In the matters we have just been considering, there is widespread agreement between the rational humanist and the neo-Thomist. Both agree on the general aims of the educative process, the nature of the teaching process, and the function of the liberal arts. There are, however, differences of opinion on certain practical aspects of curricular organization that are worth giving some attention to. Maritain has advanced certain proposals for organization of the curriculum.

According to Maritain, there are three principal stages in the educative process. These correspond with the three main stages of human growth, as well as with three distinct stages of human knowledge. Thus, childhood corresponds with the years of elementary schooling, adolescence

---

[37] It seems clear that if the proposals of the rational humanists were to be put into effect, the high school as we have known it would disappear. Part of its work would be allocated to the elementary school and part to the college. See Van Doren, *Liberal Education*, p. 98.

with the years of liberal education, and young adulthood with the years of the higher learning. Specifically, Maritain has advocated a Stage I, involving seven years of elementary education (ages six to twelve); a Stage II, covering seven years and involving the humanities (ages thirteen to nineteen); and a Stage III, which is the period of the advanced studies taken in the university. The elementary stage is divided into an initial period of four years, corresponding to primary education, and a three-year period corresponding to the intermediate grades in our conventional elementary schools. Stage II would be divided into a three-year period of secondary education and a four-year period of college. The A.B. degree would be awarded at age nineteen, the average age at which students would complete preuniversity education. In university education, the normal time required for the master's degree would be three years, with two to four years for the Ph.D. In the purely organizational sense, this does not represent any very great departure, either from the program advocated by Hutchins and the rational humanists, or from the traditional organization of American schools.[38] Within this general outline, however, are certain important differences.

Maritain stressed the difference in the mental life of the elementary school child as compared with the functioning of the adolescent or adult mind. He made much of the fact that childhood is the time of intense imagination in which knowledge must be given the child somewhat in the manner of a story. Childhood is the time in life when reason slowly gains ascendance over imagination, but this process cannot be hurried nor can it be imposed on the child. Maritain laid stress on what he called the "vitality and intuitiveness" of the child. Granted that the excess of animal spirits and lack of internal controls in the child can lead to mischief, nevertheless the "vitality of spirit" is the great resource to be used in the education of the young child. In various places in his writing, and always in the strongest terms, Maritain inveighed against the idea that a child is simply a small adult who must be stuffed with simplified, diluted adult knowledge. Even though there are many and profound differences between the educational philosophies of Maritain and Dewey, here at least they meet on common ground in forming a protest against the prevailing American essentialism.[39] The same kind of protest can be found by careful search in the literature of rational humanism, but it is usually there by implication or in the form of side remarks.[40]

---

[38] Maritain's description is in a long footnote on pp. 66–67 of *Education at the Cross-roads.*

[39] Ibid., pp. 60–61; compare with Dewey's *Democracy and Education,* p. 257.

[40] The most extensive remarks in this vein with which I am familiar are to be found in Van Doren's *Liberal Education,* pp. 88–93.

Maritain's interpretation of the liberal arts differs in certain important respects from that of the rational humanists, who tend to interpret these arts in the sense they had in the medieval period. The fact, said Maritain, that the liberal arts took the familiar form of the trivium and quadrivium was more an accident of history than anything else, and he suggested that whatever is considered to be the liberal studies in any historical period ought to depend on the kind and amount of humanistic knowledge extant in that period. Since the corpus of knowledge in our own time is far greater and very different from that of the medieval era, our conceptions of liberal learning ought also to be different.[41] In his opinion, one of the most notable additions to the liberal studies that must be made is the natural sciences.

Maritain would place first in the curriculum what he has called "the pre-liberal arts." These would include grammar and linguistics, logic, modern languages, history, and in connection with it, geography. In the liberal arts proper, the trivium would consist of eloquence (presumably rhetoric in a wide sense of that term); literature and poetry; and art, which would include not only the fine arts, but also the applied arts and technology, these being employed in a humanistic mode and not with any reference to vocationalism. The quadrivium would be made up of mathematics, including its history; physics and natural science and the history of science; social sciences and the history of civilization; philosophy, to include philosophy of nature, philosophical psychology, metaphysics, epistemology, and social philosophy (ethics, politics, and so on). Thus, Maritain has been more forthright in making the quadrivium that part of the liberal arts that is substantive in nature and not exclusively formal, as the rational humanists tend to interpret it. In a footnote to page 70 of *Education at the Crossroads*, Maritain spoke directly to a point on which rational humanists have not always been clear, namely, that the great books have other purposes than furnishing the apparatus for mental gymnastics.

There are also differences between Maritain's idea of a university and that advanced by the rational humanists. Briefly, Maritain has held that the purpose of the university is teaching universal knowledge. Hence, there would be four "orders of subjects" each of these to be taught in an "Institute" that would be organically linked with the other "Institutes." The first order of subjects would be the useful and applied sciences, for example, technology, applied arts, agriculture, business administration, and so forth. The second order would include medicine and psychiatry, law, politics, education, economics, and so forth; these are practical studies that relate to man and human society and hence belong either to the domain of art or to ethics. The third order would embrace the speculative sciences

41 See *The Education of Man,* ed. Gallagher, pp. 90–93.

and fine arts, namely, mathematics, natural science, social science, history, literatures, music, and fine arts. The highest institute in the university would teach the fourth order of subjects, which would include philosophy in all its branches together with theology and the history of religions.[42] Beyond the teaching institutes, Maritain has envisioned a series of Institutes of Advanced Research devoted to the extension of knowledge in all branches of human endeavor. He advocated that these research institutions should complement each other in their work but that they should be separate and distinct. Maritain agreed with the rational humanists that when research and teaching compete with each other in the university, it is usually teaching that suffers from neglect.

If we were to look for the greatest difference between the educational philosophy of the rational humanists and that of the neo-Thomists, we should find that it lay in the conception of the role religion and theology should play in the education of man. The neo-Thomist believes that as enlightened as the rational humanists have shown themselves to be in their understanding of the real meaning of liberal education and the purpose of the higher learning, their philosophy of education is incomplete because they fail to include theology and religion in their educational formulations. Maritain, writing as a Roman Catholic as well as a philosopher, agreed that in a society based as ours is on religious pluralism, religious instruction cannot be made compulsory in the schools, but he has suggested that ways can be found in communities to provide students with instruction in religion. And he has maintained further that if the university is really to be a center for the teaching of universal knowledge, theology must be included, for it is as much a part of knowledge as physics or mathematics.[43]

In concluding our consideration of the curriculum as it is viewed in the perennial tradition, we may make the following summary observations: First, although there are some differences over details to be found, a very wide area of agreement exists among adherents of this tradition over basic educational questions. Secondly, although perennialists are critical of progressivism on a number of important points and reject the naturalism inherent in it, their main educational criticisms are directed squarely (and necessarily) at essentialism, the prevailing tradition in America. Third, the principal difference in the educational philosophy of rational humanism and that of the neo-Thomists stems from somewhat different perceptions

---

[42] *Education at the Crossroads*, pp. 75–83.

[43] For examples of Maritain's position on this point, see *Education at the Crossroads*, pp. 71–75; 82–83; *The Education of Man*, pp. 75–81; John S. Brubacher, ed., *Modern Philosophies and Education*, Fifty-fourth Yearbook of the National Society for the Study of Education (Chicago: University of Chicago Press, 1955), pp. 83–88.

of the significance theology has for our understanding of the educative process.

## EDUCATION AND THE NATURE OF HUMAN NATURE

In beginning our inquiry into selected elements of the perennial philosophy, we do well to recall Maritain's injunction: "The chief task of education is to shape man." This means that the immediate directives for what the education of man should be emerge from a consideration of what man is in his fundamental nature. Education, therefore, is properly considered to be a branch of ethics, and specifically, a part of social ethics. However, there are also other kinds of knowledge that must be taken into account when we consider human nature; for example, biology, psychology, and epistemology are also sources of knowledge about the nature of man. And since ultimately man is part of a great world system, we must turn to metaphysics for certain important understandings. We cannot pretend to give any complete exposition of the world system as it was conceived either in Aristotelian or in Thomistic philosophy. All we can do here is to indicate in general outline the nature of man as it is conceived in those philosophies and to show the import this conception has for the philosophy of education. The exposition here will be arranged around certain propositions, which are as follows:

1.  All men share in the same human nature and this nature is constant; it does not change. (This has been mentioned but not clarified.)
2.  Since all men have the same nature, all men have the same natural powers. (This has been mentioned as being an important point, but we have not inquired very far into its meaning.)
3.  By virtue is meant the perfection of a natural power and since all men have the same natural powers, the virtues are the same for all men. (We have yet to determine what this means.)
4.  Education is concerned with the development of man's rational powers, that is, with the formation of the intellectual virtues. (We have already discussed this idea, but we shall investigate it further.)
5.  Since the aim of education is the formation of the intellectual virtues, and since these virtues are the same for all men, the aim of education is the same for all men. (This is the conclusion we shall reach.)

Thus, our chief interest is in the nature of man and what can be derived from it to guide educational policy, but before we can turn directly to specific consideration of man, we must give some heed to the nature of the world system in which this human nature exists and of which it is a part.

## MAN AND NATURE

We have already had occasion to note that a significant point of disagreement between Plato and Aristotle lay in their conception of the relation of the universal to the particular. Plato had conceived reality in terms of universal ideas, or forms, to which particular things are related in some way. Aristotle was never satisfied with the Platonic metaphysics because it separated the universal (form) from the particular, and since there seemed to be no way to get them united, it became necessary to assign an inferior status of being to the things that make up the world of sense experience. Aristotle's solution to the problem lay in his conception of substance as the union of form *in* matter. Thus, in this hylomorphic relationship, all substantial existences are composed of matter that is indissolubly linked with form. The universal therefore is always *in* the thing. Intellectually, we can conceive of "prime" matter, that is, matter that is completely unformed, but we never encounter it in nature. Similarly, we can think abstractly of pure form—the universal existing independently of matter—but this does not occur in the natural world. We have already seen that this "moderate realism" that was originally developed by Aristotle played an important part in the great medieval controversy over the character of universals and became the view accepted by Saint Thomas Aquinas and ultimately the accepted view of the Church. We should remember that both the present-day rational humanist and the neo-Thomist argue their case from the position of moderate realism.

Thus both Aristotle and Saint Thomas were realists and accepted the principle of independence quite as much as any realist today. The independently existing world is made up of substantial entities and the relations that obtain among these entities. A substantial thing, a table, for instance, is composed of matter that is given the character peculiar to a table by the union of matter with the form "tableness." In this way, the form of a thing makes it what it is. Both chairs and tables are material objects, and therefore there is a material cause involved in their existence, but tables are different from chairs, and therefore there is also a formal cause involved. The difference in the forms involved makes the difference between chairs and tables.

The universe is made up of innumerable corporeal bodies related to each other in various ways. In considering the question of how the world comes to have the character it exhibits, Aristotle maintained that a complete analysis must take into account four kinds of causation: the material cause, the formal cause, the efficient cause, and the final cause. To understand how these various kinds of causation are involved, let us consider that a miscellaneous pile of timbers, lumber, bricks, metals and so on do not constitute a house. However, in order that a house may come into existence, there must be material available. Hence, the piles of material are the *material cause* of the house. Since a house is to come into being, and not a barn or garage, there must be a plan for the house involved in its construction. This plan, which is usually the ideas of the architect preserved in the form of blueprints, corresponds to the *formal cause*, that which makes the structure the kind of thing it is. However, material causes and formal causes, though necessary, are insufficient to bring a house into existence, for the building materials must be acted on in terms of the plan. Thus, the activities of carpenters, masons, plumbers, painters, and so forth are the *efficient cause* of the house. Aristotle indicated still one other element of causation involved, namely, the use to which a house is to be put, or as he called it, the *final cause*. And as we know, the purpose or final end of a house is to be lived in. Thus, the matter that once had the forms of trees, clay, and metallic ores has assumed new forms and become a house. These four aspects of cause operate in every act of becoming, which is the development from potential to actual. Aristotle's point is that in every case, there must be something to be moved, something to move it, a course of development, and a goal towards which the whole process moves. However, if we take another look at the four forms of causation, we can see that actually there are only two causes: *the formal* (which includes the efficient, formal, and final) and *the material*. When we speak of a thing coming into being, we really mean that there is a movement from matter to form. The stack of building material becomes (takes the form of) the house; the acorn takes the form of an oak tree. Thus for any object, matter is the "stuff" that has the capacity to become that object: bronze or stone is matter for a statue, stone and wood are matter for a house. In other words, matter is *potentiality* and is capable of taking form and thereby realizing the actuality inherent in it. Aristotle gave a wider meaning to *matter* than we ordinarily do in modern speech ("timber" is the original meaning of the Greek word translated in English as "matter"). Thus, such qualities as courage and bravery are matter that can become a soldier, and even in our common speech we may speak of a statesman as "good presidential timber."

Furthermore, change is always a movement from potentiality to actuality, and therefore what a thing will become is already inherent in it. This is another way of saying that the *actual is prior to the potential.*[44] Experience indicates this to be true. If an acorn develops into anything, it becomes an oak tree, for this final end is inherent in it. Not all acorns realize their

---

[44] Aristotle's development of this idea will be found in chap. 8, book 9 of the *Metaphysics*.

potential, for some are eaten by animals and others fall on stone or barren ground. However, we know there is nothing that can be done to cause the acorn to become a petunia or a fir tree. Similarly, the final end of an egg is to become a chicken, though it may wind up as part of a potato salad and therefore never realize its potential. Thus, in nature all things change and develop according to the pattern of movement from potentiality to actuality, and all development is toward the final ends inherent in the natures of things. And this represents a teleological conception of nature, because the cause of movement is an ultimate end that lies ahead, not the efficient cause that as we may say figuratively "pushes from behind." The view of modern science, and therefore the view most familiar to us, involves a concept of causation in which there is only efficient cause, and this means that any cause must be antecedent to its effect.[45]

Thus, the Aristotelian universe is one of constant process, in which things come into being and pass away and in which the movement is from potential to actual; the whole thrust of nature, so to speak, is upward toward the realization of complete actuality. Since all becoming must have a cause, that is, must have motion imparted to it, there must be something that ultimately is the cause of all motion in nature but itself is unmoved. Otherwise, in our analysis of cause we shall fall into an infinite regress, in which cause-effect relations appear to go back and back forever with no starting point. That which is the origin of all motion and therefore the cause of all things in Aristotle's philosophy is the Unmoved Mover, which is the source of all motion, but is not itself moved. Aristotle indicated that this prime mover is uncreated, dependent on nothing else for its existence, and thus is pure actuality. In Thomistic thought, the Unmoved Mover becomes God.[46]

## DIMENSIONS OF HUMAN NATURE

If we look at nature through the eyes of a scientist—or even with the vision of common sense—we see that there are two great strata of existence in nature. We usually speak of these as the animate and the inanimate levels of nature, and more often than not, common sense seems to indicate that the distinction is an absolute one. Even if it should be discovered that a block of stone contained the same chemical elements as a squirrel, and in exactly the same proportion, common sense would indicate that a

---

[45]  Aquinas accepted Aristotle's conception of causation. In this respect, there is a certain difficulty in scholastic philosophy over the significance of "efficient cause." See, for example, Etienne Gilson, *The Elements of Christian Philosophy* (New York: New American Library of World Literature, 1963), chap. 8.

[46]  For Aristotle's discussion of the Unmoved Mover, see *Metaphysics*, book 12, chap. 6, 1072$^b$, Ross translation.

block of stone is not a squirrel and there is nothing that can be done to make it so. Common sense would say that the squirrel is "alive" and the stone is not. Things that are animate have something that inert things do not have, and this something is life *(psychē)*.[47] In operational terms, to be a living thing, that is, to have psyche, is to have certain natural powers related to living, and at some levels of organic life, to knowing, and these powers are not possessed by inanimate things. This was Aristotle's position.[48]

There are, however, differences among animate things in the natural powers they possess. Some kinds of organisms can do things that other animate bodies cannot do. Observation can be made also of this phenomenon and living things can be classified according to the powers they exhibit. According to Aristotle, there are three levels at which organisms function. These levels are the vegetative, the sensate, and the rational. At the vegetative level of organic life, living things exhibit the powers of reproduction, nutrition, and growth. A plant, for example a radish, possesses all these powers. It can take the elements in the environment (chemical elements in the soil, air, water, light, and so on) and convert them to its own form. The radish not only has the power to grow, but also the power to reproduce its kind.

As everyone knows, the natural powers of nutrition, growth and reproduction do not exhaust the natural powers possessed by living organisms, although such organisms as radishes do not possess powers beyond these. There is a level of life at which we find living things exhibiting not only vegetative powers, but also sense perception and locomotion. And we, like Aristotle, call these organisms *animals* and we distinguish them from plants (vegetables, in the wide sense of the word). Animals have, in addition to vegetative powers, the power to receive stimuli from distant objects, as for example through organs of sight and hearing, and they have certain internal powers of memory and imagination. Animals also have powers of locomotion and their actual environments are more extensive than that of a sessile plant.

---

[47]   The Greek word *psychē*, generally translated in Latin as "anima" and in English as "soul," is never conceived by Aristotle in the sense it has come to be understood in the Christian tradition. Aristotle rejected the idea that *soul* could be conceived as existing apart from a body.

[48]   Here is a fundamental difference between the Aristotelian and Darwinian conceptions of nature. Aristotle's conception involves no idea of organic evolution in which new species evolve from less complex levels of organization. Aristotle's conviction was that the species are immutable and the world has always existed in its present form. Darwinism postulates a continuity in nature in which it is impossible to make an absolute distinction between the inanimate and the animate levels of nature.

For all the species of organisms save one, the vegetative and sensate powers mark the limits of their natures. There is, however, another level of organic life at which there are other powers. These are the natural powers of responding to abstractions, of deliberation, of anticipating outcomes—in short, of behaving rationally. Only the human species is possessed of these natural powers of reason, which Aristotle referred to as *nous*. It must be understood that when Aristotle was discussing this third level he was not talking about anything mystical or supernatural. The rational powers of the human species are as much a part of nature as the reproductive or sensate powers, and we know of their existence in the same way we know about the other natural powers—through observation and analysis.

We can now conclude that in Aristotelian terms there are three principal dimensions of human nature. First, as men, part of our nature is shared with plants and animals. The human species exhibits powers of nutrition and reproduction the same as radishes and dogs do. Moreover, men have powers of sensation and locomotion, as cats and turtles have. But man also has rational powers, and no other kind of creature has these. The thing that makes man different from all other living creatures, therefore, is *nous*, the rational powers. And hence, we have the famous Aristotelian definition: "Man is a *rational* animal." Man is a member of the genus animal, but he is differentiated from other animals by his rational powers and is thus a separate species.

We need now to remember the hylomorphism on which Aristotle's analysis rests. In all things (animate or inanimate), there are two principles involved: the material and the formal, and it is the formal that gives a thing its nature and makes it different from other things. For example, a chair may be made from any number of kinds of material: steel, wood, aluminum, plastic, bamboo, or stone. A chair may be made of any of these and still be a chair. We see, therefore, that the material factor does not determine the nature of a thing. It is the form (universal) locked up, so to speak, with the matter (wood, metal, and so on) that makes an object a chair and not a table or an automobile. Thus, we can say that though there are differences among chairs, for example, between camp chairs and lounge chairs, these differences are *accidental* and not *essential*, for they are all chairs. Thus by *essence* we mean the nature necessarily possessed by a thing, as contrasted with its *nonnecessary*, or accidental, qualities.

We now begin to see what is meant when perennialists speak of human nature being everywhere the same and never changing. Obviously, this means that the *essential* nature of man does not vary; this does not mean that there are no differences *among* men. Aristotle or Aquinas or any other perennialist knew quite well as modern psychologists do that the differences within the human species are innumerable, but Aquinas and Aristotle would remind us that these differences are accidental and not essential. And certainly, one of the main criticisms of modern perennialists is that a great part of the confusion over educational policy in the modern world can be traced to failure to distinguish between essential and accidental qualities. Whether a person is male or female has nothing to do with being a member of the species *man,* and hence, sex is an accidental quality. The difference between a man and a goat, however, is an essential difference, because man is a rational animal and a goat is not, and there is nothing anybody can do to turn a goat into a man. Since the dimensions of human nature coincide at the vegetative and sensate levels with those of goats, man has the capacity to behave like a goat when he allows the appetites of sense to override his rational powers. This has been known to happen.

The neo-Thomist agrees with the essentially Aristotelian conception of the rational humanists that man is a rational animal and that the natural powers of reason differentiate man from all other species of animals. Thomists also agree that metaphysics, the science of first principles, is the highest form of rational knowledge. We know, however, that the original dimensions of human nature as seen by Aristotle must be viewed by Thomists as incomplete. Aristotle saw man as an organism, existing within nature, subject to its processes, and possessing the nature he has by virtue of the universal "manness," or "humanness." To Aristotle, the soul (in the sense of psyche) is the form of the body, linked with matter to form an individual. The soul therefore must lose its existence when the body perishes, for form is never found except in union with matter. This conception of soul is plainly in opposition to the truth revealed in the Scriptures that the soul is immortal and survives the disintegration of the body. Since the immortality of the soul is one of the most fundamental of the basic doctrines of Christian theology, a correction—or at least a reinterpretation —of Aristotle had to be made.

The general direction in which Saint Thomas argues for the immortality of the soul is that the soul of man is different from other kinds of forms in nature. This difference lies in the power of the human soul to gain abstract knowledge *in addition to* its power to inform and give motion to the body, which the souls of other animals also possess. Man is capable of abstract knowledge in which the object of knowing is *form,* not matter. In this sense, man can know in an immaterial way. Moreover, it is argued, only an immaterial substance can perform acts that produce *concepts,* which clearly are immaterial. The soul of man, then, must be an intellectual substance that has an existence of its own and does not have to be involved in matter in order to be, yet as the form of the body, it shares its own being with the body and gives unity to human nature. Aquinas then argues that intellectual substances are incorruptible and since the human soul can be shown to be an intellectual substance, it must be considered to be incorruptible. And this is to say that the human soul is immortal.[49]

Thomism maintains, therefore, that the immortality of the soul can be demonstrated philosophically, that is, through reason. The salvation of the soul, however, is a matter belonging to theology and is known through revealed truth. The import these matters have for us here is that the dimensions of human nature, as it is viewed by neo-Thomists, are considerably wider than those assumed by the present-day rational humanists, who see man largely in Aristotelian terms. Certainly one of the clearest statements of the Thomist view of man, and one that demonstrates the various elements that have gone into the making of the Thomist view, is to be found in a passage from Maritain's *Education at the Crossroads* (p. 7):

> In answer to our question, then, "What is man?" we may give the Greek, Jewish, and Christian idea of man: man as an animal endowed with reason, whose supreme dignity is in the intellect; and man as a free individual in personal relation with God, whose supreme righteousness consists in voluntarily obeying the law of God; and man as a sinful and wounded creature called to divine life and to the freedom of Grace, whose supreme perfection consists of love.

We should remember that we started our inquiry by considering the perennialist's statement that the purpose of education is "to form man." The meaning of this statement is that education is the process of developing the natural powers in human nature. We have now determined what these powers are, according to perennialists, and we have also seen that while American rational humanists are content to view man largely in philosophical terms, neo-Thomism insists that the ultimate nature of man transcends the natural powers that make him a rational animal. The ultimate educational question that must be answered is, What is the end of man?

All things in nature develop from potency to act; there is a final end inherent in all existences. If the purpose of education is "to form man," we must know what the final end of man is. This is the supreme ethical question, but it must also be the supreme educational question, for the means that are used in education are intended to assist in realizing this ultimate end.

## THE VIRTUES AND THE END OF MAN

Some natural powers, but not all, are capable of being developed and perfected through *habit*. It is necessary to make a distinction here because

---

[49] For an explanation of Saint Thomas's argument, see Etienne Gilson, *Elements of Christian Philosophy*, chap. 9.

some powers are not capable of being developed through habituation. Examples of these are the sensory powers. Experience in seeing or smelling does not make our visual or olfactory powers stronger, nor can school experience improve the innate intelligence of an individual. Education can only develop the potential that is present. There are, however, certain powers that can be developed through habituation and these fall into two categories: the intellectual and the volitional.

The perfection of these natural powers, that is, the development of them from potentiality to actuality, is what is meant by *virtue*. From the standpoint of the essential nature of man, therefore, there are two kinds of virtues: intellectual virtues and moral virtues. Intellectual virtues are the perfection of man's natural powers of reason. Moral virtues are the perfection of the powers of volition. In both cases, perfection is achieved through forming right (that is, good) habits. Thus education is the process through which the intellectual virtues are formed through good habits, and moral training is the process of habituation that leads to realization of the moral virtues. A habit is a right habit when it perfects a power in terms of the final end of that power. Since the dimensions of human nature extend below the strictly human level of intellect and will, there are also vegetative and sensate powers that can be developed through habit; in the case of these powers, however, development is necessarily in a sense different from development of the intellectual and moral virtues.

Perfection of the intellectual and moral virtues cannot be held to be the ultimate end of man. This was agreed both by Aristotle and by Saint Thomas. The final end of man must be something that exists in and of itself and is not desired for the sake of anything else. The perfection of natural powers is the means to the final end, but this is not the end itself. With Aristotle, this final end is expressed in the untranslatable Greek word *eudaemonia,* usually rendered in English as "happiness," or "well-being," by which he meant the activity of the soul's powers in accordance with reason. All men desire happiness, Aristotle maintained, but a man can achieve this state only as he is able to exercise his powers to the proper degree and in balance and harmony. Overindulgence works to prevent the attainment of happiness, but so does ascetic repression of natural powers. To attain happiness a man must have enough means to sustain himself— a hungry man can not act nobly or attain happiness, and neither can a man who must spend his days in servile work. Happiness is not a passive state; it involves the active exercise of various powers in proper proportion to each other. The highest kind of activity of which man is capable is *contemplation,* that is, thought that is concerned with the first principles of things. This is the nearest man can come to pure thought, and when he is engaged in this activity, he is nearest to the Unmoved Mover.

Since revealed truth, as well as philosophic truth, is involved in the Thomistic view of man, we can expect that Aristotle's view that the ultimate end of man is attained through perfection of the moral and intellectual virtues must be considered incomplete by Thomists. In terms of Christian theology, therefore, the ultimate end of man must be supernatural, not natural, and it must be that of attaining a supernatural and eternal union with God. The ultimate knowledge is knowledge of God. Formation of the intellectual and moral virtues is an important part of realizing man's ultimate end, but it is only part. Here we come again to the root of the difference between the educational views of the two chief groups in modern perennialism. The main differences between them on educational philosophy are owed primarily to their different conceptions of human nature.

Five propositions were stated at the beginning of this part of the discussion, and we have tried to clarify them in the light of perennialist thinking. Concerning the first proposition, we find that all members of a species have the same specific nature and this nature does not change. For example, the species *man* is differentiated from the genus *animal* by what is essential in human nature, namely the natural powers of reason. Thus, all men have the same specific nature. Further, any differences that are found among men are accidental and not essential. About the second proposition, we have seen that since all men have the same nature, they all have the same powers. We have found the dimensions of human nature to extend from the lowest level of soul, the vegetative, through the sensate, culminating in the rational. Some of these powers, particularly at the rational level, are susceptible to development through habit; these are the virtues. The most important of these are the moral and the intellectual virtues, which are the perfection of natural powers at the level of rational soul. And so, as stated in our third proposition, the virtues must be the same for all of us, since they are perfections of powers we all possess.

The fourth and fifth propositions are those with which we dealt originally in our survey of the pedagogical position of perennialism. We now can see how these propositions are related to the perennialist's view of man. The intellectual virtues are the perfection of the rational powers and the right habits through which they are perfected are formed through *education*, the activity carried on in the school. The chief aim of the school, therefore, is to contribute to realization of the ultimate end of man by helping him perfect his natural powers of reason. The school also has some responsibility for forming the moral virtues, but this is not its main concern. The family, the community, and the church also have primary obligations for developing the moral virtues.[50]

---

[50] See, for example, *The Education of Man*, chap. 5. Compare with Van Doren's *Liberal Education*, pp. 58–65.

The purpose of education is the formation of the intellectual virtues, and since these virtues are the same for all men, the purpose of education must be the same for all men. Hence, the fundamental strategy of education should never be laid around accidental differences. There should not be one kind of aim for some students and another kind for others. All men are rational beings and they have the right to the kind of education that will develop their supremely human qualities—that is, they have the right to *become men*. The school abrogates this right when it substitutes narrow vocationalism, which is really the training of the sensate powers of the animal, for liberal education, which develops the natural powers of intellect and leads to the ultimate perfection of these powers in the intellectual virtues. Human nature is complex and multidimensional. There are various levels of powers to be perfected, but in the words of one of the most distinguished perennialists of the last century: "Everything has its own perfection, be it higher or lower in the scale of things; and the perfection of one is not the perfection of another." [51]

## KNOWLEDGE AND TRUTH

A complete picture of how the perennialist views man and education must include his thinking on truth as associated with knowledge. He views the human intellect as a complex of natural powers. How does the perennialist think these powers function in perception and cognition?

In one of Maritain's most important essays on education, he said that the fundamental element underlying an educational tradition is the philosophy of knowledge inherent in that tradition. [52] By way of example, he contrasted the position of Thomism with that of empiricism on the relation of sensory knowledge and rational knowledge. Empiricism, he pointed out, denies the distinction made by perennialists between a sense knowledge that apprehends things only as singulars and "only as enigmatically manifested by the diversified physical energies they display," and an intellect that is spiritual in its nature and knows things as they are in their essential nature through its power to abstract the universal from what is presented to sense. Empiricism, therefore, according to Maritain, since it equates all knowledge with sense impression, also maintains that all human knowledge is simply animal knowledge, more complex than that of other animals, but still based on the animal level of the sensate soul. This means that as human thought is viewed in empiricism, it is simply a response to environmental stimuli, and reflective thought occurs only in the

---

[51] Cardinal John H. Newman, *The Scope and Nature of University Education* (New York: E. P. Dutton, 1958), p. 100.

[52] "Thomist Views on Education," *Modern Philosophies and Education*, chap. 3.

presence of problematic situations, as Dewey, for example, maintained. As the perennialist sees it, the results of this conception of knowledge are disastrous in the educational process. Maritain believed, with Dewey, in the power of thought to control and improve the environment, but he was sure that Dewey and all empiricists with him had a completely erroneous view of human thought:

> On the contrary, it is because every human idea, to have a meaning, must attain in some measure (be it even in the symbols of a mathematical interpretation of phenomena) what things are or consist of unto themselves; it is because human thought is an instrument or rather a vital energy of knowledge or spiritual intuition (I don't mean "knowledge about," I mean "knowledge into"); it is because thinking begins, not only with difficulties but with *insights*, and ends up in insights which are made true by rational proving or experimental verifying, not by pragmatic sanction, that human thought is able to illuminate experience, to realize desires which are human because they are rooted in the prime desire for unlimited good, and to dominate, control, and refashion the world. At the beginning of human action, insofar as it is human, there is truth, grasped or believed to be grasped for the sake of truth. Without trust in truth, there is no human effectiveness.[53]

Aristotle said in the first sentence of the *Metaphysics*, "All men by nature desire to know." Thus, there is no problem relating to the "why" of human knowledge. Men tend to know in the same sense that smoke tends to rise and unsupported bodies tend to fall. This tendency of man toward knowing is simply one of the facts of nature. The general outline of the cognitive processes is common both to Aristotle and to Saint Thomas. Any cognitive situation involves the three elements: a subject (knower), an object (that which is known), and the relation that is established between the subject and object. Since both Aristotle and Aquinas agreed to the principle of independence, they agreed that the object exists independently of the mind. The external senses (smell, sight, sound, touch, and taste) are the avenues through which the external reality impinges on the organism. All knowledge originates in sensory experience; there can be nothing in the intellect that was not first in the senses. The impression that comes from without activates the sense organ, which produces sensation. This is a very different account from that rendered by behavioristic psychology. In behaviorism, a sensory stimulus is held to be the efficient cause of a response, but in the Aristotelian and Thomistic account, an external reality is a necessary condition for an act of knowing but it is not the efficient cause of it.

The act of perception is the creation of an image in the mind of the

---

[53] *Education at the Crossroads*, p. 13.

subject identical with the external reality except that this image is spiritual (nonmaterial) whereas the external reality is material. In this process, the sensation affects the internal senses (imagination, memory, and so on) and they create an *intentional image*, which is comparable to some extent with what in modern psychology would be called a percept. Next, the active intellect, which exercises its power to eliminate accidental qualities and thus to reveal the essence of a thing, presents to the cognitive intellect the form (essence) of the object. The cognitive intellect thereupon expresses the essence of the object in terms of a concept, or universal. The acts of the intellect are apprehension (conception), that is, making the thing present in and to the intellect without affirming or denying it; judgment, which is the process of affirming or denying; and reasoning, which is the process of going from known truth to unknown truth. The criterion for the truth of our judgments is the one we have already considered in connection with modern realism—the principle of correspondence. Truth means the conformity of the mind with reality.

In this way, the perennial philosophy explains how we can know things as they really are, that is, in their essential natures; and thus perennial philosophy can demonstrate the possibility of objective truth that is known for itself and not merely for some instrumental purpose. For the human intellect, the object of knowledge is essence, the universal, which is abstracted from the numerous data of sense impression, and which, through the operations of reason, leads us to consequences. Thus, for the perennialist, the Truth exists and can be known, but this knowing is not easy and is possible only when the faculties of reason have been developed by education, the main role of the school. For those perennialists who recognize not only rational truth but also revealed truth, there is another dimension. The revealed truths of the supernatural order must be transmitted and interpreted for children and youth, for otherwise these truths would never be gained by the young.

## SUMMARY

Perennialism holds that the ultimate ends of education can be demonstrated and can be known in an absolute fashion. In this sense, there is only one *philosophy* of education, for philosophical knowledge is that knowledge that is capable of rational demonstration from first principles. We have not attempted any such complete demonstration. We have only sought to show that the main beliefs in the perennialist's educational philosophy derive immediately from the philosophy of human nature of that tradition.

Since we are concerned with the philosophy of American education, the perennial philosophy has been presented as a protest against the prevailing essentialism. In other historical periods, perennialism has been the prevailing tradition and has been influential in determining whatever educational arrangement prevailed. Perhaps in some countries of the world today this tradition is still the dominant one. It is submitted, however, that this is not the case in the United States. Perennialism has furnished the basis for a penetrating, and on occasion, a devastating criticism of educational essentialism, but it has not succeeded in making fundamental changes in the nature of American education. Whether it ever will succeed is a speculative matter.

In some respects, the protests of perennialism at the practical level of educational policy are similar to those made by Dewey and the progressives. Both these traditions are critical of the essentialist's emphasis on the transmission of organized subject matter as the primary aim of formal education, and since other practical considerations about the operations of the school follow directly from this conception, perennialists and progressives have sometimes found other common ground for practical criticism. Beyond the practical level, however, the differences in outlook between progressivists and perennialists are enormous. In a sense, both of these philosophical traditions that underlie the two bodies of educational theory are humanistic. Both of them agree that the purpose of education is "to make a man." The issue over which they differ is the question, "What is man?" The answer to this question can be strategic for educational theory.

# chapter NINE

# THE
# MARXIST
# PROTEST

*Man is the sole animal capable of working his
way out of the merely animal state—his normal
state is one appropriate to his consciousness,
one to be created by himself.*

—FRIEDRICH ENGELS

*... The education of the future ... will
combine productive labor with instruction and
gymnastics, not only as one of the methods of
adding to the efficiency of production, but
as the only method of producing fully developed
human beings.*

—KARL MARX

The established tradition in American education is an expression of a cultural pattern that is essentially middle-class in origin and character. Important elements in this pattern are capitalism, nationalism, democracy, and experimental science, together with the supernaturalism of the Hebraic-Christian tradition. Conservatism continues to try to unite in some kind of acceptable synthesis the spirit and achievements of modern science with the older supernaturalism. Educational policies developed and supported by the conservative tradition reflect the essentially middle-class character of conservatism and its eclectic approach to the problems of society. The conservative tradition in America has been severely challenged once in the present century by liberal elements, who instigated a reform movement of considerable proportions that had as one of its facets the progressive movement in education. However, the liberal reform movement itself arose from within the middle class, and its leaders generally were fundamentally middle-class in origin and outlook. Though liberals have long advocated far-reaching reforms for social institutions, including schools, they wanted these reforms not to be abrupt and revolutionary but rather a steady and persistent advance toward improving conditions in the modern industrial world. Certainly, the liberal has sought to transform society and to eliminate many elements in the conservative pattern, but he has advocated nonviolent means within the existing procedural framework. Furthermore, it is a well-established point of liberalism that the school as an institution can act in social reform and toward improving the lot of man.

However, in this century the established tradition has had to withstand another protest movement that has not been gradualistic in its strategy, a protest that has condemned the middle-class gradualism of the liberals as completely as it has the traditionalism of the conservatives. The political reality of revolutionary socialism is a product of our own century, but its origins lie in the nineteenth century. The end of February 1848 was a fateful time in the history of the West, for it was then, on the eve of the Revolution of 1848 in France, that a small pamphlet written in German was published in London. It bore the title *The Manifesto of the Communist Party*. Its authors were Germans, Karl Marx (1818–1883) and Friedrich Engels (1820–1895), and its opening lines were meant to be the death knell of the old order: "A spectre is haunting Europe—the spectre of Communism. All the Powers of old Europe have entered into a holy alliance to exorcise this spectre. . . ." The closing passage of the *Manifesto* has served for more than a hundred years to send chills down the spines of Western conservatives and liberals alike: "The Communists disdain to conceal their views and aims. They openly declare that their ends can be attained only by the forcible overthrow of all existing social conditions. Let the ruling classes tremble at a Communistic revolution. The proletarians have nothing to lose but their chains. They have a world to win. Working men of all countries, unite!" [1]

It has often been said, even by those who hate the very sound of his name, that Marx is one of the genuinely important figures in human history. There are, as C. Wright Mills has pointed out, several Marxes.[2] There is Marx the political agitator and polemicist; he has had few peers in this role. There is Marx the economist; after him, economic theory could never be the same. There is, of course, Marx the philosopher of history, and we may ask, Is there also a Marx the educational philosopher? This question is not so easily answered. Marx was concerned with educational policy but he did not write any systematic treatise about it. Consequently, his observations about education are scattered through his voluminous writings.

An important reason for including a discussion of Marxism in this book is that certain ideas of Marx provide insight into the human situation, particularly under conditions of industrial society, and into the prospect for improving man's lot in the modern world. We have considered this matter in connection with other traditions and found it important in its effect on educational theory and we propose to do the same thing with Marxism. We do not intend to make the educational system of the Soviet Union a leading subject of this chapter, even though at one time conservatives often made invidious comparisons of the American system of education with that of the Soviet Union.[3] Our principal enterprise is to study the protest that Marx and his followers launched against bourgeois society and whatever ideas about education we may find to be involved in this protest.

## MATERIALISM AND DIALECTICAL DEVELOPMENT

Marxism is undoubtedly best known—and most feared—for its economic theory, but Marx developed his theory of history long before he turned his attention to demonstrating that capitalism had within itself

---

[1] The *Manifesto* has been reprinted many times. My references are to Karl Marx and Friedrich Engels, *Selected Works*, 2 vols. (Moscow: Foreign Languages Publishing House, 1962), 1:33–69.

[2] *The Marxists* (New York: Dell Publishing Co., 1962), p. 41. See also chap. 2.

[3] For example, see *Report on Russia by Vice Admiral Hyman G. Rickover, USN*, Hearings before the Committee on Appropriations, House of Representatives, Eighty-sixth Congress (Washington, D.C.: United States Government Printing Office, 1959).

the seeds of its own destruction. In the field of philosophy, by far the greatest influence on Marx's thought was the idealism of Hegel. In Chapter Four of this volume, we saw something of the character of Hegelian thought: the Absolute Mind that is within itself the whole of reality; history as the concrete manifestation of the developing processes of this Supreme Consciousness, and the inherently logical character of the development of this Consciousness in terms of a dialectic pattern, which is the synthesis of opposing forces. Marx rejected Hegel's idealism, but he saw in Hegel's dialectical and historical method a means to the development of a scientific interpretation of history. "What distinguished Hegel's mode of thought from that of all other philosophers," Engels said in commenting on Marx's *Critique of Political Economy*, "was the tremendous sense of the historical on which it was based." [4] It is true, Engels agreed, that Hegel was thoroughly idealistic, but he always related the development of his argument to history and believed that the events of history constitute a test of the validity of the argument. What Marx and Engels proposed to do was to unite Hegel's dialectical method with materialism. In this view, the world is to be taken as it is for what it is. Its existence is not to be attributed to the creative act of some supernatural force nor dependent for its reality on any form of consciousness. The priority of matter is asserted in place of the priority of consciousness, as in idealism. Consciousness derives from matter. [5]

Marx's materialism, however, is not to be viewed as a kind of mechanism in which inert matter is pushed and pulled about by separate forces. Matter is essentially dynamic in nature, always in process of change and transformation. Development and change follow the dialectical laws inherent in the nature of things. Therefore, if we are to inquire into the nature of anything to understand it, we must inquire into its history. What a thing is seen to be at any particular time does not reveal the real nature of that thing. It is the direction and rate of development that is important. Presumably, this is true of all phenomena of nature, but Marx's great achievement was the application of this dialectical materialism to human society. In the preface to his "Contribution to the Critique of

---

[4] *Selected Works*, vol. 1, p. 372.

[5] In the preface to the second edition of *Capital*, Marx makes this observation about Hegel: "My dialectic method is not only different from the Hegelian, but is its direct opposite. To Hegel, the life-process of the human brain, i.e., the process of thinking, which, under the name of 'the Idea,' he even transforms into an independent subject, is the demiurgos of the real world, and the real world is only the external, phenomenal form of 'the Idea.' With me, on the contrary, the ideal is nothing else than the material world reflected by the human mind, and translated into forms of thought." *Capital*, vol. 1 (New York: Modern Library, no date), p. 25. All my references in *Capital* are to the Modern Library edition.

Political Economy," Marx related how he came first to a study of Hegel because of a controversy in which he was involved when he worked on a radical newspaper in the Rhineland. This experience convinced Marx of the inadequacy of his own philosophical knowledge, and in consequence of this he embarked on a critical study of Hegelian philosophy. "My investigation led to the result," he said, "that legal relations as well as forms of state are to be grasped neither from themselves nor from the so-called general development of the human mind, *but rather have their roots in the material conditions of life, . . .*" [6] Thus, if we are to understand institutions or laws of any particular time these must be studied in terms of their history—the conditions from which they have emerged and the direction in which they are tending. This is the essence of dialectical method.

From this beginning, Marx worked out the basic theses of his theory of society and history. In social life, men necessarily enter into certain kinds of relations over which they have no control. These are relations involved in economic production, and the sum total of these relations constitute the economic structure of society, the base on which everything else in that society rests. Therefore, in any given period the character of all institutions—legal, political, educational, religious, or whatever—is a function of the existing modes and forces of production current in that society. Perhaps the most momentous effect of the economic base is that it determines the class structure of a society. It is a matter of historical fact that class structure in different periods has varied, and it was Marx's point that these variations have been the result of different economic bases, that is to say, variations in the class structure of societies are the result of objective, historical conditions.

All development is dialectical in nature, and at the level of human society, the dynamic takes the form of the struggle of social classes. The conditions leading to this clash and struggle of interests were described by Marx as follows:

> At a certain stage of their development, the material forces of society come in conflict with the existing relations of production, or—what is but a legal expression for the same thing—with the property relations within which they have been at work hitherto. From forms of development of the productive forces these relations turn into their fetters. Then begins an epoch of social revolution.[7]

For example, given the economic base of capitalism in which the institution of private property is the basic element, society consequently is divided into two classes: those who own the means of production, that

---

[6] *Selected Works*, vol. 1, p. 362. Italics mine.

[7] Ibid., p. 363.

is, the capitalists; and those who have nothing to sell but their own labor, that is, the workers. One of the elements in the economic base is what Marx called, as in the quotation above, "the existing *relations* of production"; by this he meant the system of ownership, which under capitalism is private ownership of the means of production, and prevailing ways of distributing and exchanging commodities. The other element that Marx referred to as "the *forces* of production" consists of the raw materials, tools, technical skills, and so on involved in the processes of production. As the historical period of capitalism begins, the relations of production are harmonious with the forces of production and there is a period of dynamic and creative growth. But eventually the point is reached at which a contradiction develops between the forces and relations of production. The expanding productivity, which creates surpluses of goods, is inimical to the interests of the owning class. This class reacts by suppressing technological advance in various ways and in the end, it is capital itself that is the real barrier to production. The practical effect of this contradiction is that the mass of the people are without work and on the verge of starvation. The "epoch of social revolution" Marx spoke of in the quotation begins when this exploited proletarian mass becomes politically conscious and adopts revolutionary methods to change the economic base. The conflict that develops between the forces of production and property relations cannot be resolved within the institutions of capitalism. According to Marx, no amount of social reform effort, legal or other, can possibly suffice to ease the mounting tension to prevent the ultimate disintegration of the old order. In Marx's view, the transition from one historic period to another is never easy, gradual, or peaceful. Said Engels in his preface to the *Manifesto*, "The whole history of mankind (since the dissolution of primitive tribal society, holding land in common ownership) has been a history of class struggles, contests between exploiting and exploited, ruling and oppressed classes." [8]

The economic base of a society, which includes the relations and the forces of production, determines the superstructure of social institutions and relationships of that society, and hence determines the way in which society is divided into classes and the relationships that obtain among these classes. The class structure is different in feudal society, for example, from that under capitalism, and the relations of a feudal lord to his serfs are different from the relations of the owning class to the workers under capitalism. The reason for these differences is objective and historical; it derives from the character of the economic base of society.

The institutions that rise above the economic foundations as a super-

[8]  Ibid., p. 28. This refers to the English edition of 1888.

structure are not only functions of basic economic conditions in a historical period; they are always employed by the dominant exploiting class to further its own purposes. The legal structure of a society exists to protect the interests of the class in control, although its true origin and character may be hidden behind a gloss of abstractions about "natural rights" and "eternal ideals of justice." In the *Manifesto*, Marx and Engels ridiculed the pretensions of the bourgeoisie about the objectivity of law and justice. "Your jurisprudence is but the will of your class made into a law for all, a will whose essential character and direction are determined by the economical conditions of existence of your class." [9] Engels, writing at a later time and discussing the ways in which abstract legal concepts and systems of law develop, observed: "The justice of the Greeks and Romans held slavery to be just; the justice of the bourgeois of 1789 demanded the abolition of feudalism on the ground that it was unjust." [10]

In the same way, and for the same reason, the nature of the family and the character of relations between the sexes, together with the relations of parents and children, vary from one historic period to another. Bourgeois society makes its ideas about the family into holy myths and supports them with theological pronouncements about marriages being made in heaven and wedlock a holy state ordained by God. "On what foundation is the present family, the bourgeois family, based?" the authors of the *Manifesto* demand. And they answer their own question: "On capital, on private gain. In its completely developed form this family exists only among the bourgeoisie. But this state of things finds its complement in the practical absence of the family among the proletarians, and in public prostitution. The bourgeois family will vanish as a matter of course when its complement vanishes, and both will vanish with the vanishing of capital." [11] And with the question of education, the same thing holds. Bourgeois education in its aims and operations is determined by the economic structure of which it is both a product and a tool. In highly developed bourgeois societies, the educational system conceals its origin and nature behind a screen of genteel abstractions about "the pursuit of truth for its own sake" and the "general enlightenment of mankind." Lenin lashed out at this pretension:

> The more cultured was the Bourgeois state, the more subtly it deceived, asserting that the school can remain outside of politics and thus serve society as a whole. In reality the school was wholly an instrument of

---

[9] Ibid., p. 49.

[10] From "Supplement on Proudhon and the Housing Question" (1873), *Selected Works*, vol. 1, p. 624.

[11] Ibid., p. 50.

class domination in the hands of the bourgeoisie; it was permeated throughout with the spirit of caste; and its aim was to give to the capitalists obliging serfs and competent workers.[12]

In the *Manifesto*, the promise was made that under communism the influence of the bourgeoisie over education would cease, and this as a matter of historical necessity. The tenth measure for action proposed by Marx and Engels in the *Manifesto* was for free education for all children in public schools, the abolition of child labor in factories, *and the combination of education with industrial production*; this last was Marx's most important proposal for educational practice.

We have now seen something of how the superstructure of society develops in terms of the economic base. The class structure, the legal system, such institutions as the family and the school, political processes and institutions, are what they are, and what they must be because of the objective conditions that have produced them. At the top of the superstructure of society is what Marx called *the state*. In this sense, the state is not simply the government, that is, the institutions that carry on the routine and administrative affairs of society. The state is the coercive power in society, described by Marx as "the standing army, police, bureaucracy, clergy, and judicature." [13] This coercive power is always available and when the interests of the dominant class are threatened seriously and these threats cannot be contained by political or other means, the full force of the state will be invoked. Marx dismissed the idea of the state's being neutral and above class considerations as pure nonsense. "The state," said Engels, "is nothing but the organized collective power of the possessing classes, the landowners and the capitalists, as against the exploited classes, the peasants and the workers." [14] Nor will this condition change until the conditions that produce it change. Until capitalism falls, the state will be in the service of the exploiting class.

Some of the main ideas involved in Marxian theory may be summarized as follows: (1) A conception of nature as material in character, all else being derived from matter. (2) Nature developing in terms of a dialectical pattern in which the struggle and eventual synthesis of opposing forces is the dynamic factor. (3) The applications of dialectical, and hence historical, method to understanding the nature of human social organization, and an interpretation of the struggle of social classes as the dynamic element in social change. (4) The theory that the relations and forces involved in economic production are the determining factors in society and shape

---

[12] Quoted in George S. Counts, *The Soviet Challenge to America* (New York: John Day Co., 1931), p. 318.

[13] Ibid., p. 516.

[14] Ibid., p. 604.

the character of that society. These ideas were all fundamental in Marx's conception of the historical process and the rise and fall of social systems.

## THE COURSE OF HISTORY

According to Marxian thought, there are five important stages in human history. These are primitive communism, slavery, feudalism, capitalism, and socialism (that is, communism). Each successive stage has developed out of the preceding one (with primitive communism considered the initial state of human society) according to the historical process we have already considered in the preceding section. The character of each of these social systems is determined by the relations and forces of economic production in that system. The transition from capitalism to socialism is the most important question in Marxism, and it is the matter to which Marx himself gave the most attention. However, the development of socialism out of capitalism is only one (and the last) historical development of society. It is necessary that Marx's theory of history account not only for the fall of capitalism but also for previous transformations and developments of society if it is to be truly comprehensive in its conception of the historical process. There are certain difficulties involved in Marx's conceptions of the development of slavery and subsequently the transition from slavery to feudalism.[15] Briefly, historical development as Marx saw it is as follows:

As human history begins, men live under conditions of primitive communism in which the means of production is the natural environment. They are food gatherers and hunters, and to survive the rigors of nature they are forced to work together. The means of production and the proceeds of production are held in common. There is as yet no conception of private ownership of the means of production. There is no owning class, and hence there is no exploitation.

The historic period that succeeds the era of primitive communism is slavery. Now both the forces and relations of production have changed. Tools and techniques are much improved compared with their primitive counterparts. Agriculture, handicraft, and animal husbandry are well advanced. Surplus wealth appears (that is, economic goods in excess of those needed to sustain the population). The way is now clear for exchange of goods and accumulation of wealth and the division of society into an exploiting class or the owners, and an exploited class—the slaves. Thus, a class-structured society emerges, and the relations of production are those of master to slave. The slave is his master's chattel. A master can do any-

---

[15] For a more detailed discussion, see George Lichtheim, *Marxism: An Historical and Critical Study* (New York: Frederick A. Praeger, 1961).

thing with a slave he chooses to do: buy him, sell him, punish him, kill him if he wants to. Slaves receive enough for their subsistence, but that is all they get. Whatever a slave produces beyond that needed to keep himself alive and in working condition is surplus value and accrues to the owner.

Eventually, the relations and forces of production change, and humanity enters the new era of feudalism. Technological improvements have changed productive forces somewhat. The various forms of agriculture have become more efficient, the beginnings of factory production can be seen. It becomes to the advantage of the owning class that the workers have some psychological involvement in the productive process and therefore exercise some of their own ingenuity and initiative—this in contrast to the slave, who felt no involvement and whose attitude was passive. And so the slave becomes the serf who owns some of the tools of production and who pays the feudal lord with part of the fruits of his labor, keeping for himself whatever is left. Thus, the exploitation of the serf is nearly as bad as that of the slave under conditions of the previous historical period, and as was true under slavery, an intense class struggle develops between the exploited class and the owning class.

The fourth stage of historical development ushers in capitalism. The relations of production under capitalism are those of an owning class (the capitalists) to a working class (the proletariat). Members of the proletariat are free; that is, they are not owned by the capitalists and they cannot legally be bought or sold or killed. The forces of production have also changed. The simple handicraft system and the guilds of medieval craftsmen have given way to large and increasingly complex manufacturing establishments. The main source of energy is no longer human and animal muscle power, but steam, and following it, electricity. Capitalism requires much more from workers than either slavery or feudalism demands. Industrial production involves complicated machinery and processes and workers must be capable of being instructed in the use of machines. It is to the advantage of the owning class, therefore, that the workers have personal freedom and at least the illusion of a certain amount of political freedom. Under the conditions of advanced capitalism, it is also advantageous for the working class to have a certain amount of schooling—at least the elements of literacy.

In Marx's day, the desirability of popular education, however, ran counter to another important aspect of the early capitalism, the employment of children in factories. In England, which was the most advanced industrial nation in the early and middle nineteenth century, provisions were included in a series of "Factory Acts" that children employed in factories were to receive a certain amount of schooling—actually a few hours per week. Marx's comments on the quality of this "schooling" are withering. He quoted from reports of factory inspectors concerning the total lack of fitness of the teachers in the factory schools, many of whom were not sufficiently literate to keep the class register or even to spell their own names in the same way on different occasions.[16] To Marx, the sham of factory education of children was but an example of the merciless exploitation of the working classes by capitalists. However, as scornful as he was of capitalism's real contribution to the education of the common people, he did discover in the combined work-study program provided under the factory acts an idea for the universal education that would develop when capitalism and all its attendant evils have succumbed to the historical process.

The transition from capitalism to socialism is the last and most crucial episode in the historical process, according to Marxists. It is also the point of greatest interest for us. The Marxist protest is against bourgeois, capitalist society and the institutions and philosophies of that society. Hence, Marxism is in various ways a protest against all the educational traditions we have considered thus far. In thinking about Marx's ideas about the transition from capitalism to socialism, we must be sure to keep certain things in mind. For one thing, we should remember his principle that the mode of production in a society determines the institutions, processes, and ways of life of that society. In addition to this idea, which is the basis of Marxian social philosophy, two other ideas are closely associated with it.

First, since the mode of production of material life determines the character of social processes, according to Marx, "It is not the consciousness of men that determines their being, but on the contrary, their social being that determines their consciousness." [17] This is a conception of great importance in the Marxian tradition. Marx was saying that the very way in which we perceive the world is a function of the mode of production that obtains in the particular historical period in which we live. What we consider right and what we consider wrong, what is just and what is unjust, what is to be desired and what is to be avoided are all judgments made with reference to certain objective conditions that exist and serve to determine our perceptions. Hence, Marx was denying that there is some ultimate source, usually alleged to be universal and unchanging, from which our ethical principles derive. Ethical principles are emergents of history; they are naturalistic in their origin. In Marx's thought, therefore, not only were ethical conceptions relative to historical periods, they were also relative to the demands and needs of social classes. This had to be true because all social orders existing in the historical period between primitive communism and the advent of socialism were divided into opposing classes

---

[16] See *Capital*, vol. 1, p. 437. See pp. 436–40 for Marx's complete description of the education of working-class children.

[17] "Preface to the Critique of Political Economy," in Marx and Engels, *Selected Works*, vol. 1, p. 363.

whose needs and interests were diametrically opposite. Each class sought to make its own claims prevail, but neither class could seriously maintain that its claim could be justified in terms of some higher law or absolute. The last resort, said Marx, is force:

> The capitalist maintains his rights as a purchaser when he tries to make the working day as long as possible, and to make, whenever possible, two working days out of one. On the other hand, the peculiar nature of the commodity sold implies a limit to its consumption by the purchaser, and the labourer maintains his right as seller when he wishes to reduce the working day to one of normal duration. *There is here, therefore, an antinomy, right against right, both equally bearing the seal of the law of exchanges. Between equal rights force decides.*[18]

It is often maintained that there is a more or less objective community of values to which all men customarily subscribe, regardless of history or class status. After all, it is said, truth, goodness, security, love, beauty, and so on, are goods that are universally desired. In essence, Marx's answer was that perhaps they are, but the very way in which these abstractions are conceived is a function of historical circumstances. What is justice to the capitalist is injustice to the worker. The security of the owning class is bought at the expense of the insecurity of the workers. There is no community of value in the practical sense because the needs and demands of social classes cannot be reconciled so long as there is an exploiting class and an exploited class. This is the case under capitalism, and given the base on which the superstructure of capitalism rests, it cannot be otherwise so long as that system endures. The proletariat, therefore, can never be free of exploitation until class distinctions and class struggles cease, and this condition will come only with socialism.

The other matter we need to bear in mind as we consider Marx's conception of the transition to socialism is the principle he enunciated in his "Preface to the Critique of Political Economy." [19]

> No social order ever perishes before all the productive forces for which there is room in it have developed; and new, higher relations of production never appear before the material conditions of their existence have matured in the womb of the old society itself. Therefore mankind always sets itself only such tasks as it can solve; since, looking at the matter more closely, it will always be found that the task itself arises only when the material conditions for its solution already exist or are at least in the process of formation.

Each of the succeeding stages of history, therefore, beginning with

---

[18]   *Capital*, vol. 1, p. 259. Italics mine.
[19]   *Selected Works*, vol. 1, p. 363.

primitive communism, develops only as the preceding stage has exhausted itself. The transition from capitalism to socialism must occur in a country in which capitalism has run its course. Just prior to the breakdown of the old capitalistic order certain symptoms will appear. The polarization of society will be virtually complete. The two great classes, the capitalists and the proletariat, whose interests are diametrically opposed, will be in a state of continuous struggle. The owning class will have grown smaller in number and the proletariat will have grown larger, to a considerable extent because of the impoverishment of small shopkeepers, farmers, and so on, and their consequent descent into the propertyless proletariat. Economic crises grow in frequency and in severity. Riots and strikes are common. The aging capitalism no longer has the flexibility and viability to recover from periodic crisis. The owning class, feeling its domination threatened, uses the coercive power of the state without mercy to keep down the increasingly revolutionary actions of the masses, which by now have become politically conscious.

The final act in the drama is a revolution in which the capitalistic class is overthrown, the proletariat institutes a dictatorship in which the coercive power of the state is converted to the uses of the now dominant working class as it seeks the transition to socialism. The conversion from one social system to another cannot be abrupt and immediate. In one instance, Marx described the nature of the transition in this way:

> Between capitalist and communist society lies the period of the revolutionary transformation of the one into the other. There corresponds to this also a political transition period in which the state can be nothing but the revolutionary dictatorship of the proletariat.[20]

The first stage initiated by the new dominant class is state ownership of the means of production. Out of this emerges the first stage of socialism, in which workers are rewarded according to what they produce. This period has not divorced itself completely from certain aspects of capitalism, yet it is a classless society. The change that has occurred in the economic base, that is, the abolition of private ownership of the means of production, has destroyed the class basis of the old society. Hence, there is no exploitation and no class struggle. The final and highest form of society is reached in pure communism. Under these conditions, the last manifestations of the old order have disappeared and all men will "contribute according to their capacities and be rewarded according to their needs." In this final stage, the state will disappear because it will have no reason for being. The only function of the state is the protection of the interests of the dominant class, and under communism there are no social classes and

---

[20] "Critique of the Gotha Programme," ibid., vol. 2, p. 32.

no selfish interests to protect. This does not mean there will be no institutions to regulate and administer the routine affairs of society. It means
that the need to coerce has vanished. Exploitation of human labor is gone.
There is no need for extrinsic motivation for man to labor. He is now free
to express his own uniquely human nature—to live like a man. And so,
in the next stage of our inquiry, we will concern ourselves with the question
of what it means to live like a man. To answer this question we must turn
our attention to Marx's conception of human nature.

## THE NATURE OF MAN

Whatever conception of human nature Marxists may hold, we can
presume that it is consistent with the materialist philosophic position of this
tradition and also defensible in empirical and historical terms. Philosophies
of human nature, whatever their character may be, are always concerned
with describing the primary characteristics of the human species, discovering the essential differences that set man apart from other species of animals, and as a consequence of these ideas, stating some final end for man.
For example, Aristotle (and subsequently the Scholastics) saw man as an
animal, part of whose nature is identical with the nature of animals but
who in addition possesses unique powers of reason. The essence of man,
therefore, in the perennial philosophy is reason, and man is a rational
animal.

The approach of Marx and Engels to the problem of the nature of
man was historical and scientific. Human nature, and what is unique to it,
is a product of historical development. Man is what he is because of the
conditions involved in his development from less complex organisms, and
the fundamental factor is *labor*. This thesis was stated by Engels:

> Labour is the source of all wealth, the political economists assert.
> It is this—next to nature, which supplies it with the material that con-
> verts it into wealth. *But it is infinitely more than this*. It is the prime
> basic tradition for all human existence, and this to such an extent that,
> in a sense, we have to say that *labour created* man himself.[21]

Having stated his thesis, Engels then proceeded with his argument
that the human species developed from apes and that the chief factor in
this evolutionary development was labor. The decisive event in the development of the human species was the accomplishment of walking upright

---

[21]  Engels, "The Part Played by Labour in the Transition from Ape to Man," *Selected
Works*, vol. 2, p. 80. Italics mine.

and thereby freeing the hand for work. "Thus," said Engels, "the hand is not only the organ of labour, *it is also the product of labour.*" [22] The hand is only one of the members of the organism, yet the development of this one member affected the development of others, and man not only learned to labor with his hands but also to speak. And so the simple, primitive gregariousness of the ape becomes the society of human beings and work becomes cooperative, that is, social. This, in the judgment of Engels, was the crucial element in human nature and in human society. He asked, "And what do we find . . . as the characteristic difference between the troupe of monkeys and human society?" The answer, he said, is "labour." [23] An animal only uses whatever may be present in the environment but man adapts nature to his own ends—he masters it—and the fundamental element in this mastery is human labor.

We are not concerned here with the technical adequacy of Engels's evolutionary theory. The important matter is his idea of the historic role labor has played in the development of human nature and the strategic part this idea plays in Marxian conceptions of man. Marx and Engels regarded the control man had achieved over nature with the greatest respect and enthusiasm. The conquest of nature not only showed the power of human labor, they thought, but also showed the intimate relation of man with the rest of the processes of nature, and exhibited the falsity of all those philosophies that rest on the familiar dualisms of mind *and* matter, man *and* nature, soul *and* body. Man is a part of nature, an animal evolved from more primitive species. But "Man is the sole animal capable of working his way out of the merely animal state—his normal state is one appropriate to his consciousness, one to be created by himself." [24] The essence of man therefore is his urge to create and re-create his own environment, not simply to adjust to it as other animals do. The urge to labor is not simply a reaction to external stimuli; it is of the very nature of man himself. If for Aristotle man was a rational animal, for Marx and Engels he was a *working* animal. It is through labor that his fundamental nature is realized.

The role of human labor is to give man mastery over the physical world and to make possible the realization of man's own nature, but since the time of the emergence of the human species from the original condition to primitive communism, events have conspired against it. Man has conquered nature, but in having lost control of the productive forces that have given that control, he has lost himself. Said Engels in the introduction to *Dialectics of Nature:*

---

[22]   Ibid., p. 83.

[23]   Ibid., p. 84.

[24]   Engels, *Dialectics of Nature* (New York: International Publishers Co., 1940), p. 187.

In the most advanced industrial countries we have subdued the forces of nature and pressed them into the service of mankind; we have thereby infinitely multiplied production, so that a child now produces more than a hundred adults previously. And what is the consequence? Increasing overwork and increasing misery of the masses and every ten years a great crash.[25]

Such is the course of human alienation.

Ever since human society emerged from primitive communism to slavery the mass of men have been alienated from themselves; they have always worked under compulsion—first under slavery, then under feudalism, and finally under capitalism, in which the process of alienation has reached its highest point. Under capitalism, human labor is simply a commodity that is bought and sold on the market, and man becomes merely a means and not an end. Hence, the worker is most with himself when he is not working and most alienated from himself when he is at work. The work he does is not in response to the deepest urgings of his own nature, but rather is extraneous to it. Marx said the worker feels most free when he is performing purely animal functions and least free when he is performing the distinctively human activity of labor. This is the irony of history, and it can never be eliminated; man can never be united with himself until the capitalist period of history ends and mankind gains control of productive relations and processes. The historical effect of labor has been to create private property, the property of someone other than those who labored to produce it. "Capital is dead labor," Marx said, "that vampire-like, only lives by sucking living labor, and lives the more, the more labor it sucks." [26]

For most of human history, man has been exploited and hence alienated, but under the conditions of capitalism this alienation has reached its highest point. The relations of production under the factory system are such that work has become completely dehumanized. The interest of the worker is set off against the interest of the factory owner, but more than that, in their work men are set against each other. Factory management assigns to each worker a simple, routine, repetitive task that is done over and over again (in Marx's day for as long as 14 or even 18 hours a day). This simplification and routinization made it possible to employ very young children in the early factory system of production, the horrors of which Marx described and documented in great detail. The work that is natural to man—the labor that in the view of Engels has served to make the species what it is—is free spontaneous activity in which through communal effort men seek to transform the environment in accordance with

---

25   *Selected Works*, vol. 2, p. 75.
26   *Capital*, vol. 1, p. 257.

their desires. Under conditions of factory production, however, labor is neither spontaneous nor free. It is forced labor performed for another; it is wage slavery. And it is under these conditions, Marx pointed out, that "the relations connecting the labor of one individual with that of the rest appear, not as direct social relations between individuals at work, but as what they really are, material relations between persons and social relations between things." [27] And in this sense, a contradiction develops within human nature itself, for under these conditions labor is not the essence of man. It contradicts the very character of humanness, and what is at the very heart of this contradiction is acquisitiveness—greed. Man is thus engaged in a struggle with himself to free himself from the despotic rule of this inhuman and dehumanizing force, which is objectified socially in the person of the capitalist.[28]

We should remember that "it is not the consciousness of men that determines their existence, but on the contrary, their social existence determines their consciousness." Alienated man, who is not the real man, is what he is because of objective historical conditions. Before man can lose his alienated state, he must become conscious of himself. Self-consciousness is the key to freedom, and the burden of the fulfillment of this, in Marx's philosophy, is laid by history on the proletariat. The first step in this process is that the proletariat must become class-conscious. When this class consciousness has become sufficient, the proletariat will revolt and in its act of revolution change the conditions that created alienated man. Thus, when the social relations in society are brought into harmony with the forces of production, all mankind will be freed from its condition of alienation and men can live like men. As one writer has said, "The promise of the Marxist vision is of man united with himself, his comrades, and his world." [29]

In the long history of alienated man, he has turned to religion. In Marx's view, religion has always been an emotional outcry of great intensity, expressing the essential misery of the human species. It has also constituted a protest against the conditions that produce this misery. But

---

[27] Ibid., p. 84.

[28] There are marked differences of opinion about how certain ideas of Marx that concerned human alienation should be interpreted. An important point of controversy is whether the primary alienation is within the individual and subsequently projected into social relations or whether alienation in social relations is the prior condition. See, for example, Robert C. Tucker, *Philosophy and Myth in Karl Marx* (London and New York: Cambridge University Press, 1961), chap. 9; and Sidney Hook, *From Hegel to Marx* (Ann Arbor: University of Michigan Press, 1962), pp. 3–8.

[29] Robert S. Cohen, "On the Marxist Philosophy of Education," in John S. Brubacher, ed., *Modern Philosophies and Education*, Fifty-fourth Yearbook of the National Society for the study of Education (Chicago: University of Chicago Press, 1955), p. 192.

religion has also prevented men from recognizing and rising against the conditions that perpetuate their misery. Institutionalized religion has been used by the exploiters to keep the masses in subjection.[30] Engels, for example, discussing the situation in Britain remarked: "Now, if ever, the people must be kept in order by moral means, and the first and foremost of all moral means of action upon the masses is and remains—religion." [31]

In his own conception of the nature and function of religion, Marx was influenced by the German philosopher, Ludwig Feuerbach (1804–1872). Feuerbach had interpreted religion as a projection of human needs and aspirations, although, he pointed out, this projection is necessarily illusory and distorted.[32] Religion is a form of self-alienation because it involves a duality: an imaginary and ideal world portrayed by religion, and the real world in which men live and suffer. Marx was attracted by Feuerbach's naturalistic explanation of the religious phenomenon, that is, that the world portrayed by religion has its origin and finds its basis in the "real" world of secular life. But Marx also believed that Feuerbach had left the real task undone. "Feuerbach," he wrote, "resolves the religious essence into *human* essence. But the human essence is no abstraction inherent in each single individual. In its reality it is the ensemble of the social relations." [33]

Feuerbach's failure to perceive that religious feeling is itself a product of historical and social conditions allowed him to reach a conclusion that was common in those days, as well as in these, that religious feelings are a part of man's essential nature; that is, that man, we might say, is by nature "a religious animal." Since he is religious by nature, man always tends to project his needs and desires into a perfect world of illusion, and this vision—distorted though it may be—is a true expression of his longings and a protest against their lack of fulfillment. With this in mind, Marx in his earlier career wrote the famous line "Religion is the people's opium." If man has an essential nature, it is not one that is carried in the genes. Rather, Marx maintained, it derives from social life, and this means that the character of economic forces and relations is the determining factor. The religious phenomenon, therefore, is a social phenomenon and can be studied and understood in empirical and historical terms. The conditions that give rise to religion are the conflicts that develop in society and are caused by economic conflict. When these conditions disappear, that is, when men gain control over economic and natural forces, they will no longer be at the mercy of these forces and they will gain control over their own history. The alienated condition of man will pass away, and the

---

[30]   Ibid., p. 188.
[31]   "Socialism: Utopian and Scientific," in *Selected Works*, vol. 2, p. 113.
[32]   Ludwig Feuerbach, *The Essence of Christianity* (London: John Chapman, 1854).
[33]   "Theses on Feuerbach," *Selected Works*, vol. 2, p. 404.

myths and illusions of religion will no longer have a part to play. This cannot be, however, until the historic age of capitalism has spent itself and the proletariat can institute the classless society under socialism. Marx himself did not believe that the working-class movement, as he knew it, should make antireligion a part of its strategy. The energy of the working class, he maintained, should be directed against the conditions that generate religion. When those conditions have been changed, the rest will follow as a necessary course.[34]

Also in the critique of Feuerbach is the key to Marx's conception of human knowledge and truth. As a materialist, Marx necessarily rejected the idealistic account of the knowledge process, but he also found in idealism, particularly in Hegel, the element that was missing in previous materialism, whether of the ancients or of the eighteenth century. This element was the essentially active aspect of the knowledge process, which in idealism is the activity of mind. Typically in materialism, the act of cognition had been conceived as essentially passive. The mind passively receives the impact of stimuli coming from the external object, and thus, mind is simply a spectator of an independent reality. Such a view, Marx thought, was incapable of accounting for the role that human action has in the process of knowledge and consequently in social life. As he saw it, knowing always involves acting on and therefore transforming the object. In the second of his theses on Feuerbach, Marx observed: "The question whether objective ... truth can be attributed to human thinking is not a question of theory but is a *practical* question. In practice man must prove the truth, that is, the reality and power, the this-sidedness of his thinking." [35] Now the question is, How do we prove the truth?

Marx had thought the idealists right in their emphasis on the dynamic, active character of cognition, but since idealism is built on the priority of consciousness and the immateriality of the object, the only possible criterion for truth is coherence. On the other hand, the only conceivable criterion of truth available to materialism is correspondence, which involves certain difficulties; and these were sufficient in Marx's judgment to render correspondence inadequate as a theory of truth. In the last sentence of his second thesis on Feuerbach, Marx said: "The dispute over the reality or non-reality of thinking which is isolated from practice is a purely *scholastic* question." What Marx was saying here is very similar to what C. S. Peirce and subsequently John Dewey said: that a statement that cannot be put to the test of action is a meaningless statement. As in the pragmatism of Peirce and the instrumentalism of Dewey, ideas are always hypothetical. They are not simply copies of an external object. *They are plans for guiding action.*

---

[34] See on this point, Hook, *From Hegel to Marx*, p. 293. Also see in this same volume Hook's complete discussion of Marx's *Theses on Feuerbach*, pp. 272–307.

[35] *Selected Works*, vol. 2, p. 403.

To prove their truth, therefore, our ideas must be brought to action and the condition that must be satisfied is that the consequences anticipated in the idea must be realized in the experimental application of the idea. Our desires and aspirations do not constitute the truth of our ideas. As Sidney Hook has said, "There is no will to believe in Marx but a will to action, in order to test belief and set additional grounds for further action if necessary." [36] As with the pragmatists, truth is something that happens to an idea. Truth is not universal and unchanging. It must change as the conditions that generate it change. In this sense, it is historical and dialectical.

Marx's theory of knowledge and truth is consistent with his historical and social theories. If the basic motive in human nature is action, freely directed at changing the environment in accord with men's own needs and desires, then ideas are not divorced from action but are one aspect of human activity. Any effort is specious that seeks to cut theory off from practice and make it something higher and more important than mere action. This was one of Marx's fundamental objections to Feuerbach, who, he said, regarded "the theoretical attitude as the only genuinely human attitude, while practice is conceived and fixed only in its dirty-judaical form of appearance." [37] Thus, Feuerbach, for all his materialism, winds up in essentially the same position as classic Western philosophy, which consistently gives theory a separate and higher status than mere practice. Parenthetically, we foresee that Marx's theory of the relation of idea and action had important implications for his conception of education and for the protest against educational conservatism inherent in the Marxist philosophy of human nature. Philosophy itself was seen by Marx not as simply an explanation of the character of the world, nor as it sometimes seems to be, an apology for it; rather it should represent a wholehearted effort to convert the world to the needs and uses of humanity. This conviction finds expression in one of the best-known and most frequently quoted statements from Marx's writings: "The philosophers have only *interpreted* the world, in various ways; the point, however, is to *change* it." [38]

## THE EDUCATION OF MAN

Neither Marx nor Engels had much to say about education directly. Whatever statements were made were scattered through their writings in various contexts. Furthermore, there is comparatively little commentary

---

[36] Hook, *From Hegel to Marx*, p. 285. See also, on Marx's theory of knowledge, C. E. M. Joad, *Guide to Philosophy* (New York: Dover Publications, 1936), pp. 474–76.

[37] *Selected Works*, vol. 2, p. 403.

[38] This is the last of the eleven "Theses on Feuerbach," *Selected Works*, vol. 2, p. 405.

on Marxian ideas of education extant, except that emanating from the Soviet Union. In what is available, the ideas of Marx have been warped in whatever way seemed necessary to accommodate them to the prevailing line of the Communist Party of the USSR. In our consideration of the protest inherent in Marxian thought against conservative middle-class educational practice, we confine our attention to what Marx himself had to say that may be relevant to this protest.

Marx took universal education seriously. This observation may seem innocuous enough, since every tradition we have considered thus far also has taken it seriously. We should recall, however, that at the time Marx lived and wrote, the idea of free, universal education was far from being established and it also conflicted with the prevailing practice of employing young children in factory production. It is virtually axiomatic that universal education cannot exist until it is made legally compulsory and until it is completely tax supported. We can gain some idea of how radical the notion of free, universal education was in the middle of the nineteenth century if we consider that it was one of the measures the *Manifesto* called for, along with a heavy graduated income tax and socialization of industry, communication, and transportation. Marx and Engels knew well enough that the principle of free education in public schools for all children would remain a mockery unless the labor of children in factories was abolished, or at least greatly curtailed, or unless education could be combined in a humane and fruitful way with productive work.

It is a fact of history, now so well established as to be outside serious argument, that free, public education is itself a product of industrial society. In previous periods of history, it was virtually unknown even as a serious idea, and certainly unknown as a concrete reality. This means that universal education is not only a product of industrialism but of capitalism; and if Marx's thesis that the superstructure of society, which certainly would include schools, is a product of the economic base, then the character and function of education is determined by the productive forces and relations inherent in capitalism. The term *school* is simply an abstraction whose meaning is determined by the social context in which it exists and which determines its function. Thus Marx, in his critique of the program of the German Workers Party, written in 1875, pointed out the equivocative character of the party's proposition on education. The program of the party had called for: "Universal and *equal elementary education* by the state. Universal compulsory school attendance. Free instruction." [39] Marx inquired:

> What idea lies behind these words? Is it believed that in present-day society (and it is only with this that one has to deal) education

---

[39] *Selected Works,* vol. 2, p. 34.

can be *equal* for all classes? Or is it demanded that the upper classes also shall be compulsorily reduced to the modicum of education—the elementary school—that alone is compatible with the economic conditions not only of the wage-workers but of the peasants as well? [40]

Marx evidently believed these questions to be rhetorical. A society that is divided into an owning class and a working class will never have free and equal educational opportunity for all children. Such a society will not provide opportunity for education of the masses above a minimum level (in Marx's day this meant elementary schooling) and it most surely will not reduce the education of the dominant class to the common level. Furthermore, Marx raised the question of what was to happen when in some states of the United States higher education was also made free, referring presumably to the land-grant colleges established under the Morrill Act of 1862. What happens, he said, is that the upper classes have the costs of their higher education free, these costs being defrayed by the general tax revenues. The poor get nothing; and he added, "The paragraph on the schools should at least have demanded technical schools (theoretical and practical) in combination with the elementary school."

The statement in the program of the German Workers Party that Marx found most repugnant was that education should be conducted by the state. He believed that financial support, minimum qualifications of teachers, subjects to be taught, and perhaps the supervision of instruction should be prescribed in law. But he maintained that the government and the church should be excluded from any influence on the school. In this position, he approached the ideals of Jefferson and other liberals of the eighteenth century, which were that education should be carried on for the general enlightenment of mankind, and the school should not be in the services of any element of society whether it is class, state, or church. However, the Marxian view of history precludes any notion that education can serve as a true source of enlightenment for mankind so long as it goes on in a class-structured society. Marx excoriated the "factory schools" that British capitalists had been forced by the Factory Acts to establish. In his view, the school, prior to the advent of socialism, is inevitably the tool of the dominant class—it is used by the capitalists to further their own ends. Is this not immoral? This question can be answered only in the context of Marx's ethical relativism. From the standpoint of a thoroughly class-conscious proletariat, it is a monstrous immorality, but the consciousness of men is determined by their social existence and the capitalist is only doing with the school what must be done within capitalist society. This is one of those historical conditions that can be settled *only by force.*

---

[40]   Ibid.

In the period prior to the revolution the proletariat, having become socially conscious, will attempt to use the schools to further the class consciousness of the masses and pave the way for the final struggle that will transform society.

Once the complete transformation of society has been achieved, the old forms of education will disappear and man will develop his full nature by participation in social life.[41] Men will no longer be chained to machines, doing endlessly repetitive tasks that dehumanize them. They will rather be capable of doing all kinds of labor and these labors will be true expressions of the whole man. In this sense, Marx's view of the future is idyllic. He saw a man in that future "hunting in the morning, fishing in the afternoon, raising cattle in the evening, and even judging food, without ever being either hunter, fisher, herdsman, or food taster. . . ." [42] Between the last days of the old order, however, and the ultimate realization of the new historic period, there lies a time of transition—the "realm of necessity." For this transition period, Marx proposed that the old forms of education be retained but modified to meet the needs of the working class.

The modification he proposed was one of combining education with productive work. He gives credit to a British factory owner, Robert Owen, for initiating this idea in his mill at New Lanark, Scotland, in 1799. Owen opened a school for the children apprenticed to him by the poor-law authorities and sought to give them moral, physical, and intellectual training. Said Marx:

> From the factory system budded, as Robert Owen has shown us in detail, the germ of the education of the future, an education that will, in the case of every child over a given age, combine productive labour with instruction and gymnastics, not only as one of the methods of adding to the efficiency of production, but as the only method of producing fully developed human beings.[43]

Marx's objection to the plight of children in the factories was not only that they were overworked but that the work they did was completely uneducative. "The children employed in modern factories and manufactures," he said, "are from their earliest years riveted to the most simple manipulations, and exploited for years, without being taught a single sort of work that would afterwards make them of use, even in the same manu-

---

[41] In this conception, Marx reactivates the Greek idea that "the city educates the man."

[42] On this point, see Horst Wittig, "Philosophical Origins of Communist Pedagogy," *Soviet Survey*, no. 30 (October–December 1959), pp. 77–81.

[43] *Capital*, pp. 529–30. Italics mine. For Engels's description of the work of Owen at New Lanark, see "Socialism: Utopian and Scientific," in *Selected Works*, vol. 2, pp. 125–26.

factory or factory."[44] In its essence, Marx's proposal was to implement the original idea of Owen more fully and make it the standard practice in elementary education. In 1866, he prepared a memorandum on education for the German delegation to a meeting of the International Workingmen's Association. In this memorandum, he followed the general idea first advanced by Owen. Education was to have three closely related aspects: intellectual education; physical training or gymnastics; and polytechnical training, by which he meant instruction in the scientific principles underlying all production processes, together with instruction in the use of the tools of production. He proposed three levels of schooling, and at each level productive work was to be related to the intellectual learning of the children. The first level was for children of the ages from nine to twelve years, who would do two hours of productive work in a shop or at home. At the second level, there would be four hours of work for children of the ages thirteen and fourteen. The third level would include those up to seventeen years, who would do six hours of work each day.[45]

The idea of fusing knowing with doing in a polytechnical education is surely the most important of Marx's ideas on education. It is at the heart of Marxism's protest against bourgeois educational practice. As Marx saw it, not only is education the tool of the dominant class; it is also the product of the classic philosophical dualism of mind *and* body, idea *and* action. This dualism seems always to find expression in an educational theory that sets up theoretical, rational learning as the highest and most desirable (and therefore what is appropriate for free men) and then in opposition to it puts active, physical, productive work as low, base, and servile (and therefore what is appropriate for slaves). Marx condemned this educational dualism not only because it was the dominant conception of bourgeois society, but also because he thought there was evidence of its ineffectiveness. Marx had a very low opinion of the education demanded by the Factory Acts for children working in industries, but even so, he noted with approval a discovery of the factory inspectors that "the factory children, although receiving only one half the education of the regular day scholars, yet learnt quite as much and often more." He also agreed with the observation of a Mr. Senior, made at a Social Science Conference in 1863, that upper-class children wasted their time and energies in the long hours of the school that was divorced from any practical activity or productive enterprise.[46]

Marx's idea of combining theoretical and practical activities clearly was consistent with his conception of the knowledge process. He rejected

---

[44] *Capital*, p. 530.

[45] I am indebted for the details of this program to Horst Wittig, "Philosophical Origins," p. 79.

[46] *Capital*, vol. 1, p. 529.

any conception that makes mind merely a spectator of an external reality and insisted that in any act of cognition the object itself is changed. Thus, Marx's operationalism would appear almost by necessity to demand a theory of education that stressed the essentially dynamic interrelatedness of knowing and doing. Since he was confronted with the fact of child labor in factories, and since his overriding concern was with the economic system, it is perhaps only to be expected that he would work out whatever ideas about education he might have had around the factory system. This is in contrast to Dewey, who half a century later and in the context of another philosophy of society worked out the connections of his instrumentalist theory of knowledge with the theory of education. Nevertheless, this aspect of the Marxian protest against essentialism is similar to Dewey's protest, or for that matter, to the protest of any theory of education that involves an operational theory of knowledge. Marx did not believe that the purpose of education is transmitting information for absorption by learners, apart from any real social contexts, any more than he believed that human labor, when freely performed, is slavish and degrading to the personality. Marx believed that education should be to develop the powers inherent in the human organism so that man could become human and live like a man. He believed, however, that this could not be accomplished so long as capitalism endures, since for the duration of that period of history, exploitation of one man by another is inevitable.

This observation brings us to existing modes of education and their effect in human alienation. The idea of human alienation in Marx's thought is a tricky one. This is owed partly to the fact that Marx's position on it changed with the maturing of his own thought and partly to a recent preoccupation of various commentators with equating Marx's ideas to certain contemporary views on psychotherapy.[47] Marx criticized Feuerbach's acceptance of a human essence conceived apart from the complex of social relations that obtain in any historical period. This enabled Feuerbach to explain religion in terms of the essential nature of man, and to explain human alienation in terms of man's being torn between an illusory world of perfection, which by his very nature he projects, and the real world of imperfection and suffering in which he finds himself.

Now a little thought will indicate that a somewhat similar case can be made for the alienation of man by traditional modes of education. These too invariably involve a dualism consisting of a world of pure ideas, universals, forms, and so on, which are alleged to be the proper subject matter of education, and a world of process and becoming, in which there is no possibility of *truth* or of grasping truth for its own sake but only the possibility of opinion and practical action, which is animallike and

---

[47]  For example, Erich Fromm, *Marx's Concept of Man* (New York: F. Ungar Publishing Co., 1961).

servile. As is well known, the view of human nature that accompanies the former view is that man in his essence is rational; he is a "rational animal," and any mode of education that centers on practical activity and the union of idea with action alienates man from himself—since the essence of his selfhood is reason. It is easy to see that this kind of conclusion must be excluded completely in Marxian thought. But it is possible to argue the other way and maintain that classic forms of education alienate man from himself because they create an illusory world of pure thought (universals, essences, "first principles," and so forth) and ignore the world of labor and practical activity, which is the real world. Thus, under this view man is alienated, because in his education he is torn from the real world to one of illusion. Classical philosophy, and hence classical education, is a distorted projection of man's longing for a world of stability, dependability, and universal truth in the face of his real existence in a world that is precarious, changing, and in many respects unpredictable.

To argue in this vein is to repeat the error Marx found in Feuerbach; it is to escape from the clutches of one absolute only to fall into those of another. The nature, or essence, of man, according to Marx, is a product of historical conditions that can be determined and studied scientifically. In the same sense, the conclusion of classic philosophy that the essence of man is reason was produced by a determinate set of economic and social relations existing at a particular time in history—namely, in the historic period of slavery in the Hellenic world. It is the product of a class-stratified society, in which the mass of men (the slaves in the Greek world; and since the idea was carried over into the Middle Ages, the serfs in the medieval world) are systematically exploited by the dominant class. The view that the essence of man is reason is the product of the same set of social relations that produced the distinction between liberal and practical education and led Aristotle to the conclusion that some men by their nature are fit only to be slaves. Thus, the dominance of the classical dualism, and its expression in educational policy, together with the splitting of thought from action in labor, are *results* of objective conditions. One is not the cause of the other, for they are all consequences of the economic base that determines the character of a society and its institutions. As with the case of religion, these dualisms will pass away when the conditions that produce them cease to exist. This is to say that they cannot be eliminated until capitalism is eliminated. When true communism is achieved, the dualism of thinking and acting will be gone entirely, but for the "realm of necessity" it will be possible to mitigate its effects by combining intellectual education, physical training, and useful labor in the schools.

In his own protest against educational essentialism, John Dewey and many of his associates had called for a fusion of thinking and acting in the education of children. Dewey advocated active occupations in the school and developed the program of his own Laboratory School around a sequence of active enterprises. Dewey gave little weight to the actual production of commodities in the school, however, whereas Marx did. They both believed that education of the intellect could never be separated from other aspects of development with fruitful results. Marx never worked out in detail either a theory of knowledge or a theory of education, as Dewey did, but we can see that in certain respects their protests against the reigning tradition are similar. On the other hand, the differences between the two are as great as the differences between revolutionary socialism and American liberalism. Dewey believed that the school could be a means for social progress and the gradual improvement of society and the common lot of man. But Marx's historical determinism indicated that in any period before the coming of socialism, the school could only be the tool of the dominant class, and hence could have little or no influence in the direction of social reform. The school in the transition from capitalism to socialism, under the dictatorship of the proletariat, can be employed by the proletariat to further the aims of the revolution and eventually to usher in the new era in human society. It is the treasured belief of American liberalism that by bold and thoughtful political action the evils and insufficiencies that characterize the older order can be mitigated and our institutions—including our educational institutions—can be transformed so that they will serve human needs and aspirations. And it is the belief of the liberal that this can be accomplished without social upheaval, violence, and bloodshed. Marx considered these liberal beliefs naive.

## SUMMARY: THE MARXIST PROTEST

Marx's protest was not aimed exclusively at Western conservatism, although it was the outstanding example of what he considered the fundamental rottenness of the bourgeois society that he held destined by history to disappear. His protest was also against what he considered the opportunism and political naiveté of liberalism. Needless to say, he thought the perennialist philosophy reactionary, inimical to the welfare of the masses, and a dangerous hangover from feudalism. ("The mortgage that the peasant has on heavenly possessions guarantees the mortgage that the bourgeois has on peasant possessions.") [48] Marxism is thus a conscious protest against the important historic traditions of the West. Purely as an intellectual protest it is provocative enough, but the political reality that it has assumed in the USSR is the determining factor in the political character of our world. Sidney Hook has characterized Marxism as an ambiguous legacy, and truly

---

[48] Marx, "The Class Struggles in France, 1848–1850," *Selected Works*, vol. 1, p. 187.

this ambiguity seems reason enough to make us doubt that Marx could either have predicted the events that took place in Russia in this century or that he would approve of what developed there.

The fact that there are numerous insufficiencies, obscurities, and outright errors in Marx's writings has been documented in numerous sources. The highlights of the difficulties that are inherent in the Marxian tradition are as follows. First, Marx's theory of history, which was one of his most important contributions, has shown itself inadequate for interpreting the events of this century. The power of any scientific theory, and it should be remembered that Marx considered his interpretation of history to be scientific, lies in its predictive powers and only secondarily in its power to account for events that have already occurred. As has been pointed out many times, Marx's theory has been inadequate to predict that a communist revolution would occur in Russia when it did and that one would subsequently occur in China. Revolutions of this kind should never have occurred in either place, since at the time of both revolutions those countries were not well advanced into the industrial age nor into capitalistic economy. According to a fundamental principle of Marxism, no social order ever perishes until all the productive forces inherent in it have developed, but not by the widest stretch of the imagination can this be thought to have been true of either China or Russia at the time revolutions occurred in those countries. This failure of prediction in itself is sufficient to require us to doubt the adequacy of Marx's historical determinism.

In the second place, Marx's conception of the class stratification of society as being a function purely of the economic base is now seen as an oversimplification. This is not said as a denigration of Marx's contributions to scientific sociology, to which full credit is regularly given by social scientists who are not Marxists and who therefore do not think Marx said the last word about the origin and nature of social classes. Modern sociology recognizes the existence of class stratification, but finds it far more complex than the simple polarity of an all-powerful owning class of capitalists and an increasingly impoverished proletariat. Granted that economics is closely related to class structure, it still does not follow that all class structure and all class relations are determined simply by the forces of economic production. The nature of social stratification is an empirical question, and while Marx believed that his analysis of it was indeed scientific, with the perspective now available to us it is apparent that there was a kind of economic mystique inherent in his thought that in many respects effectively obscured the complexity of human relations as they existed in his time and as he predicted they would be in the future.

Third, it now seems clear that Marx completely underestimated the potency of politics and particularly the power of political democracy. It will be recalled that according to his view, politics is a part of the superstructure that develops on the economic base of a historical period, and thus the character of political life is determined by that base and cannot function independent of it. In other words, political power can never be dissociated from economic power. Perhaps it is true that politics is never separate from economics, but the history of the present century shows among other things that at least in America trade unionism did succeed in improving working conditions and remuneration of factory workers, that the horrors of child labor in industry were eliminated, and that the mass of working people—the proletariat—have improved their lot significantly instead of becoming increasingly impoverished and wretched. And it is submitted that these have been achieved almost entirely by political means and without bloodshed. Certainly they have been achieved by means that are far short of revolutionary. This is not to say that all problems are solved. Unemployment still seems to be a built-in feature of modern capitalism, although the amount of it today is far short of what Marx's predictions would have it. Poverty and economic misery are still present in our own country, which is the richest nation ever to exist. Support for public education varies greatly from state to state and is cruelly meager in some parts of the nation. The successes we have had, however, give us reason to believe that these difficulties also can be made to yield to resolute and dedicated effort that is essentially political in character. In view of all this, what can we say about the Marxist protest—Is it completely false?

In thinking about this, let us consider that nobody ever asks whether Plato is true or false. We should regard the question of whether Platonic philosophy is true or false as completely fatuous. There is not much question but that we could say the same thing about Plato's writings that we said about Marx's writings, namely, that they contained many insufficiencies, obscurities, and outright errors. The value of a philosophy lies in the power it has to help us think for ourselves about the great problems and issues of our own age. The enormous potency in Platonic thought has kept it alive and vital for nearly three thousand years, and it is this same quality in Marx that keeps his thought alive, in spite of all the outrages that have been committed in the name of it. The real question is whether in the great protest that Marx raised against the character of Western society and its institutions anything remains that is pertinent to our own times—specifically to our educational problems. The answer to be given here is in the affirmative.

In the first place, although we have a long history of dedication to the idea of free, universal education, we apparently still have to learn that in America educational opportunity is linked closely to class status. It is true that our conceptions of social-class stratification are different from those of Marx and undoubtedly more accurate, but the fact remains that for the mass of children the amount and kind of education they will receive and the life work they will pursue are determined in considerable measure by the social class into which they are born. To admit this goes directly against the basic instincts of a majority of Americans, but the fact is so well documented as to be beyond argument. It has long been a commonplace of educational sociology that the American public school is thoroughly middle-class in its orientation and that it discriminates systematically against lower-class children, usually unconsciously, and therefore unusually effectively. The plight of the black child in the slum school is the most dramatic example of this in our time, but it is only one example. This is not the place to record statistics about high school dropouts, and the few members of submerged minority groups who are enrolled in institutions of higher learning or have opportunity to enter the learned professions. But until we have put our own house in order, we shall do well to ponder Marx's biting question addressed to the German Workers Party in 1875:

> Is it believed that in present-day society . . . education can be *equal* for all classes? Or is it demanded that the upper classes also shall be compulsorily reduced to the modicum of education . . . that alone is compatible with the economic conditions not only of the wage-workers but of the peasants as well? [49]

In the second place, whether Marx was right about the source of human alienation or not, the fact remains that this is one of the realities of our own day and Marx's description of it comes close to matching the clinical accounts of psychotherapists. The loss of a feeling of self-identity on the part of modern man is a theme that is treated in somewhat different ways by those of varying philosophic viewpoints. Dewey considered it mainly in terms of the need to develop a new individualism that would be in the modern age what the old individualism was historically. Existentialists handle it entirely differently. It may well be that the loss of identity in the modern world is not a function of capitalism, which is what Marx thought it was, but a product of *industrial society*, which does not have to be equated with capitalism. Identity loss occurs in the Soviet Union as well as in capitalistic countries. Marx's observations on the effects of machines on factory production, the routinization of human effort in productive work, and the dehumanizing effects of it, were acute. Yet he did not know the production-line techniques that have transformed the industrial processes of our own day nor did he foresee emergence of the "automatic factory," in which active human labor is reduced to the vanishing point. It has long been fashionable for critics to point out that Marx failed to foresee or to predict this or that occurrence. And certainly in many ways this is correct. He foresaw the proletariat as becoming increasingly impoverished and reduced to the verge of penury and starvation. What he did not foresee is the modern industrial worker who performs

---

[49] *Selected Works*, vol. 2, p. 34.

the motions of an automaton for forty hours a week on an assembly line and spends his "free" time with a can of beer while squatting in front of a television set. It seems a fair question to ask, who is the more alienated? We shall no doubt do well to remember Marx's bitter observation, "The animal becomes the human and the human the animal."

We already see a time ahead when a large portion of the population will not engage in productive work, because this work will be done by machines. We have already been told that an electronic computer can do the work of a high school graduate. Yet there is little evidence that we have any conception of what this means for our educational efforts or what will be required of the school in the times ahead. There seems little doubt that concerning this question educational essentialism is completely without resources, and in their present state, the other traditions we have considered thus far lend little more, if any, assistance. It may be that the following lines from *Capital* are simply oracular and therefore may mean whatever they are interpreted to mean, but in the brave, new world that lies ahead, we are certain to have our own encounter with the fact that "the relations connecting the labor of one individual with that of the rest appear, not as direct social relations between individuals at work, but as what they really are, material relations between persons and social relations between things."

There remains only to be mentioned Marx's protest against the arbitrary division of theory and practice, which in educational terms is seen so clearly in the bifurcation of learning into liberal and practical. Marx took a unitary view of human nature, believing that ideas are inseparably united with action. He sketched in outline—but only in outline—a system of education that would unite thinking and doing in the form of productive work. If his ideas on this subject are outmoded, it is because the industrialism he knew is outmoded. He did not advocate "polytechnical" education in order simply to produce mechanics and technicians; rather, he said, it is the only way to produce complete human beings. In this he is reminiscent of Rousseau, who at an earlier time had said in a famous book on educational theory:

> Instead of making a child stick to his books, if I employ him in a workshop, his hands labor to the profit of his mind; he becomes a philosopher, but fancies he is only a workman.[50]

---

[50]   Jean J. Rousseau, *Emile,* trans. William H. Payne (New York: D. Appleton and Co., 1898), p. 153.

# chapter TEN

# THE · EXISTENTIALIST PROTEST

*And, to say all in a word, everything which belongs to the soul is a dream and vapor, and life is a warfare and a stranger's sojourn, and after-fame is oblivion. What then is that which is able to conduct a man?*

—MARCUS AURELIUS

*Once cut the cords of connection which bind man to nature even when he strives to improve on it and there is no escape from the agonizing view, in all its variants from the Book of Ecclesiastes to the Notebooks of Kierkegaard, that "the self [is] not merely a pilgrim but an unnaturalized and unnaturalizable alien in this world."*

—SIDNEY HOOK

About the time of the ending of World War II, Americans began to be aware that new developments in philosophical thought were taking place in Europe. The early harbingers of these events reached our shores largely as literary works—stories, novels, and plays—by certain French writers. These writings usually had an alien, somewhat gamy flavor that made them provocative and intriguing, as well as difficult to understand. This new movement went under the name of existentialism, and in the early days this term mostly raised the vision in Americans of Left Bank bohemianism and drinkers of absinthe. The principal themes of the existentialist writers were dim and murky, with anxiety, despair, death, and alienation predominating. It was thought in the beginning that these woeful expressions were simply the result of the horrors of a great war and the disillusionment and disenchantment that inevitably are the aftermath of such upheavals. In time, however, it began to be known that existentialism was more than a literary cult, much more. The realization developed that fundamentally existentialism represents an approach to philosophy that dates back well into the nineteenth century and that is different both from the classic, system-building approach and from the modern analytic schools. The effects of existentialist thought began to be felt in theology, and perhaps with good reason, since some of its main historic roots lie in that area. It also made its presence felt in psychology, particularly in psychotherapy.

In the American world of academic philosophy, however, existentialism has not fared as well. The interests of American philosophers have for more than a generation revolved mainly around technical, analytical work, particularly with analysis of language and with logic and scientific method. This preoccupation of academic philosophers with such technical and abstruse matters in many ways has been fruitful for the philosophic enterprise, but it has also caused the philosopher to lose touch with the rest of mankind. However, given some encouragement, a considerable portion and perhaps all of mankind is incurably philosophical. Crane Brinton, for example, once observed that it is as hopeless to ask people to do without metaphysics as it is to ask them to do without sex relations.[1] People are not simply "interested in" the character of the universe in which they live and the relation they have to the scheme of things; they are *concerned* with these matters. They are not only concerned in their own amateur ways with the historic categories of philosophy—with ontology and epistemology and ethics—they are also concerned, as the existentialists have demonstrated, with themselves. And this concern with the character of one's own existence is different in certain important respects from the concerns of either the classic or the modern traditions in philos-

---

[1] *The Shaping of the Modern Mind* (New York: New American Library of World Literature, 1953), p. 13.

ophy. The question of the nature of *existence* or *being* has been a matter of debate ever since the birth of Western philosophy, and the development of this question has usually taken the form of great speculative systems of metaphysics, in which the nature of man himself has been reduced to some essence that in itself not only *describes* the nature of man but also *prescribes* it. Man thus is reduced by the philosophers to an abstraction. But something apparently keeps telling common men, and perhaps also philosophers in their unguarded moments, that the real problem of existence is not one of abstraction and essences, but the problem of *my* existence, *here* in this world. The existentialist approach to philosophy is in agreement with this common feeling, or intuition, or whatever it is. Thus, in a sense, existentialism proposes to do what Socrates did for the philosophy of his own time, namely, to abandon physical nature as the center of interest and the attempt to develop some all-encompassing scheme to explain everything and instead to make *man* the central concern of philosophy. "Know thyself" was Socrates' admonition. "The unexamined life is not worth living." And in a much later day we find one of the leading figures in modern philosophical thought, Karl Jaspers, saying, "Man is everything." If existentialism is capable of being defined, and there is some question whether it can be, it is possible only to say that as philosophy it is concerned with the actual character of human existence and the calling of men to a realization of their essential freedom.

As we come to our inquiry into the general character of the existentialist protest, we are confronted immediately with two primary difficulties. In the case of the traditions with which we have dealt up to now—and this holds true whether these are educational or philosophical traditions—we have been able to work, at least for the most part, with well-developed, systematic bodies of thought. We have been able, therefore, to develop reasonably systematic surveys of the ideas involved, to indicate certain lines of argument, and to come to reasoned philosophical and educational conclusions on the basis of the argument. It is important for us to realize in the beginning that with existentialism this is exceedingly difficult. Existentialism is not a *philosophy* in the sense that idealism or pragmatism may be said to be. It is not systematic in the usual sense of that word and it has no ambitions to become so. One of the chief protests of existentialist thought against traditional philosophy is that conventional philosophers have sold out everything—particularly man—to the interests of some system. It is sometimes said that existentialism is an approach to philosophy rather than a system of philosophical thought. This view is somewhat clearer, but there is a question whether even this observation is really adequate. Existentialist philosophers, as might be expected, are individualists above all. There is some common thematic material among them, but each approaches a theme in his own way, and its development in the hands of one man is usually very different from that of another. Thus, our first difficulty is that our inquiry into existential philosophy simply cannot have a relatively neat intellectual character.

The second difficulty arises since almost nothing has been said in the primary literature of existentialism about education. It is a broad generalization to say that no important figure in existential philosophy has had anything significant to say about education, yet it is true. There simply is no indication that educational policy is regarded by existentialists as important. Existential thought has much in it that is directly relevant to religion and to what in the broad sense, at least, we should call psychology, but of education there is little said directly. Why this should be so is a provocative question to which the present author has no good answer. As a general rule, the great names in Western philosophy have found something to say about educational matters, and some of them have found a lot. In our previous inquiries, we have been able to find specific connections of one kind or another between philosophic ideas and educational ideas. In the present context, however, this is not going to be easy. We shall have either to draw inferences of our own about the relation of existential thought to educational policy or to consider inferences drawn by others. This is probably not very satisfactory, but it is the best we can manage.

Our approach is threefold. First, we give brief attention to the historical development of the existentialist tradition in philosophy so we may have some grasp of its general character. Secondly, we consider some of the themes of present-day existentialism and the ways in which they have been developed. And last, we consider what these matters may indicate for educational thought. In adopting this procedure, we are again giving up the pattern of analysis we have used for all the traditions except Marxism. In our procedure we have begun with the specific educational ideas involved in a tradition and then proceeded to more abstract matters. In most cases, we have had before us a real school or a body of practice that served as a model, for example, the existing elementary and secondary schools of the conservative tradition or the historic Laboratory School of the Dewey tradition. Such a procedure is impossible with the existentialists. Where is there to be found an "existentialist school"? For that matter, does the term *existentialist school* make any sense? Perhaps it does, but if so, we are left with the task of making our own model. Whatever this may turn out to be, it is certain that its nature must reflect in some way the historic character of existentialist thought.

## THE DEVELOPMENT OF EXISTENTIALISM

Four men are generally conceded to be the leading figures in existentialism. They are Soren Kierkegaard (1813–1855), Friedrich Nietzsche (1844–1900), Martin Heidegger (born 1899), and Jean-Paul Sartre (born

1905). Other names will arise, but in general, our attention will be addressed to these four. Modern existentialism is generally thought of as beginning with Kierkegaard, but it is possible to find existential themes in much earlier sources. Certain portions of the Bible, the Book of Ecclesiastes, for example, express ideas that have recognizable existentialist content. The same may be said for certain parts of the works of Saint Augustine and of Blaise Pascal, the French mathematician and philosopher. The Russian writer Fyodor Dostoevsky also is often considered to be a forerunner of existentialism, and his "Notes from Underground" are thought by many to be a rich mine of existentialist thought. It was the thinking of Kierkegaard, however, that more than anything else started the modern trend.

By conventional standards, Kierkegaard's life was a tragic failure. He was deformed physically, having a hunchback. His constitution was frail and he was chronically ill. Psychologically, he was introverted and solitary. He did not achieve the ordinary felicities of family life, though he seemed to long for them throughout his life. In a single act of self-denial, he broke his engagement with a young woman whom he loved deeply and the consequences of this act never left him. A fairly common interpretation holds that the character of Kierkegaard's thought is a direct product of his physical abnormalities and perhaps of his psychological crippling.[2] However this may be, we are interested in the *grounds* on which Kierkegaard's thought rests and not in the causes of it.[3]

Kierkegaard's thought was a protest and one of the greatest, matched perhaps in the modern age only by that of Marx. It was a protest not only against the age in which he himself lived, but also against the historical continuum that led up to it. In a sense, his protest was two-pronged —against philosophy (he did not consider himself a philosopher) and against conventional religion. So far as philosophy is concerned, Hegel was for him the archenemy. Yet Hegel was only the leading representative in the nineteenth century of the whole fallacious tendency of classic philosophy to submerge the individual and make of him only an abstraction whose identity rests in the fact that he is a part of something more all-embracing. This idea may have had its highest development in the hands of Hegel, but his conclusions were implicit in the whole course of Western philosophy.

In an instructive piece of analysis of Kierkegaard's protest, William Barrett has observed that there are two ways to react to Kant's analysis

---

[2] For example, Theodor Haecker, *Kierkegaard, The Cripple*, trans. C. V. O. Bruyn (London: Harvill Press, 1948).

[3] This distinction is important and always should be borne in mind in considering the contributions of any thinker.

314 PHILOSOPHIES OF EDUCATION: AN INTRODUCTION

of the term *being*.[4] Kant had maintained that there seems to be no real way to conceive of *being*. It is possible to think of a thing, a table or a lamp, for example, and then think of the table or the lamp existing, but nothing seems to be added to the first concept by the addition of the concept of being. Therefore, Kant concluded, to predicate existence of a thing adds nothing and apparently there is no way of conceiving of being as simply being. Barrett's point is that one way of reacting to this conclusion is that of the positivists and other scientific philosophers. In the view of these people, knowledge is operational—it is *about* something that can be observed and manipulated. Existence is obviously something that it is not possible to observe or experiment with, and therefore the positivists gave it up, calling it and all such matters metaphysical and hence superfluous.

Kierkegaard's reaction was diametrically opposite. It may be that existence cannot be conceived rationally, but if this is so it is not because it is amorphous and vague. It is because it is so immediate and enveloping that mind cannot cope with it. Therefore, I do not know *existence*. I *experience* it. It is the reality of the self. Existence is had, and the supreme manifestation of this having is when man is confronted with the necessity of choice. This is a primary theme in Kierkegaard's thought and in modern existentialism. Thus, the main elements in Hegel's idealism that Kierkegaard attacked are objectivity and determinism. In the Hegelian system, the dialectical workings of the Absolute are objectified in the phenomenal world. The world process is all-inclusive and completely logical in its character. Whatever happens in history *must* happen. Whatever is, is right. If the world is itself the necessary unfolding of the Idea, then what happens to individual freedom? It would appear that the only answer is that what we call individual freedom is simply our awareness and acceptance of necessity. To Kierkegaard this was the most repugnant conclusion it is possible to reach. Such a conclusion closes the door forever on the possibility of freedom of the self to choose in an uncertain world in which genuine possibilities exist. And so, in opposition to Hegel's objectivity of history, Kierkegaard emphasized the essentially subjective existence of the individual and his passionate involvement in his existence. To the determinism of Hegel, he opposed the freedom of the individual to choose and the necessity of this choosing, together with the individual's awareness of the crucial character of his choice.

Aside from Hegel and classic philosophy, Kierkegaard's main target for criticism was organized Christianity, and his protest was against the Danish state church of his time. He thought that the net effect of Western

---

[4] *Irrational Man: A Study in Existentialist Philosophy* (Garden City, N.Y.: Doubleday & Co., 1958). My references are to the paperback edition published in 1962. On the point referred to above, see pp. 158 ff.

philosophy had been to submerge the individual in the Absolute, to deny the validity of subjective truth, and to obscure the reality of individual experiences. In its own way, organized religion had done the same thing. When Greek rationalism, which insisted that the only truth is objective truth, was synthesized with Christianity, religion itself fell victim to a rationalistic reductionism. Theology became a matter of proving propositions through rational argument; and faith, which emphasizes the commitment of the individual, had to assume a secondary role. Further, the church as an institution was ignoring the individual subjective element that is always paramount in religious experience. It was engulfing the individual and the realities of his own experience. "Man," Kierkegaard said, "has forgotten what it is to be a Christian."

Religious truth can never be grasped merely through reason. There is in Christianity a paradox, one that reason can never comprehend, much less resolve. Basic to the Christian creed is the idea that God, *the eternal*, revealed Himself *in time* in the person of his Son, Jesus. In the light of reason, this is a contradiction. It is absurd. Yet this is the basic tenet of the Christian faith, for without it there is no Christianity. For Kierkegaard, therefore, there could be no rational resolution of the paradox inherent in Christian doctrine, and what is left is faith. But faith itself is a response to uncertainty; to have faith means to choose, and hence to take a risk. By faith is meant that there is an inherent contradiction between the inward passion of the self and the uncertainty of objective truth. However, when man places himself in this relationship to God he is *in* truth—which may appear to us of a later day also to be absurd, since it places a different meaning on truth from that to which we are accustomed.

Kierkegaard, however, would remind us that we are victims of the belief that truth is a matter of group opinion—of the crowd. In this view, one only has the truth, so to speak, when he has the crowd on his side. This was Kierkegaard's blow against mass society and the creeping "groupiness" we have come to know so well in our own day, but it is also more than that. By "crowd" he meant not only the mass of society in the 1850s, or for that matter, in the 1970s, to which men give their allegiance and which in turn determines their ideas and their concepts of the truth. The "crowd" is also the whole body of doctrine that holds that to be a man means to belong to a species of rational animals. Given this view, said Kierkegaard, there are no individuals, only specimens. To be with the crowd is to be in *untruth*. Truth, for Kierkegaard, lay in the individual's own unique experience. In this sense, it is subjective, for man always stands alone. His existence precedes his essence.[5]

---

[5] On this point, see Kierkegaard's "That Individual," reprinted in Walter Kaufmann, ed., *Existentialism from Dostoevsky to Sartre* (New York: Meridian Books, 1956), pp. 92–99.

The fundamental condition of man Kierkegaard found to be one of despair. This is a universal condition. He said that just as in the medical sense no man is ever completely healthy, so there is no man who is outside despair. The only possible exception is the true Christian (that is, the man who stands completely in the relation to God that Kierkegaard defined as true Christianity). But even the devout Christian, who is not completely the true Christian, is also in despair. Kierkegaard described despair in such terms as "disquietude, a perturbation, a discord, an anxious dread of an unknown something, or of a something he does not even dare to make acquaintance with." [6]

Despair is the sickness unto death, but this is not to be taken in the usual literal sense we mean when we speak of a mortal sickness for which death is the last phase. To the Christian, death is not the last thing, for it is the beginning of life in eternity. The agony of despair consists in not being able to die. The self cannot die of despair in the sense that the body can die as a result of illness. According to Kierkegaard, despair takes three forms: despair at not being conscious of selfhood; despair at not being willing to be oneself; despair at willing to be oneself. The investigation of these modes of despair constitutes Kierkegaard's most remarkable treatise on human psychology. [7] The terrible feeling of despair is the price we pay for our existence as conscious selves in a world in which all things are possible. But the experience of anguish and dread is not morbid, for it is our experience of freedom.

We may summarize Kierkegaard's original and extremely important contributions to existentialist philosophy under three categories. First, there is Kierkegaard's interpretation of the essentially subjective nature of human existence; his insistence on the complete freedom of the individual to choose and to become what he wills himself to become; and his consequent denial of determinism and of the priority of essence over existence. Secondly, there is his protest against institutionalized Christianity that seeks to understand and make clear what is paradoxical and absurd and therefore outside the possibility of human reason. The church is an institution that engulfs men as individuals, encouraging them to act like sheep, effectively preventing them from the personal encounter with God that is the only true religious experience. Third, there is Kierkegaard's analysis of the human condition as being one of despair and anxiety, at the root of which lies the necessity for choice in a world that is completely undetermined. These three themes have been taken up and developed in various ways in existentialism today. Before we come to consider the existentialist philos-

---

[6] *The Sickness Unto Death*, trans. Walter Lowie (Garden City, N.Y.: Doubleday & Co., 1954), p. 155.

[7] Ibid.

ophy of our own day, however, we must give some attention to the contributions of another historical figure, the German philosopher Friedrich Nietzsche.

Nietzsche was without doubt one of the authentic geniuses of the nineteenth century, but his genius often was as erratic as it was brilliant. His intellectual development was precocious. He assumed the university chair in classical philology at Basel when he was only twenty-four years of age. This in itself was a remarkable achievement. Like Kierkegaard, Nietzsche suffered ill health throughout his life and in the end he was engulfed in a hopeless insanity. As in the case of Kierkegaard, we can hardly escape attributing the restless, passionate, often tragic character of his philosophy to the structure of his own personality and the tragic events of his own life. Nietzsche's philosophy, however, is far more than simply the expression of a tormented soul, although it certainly is that. Nietzsche foresaw with great clarity the problems that were to haunt man in the twentieth century, problems that many of us have not even faced, much less solved. His statement of and reactions to these problems form one of the great contributions to modern philosophy, and their influence on the development of present-day existentialism is decisive. There are three thematic elements: his atheism, his ethical relativism, and "the will to power."

Nietzsche, like Kierkegaard, had a basic religious theme, but he treated it very differently. Kierkegaard was a profoundly religious man who attacked conventional organized religion, because in his judgment, it prevented the individual's confrontation with God and thus made real religious experience impossible. Nietzsche's reaction to the character of religion in the nineteenth century was different. The awful fact, he said, is that God is dead and we have killed him. There was nothing novel about atheism in Nietzsche's time, but his development of the consequences of "the death of God" in the modern world is overwhelming. We have noted in various contexts that a fundamental conflict exists in modern culture because in the postmedieval world the older supernatural view of man and the world directly conflicts with other traditions that deny such a view. It is well known that in the medieval world institutionalized religion—the church— was the great universal institution that formed the community of Western man. In our analysis we have attributed the breakup of this community to the development of new, conflicting traditions; one of the most potent of these was natural science. And so we may say that with our science we have killed God. We must, however, enlarge the meaning of *science* so that it extends beyond the currently restricted sense of that term. We have killed God with reason and with rationalistic philosophies, as well as with rationalistic science. We have killed Him with our pretensions to objective truth. Kierkegaard believed the church had killed religion, but he believed that God exists and can be known, although not in the formalistic sense that the church prescribed. Nietzsche went beyond and insisted that religion is dead because God is dead. From now on, each of us is on his own. We are no longer cuddled up with each other in an all-embracing community in which our fears and anxieties are sublimated and made to go away. We are on our own—whether we know it or not.

A prevalent reaction of modern civilization to all this is that if only we were to stop thinking about it, it would go away. The conservative tradition, for example, proceeds in the belief that there is no ultimate contradiction between the older supernaturalism and the new universe of science. Conservatism seeks to make science (in the broad sense) a kind of subdepartment of God. What the conservative tradition does not know—or at least is unable to admit—is that the subdepartment has destroyed the whole establishment, and all that is left is the *individual*. In his most powerful exposition of these events, Nietzsche portrays a madman who runs about in the marketplace crying, "I seek God! I seek God!" Various people who do not believe in God make fun of him and ask whether God has got lost or gone on a voyage or is hiding somewhere. But the madman with his frenetic stare ignores their gibes and cries, "Whither is God? I shall tell you. *We have killed him*—you and I." [8] And then come the prophetic words: "Is not the greatness of this deed too great for us? Must not we ourselves become gods simply to seem worthy of it? There has never been a greater deed; and whoever will be born after us—for the sake of this deed he will be part of a higher history than all history hitherto." But the madman saw that the people did not understand him and he ran around to several churches singing requiems for God and when he was asked why he did it, he said, "What are those churches now if they are not the tombs and sepulchers of God?" The men in the market did not believe God exists but they had no apprehension of the awful consequences of the fact that they had killed him. They had yet to learn that when He died all the alleged absolutes of conventional morality died with Him—leaving the individual.

The root of Nietzsche's ethical relativism lies in his prediction that a new episode in history is to begin, an era that will be nihilistic so far as the old, conventional values are concerned. He thought he saw the beginning of a "more manly, a warlike age," and this age was to be preparatory to a time in which men would "carry heroism into the pursuit of knowledge." For this first new stage of history new men would be required, men of valor and strength of character—in short, men whose character is marked with "style." What will not be needed are the meek conformers, the subscribers to Kant's categorical imperative, which Nietzsche described as "the highest formula of a government official." For men of the new

---

[8] "The Gay Science," reprinted in Kaufmann, *Existentialism*, pp. 104–6.

age, the imperative is "Live dangerously." Nietzsche was influenced by the Darwinian conception of nature as evolutionary. In this view, life is in a continuous process of evolutionary development, in which new types appear. Nietzsche believed that "the death of God" marked the beginning of a new historical period and the emergence of a "new" man. The fundamental motive of all life is not to adjust supinely to the pressures and necessities of the environment. The motive of all life, wherever it is found in nature, is the *will to power*.

In this conception, Nietzsche, who presumably had renounced all metaphysical absolutes of conventional philosophy, appears to have invented one of his own. The will to power is not simply the will to self-preservation. It is not the effort to experience pleasure and to avoid pain. Hedonism, Nietzsche maintained, is no answer to the question of value. It may be true that increase of power and mastery brings feelings of pleasure with it, but pleasure exists and is experienced in the increase of power. Value and power are identical, and the ethical principle for man is self-aggrandizement. An approach to ethics that equates value with power recognizes that pain and suffering cannot be avoided for they are necessary elements in the experience of those who live dangerously. What Nietzsche warns us against is the easy pessimism into which hedonists are prone to slip, since they make their value judgments on the basis of pleasure and are therefore appalled by the ubiquity of pain. He warns us also against the trap of conscience, that tool of conventional Christian morality with its mawkish, sentimental approach to morality and its exploitation of feelings of guilt that constitute a sickness in the human mind. The antidote for sickness of the spirit is the will to power. But there is a difficulty here, and apparently Nietzsche never found his way out of it. If the will to power exists only for itself, if power leads only to the striving for more power, do we not come ultimately to the brink of nihilism? If there is a final answer to the problem of nihilism, and perhaps we should admit the possibility that there is none, it is not to be found in the thought of this great precursor of modern existentialism.

The ideas of later contributors to existentialist philosophy strongly resemble those that can be identified in Kierkegaard and Nietzsche, although their detailed development has often been somewhat different. Heidegger and Sartre have been two of the leaders of this group. A paramount concern of the philosophy of Heidegger is the philosophical problem of being. In his work with this concept, Heidegger was partly influenced by the German philosopher Edmund Husserl. Heidegger was also influenced by certain ideas of Kierkegaard.

The nature of *being* is the primary concern of that branch of philosophical thought called ontology, and Heidegger has maintained that the real purpose of his philosophical studies is to develop a philosophy of *being* rather than a philosophy of existence. There are no trickier words in the philosophical vocabulary than the simple verbs *to be* and *to exist*. The interpretation of the meaning of these terms is one of the perennial problems of Western thought. Heidegger's main conclusion on the different ways in which the word *exist* can be used is that it is man alone who can be said *to exist*. Other kinds of things *are*, but they do not exist. Trees, rocks, and animals are, says Heidegger, and angels and God also are, but they do not exist. This does not mean necessarily that these things are unreal or illusory; it means that man exists in a way that is different. A fundamental difference is that man has consciousness.[9] Man can exist authentically, however, only as he dissociates himself from the world in which things merely are—what in common speech we should call the everyday world. So long as we remain in this world, we are not conscious of our own existence. According to Heidegger, the only form of being with which we truly are in contact is the being of man. Man can exist authentically, however, only by undergoing certain experiences in which he is aware of himself as one who exists. Fundamentally, these experiences are of the kind Kierkegaard had called anguish or anxiety—"the sickness unto death."

In the experience of anguish, man sees himself for what he is. He is in the world, but he does not know why he is there. God does not exist, and consequently the existence of man is forlorn. He has no home nor refuge. And as was foreshadowed in Kierkegaard, he is existence without essence. In this conclusion, Heidegger, as Kierkegaard did, departs from the well-traveled path of classic philosophy. Both Kierkegaard and Nietzsche had found that human experience was characterized by infinite possibility, although they came to this conclusion by somewhat different routes. But Heidegger emphasizes that the existence of man is limited, that for a time all things may be possible, but this time ends because the existence of man is finite. Death puts an end to all possibility, and all men must die. The authentic person is one who is able to face resolutely that his existence is a "being for death." Hence, for the authentic man the thought of death, though it pervades the whole of human existence, is not morbid, but it does account for the tragic character of the human condition.[10] In Heidegger's view, however, man should pass beyond the condition of anxiety and anguish. The world is unfriendly and it is cruel, but the point is not to attempt to reconcile man, through philosophy or science, with the fact that this is the way things are. The authentic person is one who will face the fact of his existence, and through what Heidegger called "the reso-

---

[9] This point is made in Heidegger's, "The Way Back into the Ground of Metaphysics," in Kaufmann, *Existentialism*, p. 214.

[10] For a discussion of Heidegger's position on this point, see Robert G. Olson, *An Introduction to Existentialism* (New York: Dover Publications, 1962), pp. 197–201.

lute decision" will take his destiny into his own hands. This, too, was foreshadowed in Kierkegaard and Nietzsche.

The ideas on existentialism of Jean-Paul Sartre, the French philosopher, are better known in the United States than the ideas of Heidegger. This is partly because Sartre's works have been more generally available in English translations and partly because his literary works, which are built around existentialist themes, have been read widely in this country. One of the fundamental concerns in Sartre's philosophy is the ontological question of being, which is the great concern of Heidegger. Perhaps the most important aspect of Sartre's treatment is his distinction between two forms of being: being-in-itself and being-for-itself. By being-in-itself, Sartre means the self-contained being of things. What we in common speech call objects—that is, trees, stones, chairs, tables, and so forth—are examples of being-in-itself. They are what they are in themselves. On the other hand, being-for-itself is the realm of human consciousness, and the essential fact of consciousness is that it is always outside of and ahead of itself. We project ourselves into the future, or perhaps into the past, but we are always outside ourselves. In this sense, we transcend ourselves, and the being of man is always for itself. If this were not true, we should simply be being-in-itself. This dualism of being in Sartre is similar to the dualism developed by Descartes. There is also a resemblance between Sartre's being-for-itself as the realm of consciousness and Heidegger's principle of transcendence, or "passing beyond" ourselves.

Sartre restates the theme we have already discovered in Kierkegaard and makes it an important part of his philosophy: Existence precedes essence. Sartre completely disavows the idea that there is some universal concept "Man" that exists prior to the existence of particular men and determines their nature. What this means, Sartre says, is that "man exists, turns up, appears on the scene, and only afterwards, defines himself." [11] There is no universal idea of human nature because there is nothing to conceive it. God does not exist, and therefore the idea of man does not exist in the mind of God. Man is whatever he conceives himself to be, and whatever he may become is whatever he wills himself to become. Said Sartre, "Man is nothing else but what he makes of himself. *Such is the first principle of existentialism.*" [12] It is important to understand that not only is man free to choose what he will become, but also he is *responsible* for what he chooses to become. At the beginning of this chapter, we adopted a definition of existential philosophy that indicated two objectives for existentialism: an examination and analysis of the nature of human

---

[11] *Existentialism,* trans. Bernard Frechtman (New York: Philosophical Library, 1947), p. 13.

[12] Ibid. Italics mine.

existence *and* the calling of men's attention to the fact of their freedom *and its consequences*. This second part of the definition receives powerful development in the hands of Sartre.

The conditions of existence are not only that man is whatever he has chosen to be, but that whenever we choose we are not choosing only for ourselves *but for all mankind*, and therefore the responsibility we inescapably bear is far greater than merely choosing for ourselves. "In fact," Sartre says, "in creating the man that we want to be, there is not a single one of our acts which does not at the same time create an image of man as we think he ought to be." [13] Whenever we choose, the choice made is one we affirm to be good. Choosing is never the simple matter of distinguishing good from evil and choosing one or the other. We are incapable of choosing evil anyway, and so our choices are made among competing goods. According to Sartre, "We always choose the good, and nothing can be good for us without being good for all." This being the case, the responsibility that weighs on all men is simply incalculable, and it is this fact that is the source of anguish, anxiety and despair. Sartre believes, as Kierkegaard did, that there is no man outside the condition of anguish and despair. There are people who do not exhibit the obvious clinical symptoms of anxiety, but they are hiding their anxiety and running away from it. Even when we attempt to discuss the crucial character of our decisions and maintain that we are choosing only for ourselves, we are lying, and in so doing we choose the lie for all mankind.

Sartre resembles Nietzsche and Heidegger in being an atheist. For him, the root of human anxiety is in the fact that man exists, must choose, and does not find God present to put the responsibility on. But Sartre insists that the nonexistence of God is not a matter for rejoicing among existentialists, and they do not stoop to cheap tricks to get rid of Him. Sartre comments wryly, "The existentialist is strongly opposed to a certain kind of secular ethics which would like to abolish God with the least possible expense." [14] In some ways, perhaps, it would be better if God did exist. His existence would make possible a universe of permanent and dependable values. The real point of the nonexistence of God, Sartre says, is exactly the way Dostoevsky put it, "If God didn't exist, everything would be possible." As the existentialist sees it, this is the situation precisely: God does not exist; everything is possible; and consequently, man is in despair, for there is nothing to which he can cling. Therefore, *man is condemned to be free. Condemned* is a strong word, but it is the right one to use because man did not create himself and did not ask to be thrown into the world; but being in the world he is faced with the necessity of choice and

---

[13]   Ibid., p. 20.

[14]   Ibid., p. 25.

the necessity for shouldering the responsibility for what he chooses. Thus, Sartre continues the theme that is significant in existentialist philosophy—indeterminism. Man's nature is not predetermined by any universal; existence comes first, and the behavior of man is not determined. He is what he chooses to be.

## THE PROTEST OF EXISTENTIALISM

In our historical survey of the development of existential philosophy, we have confined our efforts to the thought of two important figures in the nineteenth century, Kierkegaard and Nietzsche, and to two present-day philosophers, Heidegger and Sartre. Other men have played important roles in developing the existentialism of our own time, but there is wide agreement among students of this philosophical tradition that the contributions of the men to which we have given our attention form the basis of existential philosophy. Our review provides a base from which we can assess the protest that existentialism makes against the character of modern society and its institutions, particularly the protest of existentialism against Western conservatism. Our ultimate objective is to assess what the protest of existentialism means for educational ideas. Three themes of present-day existentialism constitute protests against the established tradition. These themes are the human situation, the fact of freedom, and alienation and authenticity.

### THE HUMAN SITUATION

As anyone who reads the papers and the popular magazines knows, ever since the close of World War II there has been a steady outpouring of sentiment about this period as "the age of anxiety." It is customary for various kinds of evidence to be brought out to prove why this should be so. Certain horrible events of the war—the death camps, the gas chambers, and the reeking piles of burning human bodies—show that what we are pleased to call civilization is simply a very thin and fragile veneer, and that when this is stripped away, underneath is revealed the savagery and brutality that is human nature. During this same war, what may well be the "ultimate weapon" emerged—or at least its ancestor did. Crude and inefficient as this ancestor may have been by modern standards of technology, it was sufficient to destroy two great cities in a matter of seconds and hence to change forever the character of warfare. Only shortly after the end of this war, technologists succeeded in partially freeing an object from the earth's gravitational field and sent it spinning in an orbit around the earth. Achievement of this feat first by Russians instead of by Americans produced a profound mass anxiety in the United States. On the basis of these facts and some others, the conclusion is reached that our age of anxiety is unique. Man is afraid of other men, but more and more *he is afraid of himself.* He now has the means to destroy himself completely— and perhaps he will. Thus, it is said, living under such awful and unprecedented conditions as these, we are prone to anxiety, and all the classic symptoms of this malady are everywhere to be seen. Our fears are not merely rational and therefore concrete. The fears of our age are in many respects insubstantial and irrational, and without any discernible reference. They are of the free-floating kind, accounts of which fill the notebooks of every psychiatrist. What all this argument boils down to—if it boils down to anything—is that the anxiety of our time is a response, although a neurotic response, to certain objective conditions that lie mostly outside the self and are explainable, therefore, in terms of the cause-effect relations of behavioristic psychology or the psychodynamics of the Freudian schools of psychology. The existentialist, however, has a different account.

Existentialism is generally willing to agree that the condition of modern man is forlorn, that he is in despair and anguish. But what makes him think he has any private option on this condition? Kierkegaard described the human condition of anguish and despair with a passion and power that probably never will be equaled, yet he knew nothing of megaton bombs and "overkill." William James, who, it is often said, comes the nearest of any American philosopher to existentialism, spoke of "metaphysical wonder" and "cosmic sickness." Yet in his day, men were still politely shooting at each other with cannon. Ours certainly is not the first age of history in which the threat of mass annihilation became a reality. The Black Death killed more men than atomic or nuclear weapons have, and its workings were as mysterious to medieval man as those of a hydrogen bomb are to most people today. It may be that crises in society in various historical periods bring to the fore philosophical thought that emphasizes the plight of the individual caught in the net of circumstance. This was true, for example, of the Stoic philosophy that flourished in the declining years of the Roman Empire. It is one thing to say, however, that social crisis emphasizes and calls our attention to the unique condition of man and quite another to say that it is the cause of it. In the view of existentialism, one of our principal difficulties is that we are prey to the hedonistic ethic Nietzsche warned against. In this view of ethics, happiness is the ultimate end and is equatable with pleasure, which itself has materialistic origins. Poor men think they would be happy if only they were rich, but if they become rich they find they are not happy. Hungry men think they would be happy if only they had food in abundance, but the satiation of hunger does not bring happiness. Insecure men think they would be happy if only they had financial security, but when they attain that security they are restless and bored to the point of nausea. Ralph Harper, in considering these same matters, concludes that "the materialistic ideals of the nineteenth century are as good as achieved. And this, of all times, is the time for the greatest anxiety, mass anxiety." [15]

The structural elements of the existentialist's position on the question of the human situation are at hand. We have already identified them in our previous inquiry into the origins of the existentialist tradition. There is agreement within this tradition that to be a man means to be in despair —to experience anguish. Presumably, this has always been the human condition but certain events in the modern world have conspired to increase the intensity of human experience. There are two things that can be said about the human situation in our day: first, we are aware of the contingent nature of existence; and secondly, we realize the inherent particularity of human existence.

First, regarding contingency, when we say that a thing or event is contingent, we mean that it may either be or not be. There is nothing that makes its existence necessary. In this sense, "nothingness," or non-being, is as much a possibility as being. It is possible to garner a great deal of evidence from our experience in the everyday world to show that contingency does seem to be a built-in character of the conditions under which we live. Pragmatists, particularly, have emphasized the inherently contingent and unpredictable character of the world with which we interact. The very way in which John Dewey defined intelligence and its methods reveals his conception of nature as always in process, unfinished, undetermined in many of its basic features. A large effort of Western traditions in philosophy, however, has been devoted to banishing contingency as a basic trait of reality and to insisting on the necessity of Being. Plato denied the reality of the world of sense, in which the contingent character of existence seems so obvious, and posited as real a perfect world of unchanging forms, whose existence is timeless and absolute. Aristotle could not conceive of a specific act of creation in which the world was created out of nothing. Therefore he subscribed to the idea that the world had always existed in the same form and the species are immutable.

On the other hand, a fundamental tenet of the Hebraic-Christian tradition is that the earth was created by God, and therefore its existence is contingent. There was a time when the world did not exist, and contingency must be an aspect of its being. Strictly speaking, there is no way of knowing why God created the world. This is something that is a mystery, forever outside the possibility of human understanding, and simply must

---

[15] Ralph Harper, "Significance of Existence and Recognition for Education," in *Modern Philosophies and Education*, Fifty-fourth Yearbook of the National Society for the Study of Education, part 1 (Chicago: University of Chicago Press, 1955), pp. 215–58; p. 217.

be accepted. There are other doctrines of the church, however, that mitigate the effects of the Christian doctrine of contingency and make the prospect more tolerable. Not so for the existentialists, however.

For the existentialist, even such Christian existentialists as Kierkegaard, it is a mistake to try to water down our awareness that contingency is of the very nature of things. Kierkegaard was a devout Christian who believed in the existence of God as ardently as any man ever did, and he believed that man had fallen from God through original sin. He did not believe, however, that man could ease his alienation from God by any act of reason or simply through good works. The nature of God's existence and His creation of the world are a mystery in which there are elements of paradox. Therefore, whether Christianity is based on an unfathomable mystery, as for Kierkegaard, or whether God is dead in Nietzsche's sense, the being of the world—and therefore the being of man—is without meaning. It is absurd. It is absurd because there is nothing to give it any meaning. That is, there is nothing outside man himself. The condition of man is that he is in the world. He does not know why, and there is no way for him to find out why. It is in anguish that man realizes that the source of value and of meaning lies within himself. He is called on to shoulder the responsibilities that once were believed to belong to God.

To this fundamental awareness of the contingency of existence, the existentialist adds the fact of the particularity of human existence. A big protest of existentialist philosophy is against the effort of Western philosophy to reduce the human being to an abstraction—an essence or universal. The net effect of this, as Kierkegaard said, is to make man a specimen instead of an individual. The fact of human life is that man exists as an individual. There is no structure of Being, call it God or anything else, that determines any essential nature of man as an individual. The existence of man is finite, and he lives in the knowledge that he must one day die. His existence, as Heidegger said, is a "being for death." Therefore, even in our moments of greatest joy and happiness, our experience is pervaded by a sense of nostalgia and despair, for we know that this joy cannot endure. The individual is unique and therefore irreplaceable. Whatever he is, he has chosen to be, and when he dies, there is no one to fill the vacant place. The way we have most often taken in our attempts to escape from the awful fact of the indeterminacy of existence and our finite nature is to run to the crowd in the hope that by submerging ourselves in the group, or in the institution, we shall find surcease. But the crowd, whatever form it may take, is always untruth.

## THE FACT OF FREEDOM

One of the most important ideas in the existentialist tradition is that man is free to choose and his choices are undetermined by external conditions. In this sense, existential philosophers emphasize the principle of indeterminism as opposed to various deterministic theories of nature and human behavior. Although freedom of human choice plays an important part in the thought of most existentialist philosophers, it has remained for Sartre to pay the closest attention to this point.

William James once made a distinction between two forms of determinism: "hard determinism" and "soft determinism." To illustrate what he meant by hard determinism, he used a verse from Omar Khayyam that expresses the thought that at the beginning of time every event was determined and there is nothing in the nature of things that can change it. Under this view, James said, "The future has no ambiguous possibilities hidden in its womb: the part we call the present is compatible with only one totality. Any other future complement than the one fixed from eternity is impossible." [16] James himself did not subscribe to the doctrine of hard determinism, but he paid it a grudging admiration because he thought it was forthright and did not try to dodge the issue. His contempt was reserved for soft determinism, a position he considered "a quagmire of evasion," in which the term *freedom* might be interpreted in any number of conflicting ways. Soft determinism, said James, because it mingles ideas about good and bad with ideas about cause and effect, always winds up in a dilemma, one of whose horns is pessimism and the other subjectivism. Neither of these alternatives is very attractive and James himself believed that the way between the horns of the dilemma is to see the world as characterized throughout by pluralism and indeterminism.

From what we have already considered in existentialism, it seems clear that existentialists must reject hard determinism. Therefore there is no point in pressing this matter any further. The concern of Sartre in discussing freedom was to eliminate soft determinism also as a possibility. His principal thesis is expressed as follows: "Man cannot be sometimes slave and sometimes free; he is wholly and forever free, or he is not free at all." [17] In our discussion of freedom and determinism in other contexts, we found that the traditional view is that two elements are always present in any act of choice: an external, objective state of affairs; and an internal, or subjective, motive. Man has powers of reason, but these powers are not capable of producing action, and therefore it is necessary to conceive of another kind of power—volition or will. In the classic view, the intellect informs the will and the will initiates an act. A virtuous act is one produced by a good will that has been informed by reason. This is to say, the action has been willed freely, and therefore the individual can be held responsible for it.

---

[16] "The Dilemma of Determinism," reprinted in *Essays in Pragmatism* (New York: Hafner Publishing Co., 1948), pp. 37–64; p. 41.

[17] *Being and Nothingness*, trans. Hazel E. Barnes (New York: Philosophical Library, 1956), p. 441.

Moreover, the classic view included, in addition to the faculties of intellect and will, the passions. The good life—the ethical life—is one in which the passions are regulated and kept in bounds by reason and will.

Objections to the classic view that have developed in modern philosophy differ mainly in the emphasis placed on the elements involved in an act of choice. Mostly, these objections involve a denial of the "freedom of the will," or perhaps the denial that there really is anything that can be called *the will*. Extreme behavioristic theories emphasize the external, objective situation and insist that all behavior is the reaction to stimuli and that man's actions are determined by external causes over which he has no control. In this view, "free will" means nothing. Logically, the ultimate position of this view is hard determinism, but most people have fought shy of the ultimate conclusion and have attempted to substitute some variant of soft determinism. Sartre's reply to this kind of determinism, whether hard or soft, is that the objective situation is never sufficient to initiate action. Our actions are always in terms of our own perceptions and apprehensions of the external situation and these are always freely chosen by us.

Another form of modern determinism places emphasis on the internal motives—the passions. In this view of behavior, whatever action we take is the result of the superior strength of one passion as compared with others. Our behavior, therefore, is determined by the relative strength of our motives. The most powerful passion wins, so to speak, and we do what we have to do. To this kind of argument, Sartre replies that the existentialist takes no stock in the power of passion. "He will never agree," Sartre says, "that a sweeping passion is a ravaging torrent which fatally leads a man to certain acts and is therefore an excuse. *He thinks that man is responsible for his passions.*" [18] In Sartre's opinion, it makes no sense to talk about the strength or weight of passions as if they were physical things capable of being submitted to measuring and weighing. If it makes any sense at all to talk about "the weight of passions," the conclusion is that a passion has just as much weight as we give it. Thus, Sartre is not denying that external circumstances are involved in our actions or that we do have motives. What he emphasizes is that our apprehension of external conditions and the character of our own motives are themselves products of our own choices.

Sartre also raises objections to the kind of psychological determinism inherent in Freud's work. A key idea in Freud is that behavior is determined by the unconscious part of psychic life, the id, which is primitive and irrational. Sartre's criticism of Freud is complex and we shall not pursue it, except to say that Sartre asks how, if Freud's theory is correct, are we

---

[18]  *Existentialism*, pp. 27–28. Italics mine.

to explain certain things that happen in psychoanalytic therapy—patient resistance, for example?

Thus Sartre dismisses fundamental theories of determinism. In a summary of his own views, we find that the fundamental premise is that man is free and makes his own choices. His behavior is self-determined and responsibility for it cannot be placed anywhere except on himself. The only limit placed on his freedom is that he cannot choose not to be free. The choices we make are made around a goal that we have set for ourselves; Sartre calls this a project of the for-itself. To understand his point here, we must consider that his views are different from those found in conventional psychology. Sartre maintains that there are two aspects of consciousness: the nonreflective and the reflective. Our original choices—our project of being—is made by the nonreflective consciousness. The part played by the reflective consciousness is not to select the project of being, but to make us aware of the motives we have. Even before we begin to deliberate, we have already made up our minds.

Sartre illustrates this with an anecdote that has been retold many times. A young man comes to Sartre and asks his advice. This young man is faced with making a decision. He can stay with his mother in Occupied France and take care of her, or he can rejoin his comrades in the Resistance and try to escape the country and join the Free French who are fighting the Nazis. Sartre's point is twofold: first there is no point in giving this young man any advice because he had already made up his mind before he sought advice; secondly, the young man made his decision at the level of nonreflective consciousness—where all such choices are made—and he himself cannot change his own choice through any process of reflection.[19] In this sense, voluntary deliberation is always deceiving oneself.

The fact that we determine our project-of-being by our own choice is the source of anguish. Given Sartre's conception of the matter, one must concede that we make this choice alone without the possibility of any help from God or from any human being. The responsibility is ours and cannot be transferred elsewhere.

## ALIENATION AND AUTHENTICITY

Two questions are of widespread interest today. They are, first, What is the meaning and the source of human alienation as it is viewed in existentialist philosophy? and second, What does it mean to live *authentically*? What is the *authentic* person? These questions are treated in various

---

[19] *Existentialism*, pp. 29–33.

ways by people of differing philosophical and psychological outlooks.

Our consideration of other philosophical traditions has revealed that human alienation is an important question. Marx, for example, treated this matter at length, and in the latter part of his career affirmed that the alienation of man is a consequence of certain objective historical and social conditions. The promise of Marxism is that in the course of historical events, when conditions change, man will overcome his alienated state and will be with himself. In this sense, at least, Marxist philosophy is optimistic about the human condition. A similar kind of optimism can be found among the pragmatists. Dewey was concerned with loss of individuality in the world of modern industrial society and he agreed that the older individualism that had its origin in the preindustrial world was no longer tenable. His middle-class liberalism indicated, however, that a new individualism is possible and organized education can play a part in helping us find our way to it. Even William James, who differed significantly from Dewey temperamentally, and to some extent philosophically, tried valiantly to maintain optimism in the face of the contingency and unpredictability of existence. Such optimism is lacking in the existentialist view. In any common meaning of the term, existential philosophy is pessimistic about the human condition.

A deep root of this pessimism is the existentialist's conviction not only that man is alienated, but that alienation is an irreducible condition of human existence and hence can never be overcome. Sartre's conclusion that "man is condemned to be free" is an eloquent statement of the case. There are at least three dimensions of this freedom and the consequent alienation of man. In the first place, man is forever alienated from the source of his being. This is explained somewhat differently by Christian existentialists and by atheistic existentialists, but their explanations turn out to be similar in the end. Christian existentialists, of whom Kierkegaard is a prime example, hold to the existence of God and the belief that for Him being does have meaning. The gulf, however, between man and God is so vast that there is no way by which man can apprehend this meaning. The significance of the Christian doctrine of the fall of man is that man has become an alien in the world—that as Heidegger has said, man is forlorn. The atheistic existentialists, on the other hand, maintain that only the existence of God could give meaning to existence, and since He does not exist, there is no possible meaning at all. In either case, man is alienated from the source of his being and this alienation cannot be overcome.

Man is not only alienated from the source of his existence; he is also an alien in the world in which he must live. Heidegger insists that man is simply thrown into the world, for no reason apparent to him. Sartre has said that the central principle of existentialism is that man simply appears on the scene, again for no known reason. Both Sartre and Heidegger emphasize the inherently contingent character of the world and maintain that this contingency indicates a complete lack of intrinsic meaning. There is no ultimate ground of being, philosophical or theological, that furnishes a source of value. The world is being-in-itself and man in his existence is hampered by the in-itself. It is his adversary. Thus, man is set against the world and there is no possibility that he can ever achieve a harmonious adjustment to it. Man is not only alienated from the world; he is irrevocably alienated from it.

Even this is not all the story, for man is not only alienated from the source of his being and from the world, he is also alienated from other selves—from society. In accepting this principle, existentialists today follow the course set by Freud rather than that taken by pragmatism, for Freud maintained that man cannot ever hope to establish the kind of social harmony with others that is implicit in pragmatic and other modern philosophies. Existentialism emphasizes individuality and that every man stands alone in the world. This does not mean, however, that existentialists think interpersonal relations are unimportant, nor does it mean that this philosophical tradition advocates a withdrawal by the individual to the existence of a hermit. Existentialists consider human relations to be a crucial problem in philosophy, but their interpretation of it is different from that encountered in most modern philosophies and psychologies. The basic condition of interpersonal relations is one of tension and conflict. "The other" is set against me as my adversary. As a subject (being-for-itself) all other selves become objects (being-in-itself), just as for another self I become an object for him. Thus my relations with other persons are marked with tension and conflict that can never be resolved. The existentialist has profound contempt for the two chief ways present-day man tries to escape the conditions of freedom that are forced upon him by the nature of existence. One of these is the escape to the crowd. The crowd, Kierkegaard said, is always untruth, but those who seek this way out try to conform to the ways of the crowd, to become "socially adjusted," which means that they never do anything without thinking first about the reactions of other people. Their main goal in life seems to be not to offend anybody. The other effort is exemplified in the behavioristic psychologists and the "group dynamics" advocates, who regard themselves as "social engineers" who can manipulate human behavior at will, and through the scientific method, create whatever human nature and whatever human society they desire. Their "social technology" is, we perceive, based on an assumption of determinism.[20] What these "engineers" do, in the judgment of the existentialist, is to make human beings into laboratory subjects and do all

---

[20]  The scientific realism and behaviorism involved in this approach are discussed in Chapter Four.

they can to eliminate subjectivity and choice. The point of existentialism is that these efforts, abhorrent as they are in themselves, always fail because the human spirit is capable of rising above them. It may be that most men today are "other-directed," but the facts of existence are such that they need not be, and it is part of the mission of existentialist philosophy to call attention to the essential freedom of man.

What does it mean to be an "authentic person," or to live "authentically"? Naturally there are differences among existentialist philosophers on this point, stemming mostly from their differences concerning the nature of human existence. However, there are also common elements. In the broadest sense, to live authentically means to live in full awareness of freedom. To achieve this, we must be aware that human existence is absolutely unlike the existence of things. We must not only understand, but take to heart, Sartre's distinction between the in-itself and the for-itself and Heidegger's insistence that the locus of human inauthenticity is the condition of being-in-the-midst-of-the-world—that is, the everyday world of things. Sartre and Heidegger have somewhat different conceptions of the nature of the everyday world of things, but they agree that the authentic person is one who transcends it, and that this can only be achieved through the experience of anguish. The authentic person is one who faces the real character of existence, who recognizes both the freedom and the necessity of choice, and who chooses freely with complete realization that he is responsible for what he has chosen.

There is an element of irony here, for it seems clear that the more authentic we become, that is, the more we are with ourselves instead of the crowd, the greater our isolation from other individuals. If the existentialists are right, if the only significant choices are those we make ourselves for ourselves, then it must be that nobody can really help us—we stand alone. The price of authenticity is anguish.

A summary of the various protests that existentialists make against modern society and the character of modern life concludes our survey of modern existentialism. First of all, we have found existentialism to be a protest against conformity in all its possible aspects. It is as much a protest against institutionalized religion as it is against the institutional character of the classic tradition in philosophy. We may add to this also the protest existentialism makes against the institutionalized science of our day and against the willingness of many people in these times to reduce man to simply a scientific object. There are many people who have switched their conformity to metaphysics for a conformity to scientism, and they have succeeded in transforming man from a metaphysical essence into a scientific specimen. The protest against conformity for which existentialism is best known today is against conformity to mass society. The problem undoubtedly is more acute now than it was in the nineteenth century, although both Kierkegaard and Nietzsche saw the situation with great clarity. The "other-directed" person was as well known to them as he is to us. The difference between the pressure to conform in their day as compared with our own may be a difference of degree rather than kind, but even as a difference of degree it is overwhelming. A whole popular literature, as well as a technical one, can be explored on this point.

A second big protest of existentialism is against determinism in any form, whether this is the mechanistic determinism of the behaviorists or the psychological determinism of the Freudian schools of psychology. Existential philosophy insists that man is free and that whether he likes it or not, he is faced with the necessity of choice. There is a radical difference between man and the rest of existence. Man, in Sartre's term, is being-for-itself; he is constantly transcending himself and hence is not subject to the law of identity. Things are whatever they are in themselves; they are being-in-itself. But man is what he becomes, and what he becomes is a matter of his own choosing. He may choose authentically as a man or inauthentically to be a member of the crowd, but he must choose because there is nothing anywhere on which he can place the responsibility. It is a common thing for us to look for something to blame for the predicament in which we find ourselves: If I had not been born in a slum; if my parents had not treated me so badly when I was a child; if my genetic inheritance had not been so unfavorable; if I had been able to go to a better college; if I were not a Jew or a black or something else; and so on and on through all the familiar litany of excuses. But the admonition existentialism addresses to us is that we are what we have chosen to be. It is easy to misunderstand this. Existentialists are not talking about magic. They are not saying that a person born into slavery could have chosen to be born into royalty or that a person born a black could have chosen to be born a white. Their point is that man can rise above history and assert his own freedom. The point is not what the content of our choices is, so much as that we make choices and shoulder the responsibility for them. How we act in the face of circumstance is our own doing.

Existentialism may also be interpreted as a protest against all efforts to reconcile man with the world. It has sometimes been said, by Dewey, for example, that the mission of Western philosophy has been a concealed effort to banish all that is harsh, banal, and annoying in existence to some limbo of nonbeing or the "merely empirical" and to enshrine the true, the good, and the beautiful as the real attributes of Being. Theology, like philosophy, has been concerned in assuring us that existence has a built-in meaning to it, that if we could only get the "big picture" we should see that what in the partial and finite view appears meaningless and even evil is but an aspect of what is complete and good. In common language, the effort of a very great deal of philosophy and theology has been to assure us that in the long run everything is going to be all right. If man is alienated in this world, he will lose his alienated condition in the next. If man is alienated under the conditions of capitalism, he will be with himself when socialism is established.

The existentialist protests against the effort to explain away what so evidently is the condition of human existence. Men can know, even without the assistance of philosophers, that there is much in human life that is without any apparent meaning, that death is the reality that confronts all men, that each man must live and choose for himself, and that the world in many respects is alien and unfriendly. The charge existentialism lays on us is to face the realities of human existence and the fact of human freedom and not to sell our birthright as men for a mess of philosophical and theological pottage. Existential philosophy is a condemnation of all the abstractions and rationalistic reductionisms that blind us to the fact that existence inherently is absurd and the only meaning life has is that with which we ourselves invest it. There is more to be learned about human existence in poetry, art, and myth than in all the intellectual posturings of the metaphysicians and the scientists.

Existentialism is also a protest against absolute norms for value, however their allegedly absolute character may be conceived. It represents a position of ethical relativism in which the individual chooses his own norms. This view does not necessarily dismiss tradition as unimportant, but it does label blind acceptance of tradition as an inauthentic choice. What is also notable is that blind rejection of tradition also constitutes an inauthentic choice. The inability of behavioristic psychology, which concerns itself with outward behavior and ignores the essentially subjective condition of human existence, to distinguish between an authentic and inauthentic acceptance of tradition (or of anything else) is evidence, to the existentialist, of the poverty of scientific psychology.

## EXISTENTIALISM AND EDUCATION

We come now to the last part of our inquiry into existential philosophy and the protest it makes against existing modes of life and education in today's American society. In seeking to locate connections of some kind between existential philosophy and ideas on education, we are at a disadvantage. This disadvantage lies in the fact that the leading figures of this tradition have had little to say about education. And it must be confessed, when some important spokesman for existentialism has said anything about education, his pronouncements have seemed to originate more in his own educational experience than in his existentialism. Further, the amount of commentary on the implications of existential thought for educational theory is not very extensive, at least in comparison with other traditions we have considered. This means that we are left, in considerable degree, to our own devices.

We have described the existentialist tradition as one that views the mission of philosophy as analyzing the basic character of human existence and calling the attention of men to their freedom. It seems reasonable to expect that existentialists would think that the educative process should take its primary direction from this principle. If this inference is correct, we should expect also that such practical aspects of education as the nature of the curriculum, the role of the teacher, and the character of educational method would be consciously designed to achieve the mission of existentialism. Generally speaking, the efforts of various commentators on existentialist ideas concerning education has been to demonstrate that this is the case.

On the character of the curriculum, for example, there seems to be considerable agreement that to achieve the aims of education, as these are stated or implied in existential philosophy, education must be conceived as liberal education.[21] The difficulty here lies in determining what is meant by the term *liberal education*. We get little help in clarifying the idea because what is offered in explanation are, on the one hand, platitudes made popular by educational essentialism ("freeing the mind from ignorance and confusion"), and on the other hand, the attempt to define liberal learning in terms of certain subject matters. In the first chapter of this book the reader was invited to try his hand at analyzing how it is that a realist, an idealist, and an existentialist can come to such close agreement on the nature of the curriculum if it is the philosophical ideas of these writers that dictate their conceptions of the curriculum. Those who did not accept the invitation originally may find it instructive to do so now.[22]

For example, in his widely read essay on existentialism and education, Ralph Harper considers the question of the curriculum. In so doing, he advocates the following ideas: (1) Everybody must be taught certain things —reading, arithmetic, writing, history, and so forth. (2) The pupil is not the one to decide what he should learn. This is the teacher's prerogative. It is not injurious to be made to learn arithmetic or read the Bible or the *Odyssey*. (3) The human mind always works in certain ways, and therefore it is essential for man to learn logic, for it leads to truth.[23] Even though the author salts his discussions of these matters with existentialistic-sounding phrases and observations, this seasoning is insufficient to mask the fundamentally conservative flavor of the discussion. It may well be that these are good and worthy ideas about the curriculum—at least conservatives have maintained for a long time that they are. The question would seem

---

[21] As examples, see Harper, "Significance of Existence," p. 227 and George F. Kneller, *Existentialism and Education* (New York: Philosophical Library, 1958), pp. 122 ff.

[22] See p. 20.

[23] Harper, "Significance of Existence," pp. 234–36.

to be, What do they have to do with existentialism? Are they even consistent with existentialist ideas? One thing at least seems certain: *One does not have to be an existentialist to accept them.*

If an existentialist does not believe that the pupil decides what he should learn, then who does he think can decide? If Sartre is right that man appears on the scene and chooses, if the authentic choice is that which one makes for himself—and which he alone can make—then what happens to authenticity in this educational scheme of things? On one occasion at least, Sartre tried his own hand with this question and was finally forced to find refuge in the last haven available to an existentialist—the paradoxical nature of existence. He defends a requirement that everyone should master the essentials, but when he is brought up against the fact that the essentials are universals, he simply says that we should do what everybody else does but be like nobody else. How this can be consistent with other aspects of his thought is something on which considerably more light is needed.[24] Simply to label the matter a paradox does not seem particularly helpful.

There is evidence in the writings of both Sartre and Heidegger of their belief that the humanistic studies are the most valuable. In various forms of art, the existence of man in all its poignant character is most clearly portrayed. Since truth for the existentialist derives from human subjectivity, since truth is a relationship in which man places himself, literature, the graphic arts, music, and myth are far more the source of truth than the sciences. There is in the literature of existentialism a strong antiscientific strain. There is evidence that Nietzsche foresaw accurately the problem of extreme specialization that is characteristic of both the pure science and the technology of our own time. He advocated the now familiar antidote of liberal education to counteract it. The main existentialist objection to science is that it is cold, aloof, and objective in its approach to nature and to man, and that as an intellectual enterprise it is concerned only with abstractions. Its effects have been unfortunate enough in warping our conception of physical nature, but when the methods of science have been applied to human nature, the results have been simply disastrous.

Those who seek to draw inferences about the role of the teacher from various principles of existential philosophy seem most often to advocate the Socratic method as a model.[25] In some ways at least, this seems to be a reasonable choice. By almost any existentialist criterion, Socrates appears to have been an outstanding example of the authentic individual. His

---

24 On this point see Kneller, *Existentialism*, pp. 122–23.

25 For example, Kneller, *Existentialism*, pp. 133–35. See also Van Cleve Morris, *Existentialism in Education* (New York: Harper & Row, 1966), pp. 135–37.

humanistic approach to philosophy and his insistence on man as the focus around which inquiry should be developed are themes that find an important place in present-day existentialism. The way in which Socrates conducted his teaching, at least as it is portrayed by Plato, and the kind of relationship he established with his students are also in apparent agreement with various ideas we have discovered in existential philosophy. It is true that Socrates did not give lectures, or prepare course outlines, or administer comprehensive examinations. There were no entrance requirements to his school; he had no school. There were no administrators and no tuition and no overhead. His method of teaching was one of asking questions, refining answers, asking more questions, and pushing the issue until some acceptable conclusion was reached. He himself did not give answers and always maintained that he was ignorant and was only asking for enlightenment from those with whom he was conversing. All of these things appear to indicate that Socrates and his famous method are an appropriate model for existentialist education. There is something more, however, that needs saying about the Socratic method.

There is, for one thing, the question of what the method of Socrates is supposed to yield. It is true that in initiating an inquiry, Socrates invariably began with some situation that was common in Athenian life. The movement of his thought was inductive, *proceeding from the immediate and particular to the abstract and universal.* Aristotle described Socrates as "busying himself about ethical matters and neglecting the world of nature as a whole *but seeking the universal in these ethical matters.*" Socrates "*fixed thought for the first time on definitions.*" [26] Socrates' example of neglecting nature and centering attention on man is something the existentialist can admire. But we should ask, What about the rest of Aristotle's observation? The method of Socrates was aimed at reaching abstractions— universals, or essences. The method itself is built on the supposition that there are universal and absolute principles of ethics, and these in the hands of Plato became the Forms. Moreover, the method also rests on the principle that ideas are innate in the individual. The ideas exist in the soul, but to be known they have to be brought to consciousness, and this is the purpose of Socrates' method. Knowing is a process of *recollection* in which the direct transmission of information can play no part at all. But knowing is the apprehension of what is already present in the soul, and what is in the soul is *abstractions.* It would appear that at this point the existentialist finds his Socratic model turning against him. Unless any methodology that involves the teacher asking questions is to be classified as Socratic, and this would appear to do violence to the Socratic-Platonic tradition, then

---

[26] *Metaphysics,* bk. 1, chap. 6. Italics mine.

there is a real question that certain principles in existentialism actually imply the method of Socrates. After all, the claim has also been made that a teaching machine can be programmed to teach like the gadfly of Athens! [27]

There is also found in the commentary on existentialism and education a strong emphasis on the character of the personal relationships between teacher and pupil. The usual thesis is that under the influence of existential ideas, the teacher-student relation will be more personal and more "interactive." [28] According to this view, the only really important thing about education is the relation established between the student and the teacher. What this relation should be—or perhaps better—*can be*, depends on whose existentialism is taken as authoritative. If, for example, Sartre's analysis of personal relationships is accepted as authoritative, it appears that the pupil-teacher relation can never be other than one of tension and conflict. Each of the persons involved is the adversary of the other. The teacher seeks to make the student an object that he can manipulate in accord with his own ideas and for his own purposes. For the student, the role is reversed; the teacher is his adversary, who stands in opposition to his own freedom. Sartre's philosophy even raises the question whether language can serve a true mediating function among individuals, and surely there is in his approach the belief that no one can really do anything important for anyone else. The same kind of question can be raised about the efficacy of student counseling and guidance, an activity that has become of great importance in present-day secondary schools. If a person's project-for-being can be made only by the individual at the level of nonreflective consciousness and if reflective consciousness serves usually as a means of self-deception, then the question is whether the counselor-client relationship can really be productive of anything. The anecdote of the young man's soliciting Sartre's advice about whether he should stay with his mother or return to his comrades in the underground is an example.

Sartre's ideas, at least when they are taken for their face value, do not seem to lend much comfort to the educational enterprise, even when this enterprise is interpreted in somewhat unconventional terms. For this reason among others, persons interested in the implications of existential philosophy for the practical affairs of education or for counseling and psychotherapy often have tended to shy away from Sartre and to pay more heed to the work of such philosophers as Karl Jaspers and Gabriel Marcel. Those readers who elect to pursue a study of the influence of these men may possibly find a closer relation between their brands of existentialism and ideas about education.[29] The question at least ought to be left open.

---

[27] Lawrence M. Stolurow, *Teaching by Machine*, Cooperative Research Monograph No. 6 (Washington, D.C.: Department of Health, Education and Welfare, 1961), p. 60.
[28] See Harper, "Significance of Existence," pp. 229–33.

The foregoing remarks, although they are somewhat critical of contemporary efforts to relate existential thought in some logical sense to
educational policy, are not meant to indicate that the existentialist protest
has no significance for those interested in the philosophy of education. In
the opinion of the present author, a primary difficulty lies in attempting to
resurrect the familiar approach to educational philosophy, that is, in taking
some principles of existentialism *a priori* and then trying to show something
that is entailed logically. It is suggested here as a possibility—if nothing
else—that a more revealing approach to the problem of existential thought
and education may be found if we consider the protest of existentialism
as essentially nihilistic in character. *Nihilism* is not a nice word to most
people, particularly to Americans, who have a way of thinking that technology can solve all problems, including those of interpersonal relations.
What is meant here is that existential philosophy offers no schemes for
social reform and progress. It does not promise us that everything is going
to be all right in some kind of future. Kierkegaard did not initiate a program to reform the Danish church; he told us how to be a Christian in
spite of the church, and how to escape from the crowd. Nietzsche did not
advocate the establishment of social democracy and communal harmony;
he said that some men could rise above the herd and become supermen.
The herd would remain. Sartre and Heidegger do not tell us that man can
be reconciled to the world; rather they insist that he can learn to live in a
world that is forever alien, and to live authentically.

Existential philosophy is a protest against an age in which the individual
is reduced to his social security number and a computer card with holes
punched in it. It is a protest against mass society, mass religion, mass
education, and mass communication. It does not tell us how to change the
character of this society. There is even reason to believe that existentialists
may not think this very important. The important thing is not what happens to a man, but how he chooses to meet it. And this, they tell us, is
solely up to us. It is suggested, therefore, that instead of attempting to
tame this rebellious offspring of philosophy, instead of trying to gentle it
and dull its bite, we should take it for the passionate, and in many ways the
irrational, protest against the established order that it is. There is no point
in looking in the literature of existential philosophy for the blueprints of a
new order in which all problems will be solved. There is the chance, however, that when we begin to think obstinately about the education of *the
individual* in mass society, the protest of existentialism will be heard and
appreciated for what it is.

---

[29] See Gabriel Marcel, *The Philosophy of Existentialism*, trans. Manya Horari (New
York: Citadel Press, 1961); Karl Jaspers, *Man in the Modern Age* (New York: Henry
Holt and Co., 1933).

## SUMMARY

We have tried to survey the historical development of existentialist philosophy and to make some estimate of its possible relation with educational policy today. The existentialist tradition itself has been portrayed as a protest movement against the character of modern society, and specifically against modern developments in science and philosophy, especially as these relate to interpretations of the nature of man. The view presented here is that the protest of existentialism is nihilistic in the sense that it presents no formula for a reconstruction of society in which the individual automatically will realize his identity and self-integrity. We have seen that a common theme developed by various existentialist philosophers is that adversity, the necessity of choice, and hence disquietude and anxiety are inherent in human experience and can never be eliminated by any means. Existentialism emphasizes the importance of our understanding that how we face events that confront us is our own choice and the responsibility for this choice can never be transferred. Hence, the emphasis is on the individual and not on the environment in which he finds himself.

The task of making some estimate of the import of existentialist philosophy for ideas about education we found exceedingly difficult. In various ways, organized education itself displays many of the qualities of mass organization, aloofness, and contempt for individuality that existentialism condemns in society at large. The conclusion offered here is that there is little or nothing in contemporary existentialism that indicates how the school as an institution might be reformed—or even any indication that such a reform might be thought by existentialists to be important. There does appear to be a possible inference that a man's education can only be a product of his own choosing, and his alone. Perhaps, there is also the promise that a man can become educated—even in spite of the school.

# chapter ELEVEN

# PROSPECTS FOR THE FUTURE

*Notwithstanding the portion of discourse which has been bestowed upon this subject, it is surprising to find, on close inspection, how few of its principles are settled. The reason is that the ends and means have not been analyzed, and it is only a general and indistinguishing conception of them which is found in the minds of the greatest number of men. Things in this situation give rise to interminable disputes; more especially when the deliberation is subject, as here, to the strongest action of personal interest.*

—JAMES MILL

What have these educational and philosophic traditions that have shown themselves pertinent to American education led to on the contemporary educational scene in America as the last quarter of the century is at hand? What do they foretell for the future? The background for the exigencies of the present to draw on is broad. The prospect for the future must be speculative.

## THE EDUCATIONAL SCENE TODAY

It surely is no news to anyone that American education is in a state of increasing confusion. Confusion has never been absent from the educational scene in this century but it has grown progressively worse in the decades since the end of the Second World War. There are various reasons for this but one of the greatest is the rapid pace of technology and industrialism and the inability, or at least the failure, of the schools to adapt themselves to these alterations in society.

The schools are in trouble, which is to say that essentialism is in trouble, since the American conservative tradition in education has managed to maintain its domination of American schools in spite of all efforts to dislodge it. It is true that over the years when occasion has demanded, essentialism has changed its tactics, but it has never changed its basic policies of purpose, organization, and educational design. Nor is it likely, or even possible, that fundamental changes in education will occur so long as education is viewed primarily as cultural transmission and preparation of the young for the future.

Although arguing the thesis on somewhat different grounds from those we have advanced, Michael B. Katz has come to substantially the same conclusion concerning the lack of any fundamental alteration in the structure and function of American education since its formative period in the nineteenth century. He observes that the purpose of the school has always been the transmission of dominant social and economic values, and that the structure that has developed is a bureaucracy. He notes further that there is always a functional relationship between the purposes the school seeks to achieve and the organization of the institution, a point we have sought to emphasize.[1]

---

[1] Michael B. Katz, *Class, Bureaucracy, and Schools: The Illusion of Educational Change in America* (New York: Praeger, 1971). Katz's argument is primarily historical. Although Katz recognizes the philosophic component, he does not develop it to any extent. However, those who are concerned primarily with philosophy of education will find this book a fertile source of ideas. Katz sees the unchanging characteristic structure of American education to be not only free and compulsory but also racist and bureaucratic. The introduction of the book will give the reader a general view of the argument and the way it is developed.

A comparison of two books published seventy-seven years apart furnishes interesting documentation for the thesis that schools have not undergone any fundamental change and that even at what might be thought a relatively superficial level they have not altered significantly. The two books are Joseph M. Rice's *The Public School System of the United States*, published in 1893, and Charles E. Silberman's *Crisis in the Classroom*, published in 1970.[2] Rice's book appeared at a time of profound discontent with the public schools, when insistent demands for reform were arising in various parts of the country. The same may be said for *Crisis in the Classroom*, for it also appeared at a time when the schools were under severe attack. Silberman's book is longer and more comprehensive than Rice's, but the volumes have two important things in common: (1) They both are based on empirical studies of what actually goes on in schools. (2) They both reach substantially the same conclusions concerning the nature and the conduct of the schools.

It is a sobering experience to compare these documents written three-quarters of a century apart. Both authors stress the sterility of the child's school experience, the rigid discipline, the lack of attention to the nature of the child and the learning process, the mechanical character of the curriculum, and the general aimlessness that pervades the life of the school. "For nearly every class that I visited," Rice wrote, "the busy-work meant little more than idleness and mischief. It was the most aimless work that I have ever found."[3] In many places in his book Silberman reports similar findings. If one makes allowance for some differences in literary style, it is difficult to know whether it is Rice or Silberman one is reading.

Both men made general suggestions for reform. Rice, who had studied in Germany, pointed to the need for adoption of "scientific pedagogy," which he had learned of in the German universities. Silberman points to the example of the British infant school as a possible direction for change. It is interesting that both men looked to other than American sources for inspiration and ideas for reform.

In our time, as in Rice's, disillusionment, confusion, and the demand for reform of education dominate the scene. The same urgency is prevalent now as at the turn of the century, when the original progressive reform movement had its start. The chief difference today is that the scale is so much greater. When Rice made his investigation, the public secondary school was not even well established and his concern consequently was with the elementary, or "common," school since it was that institution that affected the lives of the mass of children. In the intervening years,

---

[2] Reference has already been made to Rice's book in Chapter Five in our consideration of the liberal protest. Silberman's book is published by Random House.

[3] Joseph M. Rice, *The Public School System of the United States* (New York: Century Co., 1893), p. 154.

the high school has become an institution for mass education, with all the difficulties that are entailed, and the trend for higher education is the same. So the task that faces the contemporary educational reformer is far more complex than it has ever been before.

The ferment that started in the colleges and universities in the 1960s, causing so much consternation, particularly in conservative circles, seems to have subsided, although it is impossible to say whether the lull is temporary or a continuing condition. In any event, much of the rancor and rebellion that characterized the "revolt on the campus" seems now to have devolved on the secondary school, and there is not much doubt that this is now regarded as the "trouble spot" of American education. Some people have professed to see similar developments occurring even in the elementary schools.

In the face of chaos of this kind, frantic efforts at reform are inevitable. The main thing that characterizes these reform efforts is their diversity, the frenetic character of many of them, and the superficiality of most of them. They range from proposals to abolish formal schooling entirely to rebuilding the system by technological means, incorporated in some kind of systems approach. The intermediate positions are so numerous and varied that they defy enumeration, much less discussion.

One thing that stands out clearly is the typical American faith that any problem, or set of problems, will yield ultimately to two forces: *money and reorganization.* Consequently, vast sums of money have been poured into education in the effort to bring order out of chaos. A great deal of this money has come from federal sources, the rest of it from local and state governments and from private philanthropy. It has been spent among other things for research projects, for training grants, and for curriculum development, much of it on a national scale.

Likewise, in administration, a similar phenomenon has appeared. If the secondary schools are floundering, then the answer to their problems is to reorganize secondary education, create new entities—the "middle school," for example. If high schools are too large, make them smaller. If control is too centralized and unresponsive, place immediate control with the community. As a matter of fact, community control rarely seems to happen, partly because of the absence of any sense of community, particularly in large urban centers where the problems are most serious, and because real decentralization by its nature runs counter to the interests of the prevailing bureaucracy.[4]

---

[4] In the May 1972 issue of the *Phi Delta Kappan* (vol. 53, no. 9), there is a series of articles on secondary education appearing under the general title "Is There Hope for American High Schools?" These articles give a compact and useful view of the range of problems at this level of the school system and the efforts that are proposed for

In educational method, the same general approach to instructional problems is found—reorganize. Proposals for achieving this are numerous and many of them are well known, even to the general public: ungraded classrooms, team teaching, performance objectives, schools without walls, and not least, the various programs based on educational technology. Accompanying these changes in structural organization are efforts at reorganizing curricula and curriculum materials. For the most part, these developments have followed the traditional subject matter lines that have been the mainstay of conservative educational policy for decades. Under this view, the task is fundamentally reorganization of subject matter in the traditional disciplines, for example, mathematics, the sciences, the social studies, and languages. Efforts to achieve reorganization in curricula have been elaborate, involving the experts in the various academic disciplines, educational theorists, and substantial financial support. The move for curriculum reorganization began in the 1950s and continued through most of the succeeding decade. By the end of the sixties, there seemed to be a paucity of evidence to support the hopes and claims of the curriculum reformers that had appeared so bright in the beginning. The secondary schools were in worse shape, generally speaking, than they had been at the beginning of the curriculum reform period.[5]

It is appropriate to point out here that amid all the myriad activities directed toward the rehabilitation of education, the claims and counterclaims, the organizing and the reorganizing, and the researching and developing, not to mention the proliferation of gadgetry, one question was rarely raised, if ever. Yet this question is strategic beyond all others. It can be asked in deceptively simple language, but we know from the inquiry we have made in our consideration of the individual philosophies how complicated the question is and how fateful the answer given to it can be. The question is, What are the purposes education should serve? Or more simply, What is teaching for?

To put the matter briefly, this question has always been either ignored completely or dismissed as futile, irrelevant, or dull, or perhaps all three.[6] One way to assay the situation is to conclude that all of this ferment,

---

coping with them. The body of literature on the reform of secondary education is enormous and growing rapidly.

[5] Limits of space preclude a more detailed delineation of the situation here. However, Silberman, *Crisis in the Classroom*, chap. 5, presents a comprehensive discussion of what he calls "The Failure of Educational Reform." One interesting observation he makes is that the distinguished university professors who participated in the curriculum reform work actually were the source of its greatest weakness (p. 179).

[6] Examples of this attitude are furnished by James B. Conant and Martin Mayer, the latter in his book *The Schools* (New York: Harper & Brothers, 1961). See also Silberman, *Crisis in the Classroom*, p. 6.

which some have even described as constituting an "educational revolution," is simply an aimless though elaborate messing around with methodology, new tricks of the trade, and elements of the existing structure. In other words, it is an affair of all means and no ends. Now enough truth is in this view to make it reasonably tenable, but the real truth of the matter lies deeper. A thesis that offers a more comprehensive explanation of the phenomenon is that nobody says anything about educational purposes because of a tacit assumption that they are so well established, well known, and widely accepted that discussing them is an idle waste of time and a dull occupation, indeed, in contrast to the heady subject of "educational innovation."

If this is correct, it certainly is testimony to the potency of American essentialism and the hold this tradition has on education. Essentialists can afford to compromise on matters of educational method, so long as the new methods pose only a minimal threat to underlying conceptions of educational objectives. Essentialists cannot afford, however, to compromise on the objectives themselves, and there is precious little sign that they intend to or that they will find it necessary to do so, given the trend events appear to be following.

It is not a pleasant task to suggest that most of the devoted effort, good will, and money that is going into the making of "the revolution in education" will likely come to little or nothing. Every person surely has the right to be his own prophet, or philosopher of history, but let it be remembered that we have a history of efforts at educational reform and we have sufficient perspective to learn something from them. There is no guarantee that we shall do so; the probability appears to lie in the other direction. Nevertheless, a legitimate role of the philosophic enterprise is to analyze past experience to avoid the possible mistakes and pitfalls that lie in the future.

## ARE WE CONDEMNED TO REPEAT IT?

Whether what follows here can be dignified by the appellation "historical model" is unimportant. What will be done represents an effort to project events as they are likely to occur, given the situation as it is now developing in American education. This projection is not based on any particular theory of history—cyclical or otherwise. There is reason to think, however, that we are repeating (with some variation, to be sure) the experience our educational system underwent in the earlier decades of this century. We know that in these years there was a genuine educational reform movement in this country, that it was extensive, and that it developed a sophisticated philosophic base. It is granted that the highly developed educational philosophies of such men as Dewey and Bode eluded the mass of educational practitioners and that whatever modifications the progressive movement was able to effect in the schools were superficial and therefore unimportant in the effort to bring about significant alteration in the system.

It should be understood that in speaking of the earlier reform movement we are eliminating entirely the events that occurred in the years from 1955 to 1965. Although at its inception this period was heralded as "a major turning point" in education, it proved to be nothing of the kind. The "innovations" wrought were on the surface; in essential character, the schools remained as they were—only more so.[7] At this point, the cauldron of discontent and disillusion that had been quietly simmering finally boiled over. The schools found themselves in trouble.

Our effort to project future events begins with this condition. Using our understanding of what happened in the past, we may theorize that if the turmoil now disrupting the schools really constitutes the early stages of a genuine reform movement, then this development will likely pass through four stages. These stages will not be discrete, but they will overlap. However, they will be identifiable and analyzable. It may be that a genuine reform movement will not develop, that it will abort in about the same way the so-called reform era of 1955–1965 did. Events are close to us now, and consequently we lack the perspective necessary for a clear understanding. Nevertheless, if it should be the real thing, then the events herewith projected may very likely occur.

In the first stage profound dissatisfaction, disenchantment, and deep-seated hostility develop toward the established school system and its modes of education. This condition has strong political and social overtones and is an expression, both conscious and unconscious, of dissatisfaction not only with education but with the whole social scene. The pervading dissatisfaction may involve economic factors, the plight of minority groups, working-class problems, foreign policy, the rebellious attitude of the young, and any number of similar factors. Some of the hostility is directed towards well-defined targets, but a substantial part is likely to be free-floating, in which case rancor and ill temper are directed not at any specific or identifiable institution or group of individuals—a situation that the French use *ressentiment* to denote. It appears certain that this kind of social climate is a necessary condition for the developments of the second stage.

In the second stage, educational reform movements spring up and spokesmen for the reform of education appear. Typically, the latter make up a mixed bag, including sentimentalists, romantics, social radicals, serious students of pedagogy, and an assortment of crackpots. About all they

---

[7] This thesis is examined in detail and with extensive documentation in chap. 5 of Silberman, *Crisis in the Classroom*.

have in common is a burning desire to change the system. Some wish to accomplish this by relatively gradual means and by working within the system. Others advocate abrupt alteration and even outright destruction of the traditional order.

A popular strategy is the founding of "experimental schools," or in popular parlance, "alternative forms of education." In the beginning, these departures are of necessity mostly private and their sponsors must find private sources for financial support. Since schools are expensive to operate, many are short-lived. They vary considerably in ideology, programs, teaching practices, and administration. They label themselves progressive, open, or innovative, or by whatever term happens to be popular at the time, but the similarity is likely to end with the label.

Since those working in the new schools are essentially against existing institutions and practices and since their moral indignation runs high, their tendency to overreact is great. Their main effort is to eliminate as much of the regimentation, routine, and repressive control of the traditional school as possible. It appears to many of the reformers, given the heady atmosphere of the environment they work in, that the main task is to abandon all vestiges of the traditional system. In such an enterprise, the reformers receive steady reinforcement from various prophets of the new day, many of whom find it profitable in various ways—not excluding the economic—to excoriate the traditional order and its schools and to proclaim the wisdom, virtue, and what might be called the sophisticated innocence of the child.

Meantime, reports emanating from the experimental schools are uniformly ecstatic. The evangelical fervor of the reformers is such that any report of negative evidence is rare or nonexistent. The children without exception seem joyful, enthusiastic, industrious, and cooperative. Even outside observers and commentators get caught up in the jubilation. Understandably, journalists and popular writers are particularly vulnerable in this respect because educational reform almost always makes good copy. The more cautious writers sometimes insert a caveat: "To be sure, there are certain problems. . . ." But then the evaluation continues as if there were none.

Out of all this emerges a third stage of development, noted for two things: the effort to move the reform efforts out of the private sector and into the public schools, and the beginning of an awareness that all is not as idyllic as it first appeared. These two conditions are complementary. For the second, the difficulty derives from failure to define any set of objectives as basic working ideas that really are different from those of the traditional system. Many of those in the new schools fail to realize how powerful the hold of educational tradition is, even on them, and they find themselves, often without knowing it, promising that with their enlightened methodology they can produce the results that the traditional schools have failed so miserably to accomplish. This is a fatal error and plants in the reform movement the seeds of its own destruction. Doubtless various reasons can account for this fundamental mistake, but certainly many teachers and other participants in the new schools lack the necessary sense of educational history and often entertain a studied contempt for philosophy of education or any rigorous intellectual activity, or even practical pedagogy.

Furthermore, the emotional ardor of the reformers cannot be maintained at fever pitch indefinitely, and while emotional commitment may be a necessary condition for educational reform, it is hardly sufficient. Most of these schools, because of the chaotic conditions that have developed within them, will find it impossible to pay off on their promises, primarily because their program and their methodology were never designed to produce such results. Although it may have proved possible to discard the organization of the traditional school, failure to provide any alternative unifying force leads to experience for children that is atomistic, fragmented, and ultimately intolerable.

And so it is that things in the movement begin to go sour. Disenchantment develops, perhaps hardly perceptible at first; but it grows and the malaise spreads among pupils, parents, and teachers. The support that was once imagined to be available at every hand diminishes to the vanishing point.

Stage four, which is the final scene in the drama, occurs when a wave of conservative reaction sets in. This resurgent educational conservatism, like the original reform movement, is closely tied to social and political events. Now a new breed of educational critics emerges from the wings. These antagonists excoriate in their turn the excesses of the reform movement. They fulminate against the anti-intellectualism, the soft-headed sentimentality, the abysmal ignorance of the products of the schools. Many of these critics, too, will find educational criticism profitable, just as their reforming counterparts did at an earlier time. The message is simple, or can be made to seem so. It is the call for a return to conventional, time-tested modes of education, intellectual rigor, and social discipline. The emotional tide runs high among these critics, and sensing that they have considerable public support, they redouble their efforts. The supreme irony is consummated when it becomes apparent that the traditionalists are beating a dead horse. The "revolution" is over, and in spite of all the effort and dedication and idealism that went into it, the schools remain the same, except for a few superficial differences.

Before the foregoing is dismissed as simple cynicism, one ought to consider that something very like the events described has already happened once in this century. Whether essentially the same pattern will be repeated is a speculative matter. There are signs, however, that the possibility is not remote. We have already mentioned the possibility that the present state of affairs will never run the full course but will fizzle out in somewhat the same way as the so-called reform program of the fifties and sixties did.

If this proves the case, then that will be that. History can file it all away as one more example of the belief that if something is reorganized its essential character will be changed thereby.

However, the signs are that the educational reform movement that had its inception in the late sixties is different in certain respects from that of the preceding decade. The earlier movement was devoted to *academic* reform, mainly taking the form of reorganization of curriculum materials along the lines of the traditional disciplines. The essentialism of Conant and others motivated this work to a significant extent. Overtly at least, the movement was almost completely nonideological, although it rested on the social conservatism to which essentialism is so closely bound. It can be interpreted as the last stage in essentialism's effort to get the schools back on the track from which they had strayed.

There is reason to think that the newer developments are fundamentally different. They have the earmarks of a genuine protest movement. A geat deal of the ferment is colored strongly with social ideology, much of it radical in varying degrees. To many participants, the task is not only simple school reform but also far-reaching social change, in which the school will participate and through which it will be transformed. The emotional, evangelical components that historically have characterized sustained efforts at educational reform are clearly evident. In short, there is reason to believe that this movement is past the first stage described above and probably well into the second.

And now the question presents itself, Are we destined to run the same familiar course? That is, Are we condemned to repeat it? The answer to this question is that very likely we are going to repeat it *unless certain conditions can be met.*

First of all, there must be a fundamental reassessment of the purposes of education for the kind of society in which we now live and which in all probability will continue to develop along the same general lines it has followed for several decades. Specifically, the reappraisal must take into account that this is an urbanized, technological, and increasingly corporate society. In spite of the romantic rhetoric, there is little or no reason to think that this trend will be reversed, or that it can be. Whatever emerges from this reassessment must be articulated clearly; it must be understood not only by those who work in the schools, but by a substantial portion of citizens. If as a people we are still committed to social democracy, this reassessment must represent a reaffirmation of our historic ideals, but these must be reinterpreted to fit the existing social context. It is not enough that Americans—liberal, conservative, or other—are committed to such ideals as the worth and dignity of the individual, the importance of universal education, equal educational opportunity for all, and all such high-level abstractions capable of different interpretations. The important question is *what these abstractions mean in the social context in which they must work.*

Nobody can expect that complete agreement will be reached; it will probably be better if it is not, for history suggests that when agreement is too widespread it can give rise to a rigid dogmatism that is extremely resistant to change. Educational essentialism is an example of this condition. It is necessary, however, that some reasonable working agreements be reached. If this proves impossible, then the prevailing chaos is certain to continue and will probably grow progressively worse.

In the second place, in this proposed reassessment the relation of ends to means must be respected. The last thing American education needs is for a high governmental commission or other body to produce a series of abstract propositions labeled "The Aims of Education," or some similar pronouncement, with no consideration of what these proposed aims may mean in operational terms. A general reassessment, to enjoy any kind of success, will require participation of people from varied areas of the educational enterprise: practicing school people, social and behavioral scientists, academic scholars, representations of various sectors of the lay public—and *philosophers of education*.

Anyone contemplating an enterprise of this kind seriously cannot help but be appalled at its complexity and the substantial risk of failure that is inherent in it. But the alternative to such an effort is to keep on trying to muddle through, and there are good signs that we have muddled about as long as we dare. This is not the place to discuss specific patterns of strategy and organization, but a few observations may be made. First, it must be a national effort, but it must not be centralized. There is scant evidence that the federal bureaucracy, in spite of the enormous financial resources at its disposal, has been any more successful than the states or local communities in bringing about fundamental school reform. Therefore the effort, while national in scope, must be pluralistic, and to a degree free-wheeling, but at the same time coordinated. We can no longer afford the atomism that has characterized most of the educational research and experimentation that has gone on under central auspices, particularly those of the federal government.

To these observations one more should be added. We must divest ourselves of the notion that the only significant components needed for educational reform are money and reorganization. Nobody doubts that sufficient funding is a necessary condition, but as in schemes for institutional reorganization, it is only a possibility that money may effect change. There is no guarantee.

The most important matter, as we see it, concerns the need for sustained and sophisticated intellectual leadership, particularly in the normative aspects of educational reform. It seems only fair to say that currently such leadership is not very much in evidence. Ordinarily, it would be reasonable to suppose that substantive intellectual leadership, particularly in the normative sense, should come from educational philosophers, but the facts indicate that this has rarely been the case. Into the intellectual vacuum created by the apparent abdication of the philosophers, those from other fields have not hesitated to rush. There are ramifications to this situation.

## CAN IT BE THE POVERTY OF PHILOSOPHY?

In the first chapter of this book, we considered the question of the nature of philosophy of education, some common forms it has taken, and the kind of contributions that can be expected from it. In pursuing this inquiry, we considered the ways in which philosophy itself has developed over the centuries, and we paid particular attention to certain developments occurring in this century, developments that have led to the dominant position that the central, if not the only, task of philosophy is the analysis of ordinary language. This development has sparked controversy among academic philosophers themselves; it has also brought criticism from various members of the intellectual community who, while they make no pretense of being professional philosophers, nevertheless believe that philosophy has abandoned its historic role, that philosophers now talk only to each other, and that other people do not know what the philosophers are talking about and to an increasing degree could not care less.[8] For obvious reasons, academic philosophers have resented this kind of criticism, calling it not only unfair but also uninformed. It is germane to our concern to assess the effects the general situation in philosophy has had on philosophy of education.

Much has been made of the tendency of traditional philosophers of education to imitate the general system-building activity of pre-twentieth-century philosophy, that is, the effort to deduce the aims and means of education from some set of *a priori* principles in metaphysics or other conventional categories of philosophy. We have examined some of these efforts. The well-known result has been an "idealistic philosophy of education," or a "realistic philosophy of education," or some such designation. Criticism of this approach has been copious and for the most part well deserved. Much of it has come from analytic philosophers, or from those who were influenced by the analytic movement, and there is considerable agreement that this influence generally has been salutary. In its first stages, the influence of analytic philosophy tended to be negative. This is not said in any pejorative sense, but rather in the sense that the initial contribution consisted in pointing out the insufficiencies of the older approaches and advocating the development of new ways of conceiving the role of philosophy in education.

---

[8] For a sampling of this kind of criticism, see Christopher J. Lucas, ed., *What Is Philosophy of Education?* (Toronto: Collier-Macmillan, 1969), pp. 17–57.

The influence on education of philosophy conceived as analysis of ordinary language is not much more than two decades old, perhaps not even that old. It seems now to have achieved its initial objective; that is, it has succeeded in pushing philosophy of education off the dead center on which it had rested at least since the end of World War II. The success that the analytic philosophers of education experienced in this original effort, however, has created a new hazard. The future of this approach probably depends on whether the analysts can move into a constructive and significant role in education and in the reconstruction that is needed so sorely.

The danger is that philosophical analysis may succumb to the temptation to become a "system," or as is often said, a "program." [9] If it does, it likely will fall into the same error that Dewey warned about when he said that "philosophy of education is not a poor relation of general philosophy even though it is often so treated even by philosophers." [10] It is difficult to deny that there are elements in the very nature of analytic philosophy that render it susceptible to hair-splitting and the endless discussion of trivia, which can amount to little more than a torturous belaboring of the obvious. This is one criticism made about current academic philosophy and it may well apply to philosophy of education in the years ahead if the latter simply insists on applying the program of analysis to education. [11] There is not much to show that in the first part of the seventies philosophy of education made any substantial contribution to the reform and regeneration of a chaotic and perhaps a disintegrating educational system. The reason for this may be that philosophy of education had not yet mastered the new situation. It is possible that in the succeeding years it will assume the intellectual leadership that is essential if the effort to reform the schools is to have any chance of succeeding. There is nothing in the nature of things that guarantees that this will happen, but the alternative is already before our eyes. The vacuum left by the defection of the philosophers is being filled by those from other fields of endeavor. Part of this leadership is valuable and has real purpose, but a substantial part is thoroughly confused and in-

---

[9] This possibility is discussed by Abraham Edel in "Analytic Philosophy of Education at the Crossroads," *Educational Theory* 22 (Spring 1972): 131–52. He expresses the opinion that this has already happened in academic philosophy and there are signs that the same thing is occurring in philosophy of education (p. 132). On the other hand, Leonard J. Waks, writing two years earlier, indicated that the analytic philosophers of education in the United States have not shown much interest in philosophical *programs*. See his article "Philosophy, Education and the Doomsday Threat," *Review of Educational Research* 39 (December 1969): 607–21.

[10] *Problems of Men* (New York: Philosophical Library, 1946), p. 165.

[11] Sidney Hook was among the first to examine critically the possible influence of analytic philosophy on education. See his *Education for Modern Man*, 2nd ed. (New York: Alfred A. Knopf, 1963), pp. 45–53. His analysis foreshadowed such observations as those of Edel and of Waks, cited above.

tellectually unsophisticated, and stems from the "gut level." Part of it is not leadership at all but simply an endless incantation of romantic platitudes.

In the opening chapter of this book, we gave as the most important problem of the philosophy of education the ends and means of education and their interrelations. We pointed out that those interrelations are not all internal to the educational system but that there are organic connections between education and the social and cultural setting that are of ultimate importance. For this reason, in this book every effort has been made to place the various philosophies of education in the broad social setting.

If this approach to philosophy of education is tenable, if it is to profit from the new approaches and the new techniques that analytic philosophy has brought to the study of philosophy of education, and perhaps above all else, if philosophy of education is to be significant in reconstructing education, then certain conditions must be respected. They are sufficiently important to occupy the close attention of educational philosophers for a long time to come.

The view taken here is that the basic condition to be met is recognition of the empirical, the normative, and the sociocultural components of philosophy of education and their integration with analytic method. This is the view advocated by Abraham Edel in the article previously cited and it is the view implicit in the perspective of this book.[12] It is important to understand that the key idea is *integration*, and not simply *addition* of empirical and normative elements to some separate program of analysis. Edel has shown in a comparatively elaborate argument that mere addition is not only untenable on philosophic grounds but is also responsible for the sense of uncertainty and dissatisfaction found among various analytic philosophers of education today. One might say that it is the root cause for the apparent poverty of philosophy of education.

If the normative, empirical, and cultural components of education are to be integrated within the analytic approach, then certain conditions are necessary. The most obvious, certainly one of the most important, is a close working relation among philosophers and others whose scholarship is empirical and experimental, that is, social scientists, behavioral scientists, natural scientists, historians, and so on. All of these have something important to contribute to the total enterprise, each having a distinctive role. That such an integration of interest and effort does not exist today is common knowledge, and a substantial portion of the fault can rightly be laid at the philosopher's door. It may be true that education, particularly in the normative area, is too important a matter to be left to educational philosophers. But it is just as certain that it also is too important to be left to psychologists or sociologists or school administrators. It must be a *common*

---

[12] See p. 24.

concern if it is to amount to anything in the task of reconstruction that lies ahead.

In short, the fundamental policy question of the purposes of education cannot be answered by educational philosophers alone. They should not expect to do it alone and nobody should expect them to. However, the issue can be raised by philosophers, and should be, because it is normative, and therefore philosophical, and because nobody else in the field of education seems particularly interested in raising it.

If philosophy of education is to reassert itself and take the active role it rightly deserves, then the question is what educational philosophers can do to participate in the reconstruction of education. For one thing they can apply the techniques of analysis of language to current educational discourse, which is in a thorough mess. Today's literature of education—it pours from the presses at a truly astonishing rate—is not only saturated with the slogans of contending factions; it is also replete with words having the most diverse referents (when they have any at all), with concepts that are loose and slippery, and with emotive sentences disguised as statements of fact. Moreover, long lines of argument, or what purports to be argument, whose real premises are concealed, trap the unwary into agreements he would never make if he were not being misled.[13] Thus, a rigorous analytic investigation, designed for those who must decide educational policy and not primarily for the amusement of other philosophers, can be of signal service. This task is not likely to be met by people who lack training in the philosophy of education.[14] We can expect more, however, from educational philosophers, if they will rise to the occasion. As has often been observed but less frequently heeded, although empirical problems can be clarified by linguistic and conceptual analysis, they cannot be solved by analysis alone. This means that the philosopher of education must associate himself more closely with the substantive fields pertinent to education. He can do this in two ways. One way is to work more closely with scholars in the substantive fields. This has already been mentioned and seems evident anyway. The other way is for philosophers themselves to acquire a broad background

---

[13] Examples of this are too numerous to make a listing possible, and discussion of specific works obviously is out of the question here. But the interested reader need not look far for material on which he can use his analytic powers. The current literature in educational journals is replete with examples and many also will be found in publications of related fields, particularly the social sciences. For a start, one might consult *Radical School Reform*, edited by Ronald and Beatrice Gross (New York: Simon and Schuster, 1969). The blurb on the front of the book lists the contributors to the anthology as those "who are remaking American education." Let the reader judge for himself.

[14] An example of this kind of analysis that comes to mind is Philip G. Smith's article on the current preoccupation with "behavioral objectives." See "On the Logic of Behavioral Objectives," *Phi Delta Kappan* 53 (March 1972): 429–31.

of knowledge. This is not to say that they can master every field. There are no Aristotles any more. But *philosophy*, at least originally, means the love of wisdom, and wisdom involves more than a method, no matter how sophisticated that method may be.

There seems no good reason why philosophers of education should be ignorant, or profess ignorance, of the history of education, the history of philosophy and of philosophy of education, and educational practice. Nor does it seem reasonable for them to ignore such disciplines as the social and natural sciences. As Waks puts it:

> If we believe that conceptual analysis can be of practical importance in clarifying substantive issues, then this hard and fast distinction between philosophers and substantive experts must be abandoned. We must be willing to see philosophers acquire relevant substantive expertise and experts acquire considerable philosophical sophistication.[15]

It is argued here that the possibility exists for philosophy of education to move out of its poverty-stricken state, to reassert the leadership it once had in the intellectual arena, and to lend its peculiar talents in the search for an educational system that will be viable in the final decades of this century. Sad to say, it is only the possibility that can be argued with any positive conviction. The probability remains in doubt. It may well be that too much time already has been frittered away by philosophers talking to each other and by aimless dabbling in the schools on the part of well-meaning romantics, among others, and reorganizers who think that anything, including human education, will yield to the mechanics of scientific management.

It also may very well be true that the conviction is strong in this society that the question of the purposes of education has been settled and that no further attention needs to be paid to it. If this is indeed the case, then we are almost certain to repeat the experience we have already been through. It will show that we have learned little or nothing from history, and also how inadequate our simple-minded American conservatism is. If the first episode was tragedy, the next may well be farce.

---

[15]  Waks, "Philosophy, Education," p. 613. The latter part of Waks's paper is particularly pertinent to the position advocated here.

*INDEXES*

# INDEX OF NAMES

# INDEX OF SUBJECTS